Edwar

LECTURES

ON THE

DOCTRINE OF JUSTIFICATION

By JOHN HENRY NEWMAN

SOMETIME FELLOW OF ORIEL COLLEGE

Wipf and Stock Publishers
150 West Broadway • Eugene OR 97401
2001

Lectures on the Doctrine of Justification

Third Edition

By Newman, John Henry
ISBN: 1-57910-829-6

Reprinted by *Wipf and Stock Publishers*
150 West Broadway • Eugene OR 97401

Previously published by J. G. & F. Rivington, 1874.

TO THE RIGHT REV. FATHER IN GOD

RICHARD,

LORD BISHOP OF OXFORD, DEAN OF CANTERBURY,

AND

CHANCELLOR OF THE MOST NOBLE ORDER OF THE GARTER,

THIS VOLUME IS INSCRIBED

WITH A FEELING

OF VENERATION FOR HIS SACRED ORDER,

OF DUTIFUL SUBMISSION TO HIS DIOCESAN AUTHORITY,

AND OF GRATITUDE FOR KINDNESSES RECEIVED,

BY HIS LORDSHIP'S

FAITHFUL AND ATTACHED SERVANT,

THE AUTHOR.

ADVERTISEMENT TO THE FIRST EDITION.

THE present Volume originated in the following way :
It was brought home to the writer from various
quarters, that a prejudice existed in many serious minds
against certain essential Christian truths, such as Baptismal Regeneration and the Apostolical Ministry, in consequence of a belief that they fostered notions of human
merit, were dangerous to the inward life of religion, and
incompatible with the doctrine of justifying faith, nay,
with express statements on the subject in our Formularies ; while confident reports were in circulation that
the parties who advocated them could not disguise even
from themselves their embarrassment at those statements.
Moreover, it was suggested, that, though both these
lines of doctrine had in matter of fact been continuously
followed out by the great body of our divines for two
centuries and more, yet such historical considerations
did not weigh with men in general against their own
impressions ; and that nothing would meet the evil but
plain statements on the subject argued out from Scripture,—statements which, if not successful in convincing

those who refused to trust Tradition and the Church, might at least be evidence to the world, that the persons so suspected did themselves honestly believe that the doctrines of our Articles and Homilies were not at variance with what they thought they saw in the Services for Baptism, Holy Communion, and Ordination, and in other Forms contained in the Prayer Book.

These considerations have led the writer on, first to deliver, and then to publish, the following Lectures, in the hope that he might be thereby offering suggestions towards a work, which must be uppermost in the mind of every true son of the English Church at this day,— the consolidation of a theological system, which, built upon those formularies which were framed in the 16th century, and to which all Clergymen are bound, may tend to inform, persuade, and absorb into itself religious minds, which hitherto have fancied that, on the peculiar Protestant questions they were seriously opposed to one another. Such have been the occasion and the object of these Lectures ; and if in them, or in anything else he has written, there be what readers consider more severe or contentious than such an object admits, let them impute it to his firm belief that no wound is cured which is not thoroughly probed, and that the first step in persuasiveness is decision.

Since they were delivered, Mr. Faber has published his work on the " Primitive Doctrine of Justification," with a special reference to Mr. Knox's opinions. Thus the writer finds himself engaged in a discussion even more delicate and anxious than he had anticipated ; but, as he originally drew up his remarks without reference to either of those respected authors, so he has judged it best not to take part in a dispute which in no sense belongs to him, and very little to his work. How far he assents to Mr. Knox, how far to Mr. Faber, will there appear ; but while the points from which he starts are different, so too are his arguments, as being drawn not from Primitive Christianity but from Scripture.

Another recent work on Justification, Dr. O'Brien's Sermons on Faith, should also here be mentioned, from the station and reputation of the Author ; though no reason has occurred for referring to it elsewhere, as it does but advocate, in opposition to Bishop Bull and the greater number of English Divines, the pure Lutheran theory, which has been sufficiently considered in these Lectures, as far as it fell under their scope.

ORIEL COLLEGE.
March 12, 1838.

ADVERTISEMENT TO THE THIRD EDITION.

THESE Lectures on the doctrine of Justification formed one of a series of works projected by the Author in illustration of what has often been considered to be the characteristic position of the Anglican Church, as lying in a supposed *Via Media*, admitting much and excluding much both of Roman and of Protestant teaching.

Their drift is to show that there is little difference but what is verbal in the various views on justification, found whether among Catholic or Protestant divines ; by Protestant being meant Lutheran, Calvinistic, and thirdly that dry anti-evangelical doctrine, which was dominant in the Church of England during the last century, and is best designated by the name of Arminianism.

Unless the Author held in substance in 1874 what he published in 1838, he would not at this time be reprinting what he wrote as an Anglican ; certainly not with so little added by way of safeguard. Of course there are points of detail, as to which he cannot accept what these Lectures contain ; but even such incidental errors of opinion he has thought he might let stand, except where they became offensive by repetition, contenting himself with notes in brackets at the foot of the page, drawing attention to them and setting them right.

However, a few words of explanation are called for here in relation to two main propositions of the Volume, which he distinctly professed to be at variance, but (as he now believes) are not really at variance, with the doctrine held in the Roman schools of recent times on the subject of Justification. The first of these is the proposition that more than one *formal cause* can be assigned to the justified state ; and the second that one of those *forms* is the Presence of our Lord in the soul, whether the Eucharistic Presence, or a Presence cognate to it.

1. As to the former of these, it is quite true that the Fathers at Trent pronounced that there was but one formal cause of justification as a state of the soul, and that, in opposition to the Protestant view, that form was an inward gift. " Unica formalis causa justificationis," they say, " est justitia Dei, quâ nos justos facit, quâ renovamur spiritu mentis nôstræ, et verè justi nominamur et sumus, justitiam in nobis recipientes." And so far as the author of these Lectures contradicts this categorical statement, he now simply withdraws what he has said in them. But he was mistaken if he supposed that it

was thereby determined *what* the "unica forma" really was, or again that there might not be more *forms* than one (whether improper *forms*, or *forms* of the justifying justice or renovation) ; and he says so for the following reasons :—

First, Bellarmine, though he quotes the words of the Tridentine Fathers, declaratory of the "unica formalis causa" of Justification (*de Justif.* ii. 2), does not hesitate to say that it is an open question whether grace or charity is the justice which justifies ; and, though he holds for his own part that these are different names for one and the same supernatural habit, yet he allows that there are theologians who think otherwise (*ibid.* i. 2). Though, then, there be but one *formal cause* (and there never can be more than one proper form of anything), still it is not settled precisely what that form is. We are at liberty to hold that it is, not the renewed state of the soul, but the Divine gift which renews it.

And Pallavicino, as he is quoted in the Appendix (*infra*, p. 351), says "Adhibitam datâ operâ fuisse à Patribus, vocem nunc gratiæ, nunc charitatis, et interdum etiam utramque, ut se abstinerent ab eâ declaratione, duæ res an una eademque res, illa forent."

Vasquez too allows (*infra*, p. 353) that there are two possible *forms*, "per quas homo justificari possit apud Deum."

Sporer holds two partial *forms*, as making up the "unica forma," an external Divine act and internal Divine work,—" favor Dei" and "habitus justitiæ" (*ibid.*), which, with grace as an internal gift going between the two, make three *forms*, proper or improper.

Bellarmine furnishes a fourth, when he lays down that, according to the Council, living faith, "fides viva, est vera et Christiana justitia" (*de Grat.* i. 6, p. 401); and says also (*de Justif.* v. 15, p. 986), "Formalem causam justificationis . . . esse fidem charitate formatam."

Moreover, Petavius speaks of another, or fifth, viz. the substantial Presence of the Holy Ghost in the soul, as *infra*, pp. 352, etc. He speaks of the "infusio substantiæ Spiritûs Sancti, quâ . . . efficimur . . . *justi* et sancti." And he calls this substantial Presence a "tanquam *principalis*," and a "*primaria forma*," and a "*proxima* causa, et, ut ita dixerim, *formalis*." And he maintains this to be the doctrine of the early Fathers. So much on the first point.

2. With these authorities preceding him, the author went on to speak of the Eucharistic Presence, or a Presence such as that in the Eucharist, as an additional *form* of Justification ; and, in speaking of the fact of such a permanent Presence in the soul, he held nothing very different from what is taught by mystical theologians of authority such as Schram, who writes as follows :—

"Quintus modus unionis [per Præsentiam Christi personalem Eucharisticam] est, quòd, corruptis etiam speciebus, non solum maneat Christus per gratiam et charitatem unitus animæ dignè communicanti, sed etiam *personaliter penes suam hypostasim et deitatem;* ita nimirum ut, sicuti in omni justificatione, non modo per gratiam, sed etiam personaliter Spiritus Sanctus fit animæ justi præsens, . . sic etiam Christus personaliter scilicet penes suam hypostasim, virtute SS. Eucharistiæ, speciali modo, cum incremento gratiæ unionisque cum Deo, etiam corruptis speciebus, permanet."

And he goes on to mention a further "modus unionis" in the Eucharist, accorded only to very holy persons, by means of the continued Presence of the *soul* of Christ : a mode of union, "quo se Christus uniendum permanenter offert, non solùm per deitatem, hypostasim, et personam suam, sed etiam per *suam sacratissimam animam,* quatenus, *corruptis speciebus,* adeoque recedente corpore et sanguine, . . tamen . . cum [animâ] velut immediato instrumento, Verbo conjuncto, specialius quam per solam deitatem, permanet specialissime unitus nonnullis animabus valde perfectis."—*Theol. Myst.* p. 1, §§ 152, 153.

These passages do not indeed countenance the idea that the ordinary *form* of Justification is the Real Presence of the Crucified and Risen Saviour in the soul, a doctrine which was never, it is conceived, even imagined by any writer in the Catholic Church ; but they are sufficient to show that the hypothesis of a Personal Presence of our Lord in the soul, apart from His Incarnate Presence which is vouchsafed in the Eucharist, though not as a form of justification, is in itself neither preposterous nor inadmissible.

It may be well to explain the principle of succession on which these Lectures are arranged.

1. The first two introduce and open the subject which is to be discussed, by an exposition, first, of the Protestant, then of the Catholic doctrine of Christian Justification.

2. Then follows in three Lectures—the 3d, 4th, and 5th—an inquiry into the meaning of the term "Justification."

3. In the next four—the 6th, 7th, 8th, and 9th—is determined what is the real thing which is denoted by the term "Justification."

4. In the 10th, 11th, and 12th, the office and nature of Faith is discussed in its relation to Justification.

In the 13th and last, a practical application is made of the principles and conclusions of the foregoing Lectures, to the mode of preaching and professing the Gospel, popular thirty or forty years since, called " evangelical."

THE ORATORY,
    January 6, 1874.

CONTENTS.

LECTURE I.

LECTURE II.

LECTURE III.

LECTURE IV.

LECTURE V

LECTURE VI.

LECTURE VII.

LECTURE VIII.

LECTURE IX.

LECTURE X.

LECTURE XI.

LECTURE XII.

LECTURE XIII.

APPENDIX.

LECTURE I.

FAITH CONSIDERED AS THE INSTRUMENT OF
JUSTIFICATION.

TWO main views concerning the mode of our justification are found in the writings of English divines ;
on the one hand, that this great gift of our Lord's passion
is vouchsafed to those who are moved by God's grace to
claim it,—on the other, to those who by the same grace
are moved to do their duty. These separate doctrines,
justification by faith, and justification by obedience,
thus simply stated, are not at all inconsistent with one
another ; and by religious men, especially if not divines,
will be held both at once, or either the one or the other
indifferently, as circumstances may determine. Yet,
though so compatible in themselves, the case is altogether altered when one or other is made the elementary
principle of the gospel system,—when professed exclusively, developed consistently, and accurately carried out
to its limits. Then what seemed at first but two modes
of stating the same truth, will be found, the one to be
the symbol of what goes by the name of Romanism, the
other of what is commonly called Protestantism.

It shall be my endeavour in these Lectures to take
such a view of Justification, as may approve itself to

those among us who hold whether the one or the other doctrine in an unsystematic way, yet falls in with neither of them, when they are adopted as the foundation or " leading idea " of a theology. Justification by faith only, thus treated, is an erroneous, and justification by obedience is a defective, view of Christian doctrine. The former is beside, the latter short of, the truth. The former legitimately tends to the creed of the rigid Lutherans who opposed Melanchthon ; the latter to that of Vasquez, Caietan, and other extreme writers of the Roman school. That we are absolutely saved by obedience, that is, by *what we are,* has introduced the proper merit [1] of good works ; that we are absolutely saved by faith, or by *what Christ is,* the notion that good works are not conditions of our salvation.

In this and the following Lecture I propose to set down some chief characteristics of the Lutheran and Roman schemes of justification ; and first, of the Lutheran.

2.

The point at which it separates from the doctrine of our Liturgy and Articles is very evident. Our formu-

---

[1] [Catholics hold that our good works, as proceeding from the grace of the Holy Ghost, cannot be worthless, but have a real and proper value ; on the other hand, that the great reward of eternal life is due to them only in consequence of the promise of God. Good works have on this ground a claim on God's faithfulness to His promises, and thereby a claim on His justice, for it would be unjust to promise and not fulfil. The Council of Trent says : " Vita æterna est et tanquam *gratia misericorditer promissa,* et tanquam merces *ex ipsius Dei promissione fideliter reddenda.* Again : " Quæ justitia nostra dicitur, illa eadem Dei est, quia *à Deo nobis infunditur per Christi meritum.*" Sess. vi. cap. 16.]

laries speak of faith as in many ways essential to our justification, but not as the instrument of originally gaining it.[1] This peculiar instrumentality of faith is the Lutheran tenet here to be discussed; and is plainly the consequence of what has been already adverted to, the attaching an exclusive importance to the doctrine of justification by faith only. Those who hold that this doctrine declares only one out of several truths relating to the mode of our justification, even though they express themselves like the strict Lutherans, may really agree with our Church; but it is far otherwise with those who hold it as comprehending all that is told us about that mode.

This then is peculiarly the Lutheran view, viz. that faith is the proper instrument of justification.[2] That justification is the application of Christ's merits to the individual,[3] or (as it is sometimes expressed) the imparting a saving interest in Him, will not be denied by English divines. Moreover, it will be agreed that His merits are not communicated, or a saving interest secured, except through an instrument divinely appointed. Such an instrument there must be, if man is to take part in the application supposed; and it must be divinely appointed, since it is to convey what God Himself,

---

[1] The passage in the Homily on the Passion will be explained in Lecture X.

[2] Fides non justificat vel meritorie, vel per modum dispositionis, ut volunt Pontificii, sed organice et per modum apprehensionis, quatenus meritum Christi in verbo Evangelii oblatum complectitur.—Gerhard. de Justif. § 153.

[3] Beneficia Christi . . . in quorum applicatione modus ac forma justificationis consistit.—Gerhard. de Justif. § 148.

and He alone, dispenses. It is then a means appointed
by God and used by man, and is almost necessarily
involved in the notion of justification. All parties seem
to agree as far as this ; but when we go on to inquire
what it is which God has made His instrument, then, as
I have said, we find ourselves upon the main subject of
dispute between ourselves and the strict followers of the
German Reformer. Our Church considers it to be the
Sacrament of Baptism ;[1] they consider it to be Faith.

These two views indeed need not be, and have not
always been, opposed to one another.[2] Baptism may be
considered the instrument on God's part, Faith on ours ;
Faith may receive what Baptism conveys. But if the
word *instrument* be taken to mean in the strictest sense
the *immediate* means by which the gift passes from the
giver to the receiver, there can be but one instrument ;
and either Baptism will be considered to convey it
(whether conditionally or not, which is a further question), or Faith to seize, or, as it is expressed, to apprehend
it,—either Faith will become a subordinate means, condition, or qualification, or Baptism a mere sign, pledge,
or ratification of a gift which is really independent of it.
And this is the alternative in which the question has
practically issued at all times.

I am in this Lecture to consider the system of
doctrine arising out of the belief that Faith, not Baptism,

[1] Baptismus . . . est signum regenerationis, per quod, *tanquam per
instrumentum*, recte Baptismum suscipientes, Ecclesiæ inseruntur, etc.—
Artic. XXVII.

[2] Gerhard. de Justif. §§ 64, 153. Vid. Baxter, Life of Faith, iii. 8,
error 20.

is the instrument of justification. What I think of that
system may be gathered from what I say as I proceed.
I have tried to delineate it fairly ; at the same time I
am sensible that I shall seem not to have pursued the
subject to its limits. Yet I think I have reached the
limits of the meaning of those who have brought it into
discussion ; and if I am obscure, it is because I have to
use their language.

3.

Its advocates then suppose that Faith is the one
principle which God's grace makes use of for restoring
us to His favour and image. Born in sin, and the heir
of misery, the soul needs an utter change of what it is
by nature, both within and without, both in itself and in
God's sight. The change in God's sight is called justification, the inward change is regeneration ; and faith is
the one appointed means of both at once. It is awakened
in us by the secret influences of the Holy Spirit, generally
co-operating with some external means, as the written
word ; and, as embracing the news of salvation through
Christ, it thereby also appropriates salvation, becoming
at the same time the element and guarantee of subsequent renewal. As leading the soul to rest on Christ
as its own Saviour, and as the propitiation of its own
sins in particular, it imparts peace to the conscience,
and the comfortable hope of heaven ; and, as being
living, spiritual, and inseparable from gratitude towards
Christ, it abounds in fruit, that is in good works of
every kind.

Such is the first general sketch which may be given
of this doctrine, according to which *justification* means a

change in God's dealings with us and *faith* means trust. Our Article too so understands the word *justification;* so we need not stop to consider it here. Let us rather confine ourselves to the examination of what is meant by faith or trust, to which such great effects are ascribed.

It is commonly found the most ready answer to this inquiry to enlarge upon what it is *not.* Accordingly, it is not unusual to explain that faith is not mere belief in the being of a God, nor in the historical fact that Christ has come on earth, suffered and ascended. Nor is it the submission of the reason to mysteries, nor the sort of trust which is required for exercising the gift of miracles. Nor, again, is it the knowledge and acceptance of the sacred truths of the New Testament, even the Atonement, however accurate that knowledge, however implicit that acceptance. It is neither the faith of Judas who healed diseases, nor of Simon Magus who submitted to baptism, nor of Demas who might be orthodox in his creed, nor of devils who "believe and tremble." All such kinds of faith are put aside as fictitious, as not deserving the name, and as having no connection whatever, except in the accident of an homonymous term, with that faith which justifies.

Such justifying faith or trust is supposed to be, considered negatively : when a more direct account of it is demanded, answer is made as follows ;—that it is a spiritual principle, altogether different from anything we have by nature, endued with a divine life and efficacy, and producing a radical change in the soul : or more precisely, that it is a trust in Christ's merits and in them alone for salvation. It is regarded as that very feeling exercised towards our Almighty Benefactor, which we are on the contrary warned against, when directed towards anything earthly, as riches, or an arm of flesh. It is the feeling under which we flee in any great temporal danger to some place or means of refuge ; the feeling under which the servant in the parable asked forgiveness of his debt, with a simple admission that it lay solely and entirely with his lord to grant it. It consists then in a firm reliance on Christ's mercifulness towards even the worst of sinners who come to Him,— an experimental conviction that the soul needs a Saviour, and a full assurance that He can and will be such to it,— a thankful acceptance of His perfect work,—an exaltation and preference of Him above all things,—a surrender of the whole man to Him,—a submission to His will,— a perception and approval of spiritual things,—a feeling of the desirableness of God's service,—a hatred of sin,— a confession of utter unworthiness,—a self-abhorrence of what is past,—and a resolution, in dependence on God's grace, to do better in future. Some such description is often given of it ; or, in a word, it is spoken of as being, or implying all at once, love, gratitude, devotion, belief, holiness, repentance, hope, dutifulness, and all other graces.

4.

This description however, it is obvious, includes too much, as the former said too little , let us then dismiss such popular accounts as meet us in every quarter on first opening the subject, and endeavour to fix our minds on it more steadily. What then are we to say that justifying faith really is ? The Lutheran divines define

it to be a " fiduciary apprehension "[1] of gospel mercy,—
a belief, not only that Christ has died for the sins of the
world, but that He has died specially for the individual
so believing, and a sense of confident trust in consequence,[2] a claiming as one's own, with full persuasion of
its efficacy, what He has done and suffered for all. This
is an intelligible account of it certainly ; but it is not at
all sufficient for the purpose, for this plain reason ; that
justifying faith is always supposed in the Lutheran
scheme to be lively or to lead to good works, but such
a " fiduciary apprehension," or confident persuasion, may
exist without any fruit following to warrant it. Trusting faith is not necessarily living faith. The servant in
the parable knew he owed his master a large sum ; he
knew his master only could remit the debt. He applied
to him ; he appropriated to himself his mercy, in the
only way he could, by falling down and throwing himself
upon it. He did not in any degree trust in himself or in
anything else ; he discovered no pride, no self-righteousness ; his trust was absolute,—unless we choose to say
that his promise for the future interfered with it. Yet
he went away and sinned ; trust then is not necessarily
lively faith.

Shall we then define the justifying faith of the
Lutherans to be faith which *is* lively? This is a
more adequate account of it, but a less consistent one.
For what is meant by lively? is it to be explained as

[1] Propria et specifica fidei justificantis forma est *fiducialis apprehensio*
Christi Mediatoris ac beneficiorum ejus, quæ in verbo Evangelii nobis
offeruntur.—Gerhard. de Justif. § 117.

[2] Gerhard. de Justif. § 127, et seq.

merely that, which *in the event* is fruitful, without having in itself anything discriminating or characteristic? But surely that which results in good works must have some principle in it which is the cause of that result; and this is confessed by calling it lively. What then is the *life* of faith? What is that which makes it what it is? What is that, not *on account* of which it is acceptable (for we all acknowledge that Christ is the only meritorious cause of our acceptance), but what is that property in it which *makes* it (for Christ's sake) acceptable? What is the formal quality of justifying faith? Let us but ascertain this, and we shall be able to understand what the Lutherans mean when they treat of it.

Many divines accordingly, of various schools, consider this life of faith to be love; and it must be confessed that even the strict followers of the German Reformer speak in a way to sanction the notion. Thus at all times they have indulged in descriptions of faith as an adhering to Christ, a delighting and rejoicing in Him, and a giving oneself up to Him; all which seem to be nothing more or less than properties of love. Luther, however, himself, as we shall presently find, opposed himself most earnestly and vehemently to such a doctrine, under the notion that to say that love made faith living was to deny the innate life and power of faith as such, and to associate another principle with it as a joint instrument in justification.[1] Let us for argument's sake grant that love is not the life of justi-

[1] Non enim dicit [Paulus], Charitas est efficax, sed, Fides est efficax; non, Charitas operatur, sed, Fides operatur. Charitatem vero facit fidei velut instrumentum, per quod operatur.—In Gal. v. 6. (f. 407)

fying faith ; but, if so, the question recurs, *what* is the faith that justifies ?

Considering how important its office is, considering what exclusive stress is laid upon it in the School of doctrine under review, considering what severe protests

Illa charitas, vel sequentia opera, nec informant meam fidem, nec ornant ; sed fides mea informat et ornat charitatem.—In Gal. ii. 19 (f. 316). Quisquis spiritualis vitæ particeps factus per fidem, is eandem exerit per charitatem, sicut per externas operationes vita hominis naturalis manifestatur.—Gerhard. de Justif. § 153. Yet Melanchthon and Calvin take the sober tone of our Homilies in denying that justifying faith can for a moment exist without love, contrary to Luther and his school. "Fides significat fiduciam ; in fiducia inest dilectio, ergo etiam dilectione sumus justi." *Concedo in fiducia inesse dilectionem,* et hanc virtutem et plerasque alias *adesse oportere ;* sed cum dicimus, Fiducia sumus justi, non intelligatur nos propter virtutis istius dignitatem, sed per misericordiam recipi propter Mediatorem quem tamen oportet fide apprehendi. Ergo hoc dicimus *correlativè.*—Melanchth. Loc. Com. f. 213. Vid. Calv. Justific. iii. 11, n. 6. But what Melanchthon gains in reasonableness, he surely loses in the controversy with Rome. For what is the real difference between saying with him that faith is not justifying unless love or holiness be *with* it ; or with Bellarmine, that it is not so, unless love be *in* it ?—What is the distinction between the metaphors conveyed by *in* and *with ?* Nay, the approximation is nearer still, for, while Melanchthon grants that love "*inest,*" *is in* faith, Bellarmine grants that the love which makes faith living is not part of faith, but external to it. He says, "Apostolus Paulus explicat dilectionem formam esse *extrinsecam* fidei, non intrinsecam, et quæ det illi, non ut sit, sed ut moveatur."—In Justif. ii. 4. And on the other hand the Lutheran Gerhard : "Fides a dilectione sejuncta non justificat, quia non potest a dilectione nisi νοηματικῶς sejungi ; et si a dilectione sejungatur, non est vera fides."—§ 175. The sole question then is, whether love, which on all hands is allowed to be a *sine quâ non, communicates* to faith its justifying power. But what is meant by *communicates ?* Luther's doctrine, on the other hand, that justifying faith *is* without love *when* it justifies, is plain enough, and no matter of words.

are raised by that School against anything but faith, whether virtue or good work, being assigned a share in our justification, considering that the knowledge of our possessing true faith is made a characteristic of the healthy state of that true faith,[1] surely we may fairly demand in the outset, *what* faith is ; what that is, as separate from everything else, which exclusively of everything else is the instrument of so great a work. Surely it is fair to ask *whither* we are being led, before we consent to move a foot.   They who are vehement in maintaining that faith only justifies, are bound to speak only and distinctly of faith.

5.

In answer to this objection, it is usual in the first place to prohibit the consideration of it.   We are told that such inquiries are an undue exaltation of human reason, or at least an unseasonable exercise of it : that to contemplate and dwell upon faith at all, or to ask any questions about it, is a fundamental mistake, considering we should fix our eyes and rest our hearts on the Divine Object of it only.   Faith, it appears, is to be defined, not by its *nature*, but by its *office ;* not by what *it is*, but by what it *does*.   It is trust *in Christ*, and it differs from all other kinds of faith in That towards which it reaches forward and on which it rests.   Thus it differs from historical faith, or intellectual knowledge, in that it is a taking Christ for our portion, and (to use a familiar phrase) closing with His offers of mercy.   It consists, as has been already said, in this "fiduciary appre-

[1] Gerhard. de Justif. § 88.

hension " of the merits of Christ, in a willingness, most opposite to the bent of our proud nature, to be saved fully and freely with an everlasting salvation, "without money and without price," without merit, or labour, or pain, or sacrifice, or works of any kind on our part.

Or to put the subject in another point of view;— the gospel mercy is proclaimed openly and universally to all who will accept it. No special state of mind is necessary for appropriating it; a person has not to ask himself if he is fit; his warrant for making it his is the freeness of the proclamation—" Whosoever will, let him take of the water of life freely ;" if a man feels his need of being justified, and desires it, he has but to ask, he has but to look at the great work of Redemption, and it is his own in all the fulness of its benefits. Faith then as little admits of a definition as putting out the hand or receiving alms ; it has as little of a permanent form or shape as running or kneeling ; it is a momentary act or motion rather than a moral virtue or grace, though it is the work of the Spirit, and productive of all virtues, —or at least it must not be regarded as a virtue. It is the reaching forward of the heart towards Christ, deter-mining and resting in the thought of Him, as its limit, and thus deriving its character, and, as it may be called, its form from Him.[1]

This is the first answer made to the dilemma I have

[1] Ego soleo, ut hanc rem melius captem, sic imaginari, quasi *nulla* sit in corde meo qualitas, quæ fides vel charitas vocetur, sed in loco ipsarum pono ipsum Christum, et dico, hæc est justitia mea, *ipse est qualitas* et formalis, ut vocant, Justitia mea, ut sic me liberem ab interitu legis et operum.—Luther. ad Brentium Ep. apud Gerh. de Justif. § 163.

been stating, by those whom it is directed against. It
is urged on them that either faith is more than personal
trust, and if so, that addition, whatever it is, is a joint
instrument with it in our justification ; or that it is
nothing more, and then it is not necessarily living
and operative faith. And they answer, as if by way
of escaping from the dilemma, that to inquire *what*
it is in faith which *makes* it justifying, as distinct
from all other kinds of faith, is all one with asking
what it is in faith *on account* of which faith justifies ;
that the discriminating mark is the same as the meritorious cause ; and therefore that Christ Himself and He
alone, the Object of the faith, is that which makes the
faith what it is,—and to name, to hint, to look for what
it is in faith which makes it lively, is to open the door
to what Luther calls "the cursed gloss of Sophists."[1]
However, such a reply is evidently no real explanation
of the difficulty. Accordingly, when brought fairly to
consider it, they seem frankly to confess that it *is* a
difficulty, and that it must be left to itself. They seem
to allow that faith *is* in itself something more than trust,
though man may be unable to say what it is more.
"What is not really faith may doubtless," they say,
" appear to be faith ; of course there must ever be false
brethren in the church ; yet there may be true, there
must, there will be true nevertheless. If any men

[1] Pereant itaque sophistæ cum sua maledicta glossa, et damnetur
vox illa fides formata; et dicamus constanter ista vocabula, fides formata,
informis, acquisita, etc., diaboli esse portenta, nata in perniciem doctrinæ
et fidei Christianæ.—In Gal. iii. 12. (f. 347). Bp. Bull, on the contrary,
holds the doctrine of fides formata. So does Bp. Davenant *in Col.* i.
p. 28, saying that faith precedes love *naturâ*, not in fact.

pretend to faith or trust, and do not go on to obey, then they *have not* real trust. This is a proper inference, not that trust can exist without obedience.[1] Still it may be true, that the only way of becoming righteous in God's sight, the only way of becoming really fruitful in well-doing, is thus to embrace and appropriate Christ's atoning power as ours in the first instance, without standing still to speculate whether our trust is as it should be, whether we embrace and appropriate that mercy as we ought. This is God's way, and we may safely leave the difficulty to Him who has imposed it on us. We may be unskilled, if it so happen, in definitions and distinctions ; we may be unable to determine *how* true and false faith differ ; seeds which are essentially distinct may baffle the discrimination of mortal eye ; yet after all we are told, simply to look at Christ and to believe that we are justified, in order to our being so ; and this is all that concerns us."

Moreover, this supposed difficulty of distinguishing between true and false faith is not, it may be urged, in reality so great as it appears in controversy. It does not follow that faith may not admit of being ascertained, because we cannot define it in the language of human

---

[1] *Non est in arbitrio aut potestate nostra situm hanc libertatem,* per Evangelium jam invulgatam, *celare* homines aut revocare, quia Christus eam nobis donavit, ac suâ morte peperit. *Neque possumus illos porcos,* qui toto impetu ruunt in licentiam carnis, *cogere* ut corpore et rebus suis serviant aliis. *Ideo quod possumus, facimus ;* hoc est, *admonemus* diligenter eos debere hoc præstare. Si his monitis nostris nihil efficimus, *committimus rem Deo.* . . . Interim tamen hoc nos solatur, quod *labor et diligentia nostra non est inanis apud pios.* — Luther in Gal. **v.** 13. Vid also Calvin. Institut. iii. **2,** n. 11, 12.

science. If there be such a thing as a *real* apprehension
of Christ, it must necessarily be beyond explanation
It is a feeling, a spiritual taste, perception, sight, known
only to him who has the blessedness to experience it.
It is something beyond and above nature. It is a state
of mind for which no terms have been invented. We
cannot explain what sight is to the blind ; in like
manner, before the mind is enlightened by God's grace,
it cannot discern those tokens which are to the true
believer plain demonstration that he does believe and is
under no delusion. If words be attempted, they must
be used in new senses, unintelligible to the world at
large. Hence this doctrine, however true, will never
appear to advantage, or be described with justice, in controversy, which employs the language of the unregenerate. It is true its maintainers *have* attempted to argue
and refute their opponents ; but to do so was a mistake ;
they ought not to argue where they cannot refute ; for
from the nature of the case they will always appear, to
all but themselves and those who agree with them,
defective in their definitions and illogical in their
reasonings. Yet all the while it may be true, that those
who are savingly converted are converted by means of
this simple trust, which the self-deceived and carnal
misuse, and which controversialists stumble at.

6.

I have been endeavouring to represent the Lutheran, or extreme Protestant idea of justifying faith in
its *internal consistence ;* to examine how its parts hang
together, and how it disposes of objections which arise,

apart from the arguments on which it rests. What these are, will come next to be considered, but the above seems to be the doctrine which they will be required to prove, viz.—Faith, an act or motion of the mind produced indeed by Divine Grace, but still utterly worthless, applies to the soul the merits of Him on whom it looks, gaining at the same time His sanctifying aid, and developing itself in good works ; which works are the only evidence we can have of its being true. It justifies then, not as being lively or fruitful, though this is an insepa- rable property of it, but as *apprehending* Christ, which is its essence.[1]

The alleged ground of this doctrine, which of course is the principal point to be considered, is twofold,— Scripture and the reason of the thing. As to Scripture, all those many texts which speak of the freeness of salva- tion, one of which was just now cited, are brought in behalf of the principle that confident trust is the sole qualification for being justified. " Ask, and it shall be given you ; seek, and ye shall find ; knock, and it shall be opened unto you ; for *every one* that seeketh findeth ;" —" Ho, *every one* that thirsteth, come ye to the waters ;" —" What things soever ye desire when ye pray, *believe that ye receive* them, and ye shall have them." [2] No words, it is urged, can express more strongly the title of every one who hears of the great gift of God, to make it his own ; and his immediate possession of it, without any

---

[1] Gerhard. de Justif, § 179. Calvin. Institut. iii. 18, n. 10. This doctrine has sometimes been thus expressed by its defenders : " Fides, fœta bonis operibus, justificat ante partum." Vid. Bull, Harm. i. 6, § 2.   [2] Matt. vii. 7. Is. lv. 1. Mark xi. 24.

intermediate channel or instrument of gaining it, if he does but believe he has it.

To these must be added the more distinct announcements of St. Paul about faith in particular ; which, though they do not go to the extent of teaching we are justified by faith *only*, yet, as no one can deny, speak of the connection of faith with justification in a very remarkable way. I mean such texts as these :—" Being justified freely by His grace, through the redemption that is in Christ Jesus, whom God hath set forth to be a propitiation through *faith* in His blood ; and again, " Being *justified by faith*, we have peace with God through our Lord Jesus Christ ;" and again, " Therefore we conclude that a man is justified by faith *without the deeds of the law ;* "[1]—texts which certainly do speak of our being justified by faith in *some* very especial sense, and without the aid of deeds of the law, and therefore (it is urged) without the aid of any instrument, condition, or qualification at all, whether Christian grace or good work.

Scripture then, by telling us to come for the gifts of grace and that we shall at once receive them, is supposed to imply that they are dispensed without any intermediate channel between God and the soul ; on the ground that they would not be *freely* given, if given *through* any of God's servant's or ministers, Angel or Apostle, Prophet or Priest.

7.

Such is the Scripture evidence adduced for this view of justification ;—however, it is considered, instead of needing evidence from Scripture, rather to be itself an

[1] Rom. iii. 24, 25, 28 ; v. 1.

evidence of the inspiration of Scripture. Other systems (it seems) have attempted to melt the heart and restore our corrupt nature by severity, threats, or motives of expediency ; but the gospel alone has dared to trust itself to the principle of free and unconditional favour, yet with success as signal as has been the failure of all other methods ; for the mere preaching of reconciliation with God, the doctrine of pardon, the command to take and enjoy the blessings of redemption, has been found to act upon the soul in a remarkable way for its conversion and renewal. This argument has sometimes been practically considered as a substitute for elaborate Scripture evidence, as if it approved itself to men's minds at once, as a short and easy proof of the truth of the doctrine , —for though numberless conversions have been made through a long course of ages *without* the doctrine (utter revolutions indeed in the principles and framework of society, the laws of nations, and the habits both of barbarian and educated minds), still (it is said) these conversions were but outward, as not being attended by an enlightened and heartfelt perception of the free grace of the gospel, and of its abolition of all rites and ordinances ; and though doubtless, *since* this instrument has been used, multitudes have abused it to their everlasting ruin, yet all this does not interfere with the blessedness of its effects, wherever it has operated on a truly penitent heart, and been used for its legitimate purposes with meditation, prayer, watchfulness, godly fear, and a conscientious walk.

This is a practical argument in behalf of the sole instrumentality of Faith in our justification ; and it is supported by another of an abstract character, derived from (what is called) the *apprehensive* power of faith.[1] Faith alone of all the fruits of the Spirit, and not love, hope, fear, or resignation, contemplates the expiatory sacrifice of Christ ; and, as having it for its *Object*, it must be believed to have it for its *possession*. It is the instrument of appropriating the *gift*, for the very reason that it is the means by which the mind receives the *news* of it. Faith, it is argued, *sees* the purchased redemption, and therefore must be able to *take* and *apply* it. ·It is the eye, and therefore of course it is the hand. Or, in a word, it *apprehends* Christ ; a suitable, or rather convenient term as vaguely including both ideas, of accepting the message and receiving the gift, without marking the distinction between them.

8.

This however is but a portion of the argument derived from the apprehensive power of Faith. It is not

[1] Si fides, antequam sequantur opera, Christum *apprehendit,* verum esse *oportet,* solam fidem redemptionem sibi *applicare,* id quod est justificari.—Luther. Libell. ad Ed. August. Vid. also in Gal. iii. 13 (f. 351). Fides justificat apprehendendo Christum ; eadem vero justificans fides hanc habet proprietatem, quod Deo summum obsequium præstet et gloriam veritatis ei tribuat ; est ergo unicum illa medium, per quod promissionibus divinis de remissione peccatorum invitemur, et *hac ratione* bonorum in illa oblatorum participes reddimur.—Gerhard. de Justif. § 156. Nec aliud volunt nostri cum dicunt sola fide justificamur, quam quod jam dixi, gratis fide propter Christum consequimur remissionem peccatorum, non propter nostram dignitatem. . . . . . . Suntque *correlativè* intelligendæ hæ sententiæ, Fide, id est, fiducia Christi sumus justi, hoc est propter Christum sumus justi.—Melanchthon. Loci Theol. de vocab. Gratiæ. (Op. vol. i. f. 202.) Vid. also Apol. Conf. Augustan. (f. 64). Loc. Theol. in voc. Fidei (f. 197, 199).

only considered to justify *correlatively*,[1] (to use the con-
troversial expression), from the supposed *fitness* that
the principle through which the soul desires and owns
God's mercy should *ipso facto* be the instrument of
obtaining it ; but besides, something is alleged from the
very nature of faith, as well as from its function, in
proof of its being the sole justifying principle.   For, as
being the mere turning and adhering of the soul to
Christ, it may be said by a figure of speech to live in
Him in whose image it rests.   Other graces are complete
in themselves ; or at least have something in themselves
excellent and praiseworthy.   Thus they do not necessarily lead to Christ, but remain within their own limits,
contented (as it were) with themselves, and sufficient for
their own enjoyment.   But faith has no such inward
principle on which to depend ; it looks out of doors for
that in which it centres, and is altogether animated and
absorbed by its divine Object.   It depends upon, it holds
of the thought of Him ; it is alive only as the thought
of Him pervades and informs it.   Since then the
thought of Him is ever present in it, therefore He
may be said to be ever present in it, or (what is supposed to be the same thing) He is *spiritually* present
in it ; and if He is present, His merits are present in it,
and are in this way conveyed to the soul which exercises
it.   In this sense Luther seems to speak as if Christ
were the *forma fidei*,[2] or that which makes faith what it

---

[1] Gerhard. de Justif. § 163, etc. etc.

[2] Christus in me vivit : is est mea forma, ornans fidem meam, ut
color vel lux parietem ornat.—Luther. in Gal. ii. 20 (f. 318).   Fides
justificans non caret debita forma, quæ est fiducialis apprehensio

is, justifying ; for Christ being the One true Justifier,
and the thought of Him being (as it were) He himself,
and Faith being filled with the thought of Him, a justifying power is imparted to faith which in itself it has
not. On the other hand his opponents, whether of the
Roman or Anglican school, are accustomed to urge that
the thought of Christ may be possessed by those who
have not Christ, and therefore that it is in no sense the
form or characteristic principle of justifying faith ; rather
that love, as I noticed above, is the true form, the discriminating mark and moulding principle under which
belief is converted into Faith and made justifying. This
doctrine, however, Luther rejects with great abhorrence,
from the notion that it makes our thoughts centre on
ourselves, cuts off the communication between earth and
heaven, fixes our faith on that love with which it is supposed to be instinct, instead of its mounting up worthless,
rude, and unformed, to receive subsistence, fashion, and
acceptableness in Christ. By way of protest against the
doctrine, which he calls " a most pestilent and Satanical
gloss," he declares, very differently from the language of
our Homilies, that faith justifies *before* and *without* love.[1]

Christi.—Gerhard. de Justif. § 120. Vid. also § 71 (col. 505). Vid.
Calvin. Institut. iii. 11, 20.

[1] Fides . . . quando in proprio suo officio est, nullum prorsus
objectum habet, quam Jesum Christum, Filium Dei, traditum pro
peccatis totius mundi. *Non respicit charitatem ;* non dicit, Quid
fui ? quid merui ? sed quid fuit Christus ? . . . Quare quæ sophistæ
docuerunt de fide justificante, si sit charitate formata, mera verborum
portenta sunt. Ea enim fides, quæ apprehendit Christum Filium Dei,
et eo ornatur, non quæ includit charitatem, justificat. Nam fidem,
si certa et firma esse debet, nihil apprehendere oportet, quam solum

It follows that, by a strong figure, Faith may be said to *claim* the promised blessings, as if it were meritorious, that is, by virtue of the intimate correspondence and sympathy between it and Christ. Hence we may be said to be justified, not only *by* or *through* faith (as our Article words it), but on *account* of faith ; for faith is

Christum, etc. . . . . Quare, qui Christum fide apprehendit, quan-tumvis lege perterrefiat, etc. . . . . . gloriari potest se justum esse. Quomodo aut per quid? *per gemmam Christum*, quem fide possidet. Hoc adversarii non intelligunt ; ideo abjiciunt gemmam Christum, et *in locum ejus reponunt charitatem quam dicunt gemmam esse.* Luther. in Gal. ii. 4, 5 (f. 296, 7). Hic nihil te moveat impia glossa sophistarum, qui dicunt, fidem tum demum justificare si accesserit charitas et bona opera. Ista pestilenti glossa, hanc et similes senten-tias in Paulo, quibus diserte tribuit justificationem fidei, obscurarunt et depravarunt sophistæ. . . . Et pro hac sua perniciosa et pestilenti glossa comprobanda, allegant adversarii locum, 1. Cor. xiii. Si linguis hominum, etc. . . . . . Vitanda est ut venenum infernale, conclu-dendumque cum Paulo, sola fide non fide formata charitate nos justifi-cari ; quare non isti formæ gratificanti tribuenda est vis justificandi, sed fidei, quæ apprehendit et possidet in corde ipsum Christum Salvatorem. Hæc fides *sine* et *ante* charitatem justificat.—In Gal. ii. 16, (f. 309, 310). Vid. also in iii. 12. Si formatam fidem distinguerent contra falsam seu fictam fidem, nihil me offenderet ista illorum distinctio. Sed . . . . faciunt . . . duplicem fidem, informem et formatam. Hanc pestilentissimam et Satanicam glossam non possum non vehementer detestari. . . . Juxta hoc pestilens figmentum sophistarum, fides illa misera virtus erit quoddam informe chaos, nullius operis, efficaciæ, et vitæ, sed tantum passiva materia. Ista omnia blasphema in Deum et Satanica sunt . . . nam si charitas est forma fidei, ut ipsi nugantur, statim cogor sentire ipsam charitatem esse principalem et maximam partem Christianæ religionis ; et sic amitto Christum, sanguinem, vulnera, et omnia beneficia ejus, et inhæreo charitati, et diligo ac venio in facere morale, ut Papa, Gentilis philosophus, aut Turca.—In Gal. iii. 11 (f. 346). Vid. also ff. 312 (1 and 2), 316 (1 and 2), 318 (2), 347 (2). Vid. also Melanchthon. Àpol. Conf. August. (f. 67). Calvin. Institut. iii. 2, n. 8, 41, etc.

absorbed into its Object, of which it is but the outward receptacle, and consequently the symbol and representative. And in this sense faith is considered by Luther and his followers as imputed to us for righteousness, by a mode of speech; Christ really, who is spiritually present in the faith, and not the faith itself, being our sole and true Righteousness, in which our acceptance with God consists.[1] And here additional light is thrown upon the statement, as used by them, that we are justified by faith *only*, faith not thereby excluding the necessity of works, nor becoming meritorious, but the formula " by faith only, not by works," meaning simply this, " by the merit of Christ only, not of works, nor even of faith."

9.

This is an outline of a scheme of doctrine which, with more or less of system, is very prevalent at this day, and which has been usually associated with the name of Luther. The reasons which led to his insisting upon it were chiefly the two following, both arising from his opposition to the Roman doctrine concerning good works ; —first, his wish to extirpate all notions of human merit ; next, to give peace and satisfaction to the troubled conscience.[2]

---

[1] Gerhard. de Justif. § 163. For the imputation of faith, vid. Luther. in Gal. f. 335 (2), f. 417. For *propter fidem* vid. (*e.g.*) in Gal. ii. 16 (f. 308), f. 347 (2). Est Christiana justitia imputatio divina pro justitia vel ad justitiam, propter fidem in Christum, vel propter Christum.—In Gal. iii. 6 (f. 336). Vid. the whole passage. In this sense he calls faith *formalis justitia*, in Gal. ii. 16 (f. 308). See also a very eloquent passage on the same subject in f. 334, " Paulus his verbis, etc." Also Melanchth. Apol. (f. 70).

[2] These two points are treated of by Calvin, Institut. iii. 13,

In effecting these objects, however, he also adopted another tenet, which in his system is the counterpart of the sole instrumentality of Faith. He taught that the Moral Law is not binding on the conscience of the Christian; that Christ has fulfilled it by His own obedience; that He is our Righteousness, in the sense of His obedience being the substitute for ours in the sight of God's justice; and that Faith is the instrument by which that Righteousness becomes ours. Such a view of the gospel covenant met both the alleged evils against which it was provided. For if Christ has obeyed the Law instead of us, it follows, that every believer has at once a perfect righteousness, yet not his own; that it is not his own, precludes all boasting, that it is perfect precludes all anxiety. The conscience is unladen, without becoming puffed up. With a few remarks under each of these heads I shall conclude.

1. First then, as to the proper merit of works; it is urged by the school of Luther, that that doctrine is not banished from theology, so long as works are allowed to have any share whatever in our justification, in spite of St. James's affirming that they have. While they have any share in it, it is possible to *rest* in our works—they do not imply or remind of Christ's all-sufficiency; but we cannot lean upon our faith, for in fact (as I have said) it has no real substance or strength of its own, nothing to support us; it does but give way and carry us back and throw us on the thought of Christ, in whom it lives. To this argument it may be replied, that since no good works can be done but through the grace of God, those works are but evidence that that grace is with the doer;

so that to view them as sharing in our justification tends to elate us, neither more nor less than the knowledge that we are under divine influences is elating. But they answer, that we are not concerned here with formal admissions and distinctions, but with practical impressions ; that to say, that Christ is but the remote source of justification, and that our own doings, though through His grace, are the proximate cause, is in fact to fix the mind on ourselves, not on Him ; whereas to teach that He actually in His own person has obeyed the Law for each of us is a most efficacious means of deterring us from thinking about our own obedience to it at all, and faith again, however much insisted on, has so little in it to recommend it or to rest in, so little in it holy, precious, or praiseworthy, that it cannot seduce us to self-gratulation or spiritual pride or pharisaical exclusiveness, seeing our best doings in the Spirit are neither better nor more acceptable to the Divine Majesty than those natural righteousnesses, which Scripture calls "filthy rags," and "an unclean thing." On the other hand, this doctrine does not tend, they say, to widen the way which Christ has pronounced to be narrow ; for, though faith is so worthless, and therefore so safe a feeling, yet it is not easy to acquire. The pride of man resists this way of salvation from its very easiness, and is not subdued without much inward conflict.[1] In proportion, however, as faith takes

[1] Luther. in Gal. iii. 2 (f. 331). It would seem, however, as if the stricter Lutherans, who maintained that faith justified before and without love, made much more of the dignity of faith than the school of Melanchthon, who considered it to be inseparable from love, and to justify *correlative*. Vid. Bellarm. de Justif. i. 12. Gerhard. de Justif. § 163.

the place of pride, its Divine Object is contemplated by the mind,—presented, not intercepted by that which is the medium of the mind's possessing it.

Another similar use of these doctrines is to secure us against self-contemplation. Prayer, alms, fasting, and the like, which are but modes of approaching God, will be dwelt on as ends, as objects for self-complacency, and sources of those spiritual benefits which in profession are but sought through them, unless Christ's righteousness be insisted on as that in which immediately our justification lies, and faith that by which it is gained.[1]

It follows moreover, from what has been observed, that though, according to the system before us, it may be scripturally said that Faith is taken for righteousness, yet it will be safer, as well as more correct, for us to say that Christ is our righteousness ; lest we should think that our justification lies in anything of ours, and not in Christ.

10.

2. Reliance then on self, in whatever shape, is one of the two evils which it is supposed are destroyed by the doctrine of faith as the instrument, and Christ's righteousness as the form, of justification ; the other is the state of doubt about our justification which must ever attend the belief that it depends on our graces and works, though produced by divine influences. It is urged that the great end of the gospel is to give peace to the troubled conscience, to take from it the fear of eternal death, and to assure it of pardon and acceptance with God. Without the certainty of salvation,—(at least so far as to

---

[1] Luther. in Gal. ii. 20 (f. 318).

know that, were we to die at the present moment we
should be secure of heaven,[1] whatever may be our
chance of losing it in time to come),—but at least without
an assurance that we are at present accounted sinless and
unreproveable in God's sight for Christ's sake, that no
charge lies against us, that all our past sins up to this
hour are absolutely forgiven, and that no future judgment
on them need be dreaded,—without all this, the gospel has
hardly done its work, but leaves us, as far as our peace
is concerned, under the bond of the Law.[2] Now if this
certainty of our present salvation be a part of our
Christian privileges, evidently it can never be attained
by works,[3] because we can never know when we have
done enough ; whereas Faith is a principle which a person
may easily satisfy himself that he has, which is naturally
adapted to be its own evidence, and which moreover
inspires its possessor with this peculiar comfort, that he
has nothing more to do to secure his salvation, and need
but hold on as he is, looking at Christ's perfect work,
and appropriating it to himself. Christ has fulfilled the
Law for us ; faith makes that fulfilment ours ; and places
us above the Law. In observing the Law, though
we shall observe it, we are not performing a duty ;
we are merely stooping from that heavenly state in which

[1] Gerhard. de Justif. § 81, etc.

[2] Is [Christus] solus dominetur in justitia, securitate, lætitia, et
vita, ut conscientia læta *obdormiat* in Christo, *sine ullo sensu legis*
peccati, et mortis.—Luther. in Gal. iv. 3 (f. 373).

[3] Equidem si ab operibus æstimandum sit qualiter affectus sit erga
nos Dominus, id ne tenui quidem conjectura possemus assequi fateor ;
sed quum simplici et gratuitæ promissioni respondere fides debet,
nullus ambigendi locus relinquitur.—Calvin. Institut. iii. 2, n. 38.

Christ has placed us, and condescending to take part in
things of this earth.[1]   To allow we are under it, is (it is
urged) necessarily polluting our conscience with a sense
of guilt ; for, since we all sin continually, while we subject
our conscience to the Law, we can as little enjoy the
assurance of our salvation, as we can exercise implicit
faith in the all-sufficiency of Christ's merits.   Nor must
it be hence inferred that the Christian is not in fact fruitful in good works, but only that they flow naturally
from such a simple trust as has been described ; nor
that he is at liberty to violate the Law, but only that it
is not a matter of conscience to him to keep it ;[2] nor

[1] Dicimus autem supra quod lex in Christiano non debeat excedere
limites suos, sed tantum habere dominium in carnem, quæ et ei subjecta
sit et sub ea maneat ; hoc ubi fit, consistit lex intra limites suos.   Si
vero vult occupare conscientiam, et hic dominari, vide ut tum sis bonus
dialecticus, recte dividas, et legi non plus tribuas quam ei tribuendum
est ; sed dicas, Lex, tu vis ascendere in regnum conscientiæ, et ibi
dominari, et eam arguere peccati, et gaudium cordis tollere, quod habeo
ex fide in Christum, et me in desperationem adigere, ut desperem et
peream.   Hoc præter officium tuum facis, consiste intra limites tuos, et
exerce dominium in carnem.   Conscientiam autem ne attingas mihi ;
sum enim baptizatus, et per Evangelium vocatus ad communionem
justitiæ et vitæ æternæ, ad Regnum Christi, in quo acquiescit conscientia mea, ubi nulla est lex, etc. . . Hanc [justitiam Christi] cum
intus habeo, *descendo de cœlo*, tanquam pluvia fœcundans terram, hoc
est, prodeo foras in *aliud regnum et facio bona opera quæcunque mihi
occurrent*, etc. . . . Quicunque certo novit Christum esse justitiam
suam, is non solum ex animo et cum gaudio bene operatur in vocatione
sua, sed subjicit se quoque per charitatem magistratibus, etc. . . .
quia scit Deum hoc velle et placere hanc obedientiam.—Luther. Argum.
in Gal. (f. 274).   Perhaps it is a happy thing that all of Luther's
followers are not " boni dialectici " enough to carry out his principles
to this length.

[2] Quamquam sic *liber* est [Christianus] ab omnibus operibus, *debet*

that he will not labour to grow in grace, but only that he is not more acceptable to God, if he does ;[1] nor that he will not be watchful against falling away, but only that he is sure (unless his faith is weak[2]) that he has salvation at present.

And now perhaps enough has been said in explanation of a theology familiar to all ears at present, which differs from our own in these two main points among others ;—in considering that Faith and not Baptism is the primary instrument of justification, and that this Faith which justifies exercises its gift without the exercise or even the presence of love.

tamen rursus se exinanire hac in libertate, formam servi accipere, in similitudinem hominum fieri, etc.—Luther. de Lib. Christ. f. 9 (2).

[1] Episcopus sacer, templum consecrans, pueros confirmans, aut aliud quippiam officii sui faciens, non consecratur iis ipsis operibus in Episcopum, etc. . . ita Christianus per fidem suam consecratus bona facit opera, sed non per hæc *magis* sacer aut Christianus efficitur ; hæc enim solius fidei est, etc.—Luther. de Lib. Christ. (f. 8).

[2] Si . . . adest conscientiæ pavor, *signum est hanc justitiam ablatam,* gratiam amissam esse à conspectu, et Christum obscuratum non videri. -- Luther. Argum. in Gal. (f. 273).

LECTURE II.

LOVE CONSIDERED AS THE FORMAL CAUSE

OF JUSTIFICATION.

I HAVE hitherto been employed upon a view of justification which happens to be very extensively professed in our Church at this day, either systematically or
not ; and has great influence, *as* a system, in consequence
of the many religious men who hold it *without* system.
I cannot for an instant believe that so many would adhere to it, if they understood what it really means when
brought out as distinct from other views on the subject,
and made consistent with itself. They profess it, because
it is what is put into their hands, and they graft it upon
a temper of mind in many cases far higher and holier
than it.

Now I come to consider the opposite scheme of
doctrine, which is not unsound or dangerous in itself,
but in a certain degree incomplete,—truth, but not the
whole truth ; viz., that justification consists in love, or
sanctity, or obedience, or " renewal of the Holy Ghost."[1]
In describing it then, I am describing not a perversion,

---

[1] Tit. iii. 5. Hoc est *Justitia Dei*, quam non solum docet per
Legis præceptum, verum etiam *dat per Spiritus donum.*—August. de
Spir. et Lit. 56. Cum timore et tremore suam ipsorum salutem operen-
tur ; Deus est enim qui operatur in eis et velle et operari pro bona

but what Saints and Martyrs have in substance held in
every age, though not apart from other truths which
serve to repress those tendencies to error, which it, in
common with every other separate portion of the Scripture creed, contains, not in itself, but when exclusively
cherished by the human mind. But in the Roman
schools, it has often been thus detached and isolated ;[1]
to use the technical language which even the Council of
Trent has adopted, spiritual renewal is said to be the
" *unica formalis causa*," the *one and only* true description
of justification ; and this seems to be the critical difference between those schools and such divines, whether of
the Ancient Church or our own, as seem most nearly to
agree with them.—Now, however, to describe it in itself,

voluntate. *Hoc est justitia Dei, hoc est quod Deus donat* homini, cum
justificat impium. Hanc Dei justitiam ignorantes superbi Judæi, etc.
August. ad Honoratum, 53, 34, Ep. 140. Legimus justificari in Christo
qui credunt, in eum propter occultam communicationem et inspirationem
gratiæ spiritalis, qua quisquis hæret Domino, unus spiritus est.—August.
de Peccat. Rem. i. 11.

[1] [This charge only comes to this, that when the Roman schools
are treating of one point of theology, they are not treating of other
points. When the Council of Trent is treating of man, it is not treating of God. Its enunciations are isolated and defective, taken one by
one, of course. If we desire a warmer exhibition of Christian truth
than a treatise on Justification admits, we may go to mystical writers
such as Schram, whose doctrine on the Holy Eucharist, quoted above
in the Advertisement to this edition, is the supplement to an account of
formal causes. All theological definitions come short of concrete life.
Science is not devotion or literature. If the Fathers are not cold, and
the Schoolmen are, this is because the former write in their own persons, and the latter as logicians or disputants. St. Athanasius or St.
Augustine has a life, which a system of theology has not. Yet dogma
tic theology has its use and its importance notwithstanding.]

that is, so far as it may be considered as *common* to the Fathers, the Romanists, and (to say the very least) the greater number of our own writers.

2.

It is affirmed then, that since man fell, he has lain under one great need, in which all other needs are included, in supplying which all blessings are secured ; and which, in proportion as he has understood his real state, he has ever desired, ever struggled after, in vain. He is by nature born in sin, and consequently the child of wrath ; and he needs a new birth unto righteousness, that he may become the child of God. He needs a destruction of the old Adam, of the body of original death, and thereby a restoration to the light of God's countenance. What has made him hateful to Infinite Purity, what exposes him to death eternal, is disobedience ; take away that disobedience, and you take away his guilt, peril, misery, all that needs taking away ; and in proportion as you rid him of the one, you rid him of the other. This then is really our one burden ; not merely a sense of guilt, or guilt itself, but that which is the cause both of guilt and the sense of guilt. Man did not become guilty except by becoming sinful ; he does not become innocent except by becoming holy. God cannot, from His very nature, look with pleasure and favour upon an unholy creature, or justify or count righteous one who is not righteous. Cleanness of heart and spirit, obedience by word and deed, this alone in us can be acceptable to God ; that is, this alone can constitute our justification. And as certain is it, we cannot acquire it for ourselves ; but, if it is to be ours, it must come from God only. The one thing we need is the ability to please God, or to be righteous ; and it is God's gift. As His gift, good men have at all times sought it ; as His gift, it was promised under the Law ; and as His gift, it is possessed by the regenerate under the Gospel.

Till the Gospel came, with its manifold gifts of grace, there was a contrariety and enmity between the Divine Law and the heart of man : they confronted each other, the one all light, the other all corruption. They ran parallel to each other, not converging ; the Law detecting, condemning, terrifying, not influencing except for the worse ; the human heart secretly acquiescing, but not loving, not obeying. In consequence we were unable to please God by what we did, that is, we were unrighteous ; for by righteousness is meant obedience such as to be acceptable. We needed then a justification, or making righteous ; and this might be vouchsafed to us in two ways, either by our Maker's dispensing with that exact obedience which the Law required, or by His enabling us to fulfil it. In either, but in no other conceivable way, could our moral state, which by nature is displeasing, become pleasing to God, our unrighteousness become righteousness. Now, according to the doctrine I am engaged in expounding, the remedy lies in the latter alternative only ; not in lowering the Law, much less in abolishing it, but in bringing up our hearts to it ; in preserving, in raising *its* standard, and in refashioning *them*, and so (as it were) attuning them to its high harmonies. As regards the past indeed, since it cannot literally be undone, a dispensation or pardon is all that can be given us ; but for the present and future, if a gift is to be vouchsafed us, and we may anticipate what it should be, *this* is what we have to pray for,—not to have the Holy Law taken away, not to be merely accounted to do what we do not do, not a nominal change, a nominal righteousness,[1] an external blessing, but one penetrating inwards into our heart and spirit, joints and marrow, pervading us with a real efficacy, and wrapping us round in its fulness ; not a change merely in God's dealings towards us, like the pale and wan sunshine of a winter's day, but (if we may seek it) the possession of Himself, of His substantial grace to touch and heal the root of the evil, the fountain of our misery, our bitter heart and its inbred corruption. As we can conceive God blessing nothing but what is holy, so all our notions of blessing centre in holiness as a necessary foundation. Holiness is the thing, the internal state, because of which blessing comes. He may bless, He may curse, according to His mercy or our deserts ; but if He blesses, surely it is by making holy ; if He counts righteous, it is by making righteous ; if He justifies, it is by renewing ; if He reconciles us to Himself, it is not by annihilating the Law, but by creating in us new wills and new powers for the observance of it.[2]

[1] Vide John Smith, Discourse of Justification, ch. v. fin. ed. 1673. pp. 321–324.

[2] Lex ergo data est, ut gratia quæreretur ; gratia data est, *ut lex impleretur*. Neque enim suo vitio non implebatur lex, sed vitio prudentiæ carnis ; quod vitium per legem demonstrandum, per gratiam sanandum fuit. . . Propter veteris hominis noxam quæ per literam jubentem et minantem minime sanabatur, dicitur illud testamentum

3.

Nature then desires, whether it be granted or not, that that Law which we behold without us should be set up within us ; that an inward power should be imparted to us, enabling us to please God or to be justified, and converting that which is by nature an occasion of con-demnation into an instrument of acceptance. Of course, even though we did all that the Law commanded, we should after all be but unprofitable servants, and could claim nothing on the score of merit ; but, since the Great Creator deigns to accept the service of his crea-tures, we should, as giving it, be pleasing Him by our obedience. In the same sense then in which it can be said that God is *glorified* by our obedience, though His perfection is infinitely above the need of it, so can it be said that we are *justified* by our obedience, though His favour is infinitely beyond the value of it. And this great blessing, it is affirmed, really is bestowed on us in the Gospel ; which, by the gift of the Holy Ghost, works in us a new and spiritual life, such as at once glorifies God before His creatures, and justifies us before Himself.[1]

And that this will be the privilege of Saints hereafter, as of the Angels now, is, I suppose, allowed on all hands ; the characteristic of the Schools of doctrine under review, as distinct from that of Luther, being that they conceive

vetus ; hoc autem novum, propter novitatem spiritus quæ hominem novum sanat a vitio vetustatis. . . . August. de Spir. et Lit. 34, 35.

[1] Quæ [mandata] ut possit homo facere, *Deus operatur in homine* per fidem Jesu Christi, qui finis est ad *justitiam* omni credenti, id est, per *Spiritum* incorporatus factusque membrum ejus, potest quisque, illo incrementum *intrinsecus* dante, *operari justitiam.*—August. de Spir. et Lit. 50.

that in the sense in which God's grace enables us to
glorify God at present, in the same it enables us to please
God or become righteous at present ; for no obedience
can honour Him in the sight of His creatures, except
such as makes us pleasant or righteous in His own sight.

Justification, then, viewed relatively to the past is
forgiveness of sin, for nothing more it can be ; but considered as to the present and future it is more, it is renewal wrought in us by the Spirit of Him who by His
merits completes what is defective in that renewal. And
Faith is said to justify in two principal ways :—first, as
continually pleading our Lord's merits before God, and
secondly, as being the first recipient of the Spirit, the
root, and therefore the earnest and anticipation of perfect
obedience.[1]

4.

Now for the truth of these representations we are
referred to Scripture, and that not to one or two texts

---

[1] Ideo quippe proponitur justitia legis, quod qui fecerit eam, vivet
in illa, ut cum quisque infirmitatem suam cognoverit, nou per suas vires,
neque per literam ipsius legis, quod fieri non potest, sed *per fidem* con-
cilians *Justificatorem* perveniat et (ut ?) *faciat* et *vivat in eâ. Opus* enim
quod qui fecerit, vivet in eo, non fit nisi a justificato. Justificatio autem
ex fide impetratur, de qua scriptum est, "Ne dixeris in cordibus," etc.
[Rom. x. 6]. In tantum justus, in quantum salvus . . . . *Fide* igitur
Jesu Christi impetramur salutem et quantum nobis *inchoatur in re*, et
quantum perficienda expectatur in spe . . . . . Per fidem confugiat
[anima] ad misericordiam Dei, *ut det quod jubet*, atque *inspirata gratiæ
suavitate per Spiritum Sanctum* faciat plus delectare *quod præcipit* quam
delectat quod impedit. Ita multa multitudo dulcedinis ejus, hoc est,
lex fidei, caritas ejus conscripta in cordibus atque diffusa, perficitur
sperantibus in eum, ut anima sanata non timore pœnæ, sed *amore
justitiæ* operetur bonum.—August. de Spir. et Lit. 51.

only, detached from their context, as in the case of the
Lutheran view of the subject, but to an extended survey
of the inspired word in both Testaments.   Scripture in
its various portions conspires together as a whole to this
simple doctrine.   From first to last what Psalmists long
after, and Prophets promise, and Apostles announce as
given by Almighty God, is one and the same, the capacity
of serving God acceptably, or the gift of righteousness,
not a shadow but a substance, not a name but a power,
not an imputation but an inward work.

1. First, appeal is made to the book of Psalms; which,
whether in the way of aspiration, prayer, or prophecy,
so clearly assigns to the Evangelical Covenant the gift
of *inwardly* justifying, that we may as well maintain
that that Covenant has not been made as that inward justification is not accorded.   This actual inherent righteousness is the one main thought of the Psalms, not of course
to the exclusion of other blessings, but as the centre and
scope of them all.   Let us take, for instance, the 119th
Psalm, which may be considered as the standing prayer
of the Church Militant in every age, as of old time for
things longed for, so now for things pledged to it.   Now
one great gift is there contemplated again and again, in
various forms, and that is nothing short of renovation of
mind, the power to obey God, His quickening, illuminating, cleansing, comforting " Word" (as it is there called),
or " Truth," or " Law," or " Judgments," or (as the Latin
version speaks) " Justifications."   " O that my ways
were made so direct that I might keep Thy statutes !
Thy words have I hid within my heart, that I should
not sin against Thee.   My soul cleaveth to the dust, O

quicken Thou me according to thy word. Quicken Thou me in Thy way ; stablish Thy word in Thy servant, that I may fear Thee ; quicken me in Thy righteousness : Thy word hath quickened me ; my eyes long sore for Thy word, saying, O when wilt Thou comfort me ? Thy word endureth for ever in heaven. I will never forget Thy commandments, for with them Thou hast quickened me ; O how sweet are Thy words unto my throat ; my eyes are wasted away with looking for Thy health, and for the word of Thy righteousness ; when Thy word goeth forth, it giveth light and understanding unto the simple ; I opened my mouth and drew in my breath, for my delight was in thy commandments. Thy righteousness is an everlasting righteousness, and Thy law is the truth ; my heart standeth in awe of Thy word." [1]

In these passages " Righteousness " is sought after by name ; in such as the following it is promised or anticipated ; and still inward holiness is the heavenly gift which is spoken of. " Thou, Lord, wilt give Thy blessing unto the righteous, and with Thy favourable kindness wilt Thou defend him as with a shield." "The Lord alloweth the righteous." " The righteous Lord loveth righteousness ; His countenance will behold the thing that is just." " God is in the generation of the righteous." " Who shall dwell in Thy tabernacle ? even he that leadeth an uncorrupt life." " Be Thou my judge, O Lord, for I have walked innocently. Do well, O Lord, unto those who are good and true of heart." " Offer the sacrifice of righteousness, and put your trust in the Lord." " Give sentence with me, O God, according to my right-

[1] Ps. cxix. 6, 11, 25, 37, 38, etc.

eousness, and according to the innocency that is in me.
O let the wickedness of the ungodly come to an end, but
guide Thou the just. For the righteous God trieth the
very hearts and reins." [1] The sacred writer is not satisfied with an external or nominal righteousness, but he
feels a want within, and he prays for what he knows to
be the very substance of religion.

5.

If it be objected that such passages only show that
obedience is *necessary* for God's favour, which no one
denies, and that therefore an accumulation of them,
however great, is nothing to the purpose, it may be
replied, that on the contrary it is everything ; that, as
only one such text would show that obedience was *a*
condition of God's favour, so these multiplied statements
show that it is the one condition, the one thing in us
which involves acceptance on God's part, that one
requisite, in naming which all we need is named. It is
usual at the present day to lay great stress on the
distinction between deliverance from guilt and deliverance
from sin ; to lay down as a first principle that these are
two coincident indeed and contemporary, but altogether
independent benefits, to call them justification and
renewal, and to consider that any confusion between
them argues serious and alarming ignorance of Christian
truth. Now, in opposition to this, it may surely be
maintained that Scripture itself blends them together as
intimately as any system of theology can do : and that

[1] Ps. iv. 5 ; v. 13 : vii. 8-10 ; xi. 6, 8 : xiv. 9 ; xv. 1, 2 ; xxvi. 1 :
cxxv. 4.

such a system is not thereby "dark" and "ignorant," unless Scripture is so also. In truth, Scripture speaks of but one gift, which it sometimes calls renewal, sometimes justification, according as it views it,—passing to and fro from one to the other so rapidly, so abruptly, as to force upon us irresistibly the inference, that they *are* really one, and but in idea two ; that our righteousness is but a quality of our renewal. In other words, this distinction, so carefully made by many men at present, between being righteous and being holy, is not scriptural.

This might first be shown from the Psalms ; for instance, the 51st. That this is an evangelical Psalm in the fullest sense no one can doubt. It is David's prayer for restoration to God's favour after his grievous fall. It contains in it the two ideas in question, of deliverance from guilt and deliverance from sin ; but does it accurately distinguish between them ? So far from it, as to make it impossible to doubt, that in the mind of the inspired writer the one benefit immediately involved the other as being a part of it, that renewal involved external justification or God's favour, and that God's favour was given through renewal. For instance, which of the two benefits does he speak of when he says, " *Wash* me throughly from my wickedness, and *cleanse* me from my sin "? If we judge by a subsequent verse, " Thou shalt purge me with hyssop, and I shall be clean," we shall say that by " washing" he must mean renewal ; but if so, observe how the foregoing verse connects with it—" Have *mercy* upon me, O God, . . . *do away* mine offences, wash me." He says not, " *Both* have mercy *and* renew," con-

templating two gifts, but "show mercy by renewing me."
Again, "Thou shalt *wash* me, and I shall be whiter than
snow ; Thou shalt make me hear of *joy* and gladness."
What then ? does joy follow from sanctification ? The
doctrine popular at present connects joy rigidly with
justification ; as if *immediately upon* justification, and
before sanctification, "joy and peace in believing" ensued
I really do not understand how a man can read this most
important Psalm without perceiving (though I know
many do not perceive it), that we are forgiven *by being*,
or *while we are* renewed, and that the present broad
separation of justification and sanctification, as if they
were two gifts, not in idea only two, but in fact, is
technical and unscriptural.

6.

2. Now let us proceed to the Prophets, who promise the blessings which the Psalms pray for. It is
needless to observe that they name "Righteousness" continually as the great gift of the New Covenant, and the
fruit of Christ's earthly ministry. What then is this
Righteousness which is bestowed on us ? a mere external
gift, a nominal qualification for heaven ? is it the virtue of
Christ's incarnation and sufferings, not imparted to the
soul, but imputed merely ? Let us turn to a passage
from the 51st chapter of Isaiah for an answer. "A *Law*
shall proceed from Me, and I will make My judgment
to rest for a *Light* of the people. My Righteousness is
near, My salvation is gone forth, and Mine arms shall
judge the people ; the isles shall wait upon Me, and on
Mine arm shall they trust." Now the Righteousness or

salvation promised was to be a *Law* and a *Light;* how can the personal obedience which Christ wrought in the days of His flesh, by being counted as ours in God's sight, become a Law and a Light? but what follows makes this still clearer. " Hearken unto Me, *ye that know righteous-ness*, the people in whose *heart* is My *Law*." Righteous-ness then is a *Law in the heart*, and those who think otherwise do not, in the Prophet's words, "*know* right-eousness."

Again, the 35th chapter of the same Prophet might be quoted at length, as showing that the characteristic gift of the Gospel is more than the mere name of being what our Saviour really is, righteous. "*Then*," says the Prophet, " the eyes of the blind shall be opened, and the ears of the deaf shall be unstopped . . . An highway shall be there, and a way, and it shall be called, The *way of holiness;* the unclean shall not pass over it." Again, in the 26th chapter, which also is a prophecy of the Christian Church, "The way of the just is uprightness; Thou, most upright, dost weigh the path of the just. Yea, in the way of Thy judgments, O Lord, have we waited for Thee . . . Lord, Thou wilt ordain peace for us, *for Thou also hast wrought all our works in us*." Peace is made to depend on an internal work.

If it be said that there is no lack of passages in the Psalms and Prophets which speak of forgiveness as the gift of the Gospel, as David's words, "Blessed is he whose unrighteousness is forgiven," and Isaiah's, "The Lord hath sent Me to bind up the broken-hearted,"[1] this may be freely granted. All that is here maintained

---

[1] Psalm xxxii. 1. Isaiah lxi. 1.

is, that forgiveness is but a part of that one gift; that the gift relates not only to the past but to the present, not only to what is without but to what is within; that in its fulness, in its essential character, it is not pardon merely but righteousness, not merely righteousness in name but in deed and truth.

What can be more emphatic than the passage in Jeremiah, which St. Paul singles out more than once as being, what it is in its very wording, the formal announcement, or (as it were) the charter of the New Covenant? "This is the Covenant that I will make with them after those days, saith the Lord; *I will put My laws into their hearts,* and in their minds will I write them, and their sins and iniquities will I remember no more."[1] It is plain from this passage, that the *direct* promise of the Gospel, the clear intelligible view which meets us here, as in Isaiah, is a renovation of our nature, in which pardon is involved as an essential part, but only a part, of the free gift.

7.

3. Let us now, without leaving the Old Testament, turn to the Epistles of St. Paul, of whose doctrine the passage just referred to will prove to be but an ordinary specimen. St. Paul again and again speaks of our

[1] Heb. x. 16, 17.

Quid sunt ergo leges Dei ab ipso Deo scriptæ in cordibus nisi ipsa præsentia Spiritus sancti, qui est digitus Dei, quo præsente diffunditur caritas in cordibus nostris quæ *plenitudo legis* est et *præcepti finis* . . . Dicitur, "Dabo leges meas," etc., unde significavit eos non forinsecus terrentem legem formidaturos, sed *intrinsecus habitantem ipsam legis jus-titiam* dilecturos.—August. de Spir. et Lit. 36.

justification as being not from without but from within;
from God indeed as its origin, but through our own
hearts and minds, wills and powers. He attributes it to
the influences of the Spirit working in us, and enabling
us to perform that obedience to the Law, towards which
by ourselves we could not take a single step. For
instance, he describes the natural man after David's
manner, as "born in sin and shapen in iniquity," as
" brought into captivity," as having " a *law* of sin in his
members," and bearing about with him " a body of death."
And then he thanks God that in Christ he is *delivered*
from this bondage ; but how? by "the law of *the Spirit
of life* making him free from the law of *sin and death.*"
" For," he continues, " what the Law," that is the External
Law, "could not do, in *that it was weak through* the
flesh, God sending His own Son in the likeness of
sinful flesh, and for sin, condemned sin in the flesh,
that the *righteousness* of the Law might be fulfilled
in us," not independent of us, but in us, " who walk
not after the flesh, but after the Spirit."[1] Can words
be stronger to prove that the righteousness of the Law
is not abolished under the Gospel, is not fulfilled by
Christ only, but by Him as the first-fruits of many
brethren, by us in our degree after Him, that is, by Him in
us, tending day by day towards that perfection which He
manifested from the first ? Can words more conclusively
show that Gospel righteousness is obedience to the Law
of God, wrought in us by the Holy Ghost? Can we
desire a more exact counterpart to the language of the
Psalms and Prophets already pointed out ? Even if we

[1] Rom. viii. 1-4.

could otherwise interpret St. Paul's language, which we
cannot fairly, shall we be inconsistent enough to give one
meaning to the word "*righteousness*" in the prayer of
the Saints, another in the answer to them? one meaning
to it in the Prophecy, another in the fulfilment? Shall
we explain away the Apostle's language, of which
"prophets and kings" had fixed the interpretation
beforehand, and make the Epistles say the less, and the
Psalms say the more?

Again, to the Corinthians: "Ye are manifestly
declared to be the epistle of Christ ministered by us,
written not with ink, but *with the Spirit of the Living
God*, not on *tables* of stone, but in fleshly tables of the
heart." God "hath enabled us to be ministers of the
New Covenant ; *not of the Letter, but of the Spirit ;* for
the *Letter killeth*, but the *Spirit giveth Life*." [1] Can words
be clearer to show that, as the Letter or External Law is
that which condemns us to death, so the Spirit, that is
the Law written on the heart, or spiritual renovation, is
that which *justifies us ?* [2] Surely, if we may deny that
the Spirit justifies, we may, for all St. Paul says, deny
the Law condemns. But he continues more plainly :
"But if the ministration of death" (or external Law)
"was glorious . . . how shall not the Ministration *of the
Spirit* be rather glorious? for if the ministration of

---

[1] 2 Cor. iii. 3-6. *Lex Dei* non ex omni parte deleta per injustitiam,
profecto *scribitur renovata per gratiam.* Nec *istam inscriptionem, quæ
justificatio est*, poterat efficere in Judæis lex in tabulis scripta, sed
solum prævaricationem.—August. de Spir. et Lit. 48.

[2] Novi Testamenti, ministrationem Spiritus et ministrationem justitiæ dicit, quia per *donum Spiritus operamur justitiam* et *a prævarica-
tionis damnatione* liberamur.—August. de Spir. et Lit. 31.

condemnation be glory, much more doth the Ministration *of Righteousness* exceed in glory." Is it not almost too clear to insist upon, that what is first called the ministration of the Spirit, is next called the ministration of righteousness; or, in other words, that the Spirit ministers righteousness, that is, justifies? to say, as some do, that righteousness here means mere sanctification, is but a gratuitous statement to avoid a difficulty; and being so very gratuitous, shows how great the difficulty is.

8.

But this passage leads to a further remark; in it allusion is made to the tables of the Decalogue. No one can doubt that the giving of the Ten Commandments from Mount Sinai was the ministration of *condemnation;* the corresponding event then to this in the Gospel Dispensation would seem to be the ministration of *righteousness,* or justification. Now what is it? What season in the history of the Gospel answers to the Feast of Weeks on which the giving of the Law was commemorated? The day of our Lord's Crucifixion? no; the day of Pentecost; but what was the great event at Pentecost? The coming of the Holy Ghost, to write the Divine Law in our hearts: that Law then so implanted is our justification.[1]

---

[1] Ibi populus accedere ad locum ubi Lex dabatur, horrendo terrore prohibetur; hic autem in eos supervenit Spiritus sanctus, qui eum promissum expectantes in unum fuerant congregati. Ibi in tabulis lapideis digitus Dei operatus est; hic in cordibus hominum. Ibi ergo Lex extrinsecus posita est, qua injusti terrerentur; *hic intrinsecus data est, qua justificarentur.*—August. de Spir. et Lit. 29.

It accords with this view of the subject that justification, or the imparting of righteousness, is not unfrequently mentioned as an act depending on our Lord's Resurrection, and therefore, according to the analogy of faith, more naturally connected with the Holy Ghost. For instance: "who" (our Lord) "was delivered for our offences, and was *raised again for our justification.*"[1] Again, in another Epistle, the Apostle says, "If Christ be not *raised,* your faith is vain : *ye are yet in your sins;*" which surely implies that justification is through the Spirit ; for how was Christ's resurrection our deliverance from sin or our justification, unless it was so, as issuing in the mission of the Holy Ghost? And so in the Psalms : "Truth shall flourish out of the earth," Christ shall be raised in His human nature, "and *righteousness hath looked down from heaven,*" that is, the Spirit shall descend, as our Homily explains it.[2] And in Hosea, "Sow to yourselves in *righteousness,* reap in *mercy* ;"—here, even without going further, is the doctrine of justifying obedience ; but in what follows the gift of the Spirit is more distinctly implied ; "Break up your fallow ground, for it is time to seek the Lord, till He come and *rain righteousness upon you.*" With which may be compared the words of the Psalmist, "Thou art gone up on high, Thou hast led captivity captive, and *received gifts* for men : yea, even for Thine enemies, *that the Lord God might dwell among them.* Praised be the Lord daily, even the God who helpeth us

[1] Rom. iv. 25 ; 1 Cor. xv. 17 ; Ps. lxxxv. 11 ; Hos. x. 12 ; Ps. lxviii. 18, 19, 35.

[2] Sermon of the Resurrection.

and poureth His benefits upon us . . . He will give *strength and power* unto His people ; blessed be God." Is not justification a gift? therefore it must be comprised in this mission of the Spirit. With these texts let such passages of Scripture be compared as the Hymn of Zacharias, in which the inspired speaker blesses God for having "visited and redeemed His people, *as He spake by the mouth of His holy prophets,* which have been since the world began ; [1] to perform the mercy *promised,*" —"His holy covenant," and His " oath ; " and then goes on to describe the benefit to consist in our " serving Him without fear, in *holiness* and *righteousness,* before Him all the days of our life." Presently "the remission of sins " is mentioned, as if incidentally ; which brings out still more strongly the meaning of the words which I have quoted, viz. that renovation is the real gift of the Gospel, and justification is implied or involved in it.

9.

This correspondence between the giving of the Law on Sinai, and the coming of the Spirit at Pentecost, has been mentioned as conducing to the proof of the Spirit being our justification, as the Law is our condemnation ; a similar contrast is observed in Scripture between the *rites* of the Law and the *influences* of the Spirit.[2] The Jews thought to be justified by *circumcision ;* St. Paul replies, circumcision in the flesh is nothing, but *spiritual circumcision,* or renewal of heart, is all in all. Does not

[1] Luke i. 63-77.

[2] August. Ep. ad Asell. 196. Serm. 169 ; vid. also Bull, Harm ii. 14.

this imply that the renewal through the Spirit really effects what the Jewish rites attempted but in vain, justification? For instance, St. Paul says: "He is not a Jew which is one outwardly, neither is that circumcision which is outward in the flesh; but he is a Jew which is one inwardly; and circumcision is that of the heart, in the Spirit, not in the letter; whose *praise* is not of men, but of God."[1] What can God's praise mean but justification?[2] To the same purport are the following passages: "In Christ Jesus neither *circumcision* availeth anything nor uncircumcision, but *a new creature;* and as many as *walk* according to this *rule,* peace be on them and *mercy*" (and forgiveness, surely), and upon the Israel of God."[3] And the other two parallel texts, "In Christ Jesus, neither circumcision availeth anything, nor uncircumcision; but *faith which worketh by love;*" and, "Circumcision is nothing, and uncircumcision is nothing, but *the keeping of the commandments of God.*"

To the same purport too is our Lord's warning; "Except your righteousness shall exceed the righteousness of the Scribes and Pharisees, ye shall in no case enter into the kingdom of heaven." No one can doubt that an inward righteousness is here intended; that it is such as to introduce us into the kingdom of heaven; that it is that in substance which the Pharisees had only in pretence. The same doctrine is implied also in St. Paul's avowal, that he stands, not having his own right-

---

[1] Rom. ii. 28, 29.

[2] Cf. 1 Cor. iv. 4 with 5; Luke xviii. 14, with Matt. xxv. 21; 1 Thess. ii. 4.

[3] Gal. vi. 15; iv. 6. 1 Cor. vii. 19.

eousness, *which is of the Law*, but that which is through
the faith of Christ, the righteousness which is of God
by faith."[1] If *legal* righteousness is of a moral nature,
why should not the righteousness of faith be moral also?[2]

The same explanation applies to other passages of
St. Paul, the force of which is often overlooked at the
present day. For instance : " By the deeds of the Law,"
that is, by a conformity to the external Law, " there
shall no flesh be justified in His sight ; for by the Law
is the knowledge of sin. But now the righteousness of
God " (that is the new righteousness, introduced and
wrought upon the heart by the " ministration of the
Spirit)," " without the Law is manifested, being witnessed
by the Law and the Prophets, even the righteousness
of God, which is by faith of Jesus Christ, unto all and
upon all them that believe . . . whom God hath set
forth to be a propitiation through faith in His blood,
for the setting forth of His righteousness,"—a righteousness of His making, " on account of the remission of
past sins . . . that He might be just, and the justifier
of Him which believeth in Jesus ;"[3] that is, that He who

---

[1] Matt. v. 20 ; Phil. iii. 9.

[2] Qui enim crediderit in eum, non habebit suam justitiam, quæ ex
Lege est, quamvis sit bona Lex, sed *implebit ipsam legem*, non sua
justitia sed data ex Deo. Ita enim non confundetur. *Caritas* enim
est *Legis plenitudo*. Et unde ista caritas diffusa est in cordibus nostris ?
Non utique a nobis, sed *per Spiritum Sanctum* qui datus est nobis.—
August. Serm. 169.

[3] Rom. iii. 20-26. "Justitia," inquit, "Dei manifestata est."
Non dixit, justitia hominis, vel justitia propriæ voluntatis, sed
"justitia Dei," non qua Deus justus est, sed qua induit hominem cum
justificat impium. Hæc testificatur per Legem et Prophetas ; huic
quippe testimonium perhibent Lex et Prophetæ. Lex quidem hoc ipso

is righteousness in Himself, may also be a source of righteousness in all who believe.

Again, he says, in another Epistle, " By grace are ye saved through faith, and that not of yourselves, it is the *gift* of God," the great gift, even that of the Spirit ; " not of works," done by your unaided strength, in conformity to the natural Law, " lest any man should boast ; for we are His workmanship ;" He has made us a new creation, " created in Christ Jesus unto good works." Here the difference is marked between the works of the Spirit, which are " good," and those of the Law, which are worthless.

Once more : " Not by works of righteousness which we have done ;" for we have none such to produce ; all our works done in the flesh are but worthless in God's sight ; " but according to His mercy He saved us *by the washing of regeneration and renewing of the Holy Ghost,* which he shed on us abundantly, through Jesus Christ our Saviour ; that being *justified by* His grace, we should be made heirs according to the hope of eternal life."[1]

quod jubendo et minando, et neminem justificando satis indicat, *dono Dei justificari hominem per adjutorium Spiritus :* Prophetæ autem, quia id quod prædixerunt, Christi implevit adventus . . . Justitia Dei sine Lege est quam Deus *per Spiritum gratiæ* credenti confert *sine adjutorio* Legis, hoc est, non adjuto a Lege . . . Voluntas nostra ostenditur infirma per Legem, ut sanet gratia voluntatem, et sanata voluntas *impleat Legem,* non constituta sub Lege, nec indigens Lege.—August. de Spir. et Lit. 15. It must be borne in mind all along that St. Austin is arguing with the Pelagians, who said we could be justified by the Law in our natural state. " No," he answers, " we are justified only by the Spirit enabling us to fulfil the Law." This consideration makes the argument derived from his statement stronger.

[1] Rom. iii. 20-26 ; Eph. ii. 8-10 ; Tit. iii. 5-8. Cf. Gal. v. 18, etc.

And then, as before, the Apostle proceeds to speak of the necessity of those who have gained this mercy excelling in "*good* works."

10.

Such is St. Paul's testimony to the life-giving and justifying nature of the New Law ; which, unlike the External Law, is not only perfect in itself and a standard of truth, but influential also, creative as well as living, "powerful, and sharper than any two-edged sword ;" or, in David's words, "perfect, *converting* the soul ;"[1] or, as St. James calls it, "the word of truth," through which we are begotten, "the engrafted word, which is able to save our souls." Accordingly, the last-mentioned Apostle also calls it "a royal Law," and "a Law of Liberty ;" by which he seems to mean, that it is not an outward yoke, but an inward principle, a brighter and better conscience, so far as we have succeeded in realizing our evangelical state ; a law indeed, but in the same general sense in which we speak of its being a law of the mind to rejoice in, love, or desire certain objects. It is henceforth the *nature* of the mind to love God ; the Law of God is not a master set over us ; it is ourselves, it is our will. Hence St. Paul says, "Where the Spirit of the Lord is, there is *liberty* ;" and elsewhere he says, that "the Law is not made for a righteous man," not made for him, because he *is* the Law ;[2] he needs not a

---

[1] Heb. iv. 12. Ps. xix. 7. James i. 21.

[2] Sub Lege . . . vivit, in quantum quisque peccator est ; id est, in quantum a vetere homine non est mutatus. Sua enim vita vivet, et ideo Lex supra illum est ; quia qui eam non implet, infra illam est.

law to force him externally, who has the Law in his heart, and acts "not by constraint, but willingly," "not grudgingly, or of necessity," but from love.

And hence, moreover, it is that love is said to be the fulfilling of the Law, or righteousness ; because being the one inward principle of life, adequate, in its fulness, to meet and embrace the range of duties which externally confront it, it is, in fact, nothing else but the energy and the representative of the Spirit in our hearts. Accordingly, St. Paul, describing the course of sanctification, begins it in faith but finishes it in love ; "Faith, hope, charity," he says, "these three." Again, "The love of God is shed abroad in our hearts by the Holy Ghost, which is given us." Again, "the end of the commandment is love out of a pure heart, and of a good conscience, and of faith unfeigned." [1] And St. John, in like manner, "He that dwelleth in love, dwelleth in God, and God in him." Love, then, being the perfection of religion, and Love being the fulfilling of the Law, to fulfil the Law is the summit of evangelical blessedness. [2]

11.

Again, justification, as all allow, and as has been here assumed throughout, is a state in which we are acceptable and pleasing to God ; as then is the mode in

Nam justo Lex posita non est, id est imposita, ut supra illum sit ; in illa est enim potius quam sub illa.—August. in Gal. ii. § 17.

[1] 1 Cor. xiii. 13.   Rom. v. 5.   1 Tim. i. 5.   1 John iv. 16.

[2] Caritas ergo inchoata, inchoata justitia est ; caritas provecta, provecta justitia est ; caritas magna, magna justitia est ; caritas perfecta, perfecta justitia est.—August. de Nat. et Grat. 84.

which we please God, so is the mode of our justification. Now it is plain, from St. Paul, that the regenerate please God, not merely by the imputation of Christ's obedience, but by their own obedience : by their obedience therefore are they justified. If they were justified only by imputation of Christ's obedience, they could only please Him by virtue of that obedience ; but so far as they are enabled to please Him by what they are and what they do, so far may they be said, through His secret grace, to justify themselves. For instance, St. Paul says. "The God of grace . . . make you perfect in every good work to do His will, *working in you that which is well pleasing in His sight,* through Jesus Christ ;" he does not say, " *imputing to you* what is pleasing." Christ then does not keep the power of justification solely in His own hands, but by His Spirit dispenses it to us in due measure, through the medium of our own doings. He has imparted to us the capacity of pleasing Him ; and to please Him is that in part, which justification is in fulness, and tends towards justification as its limit. That this power is the characteristic of the Gospel is evident from St Paul's words elsewhere, " They that are in the flesh cannot please God ; but ye are not in the flesh, but in the Spirit." [1]

Parallel with such texts is that in the Epistle to the Philippians, on which much might be said : " Work out your own salvation with fear and trembling ; for it is God who worketh in you both to will and to do of His good pleasure." Salvation is here described, as justification elsewhere, not as coming direct from God

[1] Heb. xiii. 21 ; Rom. viii. 8, 9.

upon us, but as coming to us through ourselves, through our sanctified wills and our religious doings ; as wrought out for us by the power of God actively employed within us.

Texts which speak of our receiving a reward for our obedience enforce the same conclusion still more strongly. For what is the reward of a religious action, but God's favour, accorded to us in consequence of good things wrought in us by the Holy Spirit ?

12.

Lastly, a number of passages may be referred to, which have a peculiar cogency, as flowing spontaneously, as it would seem, from the Scripture speakers and writers, and so showing the genius of the evangelical system. As when our Lord says, " Rather give alms of such things as ye have ; and behold all things are clean unto you." " Make to yourselves friends of the mammon of unrighteousness." " This do," that is, the Commandments, " and thou shalt live." " Fear God, and keep His Commandments, for this is the whole duty of man." " Not the hearers of the Law are just before God, but the doers of the Law shall be justified." " Laying up in store for themselves a good foundation against the time to come, that they may lay hold on eternal life." " If we walk in the light, as He is in the light, we have fellowship one with another, and the blood of Jesus Christ His Son cleanseth us from all sin." " Blessed are they that do His commandments, that they may have right to the tree of life."[1]

[1] Luke xi. 41, xvi. 9, x. 27 ; Eccles. xii. 13 ; Rom. ii. 13 ; 1 Tim. vi. 19 ; 1 John i. 7 ; Rev. xxii. 14 ; James ii. 24 ; Matt. xxv. 31, etc.

" By works a man is justified, and not by faith only."
And, above all, perhaps, our Lord's declaration that the
righteousness wherein we must stand at the last day is
not His own imputed obedience, but our good works.

13.

Such is the doctrine concerning our justification,
which has the testimony of the whole Christian Church
in its favour, and which, I suppose, all sober minds would
admit at once, except from some notion that it contradicts
our Articles. What our Articles add to it, and in what
respect it is incomplete though true, and how it may be
unscripturally used, shall be considered in subsequent
Lectures ; here I will but say this, that at any rate it is
what the rival doctrine is not, a real doctrine, and contains
an intelligible, tangible, practical view which one can take
and use. That the scheme of salvation should be one of
names and understandings ; that we should be but said
to be just, said to have a righteousness, said to please
God, said to earn a reward, said to be saved by works ;
that the great wounds of our nature should remain un-
staunched ; that Adam's old sinfulness should so pervade
the regenerate that they cannot do anything in itself good
and acceptable, even when it is sprinkled with Christ's
blood,—all this would of course be matter of faith, if
Scripture declared it ; but when merely propounded
fifteen centuries after Christ came, it has no claims upon us, and might be rejected, even if it were not so very
alien as it is to the genius of the Evangelical Covenant.
That Covenant is a substance ; Judaism was the time of

shadows; it was Judaism which contained but the profession, the appearance of great things, exciting hopes which it could not gratify, and seeming to promise when it did but enforce the need. When, then, divines, however high in repute, come to me with their visionary system, an unreal righteousness and a real corruption, I answer that the Law is past, and that I will not be brought into bondage by shadows. "Shadows of religion," to use an expression of a holy Bishop,[1] these things fitly may be called; like the Jewish new-moons and sabbaths which the Judaizers were so loth to part with. Reputed justification was the gift of the Law; but grace and truth came by Jesus Christ. Away then with this modern, this private, this arbitrary, this unscriptural system, which promising liberty conspires against it; which abolishes Christian Sacraments to introduce barren and dead ordinances; and for the real participation of the Son, and justification through the Spirit, would, at the very marriage feast, feed us on shells and husks, who hunger and thirst after righteousness. It is a new gospel, unless three hundred years stand for eighteen hundred; and if men are bent on seducing us from the ancient faith, let them provide a more specious error, a more alluring sophism, a more angelic tempter, than this. It is surely too bold an attempt to take from our hearts the power, the fulness, the mysterious presence of Christ's most holy death and resurrection, and to soothe us for our loss with the name of having it.

[1] Bishop Wilson.—Family Prayers.

14.

Dismissing, however, a train of thought, which scarcely belongs to the present Lecture, I conclude by summing up the opposite characteristics of the two systems of doctrine, which have been under review, and of which Luther and St. Austin are the respective expounders.

The main point in dispute is this; whether or not the Moral Law can in its substance be obeyed and kept by the regenerate. Augustine says, that whereas we are by nature condemned by the Law, we are enabled by the grace of God to perform it unto our justification; Luther, that whereas we are condemned by the Law, Christ has Himself performed it unto our justification;—Augustine, that our righteousness is active; Luther, that it is passive;[1]—Augustine, that it is imparted; Luther, that it is only imputed;—Augustine that it consists in a change of heart; Luther, in a change of state. Luther maintains that God's commandments are impossible to man;[2] Augustine adds, impossible without His grace;[3]

---

[1] In Galat. Argum.

[2] Etsi igitur offenduntur viri politici, cum Lex Dei dicitur impossibilis, tamen id dictum verum est de hac corrupta natura. . . . . Ideo donat nobis Spiritum sanctum ut in tanta infirmitate tamen inchoetur Lex.—Melanchth. Loci Theol. de Lib. Arb. f. 169. Gerhard explains St. Austin's statements about grace enabling us to fulfil the Law, by understanding "grace" to mean *forgiveness;* or that we fulfil the Law, by God's mercy not imputing to us our non-fulfilment. Gerh. de Lege Dei, § 196.

[3] Eo quippe ipso quo firmissime creditur, "Deum justum et bonum impossibilia non potuisse præcipere," hinc admonemur, et in facilibus quid agamus et in difficilibus quid petamus. Omnia quippe fiunt facilia caritati, etc.—De Nat. et Grat. 83.

—Luther, that the gospel consists of promises only ;[1] Augustine that is also a Law ;—Luther, that our highest wisdom is, not to know the Law ;[2] Augustine says instead, to know and keep it ;—Luther says, that the Law and Christ cannot dwell together in the heart ;[3] Augustine says, that the Law *is* Christ ; — Luther denies, and Augustine maintains that obedience is a matter of conscience ;[4]—Luther says, that a man is made a Christian not by working but by hearing ;[5] Augustine excludes those works only which are done before grace given ; —Luther, that our best deeds are sins ;[6] Augustine, that they are really pleasing to God. Luther says, that faith is taken instead of righteousness ; Augustine, in earnest of righteousness ;—Luther, that faith is essential, because it is a subsititute for holiness ; Augustine, because it is the commencement of holiness ;—Luther says, that faith, as such, renews the heart ; Augustine says, a loving faith ; —Luther would call faith the tree, and works the fruit ; Augustine, rather, the inward life, or grace of God, or love,[7] the tree, and renewal the fruit. The school of

[1] Luther in Gal. iii. 11 ; f. 272.   (2.) f. 274, f. 407.   Bull, Harm. i. 3, § 3.   [2] In Gal Argum.

[3] In Gal. v. 4. Discat igitur pius Legem et Christum duo contraria esse, prorsus incompatibilia.

[4] Debemus extra conscientiam facere ex ea [Lege] Deum ; in *conscientia vero est vere diabolus. Quia in minima tentatione* non potest erigere et consolari conscientiam, etc. . . . Nullo modo sinamus eam dominari in conscientia.—Luther in Gal. iv. 3.

[5] In Gal. iii. 2.

[6] He seems to have meant that they *had sin* in them ; but his words are, Opus bonum optime factum est *mortale peccatum* secundum judicium Dei.—Gerhard. de Bon. Op. § 38.

[7] Non enim fructus est bonus, qui de caritatis radice non surgit.—

Luther accuse their opponents of self-righteousness ; and they retort on them the charge of self-indulgence : the one say that directly aiming at good works fosters pride ; the other that not doing so sanctions licentiousness.

Such are the two views of justification when placed in contrast with each other ; and as so placed, I conceive it will be found that the former is false, and the latter is true, but that while the former is an utter perversion of the truth, the latter does in some respects come short of it. What is wanting to complete it we learn from other parts of St. Austin's writings, which supply what Luther, not finding perhaps in the theology in which he had been educated, expressed in his own way. I say this, lest I should appear to be setting up any private judgment of my own against a Father of the Church, or to speak of him as I might speak of Luther.[1] St. Austin doubtless was but a fallible man, and, if in any point he opposed the voice of the Catholic Church, so far he is not to be followed ; yet others may be more fallible than he ; and when it is a question of difference of opinion between one mind and another, the holy Austin will weigh more, even with ordinarily humble men, than their own speculations. St. Austin contemplates the whole of Scripture, and harmonizes it into one consistent doctrine ;

De Spir. et Lit. 26. On the other hand, Luther says, " Qui volet fructus bonos habere, ab arbore incipiat, et hanc bonam plantabit ; ita qui vult bona operare, non ab operando, sed a credendo incipiat.—De Libert. Christ. f. 8.

[1] It is but fair to Luther to say that he indirectly renounced the extravagant parts of his doctrine at the end of his life ; (that is, the distinctive parts. Vid. above, p. 10, note). Laurence, Bampton Lectures, iv. note 14.

the Protestants, like the Arians, entrench themselves in a few favourite texts. Luther and the rest, men of original minds, spoke as no one spoke before them ; St. Austin, with no less originality, was contented to minister to the promulgation of what he had received. They have been founders of sects; St. Austin is a Father in the Holy Apostolic Church.

LECTURE III.

ENOUGH has now been said to make it appear that the controversy concerning Justification, agitated in these last centuries, mainly turns upon this question, whether Christians are or are not justified by observance of the Moral Law. I mean, this has been in matter of fact the point in dispute; whether, or how far, it has been a dispute of words, or went to the root of the question doctrinally, or ethically, are considerations which I do not now dwell upon, but mention by way of explaining my meaning. That in our natural state, and by our own strength, we are not and cannot be justified by obedience, is admitted on all hands, agreeably to St. Paul's forcible statements; and to deny it is the heresy of Pelagius. But it is a distinct question altogether, whether *with* the presence of God the Holy Ghost we can obey unto justification; and, while the received doctrine in all ages of the Church has been, that through the largeness and peculiarity of the gift of grace we can, it is the distinguishing tenet of the school of Luther, that through the incurable nature of our corruption we cannot. Or, what comes to the same thing, one side says that the righteousness in which God accepts us is inherent, wrought in us by the grace flowing from Christ's Atonement; the other says that it is external, reputed, nominal, being Christ's own sacred and most perfect obedience on earth, viewed by a merciful God as if it were ours. And issue is joined on the following question, whether justification means in Scripture *counting* us righteous, or *making* us righteous;—as regards, that is, our *present* condition; for that pardon of *past* sins is included under its meaning, both parties in the controversy allow.

2.

Now, in the foregoing Lecture, in which I stated what I consider as in the main the true doctrine, two points were proposed for proof; first, that justification and sanctification were in fact substantially one and the same thing; next, that in the order of our ideas, viewed relatively to each other, justification followed upon sanctification. The former of these statements seems to me entirely borne out by Scripture; I mean that justification and sanctification are there described as parts of one gift, properties, qualities, or aspects of one; that renewal cannot exist without acceptance, or acceptance without renewal; that Faith, which is the symbol of the one, contains in it Love or Charity, which is the symbol of the other. So much concerning the former of the two statements; but as to the latter, that justification *follows* upon sanctification, that we are first renewed, and then and therefore accepted, this doctrine, which Luther strenuously opposed, our Church seems to deny also. I believe it to be true in one sense, but not true in another, —unless indeed those different senses resolve themselves into a question of words. In the present Lecture, then, I propose to consider the exact relation of justification to sanctification theologically, in regard to which our Church would seem to consider Luther in the right : in the next Lecture I shall consider the relation of the one to the other, viewed popularly and as a practical matter, as Augustine and other Fathers set it forth : and in those which follow, returning to the subject which has already employed us, I shall show the *real connection* between the two doctrines, or rather their *identity*, in matter of fact, however we may vary our terms, or classify our ideas.

If it be asked how I venture, as I do, as regards any proposition which the doctrine of justification involves, to prefer Luther to St. Augustine, I answer, that I believe St. Augustine really would consider, that in the order of ideas sanctification followed upon justification, though he does so with less uniformity of expression than Luther, and no exaggeration, and a preference of practical to scientific statements. Nor is it in any way wonderful, supposing the two are really united together, and belong to one gift of grace committed to the heart, as its properties or qualities (as light and heat co-exist in the sun), that Augustine should not make a point of being logically correct, but should in familiar language speak of the Sun of righteousness, both as shining on us, in order to warm us, and as shining on us with his genial warmth, that is justifying unto renewal, and justifying by renewing.

In adopting the middle course I have thus prescribed to myself,—allowing Luther's statement, and maintaining St. Austin's doctrine,—I am but following our Articles; which, in one place, speak of justification as synonymous with our being "*counted* righteous before God," or as being in idea separate from sanctification, following, as I have said above, Luther : and in another as equivalent to " the *grace* of Christ and the *inspiration of His Spirit,*" or as actually consisting in sanctification, following St. Austin and the other Fathers.

3.

Now to proceed to the subject of the present Lecture, viz. that in logical order, or exactness of idea, Almighty God justifies before He sanctifies ; or that, in rigid propriety of language, justification is *counting* righteous, not *making.*

I would explain the distinction I am drawing, thus ; —to "justify" *means* in itself "counting righteous," but includes *under* its meaning " making righteous ; " in other words, the sense of the *term* is "counting righteous," and the nature of the *thing* denoted by it is making righteous. In the abstract it is a counting righteous, in the concrete a making righteous. An illustration will clear my meaning. No one doubts what the word *Psalmist* means in Scripture ; yet that one undeniable sense which it has, viewed in itself, is of course very far short of its full sense, when applied to this or that person. Then it stands for much more than this bare and abstract sense. A Psalmist is one who sings Psalms ; but *the* Psalmist may be David, a given individual, living at a certain time and place, and with a certain history attached to him. The meaning of the name is one thing ;

of the object another. If one said, "the Psalmist wept over his son Absalom," it would be absurd to maintain on the one hand that the *word* Psalmist meant "a Father," or on the other that the person signified by the word was merely " a singer of Psalms." So, again, a shepherd slew Goliath, but not *as* a shepherd ; and the " man after God's own heart " numbered the people, yet not as being after God's heart. In like manner, justification, in the mere meaning of the word, may be a counting or declaring righteous (as the 11th Article implies), yet *the* justification given under the Gospel, the concrete thing denoted by the word, may (as the 13th implies) be as much more than a mere external, reputed, conventional righteousness, as "the sweet Psalmist of Israel " was more than a Psalmist. It may be as true that it is *in fact* the giving of " the grace of Christ, and the inspiration of his Spirit," as that the Psalmist was also a king, the man after God's own heart, and a type of Christ. Justification, then, *as such*, is an imputation ; but the actual Gospel gift called justification is more, it is renewal also.

Here I am to consider it, not as it is in fact, but as it is in idea : as an imputation of righteousness, or an accounting righteous ; and I shall offer remarks in behalf of three positions, which arise out of what has been said , first, that justification is, in the proper meaning of the word, a *declaration* of righteousness ; secondly, that it is *distinct* from renewal ; thirdly, that it is the *antecedent* or *efficient cause* of renewal. "The Voice of the Lord," says the Psalm, "is mighty in operation ; the Voice of the Lord is a glorious Voice." Justification then is the Voice of the Lord designating us ;—designating us *what we are not* at the time that it designates us ; designating us *what we then begin to be.*

4.

1. Justification is "the glorious Voice of the Lord" declaring us to be righteous. That it is a declaration, not a making, is sufficiently clear from this one argument, that it is the justification of a *sinner,* of one who *has been* a sinner; and the past cannot be reversed except by *accounting* it reversed. Nothing can bring back time bygone ; nothing can undo what is done. God treats us *as if* that had not been which has been ; that is, by a merciful economy or representation, He says of us, as to the past, what in fact is otherwise than what He says it is. It is true that justification extends to the present as well as to the past; yet, if so, still in spite of this it must mean an imputation or declaration, or it would cease to have respect to the past. And if it be once granted to mean an imputation, it cannot mean anything else ; for it cannot have two meanings at once. To account and to make are perfectly distinct ideas. The subject-matter may be double, but the act of justification is one ; what it is as to the past, such must it be as to the present ; it is a declaration about the past, it is a declaration about the present.

This being so clearly the case, it is scarcely necessary to quote passages from Scripture in proof; one or two shall be adduced by way of sanction.

For example ; in the fourth chapter of his Epistle to the Romans, St. Paul makes justification synonymous with "*imputing* righteousness," and quotes David's words

concerning the blessedness of those "whose iniquities
are forgiven, and whose sins are covered," and "to whom
the Lord will not impute sin." Righteousness, then, is
the name, character, or estimation of righteousness
vouchsafed to the past, and extending from the past to
the present as far as the present is affected by the past.
It is the accounting a person not to have that present
guilt, peril, odiousness, ill-repute, with which the past
actually burdens him. If a wrong has been done you,
and you forgive the offender, you count it as though it
had not been, you pass it over. You view him as before
he did it, and treat him as on his original footing. You
consider him to have been what he has not been, fair
and friendly towards you ; that is, you impute righteousness to him or justify him. When a parent forgives a
child, it is on the same principle. He says, "I will
think no more of it this time ; I will forget what has
happened ; I will give you one more trial." In this
sense it is all one to say that he forgives the child, or
that he counts him to have been and to be a good child,
and treats him as if he had not been disobedient. He
declares him dutiful ; and thereby indirectly forgives
that past self, which lives in his present self, and makes
it a debtor.

Again : In the eighth chapter of the same Epistle,
St. Paul says, "Who shall lay anything to the *charge* of
God's elect ? It is God that justifieth."[1] Here *justifi-
cation* is contrasted with *accusation ;* accordingly it is a
judicial word, and is, therefore, concerned with the past.
It comes *upon* the past, and takes up man in his natural

[1] Rom. viii. 33.

state, as found a sinner. Whatever blessings besides are intended for him, still it is the commencement of blessing, and if so, is necessarily, in the first place, a declaring, whatever it may do afterwards. It is, as being a judicial act, an act concerning the present as influenced by the past ; they who *have* sinned *are* criminals, and they *are* justified from what they *have* done. Unless it can be shown, then, that courts of law *make* men innocent instead of *declaring* them so, justification is a declaration, not a making.

Again, in the fifth chapter : " The judgment was by one to *condemnation,* but the free gift is of many offences unto *justification.* . . . As by the offence of one, judgment came upon all men to *condemnation,* even so by the righteousness of One the free gift came upon all men *unto justification* of life."[1] Now here it is objected by members of the Church of Rome and others, that Adam's condemnation included an inward destitution, and therefore justification includes an inward gift. I grant it, but this is a further question ; whatever condemnation or justification may or may not *involve* or *imply,* the point before us is, not this, but what the *word* means. A *declaration* on the part of God may in itself presuppose, or involve, or attend, or cause, or in any other way imply, the actual communication of the thing declared : still it does not thereby cease to be a declaration, and justification need not cease to be in itself an accounting, though it may involve a making righteous. Condemnation, in like manner, though it implies, surely does not *mean* making guilty, but what follows upon guilt ; and so

[1] Rom. v. 16-18.

justification does not mean cleansing, even though it
turn out to be the antecedent or cause of it.

In like manner our Lord says to the Pharisees, "Ye
are they which justify yourselves before men ;" does
this mean " make yourselves righteous," or merely
" declare, profess yourselves " so ?

These are one or two out of various passages from
the New Testament, which show the sense in which the
word justification is to be taken ; indeed, but one passage
can be produced where it is used for "making righteous,"
and there the reading is doubtful.[1] I mean St. John's
words at the end of the Apocalypse, "He that is righteous,
let him be righteous still ; " which in the Greek runs,
" let him be justified still."

5.

There are many collateral arguments leading us to
the same conclusion. For instance ; St. James says
" that Abraham believed God, and it was *imputed* unto
him for righteousness ; and he was *called* the friend of
God." No one can doubt that these phrases are synonymous with being justified ; justification, then, is a " *calling*," that is, a declaring, accounting, treating as the friend
of God. That he also *was* the friend of God, and well-
pleasing to Him, is certain too ; but his justification was
his being *declared* so.

Again ; the Jews considered they were justified by
the rites of the Law, such as circumcision, observing the
Sabbath, paying tithes, and the like ; and St. Paul says,
" By the works of the Law shall no flesh be justified.'

[1] Bull, Harm. i. 1, § 6.

Now, the Jews did not consider such works *made* them holy, but made them holy *towards God*, or *recommended* them to Him ; and St. Paul condemns them for *substituting* them *for* holiness. The Apostle goes on to say, that the only true justification is the being *made* holy or renewed ; does not this imply, from the very nature of the case, that renewal is not just the same thing *as* justification, but that *in* which God justifies men, instead of justifying *in* the observance of rites ? What the Jews thought justification through ceremonies to be, that gospel justification really is, acceptableness ; and as the word was *attached* to circumcision among the Jews without being synonymous with it, so it attaches to renewal now, without standing for it, or being an equivalent expression.

The same distinction is seen in passages where mention is made of being "*counted* worthy of eternal life : " —for instance, when our Lord speaks of those " which shall be *accounted* worthy to obtain that world, and the resurrection from the dead ; "[1] or bids us watch and pray that we " may be *accounted* worthy to escape all these things which shall come to pass ;" and when St. Paul speaks of our " being *counted* worthy of the kingdom of God,"[2] no one can deny two things ;—on the one hand, that those who are *counted* worthy, *are* worthy (for our Lord says in the Apocalypse, " They shall walk with me in white, for they *are* worthy ; "[3]) on the other, that to be " counted worthy " does not, in the very sense of the words, *mean* to *be* worthy, though it implies it,

---

[1] Luke xx. 35, and xxi. 36.
[2] 2 Thes. i. 5.   [3] Rev. iii. 4.

but means a *declaration* of that which really *is, though,* or rather *because,* it is declared. In like manner, justification, as such, may properly be a *declaration,* though it involves in fact a *gift* of righteousness.

6.

2. And secondly, it not only declares, but in order of ideas it is *distinct* from the gift which it declares; it is the "Voice of the Lord," calling righteous what is not righteous till He calls it so. This will appear from examining what justification is, as a real and gracious act on God's part towards us sinners. Now, the doctrine of our justification not only implies, but derives its special force from our being by birth sinners and culprits. It supposes a judicial process, that is, an accuser, a judgment-seat, and a prisoner. Such is our condition by nature , the devil is our accuser, as of old time he accused Job; and the natural man, not being righteous as Job, has so much more cause for amazement and confusion. Yet even Job says, "Behold I am vile, what shall I answer Thee? *I will lay my hand upon my mouth.* Once have I spoken, but I will not answer; yea twice, but I will proceed no further." Or as Ezra speaks, "We are *ashamed and blush* to lift up our faces to God, for our iniquities are increased over our heads, and our trespass is grown up unto the heavens."[1] If this be the case with holy men, what should it be with the world at large, when the heavy catalogue of their sins is spread out in the sight of Divine Holiness! Then, as St. Paul says, "*Every mouth is stopped,* and all the world is guilty

[1] Job xl. 4, 5. Ezra ix. 6.

before God." Under these circumstances, when there is no health or hope in us, when we hide our faces and are speechless, the All-merciful God, as we are taught in the Gospel, for Christ's sake, freely pardons and *justifies* us. He justifies instead of condemning; that is, He exalts us by how much we were overwhelmed and cast down, by a salvation as strange as the peril was imminent.

This correspondence between the depth of our misery and the fulness of our recovery will enable us to estimate the wonderful character of the latter. It is an act as signal, as great, as complete, as was the condemnation into which sin plunged us. Whether or not it involves renewal, it is evidently something of a more formal and august nature than renewal. Justification is a word of state and solemnity. Divine Mercy might have renewed us and kept it secret; this would have been an infinite and most unmerited grace, but He has done more. He *justifies* us; He not only makes, He declares, acknowledges, accepts us as holy. He recognises us as His own, and publicly repeals the sentence of wrath and the penal statutes which lie against us. He sanctifies us gradually; but justification is a perfect act,[1] anticipating at once in the sight of God what sanctification does but tend towards. In it, the whole course of sanctification is summed, reckoned, or imputed to us in its very beginning. Before man has done anything as specimen, or

[1] [*i.e.* Perfect in relation to the past, as being a simple reversal of the state of guilt, and a bringing into God's favour; but as God's favour towards us will grow as we become more holy, so, as we become more holy, we may receive a higher justification. The words in the text are inconsistent with an increase of justification, which Catholics hold.]

paid anything as instalment, except faith, nor even faith in the case of infants, he has the whole treasures of redemption put to his credit, as if he were and had done infinitely more than he ever can be or do. He is "declared" after the pattern of his Saviour, to be the adopted "Son of God with power, by a" spiritual "resurrection." His tears are wiped away ; his fears, misgivings, remorse, shame, are changed for "righteousness, and peace, and joy in the Holy Ghost ;" he is clad in white, and has his crown given him. Thus justification is at first what renewal could but be at last ; and, therefore, is by no means a mere result or consequence of renewal, but a real, though not a separate act of God's mercy. It is a great and august deed in the sight of heaven and hell ; it is not done in a corner, but by Him who would show the world "what should be done unto those whom the King delighteth to honour." It is a pronouncing righteous while it proceeds to make righteous. As Almighty God in the beginning created the world solemnly and in form, speaking the word not to exclude, but to proclaim the deed,—as in the days of His flesh He made use of the creature and changed its properties not without a command; so does He new-create the soul by the breath of His mouth, by the sacrament of His Voice. The declaration of our righteousness, while it contains pardon for the past, promises holiness for the future.

7.

Such is the force of passages like the following :— " *To show forth* His righteousness for the remission of sins that are past—*to show forth*, I say, at this time His

righteousness." " *Who* shall lay anything to the charge
of God's elect? *who* is he that condemneth?" as if
publicly challenging the world. " Having spoiled prin-
cipalities and powers, *He made a show of them openly,
triumphing over them by*" the Cross. Or let us consider the vision in the book of Zechariah:—" He showed
me Joshua the High Priest standing before the Angel of
the Lord, and Satan standing at his right hand to resist
him. *And the Lord said* to Satan, The Lord rebuke thee,
O Satan, even the Lord that hath chosen Jerusalem, rebuke thee ; is not this a brand plucked out of the fire?
Now Joshua was clothed with filthy garments, and stood
before the Angel. And *He answered and spake* unto
those that stood before Him, saying, Take away the filthy
garments from him ; and unto him he said, *Behold*, I
have caused thine iniquity to pass from thee; and I will
clothe thee with change of raiment. And I said, Let
them set a fair mitre upon his head. So they set a fair
mitre upon his head, and clothed him with garments."[1]
The parable of the Prodigal Son would supply another
illustration in point.

Hence, again, so much stress is laid upon taking our
shame away, this being one characteristic benefit of
justification as distinct from renewal. Guilt makes us
veil our eyes in the sight of God and His Angels ; when
God justifies, He clears us from reproach, from the suspicions of holy creatures and the accusations of the
devil. The Psalmist, for instance, says, " They looked
unto him, and were lightened, and *their faces were not
ashamed.*" " All they that hope in Thee, *shall not be*

---

[1] Rom. iii. viii. 33, 34. Col. ii. 15. Zech. iii. 1-5.

ashamed." And the Prophet, in like manner, " For your *shame* ye shall have double, and for *confusion* they shall rejoice in their portion." " My people shall never be *ashamed.*" And so again St. Paul, quoting Isaiah, Whosoever believeth in Him shall not be *ashamed.*" In these, and similar passages, the great recovery or justification of the sinner in God's sight is not the silent bestowal of a gift, but an open display of His power and love.

This particular force, as belonging to the idea of justification, might be illustrated in other ways from the Psalms. I will but refer, as a specimen, to a verse of the 37th, as commented on by St. Athanasius. The Psalmist says, " He will *bring forth* thy righteousness *as clear as the light,* and thy just dealing *as the noonday.*" Now in this particular case obedience goes *before* justification, so it is not an exact parallel of the justification of a *sinner.* I quote it then merely as illustrating what is meant by the word justification ; and with that view, add the words of the illustrious Father in question. " ' Then will He bring forth,' that is, He will establish *manifestly,* and make clear in the sight of all ; not suffering the beauty of holy living to lie hid. For thy righteousness shall be evident to all, shining forth as the light, the light of the noon-day. Not only doth He justify him who confesses, and apply to him a merciful judgment, but He bringeth his righteousness to the light ; that is, *He makes known to all* that He hath justified him. So it was with the penitent thief, whose sentence Jesus, when on the Cross at mid-day, thus *published* at noontide; and the righteousness which was upon him He brought into the light, that is, to the knowledge of all. For when He said

of him, ' Verily I say unto thee, To-day shalt thou be with
Me in paradise,' it became clear to the whole earth, or
rather it became a light to the earth ; an encouragement
to all who were in a state of penitence. 'The brightness
of righteousness,' says the Psalmist, 'shall not be hidden,
as now ; but shall be very manifest, as the sun at noon-
day,' or, in our Lord's words, 'Then shall the righteous
shine forth as the sun in the Kingdom of their Father.'"

Our Lord's justification, as St. Paul terms it, which
took place upon His resurrection, to which I referred
just now, supplies another illustration. Christ differs
from us in this, that He was the true and eternal Son,
we sons only by adoption ; He holy by nature, we made
holy beyond nature ; but He does not differ in His
justification, which, simply considered, was what I have
been showing ours to be, an open acknowledgment of
Him by the Father as righteous and well beloved, yet
not nominally such (God forbid) but really. St. Paul, who
in one place says that Christ was "*justified* by the Spirit,"
explains himself elsewhere by saying that he was "*declared*[1] to be the Son of God, with power, according to
the Spirit of Holiness, by the resurrection from the dead."
With this agree the words of the Psalm, " I will *declare
the decree ;* the Lord hath *said* unto Me, Thou art My Son,
this day have I begotten Thee." As then, Christ's justification did not supersede but implied His inherent
righteousness, yet was in itself distinct from it, and a
testimony to it, so is our justification God's announcement,
concurrent with His own deed so announced ; yet in our
case, preceding, not following, His deed, because we are

---

[1] ὁρισθέντος. Cf. Luke xxiii. 47.

but *made* righteous, and not as Christ, righteous from our birth.

8.

3. In His case, indeed, justification could be but a witness to what was true from everlasting ; but in ours it is much more than a witness, nay more than an antecedent, as indeed has been already intimated. Our justification is not a mere declaration of a past fact, or a testimony to what is present, or an announcement of what is to come,—much less, as those who follow Luther say, a declaration of what neither has been, is, nor ever will be,—but it is the *cause* of that being which before was *not*, and henceforth *is*.[1] Strange it is, but such is the opinion of one of the two schools of divinity which have all along been mentioned, that God's calling us righteous implies, not only that we have not been, but that we never shall be, righteous. Surely it is a strange paradox to say that a thing is not because He says it is ; that the solemn averment of the Living and True God is inconsistent with the fact averred ; this His accepting our obedience is a bar to His making it acceptable, and that the glory of His pronouncing us righteous lies in His leaving us unrighteous. Surely it is a paradox to maintain that the only safeguard of the doctrine of our being accepted freely and without price, is that of our

---

[1] Est differentia attendenda circa gratiam Dei et gratiam hominis ; quia enim bonum creaturæ provenit ex voluntate divina, ideo ex dilectione Dei quæ vult creaturæ bonum, profluit aliquod bonum in creatura. Voluntas autem hominis movetur ex bono præexistente in rebus, et inde est quod dilectio hominis non causat totaliter rei bonitatem, sed præsupponit ipsam vel in parte vel in toto.—S. Thom. Quæst. 110, 1.

hearts being left odious and offensive to God. How does
it diminish the freedom of the gift that He does more?
how does it exalt His grace, to say that He lets remain
in the "filthy rags" of nature those whose obedience
His omnipotence surely might make well-pleasing to
Him, did He so will? We, indeed, can claim nothing;
and if it be proved that Scripture promises no more,
then it is presumptous to seek it; but it is very certain
that Scripture, again and again, speaks of our hearts and
bodies, our thoughts, words, and works, as righteous; so
it is not for want of Scripture warrant that we shrink
from believing this gracious truth, but we are determined
that the word righteous, in such passages, shall not really
mean righteous; we put a second sense upon the word,
we explain away the sacred text, and deny a sacred doctrine, all because we have a notion that we are exalting
the fulness and richness of God's mercy by circumscrib-
ing it.

Alas! it is an opinion too widely spread, too
pertinaciously held, to need formal statement, that if God
be supposed to impart any intrinsic acceptableness to
our services, this must diminish our debt to Him; that
the more He does for us, the less we must necessarily
feel indebted to Him; and, though He give us all other
graces, He cannot give humility with them. Far be from
us notions as contrary to Scripture as they are disparaging to God's love; no, let us believe the comfortable
truth, that the justifying grace of God effects what it
declares. "The Voice of the Lord is mighty in *operation*,
the Voice of the Lord is a glorious Voice." It is not
like some idle sound, or a vague rumour coming at random,

and tending no whither, but it is "the Word which goeth forth out of His mouth;" it has a sacramental power, being the instrument as well as the sign of His will. It never can "return unto Him void, but it accomplishes that which He pleases, and prospers in the thing whereto He sends it." Imputed righteousness is the coming in of actual righteousness. They whom God's sovereign voice pronounces just, forthwith become in their measure just. He declares a fact, and makes it a fact by declaring it. He imputes, not a name but a substantial Word, which, being "ingrafted" in our own hearts, "is able to save our souls." [1]

---

[1] Quando Deus justificat impium, declarando justum, facit etiam justum, quoniam judicium Dei secundum veritatem est.—Bellarm. de Justif. ii. 3. Verbum Domini ejusque voluntas efficax est, et hoc ipso qaod aliquem justum esse pronunciat, aut supponit justum eum esse, aut re ipsa justum facit, ne verbum ejus mendax sit.—Vasquez, Quæst. 112, Disp. 202, c. 5. Vid. also Ysambert de Grat. ad Quæst. 113, Disp. 1, Art. 2. Davenant, though a Calvinist, says Cum Deus ineffabili amore complectatur filios suos, *necesse est* ut *notam seu characterem* paterni sui amoris illis imprimat et insculpat. Hoc autem aliud non est quam imago quædam et similitudo sanctitatis suæ.—De Habit. Just. c. 3. Nay, Calvin himself, Fatemur ergo simul atque justificatur quispiam, *necessario* innovationem quoque sequi.—Antid. p. 324. But then he adds that it is only a necessary *accident.* Denique ubi de *causâ* quæritur, quorsum attinet *accidens inseparabile* obtrudi? Vid. also Chemnitz de Justif. p. 128, fin. This then it seems, after all, is the point at issue ; God speaks, and a new creation follows : is this new creation involved in the *essence* of the justifying *act,* or only joined as a *necessary accident ?* [Cordis renovatio] justificationis obtentæ non *causa* (no one says it is a "cause" *except* in the philosophical sense, that whiteness is the cause of a white wall, to take the common illustration) *sed comes, simul tempore adveniens, sed ordine causalitatis subsequens.* —Davenant de Habit. Justit. c. 24. Cf. Bitontinus's language at Trent, quoted below, in Appendix, § 14, also Ysambert de Gratia, Disp. iv. Art. 4.

9.

God's word, I say, effects what it announces. This is its characteristic all through Scripture. He "calleth those things which be not, as though they are," and they are forthwith. Thus in the beginning He *said*, "Let there be light, and there *was* light."[1] Word and deed went together in creation ; and so again " in the regeneration," " *The Lord gave the word*, great was the company of the preachers." So again in His miracles, He *called* Lazarus from the grave, and the dead arose ; He *said*, "Be thou cleansed," and the leprosy departed ; He *rebuked* the wind and the waves, and they were still ; He *commanded* the evil spirits, and they fled away ; He said to St. Peter and St. Andrew, St. John, St. James, and St. Matthew, "Follow Me," and they arose, for "His word was with power ;" and so again in the Sacraments His word is the consecrating principle.[2] As He "blessed" the loaves and fishes, and they multiplied, so He "blessed and brake," and the bread became His Body. Further, His voice is the instrument of destruction as well as of crea-

---

Chamier de Sanct. x. 2, § 16, well states the case, " Quærebatur an homo, cum justificatur, acquirat justitiam et sanctitatem inhærentem ? Immo, inquam, illud *cum justificatur* sophisticum quia ambiguum ; itaque ineptum constituendo statui controversiæ. Potest enim signifi-care *conjunctionem temporis*, ut sensus sit, an simul ac justificatur homo, acquirat etiam illam sanctitatem, ut quum quis deambulans in sole simul calefit, et colorem mutat in fuscum. Potest etiam *identitatem*, ut ita loquar, *rei ;* ac si dicam, utrum cum ambulat, moveatur homo." The latter alternative is the Roman, the former the Calvinistic ; that in the text follows St. Chrysostom, who says, Ὁ μὲν σταυρὸς τὴν κατάραν ἔλυσεν, ἡ δὲ πίστις τὴν δικαιοσύνην εἰσήγαγεν, ἡ δὲ δικαιοσύνη τοῦ πνεύ-ματος τὴν χάριν ἐπεσπάσατο.—In Gal. iii. 5.

[1] The same illustration is made use of by Mr. Knox, Remains, vol. i. p. 265.   [2] Vid. also Rom. iv. 17.

tion. As He "upholds all things by the word of His power," so "at the Voice of the Archangel, and at the trump of God," the visible world will dissolve ; and as His "Voice" formerly "shook the earth," so once more "the Lord shall roar out of Zion, and utter His Voice from Jerusalem, and the heavens and the earth shall shake." [1]

It would seem, then, in all cases, that God's word is the instrument of His deed. When, then, He solemnly utters the command, "Let the soul be just," it becomes inwardly just ; by what medium or in what manner or degree, is a further question not now to be discussed.[2] Here it will be more in place, in conclusion, to mention another instance of God's dealings with us, which is ana- logous to the process of justification as above considered ; I mean, the mode in which prophecy is introduced in Scripture, and the purposes which it is made to answer in sacred history. It has been noticed before now,[3] as a characteristic of Scripture prophecy, that it precedes and introduces into the world the great providences of God's mercy. When He would set apart a family or people for some extraordinary end, He reveals His pur- pose in the case of the first father of the line. He puts His word upon it in its origin, and seals up for it its destinies in that word, which, like some potent charm, works secretly towards the proposed end. Thus, when the chosen people were to be formed, Almighty God not only chose Abraham, but spoke over him the promises which in due time were to be accomplished. The twelve tribes had each its own character and history stamped on it from the first. When the royal line of the Messiah

[1] Joel iii. 16.   [2] Vid. Lecture VI.   [3] Vid. Davison on Prophecy.

was to be begun in Judah and renewed in David, on each patriarch in turn did Providence inscribe a prediction of what was to be. Such as this is justification as regards an individual. It is a sort of prophecy, recognizing God's hidden election, announcing His purposes before the event, and mysteriously working towards their fulfilment; even "the oath which He sware" to us, "more abundantly to show unto the heirs of promise the immutability of His counsel," "that we might have a strong consolation who have fled for refuge to lay hold upon the hope set before us." And in thus openly setting forth what is secretly in course of operation, it is an appointment especially characteristic of that supernatural system which we call Revealed Religion. As God conducts His Scripture Dispensations by Prophecy, and anticipates Nature by Miracle, so does He in a parallel way infuse holiness into our hearts through justification.

10.

On the whole then, from what has been said, it appears that justification is an announcement or fiat of Almighty God, which breaks upon the gloom of our natural state as the Creative Word upon Chaos ; that it *declares* the soul righteous, and in that declaration, on the one hand, conveys *pardon* for its past sins, and on the other *makes* it actually *righteous.*[1] That it is a declaration,

[1] What is here called a *declaration,* Calvin calls an *acceptation ;* with this verbal difference, the following passage from him, as far as it goes, expresses what is stated in the text ;—"Tota nostra disceptatio est de *causa* justificationis. Hanc Tridentini patres duplicem esse fingunt ; ac si partim *remissione peccatorum,* partim *spirituali regeneratione* justi essemus . . . . . Ego autem *unicam* et *simplicem* esse assero, quæ tota continetur in *gratuita* acceptione."—Antid. p. 324.

has been made evident from its including, as all allow, an amnesty for the past ; for past sins are removable only by an imputation of righteousness. And that it involves an actual creation in righteousness has been argued from the analogy of Almighty God's doings in Scripture, in which we find His words were represented as effective. And its direct statements most abundantly establish both conclusions ; the former, from its use of the word justification ; the latter, from its use of the word just or righteous ; showing, that in matter of fact, he who is justified becomes just, that he who is declared righteous is thereby actually made righteous.[1]   Lastly, as I have said, both doctrines are laid down in our Articles : the former in the eleventh Article, the latter in the thirteenth.

[1] Davenant's statement on the subject may be entirely received, though he was a Calvinist :—" Ex usu quotidiani sermonis, qualitas inhærens, præsertim si prædominans sit, denominat subjectum, licet simul inhæreat aliquid contrariæ qualitatis. Dicimus enim non modo nivem album, aut cygnum candidum esse, sed candida tecta vocamus et vestimenta candida, quibus tamen sæpissime maculæ aliquæ offusæ sunt, et aspersiones nigredinis. Sic etiam aquam calidam vocamus, non modo eam quæ ebullit præ fervore, sed etiam quæ acquisivit gradus aliquot caloris, frigore nondum totaliter expulso. Ex quibus patet, eadem ratione renatos omnes ab inhærente justitia *vere* nominari et censeri justos, quamvis ea inchoata adhuc sit et imperfecta. Justos dico non justificatos, quia justi vocabulum, ut nunc loquimur de justo, nihil aliud designat quam præditum infuso habitu seu inhærente qualitate justitiæ, et justificati vocabulum includit absolutionem ab omni peccato et acceptationem ad vitam æternam."—De Habit. Just. c. 3, fin.   It must be carefully kept in view, that the object proposed in these citations from divines of very various sentiments, is that of showing how they one and all converge and approximate to one main clear and consistent doctrine, whatever be the precise language of their respective schools.

LECTURE IV.

IF justification be God's great act declaring us righteous, and thereby as its direct, necessary, and instantaneous result making us (in our degree) righteous,—if it
be an act external to us, continued on into an act within
us,—if it be a divine Voice issuing in a divine work,
acceptance on the one part leading to acceptableness on
the other, imputation to participation,—it requires very
few words to explain how it comes to have been taken
for what it involves ; in other words, how justification
has been said to be renewal, or to follow on or consist
in renewal, or renewal said to be justification. And yet
not a few words may be necessary to make familiar to
our imaginations what is so obvious to the reason,—nay,
to allay the feelings of distrust with which the very
notion of such an attempt is commonly received at this
day. Little indeed can anyhow be effected in the course
of a single Lecture, yet suggestions on the subject may
be of service to inquirers.

I say, then, if the direct result of pronouncing righteous be actual righteousness, it is not at all unnatural
or strange, that righteousness or renewal should be called
our justification (as little as saying, as we do without
scruple, that a man has no "life" in him, when we mean

no " activity " or no " heat,"—heat and activity being
effects of life,—or in using " animation " first for life, then
for liveliness); nor is it at all justifiable, after the fashion
of the day, to set down such a mode of speech to spiritual
blindness, and to stigmatize it as perilous to its maintainers.   My reasons are as follow :—

2.

1. Justification renews, therefore I say it may fitly
be called renewal.   Is not this an allowable variety of
expression which is exemplified every day?   For instance, to *tempt* is to solicit or assail with temptation, to
invite towards evil; yet it not unfrequently means to
overcome by temptation, or to seduce.   To *persuade*
means either to use persuasives or to succeed in persuad-
ing.   To *cure* a patient, that is, to heal or restore to
health, is properly nothing more than to take care of him.
To gain a *battle* means to gain a victory, conquest being
the intended object of engaging.   A *commander* is one
who is obeyed as well as commands.   To *call* spirits from
the deep is not merely to call, but so to call that they
come, or to evoke.   In such cases we anticipate the
result of an action from its beginning, and contemplate
it in its completeness.   Certain implications or effects
are necessary for the adequate notion of a thing, and
in speaking of it we take their presence for granted ; we
realize the thing itself in our minds by affixing to it
names which properly belong to its effects.   To call
spirits implies an effectual call ; and to declare just is to
make just.

It is a parallel mode of speaking, to say that justification *consists* in renewal, or that renewal *constitutes* justification. This is much the same as saying, which we are apt to do, that a certain remarkable event is a *Providence.* It is a result, a manifestation of Divine Providence. And so our works of obedience are said to be a justification or a declaring righteous, as being the result and token of that declaration. To be justified *by* or *through* works is nothing more or less than to be justified *in* works ; and it may suitably be urged against the thoughtless, lukewarm, formal, and superstitious, how they can suppose themselves justified, seeing that God justifies in works, or that works are the mode, medium, or state of justification.

I have before now spoken of justification as a sort of sacrament ; it is so, by a figure of speech, being an external word effecting an inward grace. Here, then, we shall have another illustration of the matter in hand, which is the more apposite because our Catechism becomes a party to it, allowing itself, as it so happens, in the same verbal inaccuracy, in explaining the nature of a sacrament, as is committed when justification and renewal are made equivalents of one another. A sacrament, it will be recollected, is there defined to be "an *outward visible sign* of an inward spiritual grace." But if so, the inward grace is *not* part of the sacrament, but a result distinct from it. Yet in the very next answer, upon the question, " *How many parts* are there *in* a sacrament ? " we are told there are " *Two ;* the outward visible sign, *and* the *inward spiritual grace,*" as if the inward *grace* were *not* distinct, but an internal result or essential *part* of the sacrament. Who does not see the real meaning

in spite of this apparent inconsistency ? viz. that the act
of administering a sacrament so involves and secures the
inward grace, that the grace comes under the meaning
of the term, so that whether or not it be *part* of the
sacrament, is a mere question of words, the term in its
elementary sense denoting the outward act, in its full
meaning comprising the inward grace also.   And in like
manner we may say, without any inconsistency and with
truth, first, that justification is *only* that acceptance on
God's part, which is the earnest of renewal; next, that
it consists of *two* parts, acceptance and renewal.   Justification tends to sanctify ; and to obstruct its sanctifying
power, is as if we stopped a man's breath ; it is the death
of that from which it proceeds.

Again, we speak of being *baptized* with God's *grace ;*
and thus we may allowably say that we are *justified* or
accepted by *obedience*.   And we might of course with
propriety urge that *baptism* is not a mere outward rite,
but an *inward* power ; and so we may say that *justification* is a *change of heart.*

3.

2. I have been arguing from the essential union
between justification and renewal, that they are practically convertible terms ; but there are still more urgent
reasons why they should be so.   God's justification does
not merely work *some* change or renewal in us; but it
really makes us *just*.   But how can we, children of Adam,
be said *really and truly* to be righteous, in a sense distinct from the *imputation* of righteousness ?   This requires a word or two in explanation.

I observe, then, we become inwardly just or righteous in God's sight, upon our regeneration, in the same sense in which we are utterly reprobate and abominable by nature, or (to use the strong language of the Homilies) as we are since Adam's fall " corrupt and naught," " without any spark of goodness in us," " without any virtuous or godly motion," " the image of the devil," " firebrands of hell and bondslaves to the devil," " having in ourselves no one part of our former purity and cleanness ;" but being " altogether spotted and defiled," and " nothing else but a lump of sin."[1] Now these fearful words, however true, do not imply that our original nature is pure evil, as Satan's now is, though even to Satan's nature, left to itself, it assuredly tends ; they are not inconsistent with an admission that the natural man may have many high thoughts and wishes, and may love and do what is noble, generous, beneficent, courageous, and wise. But the writer means that, whatever good principles there be, in whatever degree, remaining to us since Adam's fall, they are, to use his own expression, " altogether *spotted and defiled,*" thoroughly and hopelessly steeped in evil, saturated with evil, dissolved in evil. They do not exist by themselves in their unmixed nature, as if we could act on them and nothing but them, whatever might be their worth if so exerted ; but though good, viewed in themselves, still they are, in fact and as found in us, of a sinful nature. All that we do, whether from better principles or from worse, whether of an indifferent nature or directly moral, whether spontaneously, or habitually, or accidentally, all is pervaded with a quality of evil so

[1] Sermons of the Nativity, Passion, and Whitsunday.

odious to Almighty God, as to convert even our best
services almost into profanations ; or, in the expressive
words of St. Paul, "They that are in the flesh cannot
please God." This, I conceive, is a definition of unrighteousness,—to call it a moral condition *displeasing*,
offensive to God ; or, again, of original sinfulness,—a
state of *wrath* and alienation. Hence our Article says,
"Works" done in this state, or "before justification,"
" are not *pleasant* to God," but "have the *nature* of sin."
It is true He has before now, in His great mercy,
accepted such works, as the zeal of Jael, the self-abasement
of Naaman, or the faith of the widow of Sarepta ; but
(as the last-mentioned expresses it in her own case) their
" sin " was still in " remembrance ;" it was not abolished,
it still " stank " before God and was loathsome; and if
He vouchsafed to admit them to any measure of His
favour, He did so from respect to the merits of that
Atonement which was to be made, and in consideration
of those good feelings,—good in the abstract, not in the
concrete,—which lay in their souls, only as precious metal
in the ore, or as generous liquor or sweet fruit in corruption. Also those good feelings came from the grace of
God, as their first source ; but still they were not such
as to sanctify their persons, or make their works pleasing,
or good and righteous in the sight of God.

This, then, is the sense in which we are unrighteous
or displeasing to God by nature ; and in the same sense,
on the other hand, we are actually righteous and pleasing
to Him in a state of grace. Not that there is not abundant evil still remaining in us, but that justification,
coming to us in the power and " inspiration of the Spirit,"

so far dries up the fountain of bitterness and impurity, that we are forthwith released from God's wrath and damnation, and are enabled in our better deeds to please Him. It places us above the line in the same sense in which we were before below it. By nature we were not absolutely devilish, but had a curse within us which blighted and poisoned our most religious offerings ; by grace we are gifted, not with perfection, but with a principle hallowing and sweetening all that we are, all that we do religiously, sustaining, hiding, and (in a sense) pleading for what remains of sin in us, " making intercession for us according to the will of God." As by nature sin was sovereign in us in spite of the remains of heaven, so now grace triumphs through righteousness in spite of the remains of sin.

4.

The justifying Word, then, conveys the Spirit, and the Spirit makes our works " pleasing " and " acceptable " to God, and acceptableness is righteousness ; so that the justified are just, really just, in degree indeed more or less, but really so far as this,—that their obedience has in it a gracious quality, which the obedience of unregenerate man has not. And here we see in what sense Christians are enabled to *fulfil* the Law, which they certainly are, in spite of modern divines, because St. Paul says so. He says expressly, that Christ came that " the *righteousness of the Law* might be *fulfilled in us,* who walk not after the flesh, but *after the Spirit.*" He says, " *in us,*" not only *externally to us.* And to make his statement still more certain, and to explain it, he adds, " The minding of the flesh," our natural state is " enmity against God ; for *it* is *not subject to the Law of God,* neither indeed can be. So, then, they that are in the flesh, *cannot please God.*" " *But ye,*" he continues, " *ye are not* in the flesh, but *in the Spirit,* if so be the Spirit of God dwell in you ;" that is, Ye who have the Spirit *are* subject or obedient to the Law, and you *can* please God ; in you the *righteousness* of the Law *is* fulfilled. Christians, then, fulfil the Law, in the sense that their obedience is pleasing to God ; and "pleasing" is a very significant word when well weighed. Not that we are able to please Him simply and entirely (for " in many things we offend all ;" and " if we say we have no sin, we deceive ourselves, and the truth is not in us "), but that the presence of the Spirit is a sanctifying virtue in our hearts, changing the character of our services, making our obedience new in kind, not merely fuller in degree, making it to live and grow, so that it is ever tending to perfect righteousness as its limit, and in this sense making it a satisfying obedience, rising up, answering to the *kind* of obedience which is due from us,—to the *nature* of the claims which our Creator, Redeemer, and Sanctifier has upon us.

And this, surely, is St. John's doctrine as well as St. Paul's, though brought forward by him in the way of warning, rather than encouragement. He declares solemnly in his general Epistle, that " He that *doeth righteousness* is righteous ;" as if doing righteousness was that in which righteousness consists. And then, that there may be no mistake, he adds, " *even as He* is righteous." What very strong words ! implying that our righteousness is a resemblance, and therefore a partial communication or infusion into our hearts, of that superhuman righteousness of Christ, which is our true justification. Again, presently, after saying that our possessing "love" gives us "boldness in the day of judgment," he adds, "because as *He is,* so are we in this world." That love, then, which He had in infinite perfection, and which, as being in him the fulfilling of the Law, is imputed to us for our justification, is also actually given us in measure, "shed abroad in our hearts by the Holy Ghost" as an earnest of what will be given without measure hereafter.

It seems, then, that a Christian's life is not only moral as opposed to vice and crime, not only religious as opposed to unbelief and profaneness, not only renewed as opposed to the old Adam, but is spiritual, loving, pleasing, acceptable, available, just, justifying ; not of course the origin or well-spring of our acceptableness (God forbid!) but we believe this,—that He who eighteen hundred years since purchased for us sinners the gift of life eternal, with His own blood, and who at our baptism spoke over each of us the Word of acceptance, and admitted us at once to His presence, by the same Word forthwith proceeded to realize His gracious purpose ; that "His word ran very swiftly," as being ' living and powerful, and sharper than any two-edged sword ,'' that it reached even to our hearts, conveying its virtue into our nature, making us what the Almighty Father can delight in, and so returning to Him not "void," but laden with the triumphs of His grace, the fruits of righteousness in us as "an odour of a sweet smell," as "spiritual sacrifices acceptable to God, by Jesus Christ." He works out His justification towards us, in us, with us, through us, and from us, till He receives back in produce what He gave in seed. It was His very purpose from the beginning, as announced by His Prophets, to form a people to Himself, who might show forth His praise, and magnify Him, and be as jewels in the robe of His glory, who might be a " chosen generation, a royal priesthood, a holy nation, a peculiar people." Saints, not sinners, are His delight and His honour.

5.

3. There is yet a third sense which has naturally led to statements of our being justified by renewal of mind or by obedience, which I will briefly notice. We can do nothing good of ourselves ; with God's grace we can do what is good. This is what I have been hitherto saying; but this is not all,—*with* His grace we are gifted not only with the capacity of being led into truth and holiness, but with the power of co-operating with Him. God's grace unfetters the will which by nature is in bondage, and thus restores to us the faculty of accepting or rejecting that grace itself. It enables us to obey, not as instruments merely, but as free agents, who, while they obey, are not constrained to obey, except that they choose to obey ; and whose obedience is for that reason more pleasing to God, as proceeding more entirely from themselves, " not by constraint," but " willingly" and "heartily." It does not follow from this, that there is any one good thought, word, or deed of ours, which proceeds from ourselves only, and which we present to God *as* ours ; but the circumstance that in such acceptable offerings as we render to Him, there has been a co-

operation on our part, has proved a reason, over and above those already mentioned, why justification has been said to consist in our services, not in God's imputation ; those services forming a concurrent cause of that imputation being ratified. Without such co-operation, that imputation would be void ; as the grace of a sacrament is suspended when the recipient is not duly prepared. Hence, St. Peter urges us to "make our calling and election *sure ;*" St. Paul, to "*work out* our own salvation with fear and trembling ;" and St. John declares that " whatsoever we ask, we receive of Him, *because we keep His commandments*, and do those things *that are pleasing in His sight.*"

For these reasons, then, though justification properly means an act external to us, it may be said to consist in evangelical obedience ; first, because obedience is one with God's imputation by association ; next, because they are one in fact, since He implants in part within us the very thing which in its fulness He imputes to us ; and, lastly, because our concurrence in being justified is a necessary condition of His justifying.

6.

Further light will be thrown on what has been said by considering certain circumstances, which have tended still more to vary the language of theology on the subject.

1. Over and above the various senses attached to the word *justify*, the word *justification* varies in its grammatical force, and gives rise in consequence to no small apparent difference between parties who really agree together. I mean, it has two senses, an active and a

passive; and though it is not always plain in which sense writers use it, yet on the whole, one class of divines use it actively, and another passively. The word may either mean *justifying,* or *being justified;* in the latter sense it is what man receives, in the former what God gives. This holds in the case of many other words; we speak, for instance, of a Bishop's confirmation and a child's confirmation; but the child is confirmed, the Bishop confirms.[1] In like manner justification sometimes stands for an act on God's part, sometimes for an event or a state which comes upon man. Now it so happens that Protestant writers, for the most part, take the word to mean God's justifying us; whereas Roman writers seem to use it for our being or continuing justified. For instance, the Council of Trent defines it to be "not the mere remission of sins, but the *sanctification* and the *renovation* of the inner man by the voluntary acceptance of grace and gifts." And St. Thomas speaks of it as a *change, passage,* or *motion* of the soul from one state to another. Here the word is used in a passive sense. On the other hand, our own controversialists, of whatever cast of opinion, following the Protestants of the Continent, understand by justification the *act* on God's part, whether instantaneous or sustained, by which He justifies the sinner. Melanchthon used the word in both senses; —so do our Homilies, as the following passages will show. When, for instance, they declare that "justification is not

---

[1] [In like manner Voss of the word "creation:" "Creatio nunc active sumitur, ut est volitio divina .. res creans; nunc passivè, ut est ortus rei cum relatione quam ad creantem habet, ut effectus ad causam."—Thes. Theol. i. p. 1, ed. 1558.]

the *office* of man, but *of God*," they adopt its active sense ;
yet, elsewhere, they speak of " this justification or *righteousness,* which we so receive of God's mercy and Christ's
merits embraced by faith," as being *" taken, accepted,* and
allowed of God for our perfect and full justification,"
where the word denotes our *state* of acceptance, or that
in which acceptance consists.[1]

7.

Now this difference affects the language of the controversy in the following respect among others. Justification, I have said, is in its fulness a great appointment
of God towards an individual, beginning in His Word
spoken, and returning back to Him through him over

---

[1] Nimirum illi [Pontificii] *justificatum* considerant, nos potius in
abstracto *justificationem.*—Chamier de Justif. xxi. 1. Dicendum quod
justificatio passive accepta importat *motum* ad justitiam. . . . . . .
Justificatio [impii] importat *transmutationem* quandam de statu
injustitiæ ad statum justitiæ prædictæ.—S. Th. quæst. 113, Art. 1.
Ysambert, ibid. Disp. ii. Art. ii. S. Th. also uses it actively. Augustine says, Donec ad Christum transeatur et auferatur velamen, id est
transeatur ad gratiam, et intelligatur ab ipso nobis esse justificationem,
qua faciamus quod jubet.—De Sp. et Lit. 30. Justificatio est *acceptio*
remissionis peccatorum et reconciliationis seu acceptationis gratuitæ
propter Filium Dei.—Melanchth. Exam. (tom. 1, f. 312). In this
passage the word is taken *passively ;* but in the following, *actively.*
Justificatio est *remissio* peccatorum et *acceptatio* coram Deo, cum qua
conjuncta est donatio Spiritus sancti. — Melancth. Catech. Art. de
Justif. Nos justificationem simpliciter interpretamur *acceptionem* qua
nos Deus in gratiam receptos pro justis habet.—Calvin. Justif. iii. 11,
2. Apparet justificationem . . . nihil aliud esse quam gratuitum Dei
actum, etc.—Bull, Harm. Diss. 1, i. § 4. Vid. also Perkins, Ref. Cath.
4. Davenant de Just. Hab. 34, p. 329. Barrow, vol. ii. Serm. 5, p.
55. Forbes, Inst. Hist. Theol. viii. 23, etc. etc.

whom it is spoken, laden with fruit. It is a Word having a work for its complement. Such is the characteristic of God's doings, as manifested in Scripture, that what man does by working, God does by speaking. Man labours, and a work follows; God speaks, and a work follows. When man would raise a fabric, or achieve an object, he exerts himself by hands and strength, by thought and tongue, by ingenuity of contrivance, and multiplicity of resources, by a long and varied course of action, terminating in the work proposed. All the acts of the Divine Mind are of course an incomprehensible mystery to worms such as we are; but so much Scripture tells us, whatever it means, that God accomplishes His work not by a process, but by "the word of His power." When man makes a thing, it is an effort on his part passing into a result; when God creates, it is by His fiat, by a word issuing in a work. He does not make, He says, "Let it be made." The Hebrew style accurately sets forth this token of Divine Majesty. The Psalmist says, not "He spake, and He did," but "He spake, and *it was done*." It was only a word on His part, but a substantial Word, with a work close upon it as its attendant shadow. In like manner it seems a true representation of the Scripture statements on the subject, to say, that He does not make us righteous, but He *calls* us righteous, and we are forthwith *made* righteous. But, if so, justification, which in its full meaning is the whole great appointment of God from beginning to end, may be viewed on its two sides,—active and passive, in its beginning and its completion, in what God does, and what man receives; and while in its passive sense man

is made righteous, in its active, God calls or declares.
That is, the word will rightly stand either for imputation
or for sanctification, according to the grammatical use of
it. Thus divines, who in the main agree in what the
great mercy of God is *as a whole,* may differ as to what
should be called justification ; for according as they view
it as active or passive, God's giving or man's receiving,
they will consider it God's accounting righteous or man's
becoming righteous. One party, then, in the controversy
consider it to be a mere acceptance, the other to be mainly
renewal. The one consider it in its effects, the other in
its primary idea. St. Austin, that is, *explains* it, and
Protestants *define* it. The latter describe it theoretically,
and the former practically. The Protestant sense is more
close upon the word, the ancient use more close upon the
thing. A man, for instance, who described bread as "the
staff of life," need not disagree with another who defined
it only chemically or logically, but he would be his in-
ferior in philosophy and his superior in real knowledge.

If God's word and work be as closely united as action
and result are in ourselves, surely as we use the word
" work " in both senses, to mean both the doing and the
thing done, so we may fairly speak of justification as if
renewal, as well as mere acceptance. Serious men, dealing with realities, not with abstract conceptions, entering
into the field of practical truth, not into the lists of controversy, not refuting an opponent, but teaching the poor,
have ever found it impossible to confine justification to
a mere declaring of that, which is also by the same grace
effected. They have taken it to mean what they saw,
felt, handled, as existing in fact in themselves and others

When they speak of justification, it is of a wonderful grace of God, not in the heavens, but nigh to them, even in their mouth and in their heart, which does not really exist at all unless brought into effect and manifested in renewal ; and they let their idea of it run on into renewal as its just limit, there being no line of demarcation, no natural boundary in its course till it reached renewal. Till then, it was in their minds but a deed inchoate (as it is called) ; not complete, till it had sought and found, and assimilated to itself, the soul which was its subject. Unless it was thus ratified it passed away, as rays of light where there is nothing to reflect them, or a sound where there is lack of air for it to vibrate upon.

Such is the contrast existing between the practical and the exact sense grammatically of the word *justification ;* and it is remarkable that both the one and the other have been adopted by our standard writers, as has been already instanced from the Homilies. As controversialists they are Protestants, as pastoral teachers they are disciples of the Ancient Church. Who, for instance, is more clear than Bishop Bull in laying down that justification means *counting* righteous ? yet who more strenuous in maintaining that it consists in *being* righteous ? What he is, such are Hammond, Taylor, Wilson, and a multitude of others ; who in this day are called inconsistent, as if holding two views, whereas those two views are rather proved to be one, because the same divines hold them.

8.

2. This difference, I say, in the grammatical sense attached to the word *justification,* even by those who

mainly agree what it is to *justify*, is one additional cause of misunderstanding in the controversy. Another is the difference of aspect under which justification appears, according as this or that stage is taken in the whole period through which it continues. For we must consider that since we are ever falling into sin and incurring God's wrath,[1] we are ever being justified again and again by His grace. Justification is imparted to us continually all through our lives. Now though it is substantially the same from first to last, yet the relative importance of its constituent parts varies with the length of its continuance. Its parts are differently developed as time goes on ; and men may seem to differ as to what they understand by it, when they are but surveying it at a different date, and therefore in a different light. A very few words will show this.

The great benefit of justification, as all will allow, is this one thing,—the transference of the soul *from* the kingdom of darkness *into* the kingdom of Christ. We may, if we will, divide this event into parts, and say that it is *both* pardon *and* renovation, but such a division is merely mental, and does not affect the change itself, which is but one act. If a man is saved from drowning, you may, if you will, say he is *both* rescued from the water *and* brought into atmospheric air ; this is a discrimination in words not in things. He cannot be brought out of the water which he cannot breathe, *except* by

---

[1] [This is incorrect. If by "sin" is meant grievous sin, those who are in the grace of God need not ever be falling into it ; and if lighter sins are meant, these do not bring us back again under "God's wrath."]

entering the air which he can breathe. In like manner, there is, in fact, no middle state between a state of *wrath* and a state of *holiness*. In justifying, God takes away what is past, *by* bringing in what is new. He snatches us out of the fire by lifting us in His everlasting hands, and enwrapping us in His own glory.

Such is justification as manifested in us continually all through our lives; but is it not plain that in its beginnings it will consist of scarcely anything but pardon? because all that we have hitherto done is sinful in its nature, and has to be pardoned; but to be renewed is a work of time, whereas as time goes on, and we become more holy, it will consist more in renewal, if not less in pardon, and at least there is no original sin, as when it was first granted, to be forgiven. It takes us then at Baptism out of original sin, and leads us all through life towards the purity of Angels. Naturally, then, when the word is used to denote the beginning of a justified state, it only, or chiefly, means acceptance; when the continuance, chiefly sanctification. Writers, then, of congenial sentiments, or the same writers on different occasions, will speak of it first as consisting in the remission of sins, with Calvin or Melanchthon, next, with the Roman Catholics, as consisting in renewal.

To conclude : all these things being considered it does seem like a want of faith not to hold, and a superstition not to profess, that in some sufficient sense Christ, as our righteousness, fulfils the Law *in us* as well as for us : that He justifies us, not only in word, but in power, bringing the ark with its mercy seat into the temple of our hearts ; manifesting, setting up there His new kingdom, and the power and glory of His Cross.[1]

[1] Chemnitz makes the following curious confession, that common sense is against the Lutheran doctrine :—" Et sane, *si humana consulenda essent judicia,* novitati renatorum *omnium calculis* tribueretur gloria justitiæ coram Deo ad vitam æternam. Non enim est opus seu effectio humanarum virium, *sed est donum et operatio Spiritus sancti,* unde bona opera vocantur fructus Spiritus (Eph. v.) Et est *beneficium Dei Mediatoris,* propter cujus meritum credentes renovantur spiritu mentis suæ, ut per Spiritum sanctum *inchoetur* in ipsis conformitas cum lege Dei, secundum interiorem hominem (Rom. vii.) *Et illa novitas vocatur justitia* (Rom. vi. 1 Joan. iii.) De renatorum etiam bonis operibus dicit Scriptura (Tit. iii.), ' Hoc acceptum est coram Deo,'" etc. (1 Joan. iii.) " Ea quæ placita sunt coram ipso facimus," etc. " Hæc profecto valde magna et præclara sunt."—Examen, de Justif. p. 134. And then he goes on to argue that other passages of Scripture negative the idea.

LECTURE V.

MISUSE OF THE TERM JUST OR RIGHTEOUS.

PLAINER words can hardly be found than those of Scripture itself, to express the doctrine I have been insisting on. Christ, who is the Well-beloved, All-powerful Son of God, is possessed by every Christian as a Saviour in the full meaning of that title, or becomes to us righteousness ; and in and after so becoming, really communicates a measure, and a continually increasing, measure, of what He is Himself. In the words of the Apostle, " We are *complete* in Him," and again, of the Evangelist, " Of His fulness have all we *received*, and *grace for grace.*" He makes us gradually and eventually to be in our own persons, what He has been from eternity in Himself, what He is from our Baptism towards us, righteous. That acceptableness, which He has ever had in the Father's sight, as being the reflection of the Father's perfections, He first imputes, then imparts to us.

This especially St. Paul lays down, when he says in the fifth chapter of his Epistle to the Romans, " As by one man's disobedience many were made sinners, so by the obedience of One shall many be made righteous." He says that by Christ's righteousness we are made righteous ; made, not accounted merely. Christ, who is the Son by birth, makes us sons by adoption ; Christ, who is "the righteous" in Himself, makes us righteous by communication, giving us first the name, then causing the name to change into the substance.

Now, over and above what is so plain that the phrase "*made* righteous," in this passage of St. Paul, is something beyond being *accounted* righteous, two circumstances may be mentioned as making it still plainer. In the original Greek the word means not merely *made,* but brought into a *state* of righteousness. It is the same word as is used by St. Peter, when he says, "If these things," faith, charity, and other graces, "be in you and abound, they *make* you," that is, *constitute* you as being "neither barren nor unfruitful in the knowledge of our Lord Jesus Christ." It is the word used also by St. James, when he says that "so *is* the tongue," has such a place, "among our members, that it defileth the whole body;" and again, when he says that "whosoever will be a friend of the world, *is,*" or is constituted "the enemy of God." Is the world's friend but *accounted* God's enemy? or is the tongue *accounted* a defilement? or are mature Christians but *accounted* fruitful in the knowledge of Christ? When, then, St. Paul says that we "become righteous" by Christ's obedience, he is speaking of our actual state through Christ, of that internal nature, frame, or character, which Christ gives us, nor gives only but *constitutes* ours. He speaks of our new nature as really righteousness.

But, again, he parallels our privilege in Christ to our loss in Adam; "*as* by one man's disobedience," he says, "many were made sinners; *so* by the obedience of One shall many be made righteous." Now, who will deny that Adam's sin is both imputed and imparted to us ? If any one did, we should call him a Pelagian. So indeed we should *consider* him, and justly ; but how shall we *argue* with him if we deal with the latter half of the verse, as he disposes of the former ? We cannot take just so much as we will of a free interpretation ; we may open the door to heresy, we cannot close it.

Though these words of St. Paul, then, were the only passage of Scripture adducible, it would be clear, I think, that Christ's obedience, which is All-righteousness, does also work righteousness in us, according to our measure.

2.

But here another line of argument is commonly taken, which will furnish matter for the present Lecture. It is said that, though it be true that our Lord not only is our righteousness by imputation, but works righteousness in us, still there two distinct and unconnected senses in which the word "righteous" may be taken, one of which belongs to Him, the other to us. It is owned that Christians really *are* righteous, but then not righteous *in the sense* in which Christ is righteous, but in another sense. Now if by this is merely meant that He has an incommunicable righteousness, as He has an incommunicable wisdom, holiness, and bountifulness, it is of course most true. None but He has infinite perfection in any respect. Yet He does impart to us a measure of these latter excellences notwithstanding, and in like manner He may impart to us a measure of His righteousness. There is no controversy what righteousness means ; and certainly it is an attribute which admits of being imparted. All parties seem to allow that the word denotes, as I have already intimated, what is *intrinsically* good, what admits of being contemplated and accepted as such by Almighty God. In this sense Christ is Righteousness in God's sight ; He is the Well-beloved Son, in whom the Father is well pleased, as being "the Brightness of His glory, and the express Image of His Person," "the unspotted Mirror of the power of God, and the Image of His goodness." Nothing can He absolutely delight in, but what is like Himself ; hence he is said to "put no trust even in His servants, and to charge His Angels with folly." None but the Eternal Son, who is incommunicably like the Father, can be infinitely acceptable to Him or simply righteous. Yet in proportion as rational beings are like the Son, or partake of His excellence, so are they really righteous ; in proportion as God sees His Son in them, He is well pleased with them. Righteousness is nothing else than moral goodness regarded in its intrinsic worth or acceptableness, just as love, truth, and peace, are other names for the same moral goodness, according as it is viewed in different aspects. It is love, or truth, or goodness, viewed relatively to God's judgment or approval of it ; or, in words already used, it is the quality in love, truth, or goodness, of being intrinsically pleasing to Him. And, being acceptableness, it is surely as capable of being imparted to man, as love, truth, or goodness ; and that in fact it is so imparted, and imparted from and through the Eternal Son, is the literal and uniform declaration of Scripture. Not only is the *word* "righteous" applied to Christians in Scripture, but the *idea* is again and again, in various ways, forced upon us. We read, for instance, of " God working *in us* that which is *well-pleasing in His sight;*" of our being " holy and *without blame before Him* in love ;" of Christ, "who is His image," " shining" and "living" in our hearts ; of His " making us *accepted*" or *gracious* " in the Beloved ;" and of His " *knowing what is the mind of the Spirit* " in our hearts, because " He *maketh intercession* for the saints *in God's way.*"[1]

Such passages, I say, make it clear that acceptableness or graciousness is imparted to us as really as any other excellence belonging to Christ ; and if acceptableness be what is meant by righteousness, it follows that the *thing* as well as the *word* righteousness is ours in the sense in which it is Christ's. Christ's righteousness, which is given us, makes us righteous, because it *is* righteousness ; it imparts *itself,* and not something else. In other words, such texts as the above show that the word has not two different senses, according as it is applied to Christ or to us, but one ; as St. John expressly declares, if we will listen to him, " He that doeth righteousness, is righteous, *even as* He is righteous." This, however, is denied by the majority of Protestant divines, who grant indeed that we are made righteous, yet, not righteous, as He is righteous, but in an entirely different sense, as distinct from what is meant by His righteousness, as foresight or ingenuity, as possessed by brute animals, differs from the same properties when belonging to rational beings ; Christ's righteousness having intrinsic excellence, ours, though the work of the Spirit, being supposed to have none. This they maintain ; and as if

[1] Heb. xiii. 21. 2 Cor. iv. 4. Eph. i. 4, 6. Rom. viii. 27.

distinctions would serve instead of proof, they lay down, as a principle to start with, that there are two kinds of righteousness, the *righteousness of justification*, or intrinsic acceptableness, which Christ alone has, and *the righteousness of sanctification*, which is the Christian's.[1] Now, then, let us consider the principle of interpretation which such a distinction involves.

3.

Considering, then, that St. Paul all through the chapter in his Epistle to the Romans, to which I have referred, has been speaking of justification and righteousness simply in its higher sense, as sustaining God's judgment, as involving pardon, favour, acceptableness, praise, worth, a title to heaven, and the like, I do not see on what plea it can be urged, that all at once he changes the meaning of the word, and makes it stand for an obedience which is not thus intrinsically approvable. He has spoken of our "being justified by faith," "justified by His blood," of "the free gift being of many offences unto justification," of "the gift of righteousness," of "the righteousness of One," and of "justification of

---

[1] Justitia, alia justificationis, sanctificationis alia.—Chamier, de Justif. xxi. 17, § 5. It is deeply to be regretted that a work like Davenant's *de Just. Habit.* should have been written under the influence of the same theology. Yet with him it is in a great measure a matter of words. He lays it down as an axiom, that the words righteousness and just cannot be used except in that sense in which they belong to God, (*i.e.* to denote the highest possible perfection), and *therefore* when applied to us they must have a different sense. He allows that in Christians righteousness is *begun*, but says it cannot be *called* righteousness till it is perfected, which it is not while on earth.

life ;" and at the end of the chapter, he speaks of "grace reigning through righteousness unto eternal life ;" can we suppose that just in one place, in this continuous argument, he should without notice use the word in a sense perfectly distinct? He says that Christ is our righteousness, and that thereby we are made righteous ; why is this not to mean " Christ stands for our acceptableness before we have it, and then imparts it to us"? An intelligible argument, indeed, *may* be raised, whether justification means making or imputing righteous, but there can be none, one would think, what just or righteous means in itself. In short, what reason is there for this change of meaning, except the exigences of the theory making it?

Yet, in spite of this fundamental objection, the supposed distinction between the two senses of the word is laid down as a great and observable canon of interpretation by one divine after another. In vain does St. Paul declare again and again, that we *are* righteous ; the Protestant Masters have ruled that we are not really so. They have argued that, *if* we were really made righteous, Christ would cease to *be* our righteousness, and *therefore* we certainly are not really made righteous ; which is much the same as arguing, that Christ must cease to be our " sanctification," because we are made holy, or that we are not made holy because He is our " sanctification ;" in a word, that He in his infinite fulness cannot give without a loss, and we in our utter nothingness cannot be in the continual receipt of benefits without thereby ceasing to be dependent.

4.

It is, perhaps, not too much to say that the whole structure of this modern system is made up of reasonings such as these, and interpretations in conformity ; and that it dare not trust itself freely to any text of Scripture,—dare not, without the protection of some antecedent principle, and that an assumed one. For instance, St. Paul bids us " yield our members as instruments of righteousness unto God ;" he tells us we are " servants " or slaves " of righteousness," that " the kingdom of God is righteousness and peace, and joy in the Holy Ghost ;" he speaks of " the fruits of our righteousness," of " ministers of righteousness," of " the new man being created in righteousness and true holiness," of " the fruit of the Spirit being in all goodness, righteousness, and truth ;"[1] yet all these testimonies, and many more, whether found in him or in the other Apostles, in behalf of the doctrine of God's really giving us in due season and measure what He begins by imputing to us, are, I say, put aside summarily by the gratuitous position, that righteousness *cannot* in such texts mean what (if so be) it means in the verse before and the verse after.

Again : we read of " righteous Abel ;" we are told that " Noah was a just man, and perfect in his generations ;" that Job was " perfect and upright," that Lot was " righteous," that Moses was " faithful in all God's house," that Elias was " a righteous man," that Daniel was " righteous " and " greatly beloved," that Zacharias and Elizabeth were " both righteous," that Joseph was

[1] Rom. vi. 13, 18 ; xiv. 17. 2 Cor. ix. 10 ; xi. 15. Eph. iv. 24.

"a just man," that Simeon was "just and devout," that Joseph of Arimathea was "a good man and a just," that St. John the Baptist was "a just man and an holy," that Cornelius was "a just man, and one that feareth God," that "the righteous shall shine forth as the sun in the kingdom of their Father," that "the righteous" shall go "into life eternal," that there shall be "a resurrection of the just," that "the Law lieth not against a just man," that a "Bishop must be sober, just, holy, temperate." We read of the "spirits of the just made perfect," of "the righteous scarcely being saved," and of "him who is just becoming more just;"[1] but when we would apply these statements to the great evangelical canon, "The *just* shall live by faith," as explaining who are the "just" there spoken of, we are forbidden, on the arbitrary assumption that such texts speak of a sort of Jewish righteousness, even though some of them relate to times before the giving of the Law; or that they mean Christ's imputed righteousness, even though containing in them other epithets which undeniably are personal to us.

Again : when our Lord says to the scribe who had rehearsed to Him the commandments, "This do and thou shalt live," it is replied that He spoke in a sort of irony.

Again, when He says, that unless our righteousness exceed that of the Scribes and Pharisees, we shall in no

---

[1] Matt. xxiii. 35. Heb. xi. 4. Gen. vi. 9. Job. i. 1. 2 Pet. ii. 7, 8. Num. xii. 7. James v. 16. Ezek. xiv. 14. Dan. ix. 23. Luke i. 6. Matt. i. 19. Luke ii. 25. Mark vi. 20. Acts x. 22. Matt. xiii 43 ; xxv. 46. Luke xiv. 14. 1 Tim. i. 9. Tit. i. 8. Heb. xii. 23. 1 Pet. iv. 18. Rev. xxii. 11.

case enter into the kingdom of heaven ;[1] and pronounces them blessed "who hunger and thirst after righteousness," and who "are persecuted for righteousness' sake," and bids us "seek the kingdom of God and His righteousness ;" it is sometimes openly, often by implication, answered, that all this was spoken by our Lord before St. Paul wrote.

Again : when St. Paul, who is thus appealed to, says expressly, that "the righteousness of the Law *is* fulfilled in us," then Luther is summoned to lay it down as a first principle, that the doctrine of our justification without any inherent righteousness is the criterion of a standing or falling church ; or an appeal is made to our Articles, as if they too (which is quite otherwise) were committed to so artificial a theory.

Again : when St. Paul says, " I can do all things through Christ which strengtheneth me," this is supposed to mean all things except fulfilling the Law ; and when he says, in another place, that "love *is* the fulfilling of the Law," and that love is not only attainable, but a duty, we are arbitrarily answered by a distinction, that such love as suffices for the fulfilling of the Law is one thing, and such love as is enjoined as a Christian grace is another.

Again : when we urge what Hezekiah says, " Remember now, O Lord, I beseech Thee, how I have walked before Thee in truth and with a perfect heart, and have done that which is *good in Thy sight ;*" or Nehemiah, "Remember me, O my God, concerning this, and *wipe not out my good deeds* that I have done for the

[1] Matt. v. 20.

house of my God, and for the offices thereof;"[1] all the answer we obtain is, that, whatever comes of Hezekiah and Nehemiah, it is evidently self-righteous and a denial of the merits of Christ, and shocking to the feelings of the serious mind, to say that we *can* do anything really good in God's sight, even with the grace of Christ, anything in consideration of which God will look mercifully upon us.

Again : St. Paul speaks of things "just," of " virtue " and of " praise," of providing " things honest *in the sight of the Lord*," of being " acceptable to *God;*"[2] but in vain does he thus vary his expressions, as if by way of commenting on the word " righteous," and imprinting upon our minds this one idea of inherent acceptableness ; —no, this has become a forbidden notion ; it must not even enter the thoughts, though an Evangelist plead and a Prophet threaten ever so earnestly.

Again : " Work " must have two senses ; for though we are bid to work out our salvation, God working in us, this cannot *really* mean " Work out your salvation through God's working in you ;" *else* justification would be, not of grace, nor of faith, but of works of the Law.

And " reward " too, it seems, has two senses ; for the reward which Scripture bids us labour for, cannot, it is said, be a reward in the real and ordinary sense of the word ; it is not really a reward, but is merely *called* such, by way of animating our exertions and consoling us in despondency.[3]

---

[1] Isaiah xxxviii. 3.   Neh. xiii. 14.
[2] Phil. iv. 8.   2 Cor. viii. 21.   Rom. xiv 18.
[3] Calvin. Instit. iii. 18, § 3.

5.

Many other reasons are offered by the Protestant school in behalf of "righteous" and kindred words having two senses in Scripture, but without being more conclusive than those which I have already given. For instance, "To him that worketh not, but believeth on Him that justified the ungodly, his faith is counted to him for righteousness:" from these words it is argued, that, since God justifies those who are as yet ungodly *when* justified, therefore they cannot be righteous *after* justification, nay, not even really godly, but only accounted godly.[1]

Again: the "righteousness," which justifies, though spoken of as a quality of our souls in Scripture, cannot mean anything *in us*, because the Jews sought a justifying righteousness, *not* "through Christ, *but* by the" *external* "works of the Law;" and therefore if we seek justifying righteousness solely from Christ, and not at all from works done in our own strength, in inward renovation not external profession, we shall stumble and fall as the Jews did.

---

[1] "All they whom God justifies," says Mr. Scott, "are *considered as ungodly.* True faith *is* indeed the effect of regeneration, an important part of *true* godliness, and inseparable from all other holy exercises of the soul towards God; yet the believer, considered as he is in himself, according to the Holy Law, is liable to condemnation as ungodly, and is justified solely and entirely, as viewed in Christ according to the Gospel."—Essays, *On Justif.* That is, not only are we to believe that Christ accounts us just without making us just, but that He accounts us ungodly when He has made us godly. When are these conventional representations to end? When are we to escape from the city of Shadows, in which Luther would bewilder the citizens of the Holy Jerusalem?

Another argument is drawn from St. Paul's saying that "righteousness" is "*without* the Law ;" for it is argued, since our righteousness is without the Law, therefore it is without the Law for justification, and with the Law for sanctification.

Again : "Righteous" cannot be applicable to us in the sense of justifying, because St. Paul had " counted all things but dung," that he might " win Christ, and be found in Him, not having his own righteousness which is of the Law, but that which is of the faith of Christ, the righteousness which is of God by faith." If, then, the Apostle rejects the righteousness of works done in his own strength, before faith, and without grace, as worthless, and desires a righteousness of God, it is supposed to follow that that new righteousness cannot consist in works, *though* done in consciousness of their manifold imperfections, and in faith, and by the grace of Christ.

Again : it is argued that justifying righteousness cannot be of the Law, because if a man " offend in one point, he is guilty of all ;" that is, since St. James says, that, when love is *away*, we offend the Law in many points, therefore when love is *present*, we cannot fulfil it consistently, however imperfectly, like Zacharias.

Lastly : " Righteousness " is said to have two senses, because St. Paul declares, that *as* " Christ was made sin for us who had known no sin," *so* " we are made the righteousness of God in Him ;" for, it is argued, since when we *were* unrighteous, Christ was imputed to us for righteousness ; therefore, now that Christ *has been* imputed to us for righteousness, we *shall* ever *be* unrighteous still.

6.

Such is the nature of the arguments on which it is maintained that two perfectly separate senses must be given to the word "righteousness;" that justification is one gift, sanctification another; that deliverance from guilt is one work of God, deliverance from sin another; —that reward does not mean really reward, praise not really praise, availableness not really availableness, worth not really worth, acceptableness not really acceptableness; —that none but St. Paul may allowably speak of "working out our salvation;" none but St. Peter, of "Baptism saving us;" none but St. John, of "doers of righteousness being righteous;"—that when St. Paul speaks of "*all* faith," he means all *but* true faith; and when St. James says, *not by faith only*,"[1] he means nothing *but* true faith;—that it is *not* rash to argue, that justification cannot be by works, because it is by faith, though it *is* rash to conclude that Christ is not God, because He is man; and that, though it is a sin, as it surely is, to infer that Christ is not God, because Scripture calls the Father the *only* God, yet it is no sin to argue that works cannot justify, because Luther, not Scripture, says that faith only justifies.

Surely, all this is very arbitrary; and though not so intended by the multitude of persons who give in to it, yet in itself very disrespectful (to say the least) to the sacred text. It goes in fact far beyond what is claimed by the most strenuous advocate of the right of private judgment; being nothing less than the attempt to subject Scripture to a previously-formed system; for no one can maintain that such a system is really gained

[1] 1 Cor. xiii. 2.   James ii. 24.

from Scripture. It is to make Scripture not a volume of instruction to which we must reverently draw near, but at best a magazine of texts in behalf of our own opinions ; and no maintainer of private judgment has gone these lengths. Let any candid person decide *why*, in the passages just now quoted, two distinct senses are assigned to the word "righteousness ;" whether because Scripture intimates it, or because a particular human system requires it. Such modes of interpretation then call for a very serious protest from all who are jealous of the pure and unmutilated *sense*, as well as the letter of the Bible. It is but a Jewish blindness to count syllables, while we are heedless about their import ; to guard the text from addition or diminution, yet not from glosses ; to be busy in versions, yet helpless in interpretation ; to be keepers of a treasure, yet not to use it. Except to those who know its meaning, Scripture is as a sealed book, though translated into every language under heaven ; and its words surely *have* their own particular and absolute meaning over and above the accident of their being in Greek, or Latin, or English ;— and as all this, it seems to me, is forgotten in the scheme of doctrine under review, I shall endeavour in the rest of this Lecture to enforce it.

7.

I say, then, that the words of Scripture, as of every other book, have their own meaning, which must be sought in order to be found. St. Paul does not use his words indiscriminately ; he does not mean by "righteous" at one time really, at another nominally righteous, at

random and without a reason. If it be as great a peril
as it is often now thought, to confuse these supposed
two distinct senses of the word, it is an equal improbability that St. Paul should have given it two senses so
distinct. Words stand for one idea, not two ; if the same
word seems to have several, these are really connected
together. The words of Scripture were appropriated to
their respective senses by their *writers;* they had a
meaning before we approached them, and they will have
that same meaning, whether we find it out or not. And
our business is to find the real meaning, not to impose
what will serve for a meaning. Abstract antecedent
reasonings will never help us to the real meaning ;
systems of the schools are not comments on the text.
The minds and the meaning of the inspired writers were
deeper than ours are. Such remarks will be called
truisms, yet they almost immediately apply to the subject
in hand ; for what but neglect of them can account for
the common interpretation of such verses, for instance,
as that with which this Lecture began ? When St. Paul
says that we are *made righteous,* what but antecedent and
established theories could be strong enough to persuade
men either that "*righteous*" does not imply " acceptableness," or else that "*made*" means nothing but accounted ?

We must not then interpret the terms used in
Scripture by our scholastic theories ; but again, neither
can we always interpret them by some one or other
particular passage of Scripture in which they are
found. Of course, to consult the context in which a
word occurs is a great advance towards the true interpretation, but it is not enough. In Scripture, as else-

where, words stand for certain objects, and are used with reference to those objects, and must be explained by them.   They may severally have many shades of meaning, but these, though manifold, are of one family, and but varieties of one meaning, if we could find it. In this or that passage where the word occurs, it may disclose its one full sense more or less ; but the degree in which it is brought out by the context depends on the accident of those other words with which it there stands connected.   Therefore, I say, we shall never arrive at its real and complete meaning, by its particular context; which generally comes in contact with but two or three points, or one aspect of it.   What would be thought of the commentator (to recur to a former illustration) who decided that *Psalmist* meant *father*, because the Psalmist wept over his *son ;* or meant *shepherd*, because he rescued a *lamb* from the lion and bear ; or meant *king*, because he was a type of the *Messiah ?*   Yet, in this way are the sacred terms of the Apostles treated; and not only by those who interpret on a theory, of whom I have been hitherto speaking, but by others also who are clear-sighted enough to disown the bondage of modern systems, or too heedless or self-willed to learn them.   The words of Scripture are robbed of their hidden treasures, and frittered away among a multitude of meanings as uncertain, meagre, and discordant, as the one true sense, like a great luminary, is clear and gracious.   *Righteousness* sometimes is to mean God's strict justice, sometimes His merciful acceptance, sometimes superhuman obedience, sometimes man's holiness, without any attempt at harmonizing these distinct notions ; *faith* is interpreted by trust, or obedience, or conscience, or unconditional assent ; *justifying* is said to be used by St. Paul for declaring righteous, by St. James for evidencing that God has declared us righteous ; the *Law* is sometimes the moral law, sometimes the ceremonial, sometimes the Christian. What account is to be given of such changes ? none is attempted. Yet I repeat, surely if a word has so many senses at once, this is because those senses are but modifications of one and the same idea, according as it is viewed : and our business is to find out, as far as may be, what it is which admits of such diversified application. Our business is, if so be, to fix that one real sense before our mind's eye, not to loiter or lose our way in the outward text of Scripture, but to get through and beyond the letter into the spirit. Our duty is to be intent on things, not on names and terms ; to associate words with their objects, instead of measuring them by their definitions ; to speak as having eyes, and as if to those who have eyes, not as groping our way in the dark by intellectual conceptions, acts of memory, and efforts of reason—in short, when we speak of justification or faith, to *have* a meaning and grasp an idea, though at different times it may be variously developed, or variously presented, as the profile or full face in a picture.

Here is the especial use of the Fathers as expositors of Scripture ; they do what no examination of the particular context can do satisfactorily, acquaint us with the *things* Scripture speaks of. They tell us not what words mean in their etymological, or philosophical, or classical, or scholastic sense, but what they do mean actually, what they do mean in the Christian Church and in theology.

It is an objection frequently made to the orthodox interpretation of certain passages, that they *need* not mean what they are said to mean, as far as the wording goes ; that there is nothing in the passage itself to force such a meaning upon it.   For instance, when Christ is called the Son of God, this (it is objected) does not *prove* His divinity, because we are sons also ; and when He declares that " He and the Father are one," this *need* only refer to unity of will, as Paul and Apollos were " one ;" and when He says, " I am with *you* always," He *may* mean the Apostles only, or at least only those, and all those, who have living faith ; and when He says, that He gives us " His flesh to eat," this *admits* of being figuratively taken for the benefits of His death generally ; and when St. Paul says, that " in Adam all die," it is enough to suppose he means "after the pattern of Adam," as Pelagius thought ; and when he says, that we are "justified by faith," the abstract word "justified" only means, and therefore St. Paul need only take it to mean, juridically justified or acquitted.   Let us grant all this for argument's sake ;—certainly such objections would tell against our proof, if we professed to argue merely from the context ; they might prove we were bad reasoners ;—but is there not also a further question, and one more to the point, not what the sacred text *may* mean, but what it *does* mean ?   Does the word *Psalmist* necessarily involve father, shepherd, and king ?   Yet, I suppose, the most minute measurer of terms will grant " the sweet Psalmist of Israel " *was* all three ; and in like manner, if it so happen, other words too may mean more than they need mean grammatically or logically ; and what they do mean may be determinable historically, that is, by the records of antiquity, as we do explain words and statements when they relate to matters of this world. If no word is to be taken to mean more than its logical definition, we shall never get beyond abstract knowledge, for it cannot possibly carry its own explanation with it. They who wish to dispense with Antiquity, should, in consistency, go further, and attempt to learn a language without a dictionary. This, then, is the use of the Fathers in interpreting Scripture ;—those who always go by the particular context, proceed argumentatively, but come to no conclusion ; those who go by scholastic systems come to a conclusion, but without sure premisses ; but those who consult Antiquity, gain at once an authority and a guide.

8.

I will go further ; not only is the context insufficient for the interpretation of the Scripture terms and phrases, but a right knowledge of these is necessary for interpreting that context. Acquaintance with the subject spoken of can alone give meaning to the connective particles, the turn of the sentence, and the cast of the argument. What can St. Paul be supposed to mean by his contrasts, arguments *à fortiori*, or climaxes, by those who have no clear understanding what he is speaking of? What does he mean by "like as," and "much more," and "not only," and "even," in the judgment of those who have dim and partial notions of what justification means, or the law, or righteousness, or the spirit, or faith, or works? It must, I should think, come home to most

thoughtful persons, if not from their own experience, at
least on consulting commentaries, that we very little enter
into the course and substance of the Apostle's teaching.
The utmost attempt commonly made is to comprehend an
isolated sentence here and there, and we make the most
of such success in interpreting, whatever it be, from its
rarity.   What do the average of those readers, who profess they see into Scripture with a certainty which the
mass of men have not,—what do they understand by
" Who was delivered for our *offences*, and raised again for
our *justification*"? or " While we were yet sinners, Christ
died for us ; *much more* then, being now justified by His
blood, we shall be saved from wrath through Him"? or
" The Spirit is life, *because* of righteousness "? or " Ye
are all the children of God by faith in Christ Jesus, *for*
as many of you as have been baptized into Christ, have
put on Christ"?

There are, doubtless, difficulties in Scripture in proportion to its depth ; but I am speaking of a mode of
interpretation which does not feel depth nor suspect
difficulty.   And this contented ignorance not only implies a very superficial state of mind, because it is contented, but great indifference towards the sacred writers.
Surely, it is not only shallow, but profane, thus to treat
the argumentative structure of an inspired volume.   If
"much more," and " not only," and the like, be what this
exegetical method supposes them to be, then the Apostles
give less force and meaning to words than ordinary
reasoners.   On this explanation, St. Paul must be supposed to use his contrasts and analogies as rhetorical
ornaments, rather than as matters of fact and serious

reasoning. This is in fact the conclusion which is forced
on those who are more consecutive and daring thinkers
than the generality of men. They seem to allow that
St. Paul does abound in mere oratory or poetry ; and
having so decided, no wonder they go on to look upon
the science of Catholic doctrine also as a great system
of words for things, a vast labyrinth of dogmas without
meaning, of reasonings without conclusions, of maxims
without point, of logical compensations for logical difficulties, of shadow opposed to shadow, one against another.
I am sure a large part of Hooker's teaching, for instance,
about the Holy Trinity, the Incarnation, and the Sacraments, appears to acute reasoners of the Protestant school
to be a mere arbitrary and artificial arrangement of
notions. Nay, that they do in like manner so regard
St. Paul's inspired pages is plain from the remarks of
some of them, who have been desirous to relieve Christianity of the burden thence, as they suppose, attaching
to it. This they have done, as they think, by surrender-
ing his arguments, on the ground that these did not fall
under the province of inspiration, and were fair subjects
for criticism in this searching and sifting age, as it is
called ;—searching and sifting, because it shuts out the
sun, gropes about in the dark, and has the fitting fruit
of its wilfulness in never grasping what it professes to
be searching after. But supposing, for argument's sake,
the Apostle's reasonings are separable from his conclusions, and he is only inspired in the latter, yet, is it
indeed come to this, that, in order to defend the Gospel,
an Apostle must be supposed to indulge in words and
arguments which mean nothing ? Is one who is greater

than man so far forth as he is inspired, less than man
so far as he is not? Are his antitheses, and amplifica-
tions, and similitudes, are his words of emphasis and
weight, are " light," " power," " glory," " riches," " height
and depth," " inward working," " spirit," " mystery," and
" Christ indwelling," to stand for nothing? Are they
random words uttered for effect, or from a sort of habit,
as sacred names are now habitually used by sinners to
make their language tell? Are his expressions glowing,
not because his subject is great, but because his temper-
ament was sanguine? Is he antithetical, not because he
treats of things in real contrast, but because he was
taught in the schools of Tarsus? or does he repeat his
words, not from the poverty of human language, but from
the slenderness of his vocabulary? Yet this age is dis-
posed, out of mere consideration for St. Paul, to adopt
the latter alternative, choosing rather that he should
speak beyond or beside his own meaning than beyond
its comprehension ; so that it has become a fashion almost
to give over searching for any particular meaning in discourses, which the Angels desire to look into. To
acquiesce in a confined idea of them, has been thought a
sign of deference rather than of neglect ; as if to seek
more were unfair to the great Apostle,—I had almost
said, ungenerous.

9.

Thus a popular writer protects the inspired Teacher
of the Nations, by the following considerations :—" St.
Paul, I am apt to believe, has been sometimes accused of
inconclusive reasoning, by our mistaking that for reason-

ing which was only intended for illustration. He is not to be read as a man, whose own persuasion of the truth of what he taught always or solely depended upon the views under which he represents it in his writings ; ˮ otherwise, of course, his faith would have been illogical. The writer continues : " Taking for granted the certainty of his doctrine, as resting upon the revelation that had been imparted to him, he exhibits it frequently to the conception of his readers, *under images and allegories, in which, if an analogy may be perceived, or even sometimes a poetic resemblance be found, it is all perhaps that is required.*" [1] This able writer is evidently afraid lest Christianity, as it stands integrally in the Bible, should fail under the ordeal of this educated age.

Again : " There is such a thing as a peculiar word or phrase cleaving, as it were, to the memory of a writer or speaker, and presenting itself to his utterance at every turn. When we observe this, we call it a *cant* word, or a *cant* phrase. It is a natural effect of habit ; and would appear more frequently than it does, had not the rules of good writing taught the ear to be offended with the iteration of the same sound, and oftentimes caused us to reject, on that account, the word which offered itself first to our recollection. With a writer who, like St. Paul, *either knew not these rules, or disregarded them,* such words will not be avoided. The truth is, an example of this kind runs through several of his Epistles, and in the Epistle before us," to the Ephesians, " abounds ; and that is in the word *riches,* used *metaphorically as an aug-*

[1] Paley's Horæ Paul. vi. 1.

mentative of the idea to which it *happens* to be sub-
joined." [1]

Elsewhere, he thus remarks :—"Their doctrines," those
of the Apostles, " came to them by revelation, properly so
called ; yet in propounding these doctrines in their
writings or discourses, they were wont to illustrate,
support, and enforce them by such *analogies, arguments,*
and *considerations* as their own thoughts suggested. . . .
The doctrine" [of the call of the Gentiles] " must be received ; but it is not necessary, in order to defend Christianity, to defend the *propriety* of every *comparison,* or
the *validity* of every *argument,* which the Apostle has
brought into the discussion." [2]

These conclusions, I doubt not, will be painful to
many a man who adopts the principles from which they
follow. For we have all been detained by circumstances
or, as I may say, are frozen, in an intermediate state between Protestant premises and their rightful inferences.
Those circumstances are now, after several centuries,
dissolving, and we are gradually gaining a free course,
and must choose our haven for ourselves. We must
either go forward on a voyage where we can discover
only barrenness, or return home to our ancient country,
and the sepulchres of the prophets. To see where we
shall end, if we go forward, may, through God's mercy,
persuade us to go back.

To conclude ; what has been said concerning the interpretation of the sacred terms of Scripture comes to

[1] Paley's Horæ Paul. vi. 2.
[2] Evidences. Part iii. ch. 2, fin.

this ; that we must not distort the sense of those terms by our own antecedent theories and systems ; that we must not so interpret them, as to make Scripture inconsistent with itself ; that we must not think of determining their meaning by one or two particular passages, in which they occur, instead of seeking it in a large survey of the inspired text.

These are the cautions with which I pass on from considering the word "righteousness," to consider the thing which the word denotes.

LECTURE VI.

JUSTIFICATION, being an act of Divine Mercy exerted towards the soul, does not leave it as it found it,—cannot but make it what it was not before, as has been shown at length. It stands to reason that a soul that is justified is not in the same state internally as if it had not been justified,—is not in the state of others which are not justified. No one would assert that one who is justified is in all respects the same in his inner self as another who is not ; even a professed Antinomian will generally allow that he has certain spiritual feelings, as he falsely calls them, or experiences, or an assurance, or the consciousness of renouncing merit, to distinguish him from those who remain in a state of wrath.

We know well what that state of wrath consists in, or what is the formal character and condition of those who are in it ; disobedience, an evil heart of unbelief, hatred of the truth, guilt, fear of judgment to come, hardness of heart ; such as these are the constituting parts of that state, and go to make up or define it. Now, on the other hand, what is the state of a justified man ? or in what does his justification *consist ?* This is the question which is now more exactly to be treated, as was proposed in a former place ; and it is one of no small importance.

2.

As far as the *name* is concerned, there is a general agreement among all parties ; it is called " righteousness." But this is not the question ; nor, again, what the meaning of the name is, which all allow to be equivalent to acceptableness, or acceptable obedience, though one school of opinion puts a second sense upon that word, and understands it also to mean an obedience which is short of acceptable, or a righteousness of sanctification. Nor is it now the question what is meant by justification, which some take for accounting, others for being made, righteous. But the question is, what is *that* which is *named* righteousness ? what is that object or thing, what is it in a man, which God seeing there, therefore calls him righteous ? what is the state in which a justified person is, or that which constitutes him righteous in God's sight ? just as one might ask what is really meant when it is said that a man is alive, what is the thing denoted by Scripture in saying that God " breathed into Adam the *breath* of life "?—the sense of the word *breath* being indisputable.

Now Luther, as we have seen, considers it to be Christ's obedience imputed ; the Roman Schools consider it to be the new and spiritual principle imparted to us by the Holy Ghost. But before entering upon the subject, I wish to insist that there really must be, as I have said, in every one who is justified, some such token or substance of his justification ; I insist upon it, because many persons will try to slip away from so plain a truth. They so greatly dread our priding ourselves on anything that is good in us, that one cannot assert that there are distinctions between the justified state and the state of nature, without being at once accused of treating these as meritorious causes ; therefore, I will insist on the point at the hazard of being tedious.

It is certain, then, that all men are not justified ; some are, some are not ; what is it they differ in ? To justify is to *account* or *declare* righteous ; this is God's act ; this is a movement of the Divine Mind, and altogether external to the *subject* of that justification. If the only real difference between a justified man and a man unjustified, be Almighty God's thoughts concerning him, then those who are justified are justified from eternity, for God sees the end from the beginning. They are in a justified state even from the hour of their birth ; before their conversion, while they are wallowing in all sin and unholiness, they are justified, if justification be an act of the Divine Mind and nothing more,—a conclusion which has before now been maintained. Yet, unless we go these lengths, we must allow that there is a certain distinctive state of soul to which the designation of righteousness belongs. What, then, is the criterion within us, which God sees there (of His giving surely, but still given) the seal and signature of His elect, which He accepts now, which He will acknowledge at the last day ?

In asking, then, what is our righteousness, I do not mean what is its *original source,* for this is God's mercy ; nor what is its *meritorious cause,* for this is the life, and above all the death of Christ ; nor what is the *instrument* of it, for this (I would maintain) is Holy Baptism ; nor what is the *entrance* into it, for this is regeneration ; nor what the *first privilege* of it, for this is pardon ; nor what is the *ultimate fruit*, for this is everlasting life. I am not inquiring about anything past, or anything future, or anything on God's part, but of something present and inward. We should not say that animal life consisted in being born, or in having parents, or in breathing, or in sensation, or in strength, or in a certain period of years, or in God's will, or in God's attributes, or in God's knowledge of us. We should feel that nothing past, or to come, or external, could be a fit account of that which we call animal life, and that all answers so framed were beside the mark. It would be intelligible, for instance, to say that life consisted in the presence of the soul ; but whether we said this or anything else, in any case we should fix on something in us, not out of us. And in like manner, when I ask what is that called righteousness, which God first clothes us with as with a robe, then looks upon and accepts, I do not ask why God so looks upon it, but *what* it is He looks upon.

3.

1. This being the case, we may pronounce that Luther's answer to the question—viz., that Christ's obedience imputed to us is our righteousness—is in itself no answer at all, and needs explanation before it will apply. Properly speaking, I suppose it means, not that Christ's obedience imputed, but that the imputation of His obedience, is our righteousness. Christ's obedience in the days of His flesh, centuries since, must be brought near to the soul of the individual ; therefore that present applying or imputing of His obedience must be meant, when it is called our righteousness, not what is

past. But that applying or imputing is the act of God ; and the question now before us is, not what is God's act in justifying, but what is the state of the justified soul. It is perfectly intelligible to say that Christ's obedience is the procuring, or the meritorious cause of our righteousness ; but to say that our present state of being accounted righteous is nothing else than the fact of Christ's having obeyed the Law eighteen hundred years since, if literally taken, is like saying that our animal life consists in the creation of Adam, or that the pangs of guilt consist in the fall of Satan, which are words without meaning.

For the same reason, it is no answer to the present question to say that a state of justification consists in the forgiveness of sins, or in acceptance, or in adoption, all these being God's acts, and as little in point here, as if I said that obedience was divine aid.

Again : if it be laid down that our justification consists in union with Christ, or reconciliation with God, this is an intelligible and fair answer ; and then the question will arise, what is *meant* by union with Christ ? It may or may not be possible to explain it ; if we consider Scripture to be silent on this point, then we shall say that justification consists in an *unknown, unrevealed, mysterious* union with Christ ; if we do not allow that there is a mystery, then we shall be bound to say what that union does consist in.

For the same reason, to say with Roman divines, that justification consists in spiritual renovation, whether correct or incorrect, is perfectly intelligible. It is a real answer.

And Protestants, who say that it lies in Christ's obedience, seem to have felt this ; for when pressed, they have sometimes said that faith is the discriminating mark of justification, or that in which it consists. But for the most part, only *when* they were pressed ; for though such an answer, whether correct or not, is clear and apposite, yet they seem to have feared that it was all one with saying that faith had merit, or an intrinsic expiatory power in the remission of sins. At the same time, this has not hindered some of them from so resolving the question ;[1] and as it is the only serviceable answer which

[1] " The difference betwixt the justification and obedience required by the Old and New Covenant, doth not consist, as the Bishop" [Beveridge] "saith it is, in this, that, in the first, obedience in our own persons was required as absolutely necessary ; in the second, obedience in our surety is accepted as completely sufficient ; but in this, that whereas the Old Law required perfect obedience, in order to our justification, allowing no pardon for sins committed, but leaving all under the curse, who 'continue not in all things written in the Law to do them,' the New Covenant *requires only faith* in the blood of Christ, for the remission of our past sins." Again, " What interpretation of the Apostle's words can be more uncouth and unsound than this, 'Faith is imputed to us for righteousness,' that is, it is not faith, but Christ's active righteousness, which is imputed to us for righteousness ? "—Whitby, Discourse on Imputed Righteousness. Melanchthon puts the objection made to his doctrine clearly and pointedly, but is very circuitous in his reply. " Sed dicat aliquis, Si per misericordiam salvandi sumus, quid interest inter nos quibus contingit salus et quibus non contingit ? Num pariter sperabunt misericordiam boni et mali ? Hoc argumento videntur moti Scholastici ad quærendum meritum condigni. Necesse est enim discrimen esse inter salvandos et damnandos." . . He answers, that in order for the conscience to be at rest, it must have a "certa spes ;" and a "certa spes" can only come from God's mercy ; and God's mercy is given to faith. " Fides justificat, quandocunque et quocunque tempore apprehendunt eam homines."—Apol. f. 77.

I can find on the Lutheran side of the question, I shall make use of it.

These then are the two views which at first sight come into consideration, whether our state of justification, or righteousness in God's sight, consists in faith or in renovation.

4.

Now, however intelligible each of these answers may be, neither will be found sufficient and final. I mean, neither seems to pursue, and, I conceive, neither does pursue, the inquiry so far as it might ; neither traces up the criterion of a justified state to its simplest and most elementary form.   When Faith is said to be the inward principle of acceptance, the question rises, what gives to faith its acceptableness ?   Why is faith more acceptable than unbelief? cannot we give any reason at all for it ? or can we conceive unbelief being appointed as the token, instrument, state, or condition (it matters not here which word we use) of justification ?   Surely not ; faith is acceptable as having a something in it, which unbelief has not ; that something, what is it ?   It must be God's grace, if God's grace act *in* the soul, and not merely externally, as in the way of Providence.   If it acts in us, and has a presence in us, when we have faith, then the having that grace or that presence, and not faith, which is its result, must be the real token, the real state of a justified man.

Again : if we say that justification consists in a supernatural quality imparted to the soul by God's grace, as Roman writers say, then in like manner, the question arises, is this quality all that is in us of heaven? does not the grace itself, as an immediate divine power or presence, dwell in the hearts which are gifted with this renovating principle? It may or it may not; but if it does, then surely the possession of that grace is really our justification, and not renewal, or the principle of renewal.

And thus, by tracing farther back the lines of thought on which these apparently discordant views are placed, they are made to converge; they converge, that is, supposing there to be vouchsafed to us, an inward divine presence or grace, of which both faith and spirit ual renovation are fruits. If such a presence be not vouchsafed, then certainly faith on the one hand, reno- vation on the other, are the ultimate elements to which our state of righteousness can be respectively referred in the two theologies. But if it be vouchsafed, neither Protestant nor Romanist ought to refuse to admit, and in admitting to agree with each other, that the presence of the Holy Ghost shed abroad in our hearts, the Author both of faith and of renewal, this is really that which makes us righteous, and that our righteousness is the possession of that presence.

2. So much is gained from the views of the con- tending parties; next, I observe, in corroboration of the conjectural inference to which they have led us, that justification actually *is* ascribed in Scripture to the presence of the Holy Spirit, and that immediately, neither faith nor renewal intervening. For instance, St. Peter speaks of our being "elect through sanc- tification," or consecration "of the Spirit, *unto*," that is,

in order to, "obedience and *sprinkling of the blood* of Jesus Christ," that is, the Holy Ghost is given us unto, or in order to, renovation and justification. Again : we are said by St. Paul to be "washed, sanctified, and *justified*, in the Name of the Lord Jesus, and by the *Spirit of our God.*" The same Apostle says, "Ye have not received the spirit of bondage again to fear, but ye have received the *Spirit of adoption*, whereby we cry, Abba, Father." Again : "The law of the *Spirit of life* hath made me free from the law of sin and *death.*" Again : Christ says, "It is the *Spirit* that giveth life,"[1] *life* being the peculiar attribute or state of "the *just*," as St. Paul, and the prophet Habakkuk before him, declare. These passages taken together, to which others might be added from a former Lecture, show that justification is wrought by the power of the Spirit, or rather by His presence within us. And this being the real state of a justified man, faith and renewal are both present also, but as fruits of it ;—faith, because it is said, "We through the Spirit wait for the hope of righteousness *by faith ;*" and renewal, because in another passage, "*renewing* of the Holy Ghost" is made equivalent to "being justified by His grace."

Such is the doctrine of Scripture, which our Church plainly acknowledges, as is evident from the following passages in her formularies. In the 13th Article, for instance, which I have already cited, what in the title are called "works before justification," are in the body of the article called "works done before the *grace* of

[1] 1 Pet. i. 2. 1 Cor. vi. 11. Rom. viii. 2, 15. John vi. 63. Gal. v. 5. Tit. iii. 5-7.

Christ, and the *inspiration of his Spirit;* " that is, justification may fitly be called an "inspiration of the Spirit of Christ," or a spiritual presence. Again in the Baptismal Service. in which we pray God that the child to be baptized may " receive remission of his sins," which surely implies justification, "*by spiritual regeneration,*" which is as surely the gift of the Spirit. The Homilies are in accordance; in which we are told, by way of comment upon St. Paul's words, " Who rose again for our *justification,*" that Christ " rose again to send down *His Holy Spirit* to rule in our hearts, *to endow us with perfect righteousness;* " and that in this way David's words in the 85th Psalm are fulfilled, " Truth hath sprung out of the earth, and righteousness hath looked down from heaven," in that "from the earth is the Everlasting Verity, God's Son, risen to life, and *the true righteousness of the Holy Ghost,* looking out of heaven, and in most liberal largess dealt upon all the world." Justifying righteousness, then, consists in the coming and presence of the Holy Ghost within us.

5.

3. But further, Scripture expressly declares that righteousness is a definite inward gift, while at the same time it teaches that it is not any mere quality of mind, whether faith or holiness ; as I shall now proceed to show.

By a gift I mean a thing given. Now, there are four words[1] used in Scripture to describe the special abiding gift of the Gospel, which either is, or at least

---

[1] χάρισμα, δῶρον, δωρεὰ, and δώρημα.

includes justification, nay, which is expressly said to be justification, and they all signify a thing given, not a mere giving ;—not a favour (as if we should say, " it is a great *mercy* we are saved," that is, an act, display, proof of mercy), but, as indeed the word gift means in English, a possession ; as when you say a man has the gift of languages, it is a faculty in him ; whereas you would not say that popularity was a gift, which is something external, but rather the talent of becoming popular, or influence, is the gift ; nor would you say acceptance was a gift, but acceptableness.

For instance, in Rom. v. 17 we read, " They that receive the abundance of grace, and of the *gift*[1] of righteousness, shall reign in life by One, Jesus Christ." The word *gift* here used certainly must mean a thing given ; implying that the righteousness of justification, whatever it turn out to be, is a real and definite something in a person, implanted in him, like a talent or power, and not merely an act of the Divine Mind externally to him, as the forgiveness of sins may be.

But the preceding verses contain a still more convincing statement, on which indeed one might not be unwilling to rest the whole question. St. Paul says, " Not as the offence, so also is the *gift*[2] . . . . the *gift* is of many offences *unto* justification." Here, observe, he distinctly declares that justification is the result of a *gift*. Now the word used for " gift " in the original, is the very word used elsewhere for extraordinary gifts, such as of healing, of tongues, and of miracles ; that is, a definite power or virtue committed to us. Nowhere

[1] δωρεᾶς.　　　　　[2] χάρισμα.

else does the word occur in Scripture without this meaning; indeed, it necessarily has it from its grammatical form. For instance, St. Paul says, he "longs to see" the Romans, "that he may impart unto them *some spiritual gift;*" again, that "the *gift* of God is eternal life." He enumerates as gifts, prophecy, ministry, teaching, exhortation, giving, ruling, and showing mercy. Speaking of continence, he says, "Every man has his proper *gift* from God." He says, there are "diversities of *gifts*, but the same Spirit." He exhorts Timothy "not to neglect the *gift* that was *in him,*" but to stir up, to re-kindle, "the gift of God which was in him." St. Peter too speaks of our "ministering" our "gifts as good stewards." [1]

If, then, by a gift is meant a certain faculty or talent, moral, intellectual, or other, justification is some such faculty. It is not a mere change of purpose or disposition in God towards us, or a liberty, privilege, or (as it may be called) citizenship, accorded to us, but a something lodged within us.

To the same effect is St. Paul's intimation, that righteousness is *ministered* or *dispensed* by the Spirit; [2] for surely the idea of dispensing, as well as the general office of the gracious Dispenser, lead us to conclude that the righteousness dispensed is a thing, and not a name.

6.

To these passages we shall be right in adding a number of others which speak of the Gospel Gift, though

[1] Rom. i. 11 ; vi. 23 ; xii. 6-18. 1 Cor. vii. 7 ; xii. 4. 1 Tim. iv. 14. 2 Tim. i. 6. 1 Pet. iv. 10.   [2] 2 Cor. iii. 8, 9.

not calling it justification. For they speak as if there was *one* great benefit given to us under the Gospel ; and so great and essential is justification, that it must be either this or must be included in it.

For instance, our Lord says to the Samaritan woman, "If thou knewest the *gift* of God, and who it is that saith to thee, Give Me to drink, thou wouldst have asked of Him, and He would have given thee living water." The water was a real thing to be given and received.

Again : St. Peter says to the multitude, " Repent and be baptized every one of you in the name of Jesus Christ for the remission of sins, and ye shall receive the *gift* of the Holy Ghost ;"[1] can we doubt that this is identical with the abundance of grace and of the *gift* of righteousness of which St. Paul speaks ?

Again: the latter Apostle alludes elsewhere to " those who were once enlightened and have tasted of the heavenly *gift*."[2] Will it be said this means sanctification ? then is sanctification represented as greater than justification ; else why is not justification mentioned in a passage which is expressly speaking of a case in which a second justification is pronounced to be impossible ? The contrast surely requires that justification should be mentioned ; yet unless included in "the heavenly gift," it is passed over. We may add such passages as the following : " The water that I shall give him shall be *in him* a well of water springing up into everlasting life." And " He that believeth on Me, as the Scripture hath said, out of his belly shall flow rivers of living water." With such compare the words in the Prophet : " Then will

[1] John iv. 10.   Acts ii. 38.   [2] Heb. vi. 4.

I sprinkle clean water upon you, and ye shall be clean ; from all your filthiness, and from all your idols, will I cleanse you."[1] This means justifying purification, for renewal is not mentioned till the next verse :—" A new heart *also* will I give you, and a new spirit will I put within you." By water, I say, is typified justification, which accordingly is a something applied and communicated, not a change in the Divine Mind merely.

The same doctrine is implied in the Sacrament of Baptism, which certainly typifies the justifying gift. But if so, that gift is not an act merely on God's part, but a something, proximate and one, received and embraced by us.

Once more : whatever be the more precise meaning of the words, does not " the Bread of Life " which is to be " eaten," imply an *inward* gift, not merely an imputation ? Yet who can deny that that gift carries with it the application of Christ's merits to the soul, that is, justification ?

Moreover, these passages show that this gift, whatever it is, is not any moral excellence or grace, such as faith or a renewed state. For instance, to recur to the last instance, faith is but the *recipient* of the heavenly Bread, and therefore cannot be identical with it.

Thus an examination of the promises made to us in Scripture bears out the conclusion I had already drawn on other grounds, that the righteousness, by virtue of which we are called righteous, or are justified,—that in which justification results or consists, which conveys or applies the great gospel privileges,—that this justifying

[1] John iv. 14 : vii. 38.   Ezek. xxxvi. 25.

power though *within* us, as it must be, if it is to separate us from the world, yet is not properly speaking *of* us, not any quality or act of our minds, not faith, not renovation, not obedience, not anything cognizable by man, but a certain divine gift in which all these qualifications are included.

7.

4. Now to proceed a step further. I have said that, while justification is the application of Christ's *merits* to the individual, that application is the imparting of an inward gift ; to this conclusion I have come chiefly by a consideration of the language of St. Paul. Now, turning to the gospel we shall find that such a gift is actually promised to us by our Lord ; a gift which must of necessity be at once our justification and our sanctification, for it is nothing short of the indwelling in us of God the Father and the Word Incarnate through the Holy Ghost. If this be so, we have found what we sought : *This* is to be justified, to receive the Divine Presence within us, and be made a Temple of the Holy Ghost.

God is everywhere as absolutely and entirely as if He were nowhere else ; and it seems to be essential to the existence of every creature, rational and irrational, good and evil, in heaven and hell, that in some sense or other He should be present with it and be its life. Thus we are told concerning mankind, that " in Him we live, and move, and have our being." And He who lives in all creatures on earth in order to their mortal life, lives in Christians in a more divine way in order to their life immortal ; and as we do not know how the creation exists and lives in Him as a Creator, and use words about it beyond our comprehension, so much more (were not comparison out of the question) are we ignorant of the mode or nature of that life of God in the soul, which is the wellspring of the Christian's sanctity, and the seed of everlasting happiness. If this notion of the literal indwelling of God within us, whether in the way of nature or of grace, be decried as a sort of mysticism, I ask in reply whether it is not a necessary truth that He is with and in us, if He is everywhere? And if He is everywhere and dwells in all, there is no antecedent objection against taking Scripture literally, no difficulty in supposing that the truth is as Scripture says,—that as He dwells in us in one mode in the way of nature, so He is in us in another in the way of grace ;[1] that His infinite and incomprehensible Essence, which once existed by and in itself alone, and then at the creation so far communicated itself to His works as to sustain what He had brought into existence, and that according to the different measures of life necessary for their respective perfection, may in the Christian Church manifest itself in act and virtue in the hearts of Christians, as far surpassing what it is in unregenerate man, as its presence in man excels its presence in a brute or a vegetable. And those who without any antecedent difficulty still refuse to accept the literal interpretation of Scripture, should be reminded, that, since the promise expressly runs that we shall be made one *as* the Father

[1] The angelic appearances in the Old Testament, to which divine titles are given and divine honours paid, may be taken as an instance of such a presence of Almighty God in a created nature.

and the Son are one, we are necessarily led either to think highly of the union of the Christian with God, or to disparage that of the Father and the Son ; and that such schools of religion as maintain that the former is but figurative, will certainly be led at length to deny the real union of our Lord with His Father, and from avoiding mysticism, will fall into what is called Unitarianism.

With these thoughts let us turn to the review of the texts in which this wonderful promise is made to us.

Our Saviour, then, thus speaks of our communion with the Father and Son ;—" At that day ye shall know that I am in My Father, and ye in Me, and I in you." " He that loveth Me, shall be loved of My Father ; and I will love him, and will manifest Myself to him. . . My Father will love him, and We will come unto him, and make Our abode with him." Again, He prays to His Father that His disciples " all may be one, as Thou, Father, art in Me and I in Thee, that they also may be one in Us. . . . I in them and Thou in Me, that they may be made perfect in one." [1]

Accordingly, St. John says, in his General Epistle, that " if we love one another, God dwelleth in us, and His love is perfected in us. . . . . He that dwelleth in love, dwelleth in God and God in him. . . . He that keepeth His commandments dwelleth in Him, and He in him." " We are in Him that is true, even in His Son Jesus Christ." " Truly our fellowship is with the Father and with His Son Jesus Christ." [2]

Further, this fellowship with the Son, and with the

---

[1] John xiv. 20, 21, 23 ; xvii. 21-23.
[2] 1 John iv. 12, 16 ; iii. 24 ; v. 20 ; i. 3.

Father in the Son, is made through the Spirit. " Hereby
we know that we dwell in Him and He in us, because
He hath given us of His Spirit." Hence St. Paul speaks
of the " fellowship of the Holy Ghost ;" and that " we
are the temple of God, and that the Spirit of God
dwelleth in us ;" and that " our body is the temple of
the Holy Ghost which is in us, which we have of God,
and we are not our own."[1] Agreeably to which are our
Saviour's words, who, when He promised the indwelling
of Father and Son in His followers, said also, " I will
pray the Father, and He shall give you another Comforter
that He may abide with you for ever, even the Spirit of
Truth. . . . . He dwelleth in you, and shall be in you."
And then He adds : " I will not leave you comfortless,
I will come to you."

Moreover, this indwelling had been promised as the
distinguishing grace of the Gospel. St. Paul declares
both the prophecy and its fulfilment, when he says : " Ye
are the temple of the Living God ; as God hath said, I
will dwell in them, and walk in them ; and I will be
their God, and they shall be My people." Again, in our
Saviour's words, " He that believeth on Me, as the
Scripture hath said, out of his belly shall flow rivers of
living water ; but this spake He of the Spirit, which
they that believe on Him should receive ; for the Holy
Ghost was not yet given, because that Jesus was not
yet glorified."[2] Accordingly, in some of the texts just
quoted, He who dwells in Christians is called " He that

[1] 1 John iii. 24 ; iv. 13. 2 Cor. xiii. 14. 1 Cor. iii. 16 ; vi. 19.
John xiv. 16-18.

[2] 2 Cor. vi. 16. John vii. 38, 39.

is *True,*" and the Comforter is "the Spirit of *Truth,*" grace and *truth* being the characteristics of the New Covenant.

And further let it be remarked that the Divine Presence vouchsafed to us, besides being that of the Holy Trinity, is specially said to be the presence of Christ ; which would seem to imply that the " Word made flesh " is in some mysterious manner bestowed upon us. Thus He says : " If any man hear my voice, and open the door, I will come in to him, and will sup with him, and he with Me." [1] This allusion to a feast is conveyed in still more sacred and wonderful language in the following passage, to which I have already referred : " I am the Living Bread which came down from heaven ; if any man eat of this Bread, he shall live for ever, and the Bread that I will give is My flesh, which I will give for the life of the world." . . . . " He that eateth My flesh and drinketh My blood, dwelleth in Me and I in him." Again : " We are members of His body, from His flesh and from His bones." [2]

8.

Such, as far as the words of Scripture go, is the great gift of the Gospel which Christ has purchased for all believers ;—not many words are necessary to connect it with justification. I observe then—

1. First, this indwelling accurately answers, as I have already said, to what the righteousness which justifies has already been shown to consist in ; an inward

[1] Rev. iii. 20.
[2] John vi. 51, 56. Eph. v. 30. Vid. also 2 Pet. i. 4.

gift conveying the virtue of Christ's Atoning Blood. The coincidence of one and the other in such a definition proves their identity ; if to justify be to impart a certain inward token of our personal redemption, and if the presence of God within us is such a token, our justification must consist in God's coming to us and dwelling in us. It were the same to maintain, though knowing that God lives in us in the way of nature, that our mortal life does not consist in that indwelling, as to allow that He dwells in us Christians in a supernatural and singular way, yet deny that our new life of privilege and blessing depends on that Mystical Presence,—to believe that we are temples of God, yet are not justified thereby. On the other hand, since this great gift is the possession of all Christians from the time they become Christians, justification, whatever be the measures of increase which it admits, as certainly presupposes the gift, as the gift involves justification. In a word, what is it to have His presence within us, but to be His consecrated Temple? what to be His Temple, but to be set apart from a state of nature, from sin and Satan, guilt and peril? what to be thus set apart, but to be declared and treated as righteous? and what is this but to be justified?

2. Next, it may be remarked that whatever blessings in detail we ascribe to justification, are ascribed in Scripture to this sacred indwelling. For instance, is justification *remission of sins?* the Gift of the Spirit conveys it, as is evident from the Scripture doctrine about Baptism : " One Baptism for the remission of sins." Is justification *adoption* into the family of God ? in like

manner the Spirit is expressly called the Spirit of adoption, "the Spirit whereby we cry, Abba, Father." Is justification *reconciliation* with God? St. Paul says, "Jesus Christ is in you, unless ye be reprobates." Is justification *life?* the same Apostle says, "Christ liveth in me." Is justification given to *faith?* it is his prayer "that *Christ* may dwell in" Christian "hearts by faith." Does justification lead to holy *obedience?* Our Lord assures us that "he that abideth in Him and He in him, the same bringeth forth much fruit." Is it through justification that we rejoice *in hope of the glory* of God? In like manner "Christ in us" is said to be "the hope of glory." Christ then is our Righteousness by dwelling in us by the Spirit: He justifies us by entering into us, He continues to justify us by remaining in us. *This* is really and truly our justification, not faith, not holiness, not (much less) a mere imputation; but through God's mercy, the very Presence of Christ.

3. It appears, moreover, that this inward presence is sometimes described as God's presence or indwelling; sometimes that of Father and Son; sometimes of the Holy Ghost; sometimes of Christ the Incarnate Mediator; sometimes "of God through the Spirit;" sometimes of Christ, of His Body and Blood, of His Body in "flesh and bones," and this through the Spirit. Different degrees or characteristics of the gift are perhaps denoted by these various terms, though to discriminate them is far beyond our powers. What is common to all Christians, as distinguished from good men under other Dispensations, is that, however the latter were justified in God's inscrutable resources, Christians are justified by the

communication of an inward, most sacred, and most mysterious gift. From the very time of Baptism they are temples of the Holy Ghost. This, I say, is what is common to all ; yet it is certain too, that over and above what all have, a still further communication of God's glory is promised to the obedient, and that so considerable as sometimes to be spoken of as the special communication, as if there were none previously. "He that loveth Me," says our Lord, "shall be loved of My Father, and I will love him, and will manifest Myself to him ;" and "Blessed are the pure in heart, for they shall see God."

9.

4. Further, we here see in what sense it is true that justification admits of increase, and in what not. The fact that we are the temple of God does not admit of more or less ; such words have no meaning when applied to it. Righteousness then, considered as the state of being God's temple, cannot be increased ; but, considered as the divine glory which that state implies, it can be increased, as the pillar of the cloud which guided the Israelites could become more or less bright. Justification being acceptableness with God, all beings who are justified differ from all who are not, in their very condition, in a certain property, which the one body has and the other has not. In this sense, indeed, it is as absurd to speak of our being more justified, as of life, or colour, or any other abstract idea increasing. But when we compare the various orders of just and acceptable beings with one another, we see that though they all

are in God's favour, some may be more "pleasant," "acceptable," "righteous," than others, and may have more of the light of God's countenance shed on them; as a glorified Saint is more acceptable than one still in the flesh. In this sense then justification does admit of increase and of degrees; and whether we say justification depends on faith or on obedience, in the same degree that faith or obedience grows, so does justification. And again (to allude to a point not yet touched on), if justification is conveyed peculiarly through the Sacraments, then as Holy Communion conveys a more awful presence of God than Holy Baptism, so must it be the instrument of a higher justification. On the other hand, those who are declining in their obedience, as they are quenching the light within them, so are they diminishing their justification.[1]

5. And this view of the subject enables us to understand how infants may be regenerate, though they give no indications of being so. For as God dwelt secretly in His material Temple, ever hallowing it, yet only in season giving sensible evidences of what was there, so may He be present with their souls, rescuing them from Satan, and imparting new powers, manifesting new objects, and suggesting new thoughts and desires, without their being conscious, or others witnesses, of His work.

6. Moreover, if justification be the inward application of the Atonement, we are furnished at once with a sufficient definition of a Sacrament for the use of our Church. The Roman Catholic considers that there are seven; we do not strictly determine the number. We

---

[1] Vid. Jerom. in Jovinian. ii. 27-29.

define the word generally to be an "outward sign of an inward grace," without saying to how many ordinances this applies. However, what we do determine is, that Christ has ordained two Special Sacraments, as *generally necessary to salvation.* This, then, is the characteristic mark of those two, separating them from all other whatever; and what is this but saying in other words that they are the only *justifying* rites, or instruments of communicating the Atonement, which *is* the one thing necessary to us? Ordination, for instance, gives *power,* yet without making the soul *acceptable* to God ; Confirmation gives light and strength, yet is the mere completion of Baptism ; and Absolution may be viewed as a negative ordinance removing the barrier which sin has raised between us and that grace, which by inheritance is ours. But the two Sacraments "of the gospel," as they may be emphatically styled, are the instruments of inward life, according to our Lord's declaration, that Baptism is a new *birth,* and that in the Eucharist we eat the *living* Bread.[1]

---

[1] "As for the number of them [the Sacraments], if they should be considered according to the exact signification of a Sacrament—namely, for *visible signs expressly commanded in the New Testament, whereunto is annexed the promise of free forgiveness of our sins, and of our holiness and joining to Christ*—these are but two ; namely, Baptism, and the Supper of the Lord. For, although Absolution hath the promise of forgiveness of sin, yet by the express word of the New Testament it hath not this promise annexed and tied to the visible sign, which is imposition of hands. For this visible sign (I mean laying on of hands) is not expressly commanded in the New Testament to be used in Absolution, as the visible signs in Baptism and the Lord's Supper are,—and, therefore, Absolution is no such Sacrament as Baptism and the Communion are. And though the ordering of ministers hath this visible

10.

7. Lastly, We now may see what the connection really is between justification and renewal. They are both included in that one great gift of God, the indwelling of Christ in the Christian soul. That indwelling is *ipso facto* our justification and sanctification, as its necessary results. It is the Divine Presence that justifies us, not faith, as say the Protestant schools, not renewal, as say the Roman. The word of justification is the substantive living Word of God, entering the soul, illuminating and cleansing it, as fire brightens and purifies material substances. He who justifies also sanctifies, because it is He. The first blessing runs into the second as its necessary limit ; and the second being rejected, carries away with it the first. And the one cannot be separated from the other except in idea, unless the sun's rays can be separated from the sun, or the power of purifying from fire or water. I shall resume the subject in the next Lecture.

sign and promise, yet it lacks the promise of remission of sin, as all other sacraments besides the two above named do. Therefore, neither it, nor any other sacrament else, be such sacraments as Baptism and the Communion are."—Homily of Common Prayer and Sacraments.

[Catholics hold that there are two justifying Sacraments, in the sense in which the word "justification" is mainly used in this volume —that is, Sacraments which reconcile the sinner to God, or *sacramenta mortuorum*—viz. Baptism and Penance. The other five are *sacramenta vivorum*, that is, they presuppose the subject of them to be in a state of grace, or justified, and increase his justification. To regard the Holy Eucharist as justifying, in the same light as that in which Baptism justifies, is to confuse the first justification of the sinner with the farther justification of the already just.]

LECTURE VII.

THE CHARACTERISTICS OF THE GIFT OF

RIGHTEOUSNESS.

IT is not uncommon in Scripture, as all readers know, to represent the especial gift of the Gospel as a robe or garment, bestowed on those who are brought into the Church of Christ. Thus the prophet Isaiah speaks of our being "clothed with the garments of salvation, covered with the robe of righteousness," as with a rich bridal dress. A passage was quoted in a former place from the prophet Zechariah to the same purport ; in which Almighty God takes from Joshua the high priest his filthy garments, and gives him change of raiment, and a mitre for his head. In like manner, when the prodigal son came home, his father put on him "the best robe," "and a ring on his hand, and shoes on his feet ; " agreeable to which is St. Paul's declaration that " as many as have been baptized into Christ, have *put on* Christ."

Now such expressions as these in Scripture are too forcible and varied to be a mere figure denoting the *profession of Christianity ;* as if our putting on Christ were a taking on us the name and responsibilities of a Christian :—this I shall take for granted. It is much the same kind of evasion or explaining away, to say that by God's clothing us in righteousness is only meant His *counting* us as if righteous ; all the difference being that in the former interpretation the clothing is made to stand for our calling ourselves, and in the latter for God's calling us, what really we are not.

Nor, again, can these expressions be very well taken to mean newness of life, holiness, and obedience ; for this reason, if for no other, that no one is all at once holy, and renewed, in that full sense which must be implied if the terms be interpreted of holiness. Baptized persons do not so put on Christ as to be forthwith altogether different men from what they were before ; at least this is not the rule, as far as we have means of deciding. Thus there is a call on the face of the matter for some more adequate interpretation of such passages of Scripture, than is supplied either by the Roman or the Protestant schools ; and this surely is found in the doctrine of the last Lecture. If that doctrine be true, the robe vouchsafed to us is the inward presence of Christ, ministered to us through the Holy Ghost ; which, it is plain, admits on the one hand of being immediately vouchsafed in its fulness, as a sort of invisible Shekinah, or seal of God's election, yet without involving on the other the necessity of a greater moral change than is promised and effected in Baptism.

With this, too, agrees what is told of our own duties towards this sacred possession, which are represented as negative rather than active ; I mean, we are enjoined *not* to injure or profane it, but so to honour it in our outward conduct, that it may be continued and increased in us. For instance, our Lord says, " Thou hast a few names even in Sardis, which have not *defiled* their garments ;

and they shall walk with Me in white, for they are worthy."[1] Such words are more naturally interpreted of an inward gift than of a mere imputation ; and scarcely admit of being explained of a moral condition of heart, attained (under grace) *through* our own exertions. They are parallel to St. Paul's warning against "grieving the Spirit of God ;" which may just as reasonably be interpreted of mere moral excellence, as in some heretical schools has been done. Of the same character are exhortations such as St. Paul's, not "to defile the temple of God ;" to recollect that we are the temple of God, and that the Holy Ghost is in us.

2.

Moreover, it may throw light on these metaphors to inquire whether (considering we have gained under the Gospel what we lost in Adam, and justification is a reversing of our forfeiture, and a robe of righteousness is what Christ gives) it was not such a robe that Adam lost. If so, what is told us of what he lost, will explain to us what it is we gain. Now the peculiar gift which Adam lost is told us in the book of Genesis ; and it certainly does seem to have been a supernatural clothing. He was stripped of it by sinning as of a covering, and shrank from the sight of himself. This was the sign of his inward loathsomeness ; and accordingly all through Scripture we find stress is laid on one especial punishment, which is hereafter to result from sin, of a most piercing and agonizing character, the manifestation of our shame. When we consider what our feelings

[1] Rev. iii. 4.

are now as connected with this subject, we may fancy what an inexpressibly keen anguish is thus in store for sinners, when their eyes shall be opened, who at present "glory in their shame, and mind earthly things." Such then was Adam's loss in God's sight, as visibly typified; and, therefore, such as what he lost is the nature of the Gospel gift, so far as it is a return to what he lost. And as such our Lord speaks of it in the Apocalypse, warning us, as of our natural destitution, so of His power and willingness to remedy it. " I counsel thee," He says, "to buy of Me gold tried in the fire, that thou mayst be rich ; and white raiment, that thou mayst be clothed, and that the shame of thy nakedness do not appear." [1] And again, " Blessed is he that watcheth, and keepeth his garments, lest he walk naked, and they see his shame." [2] Christ then clothes us in God's sight with something over and above nature, which Adam forfeited.

Now that Adam's supernatural clothing was not a mere imputed righteousness, need not formally be proved ; it was a something, of the loss of which he was himself at once conscious, which he could not be of acts passing in the Divine Mind. Nor was it real inherent holiness ; at least we may so conjecture from this circumstance, that such a habit is the result of practice and habituation, and, as it would be attainable but gradually, so when attained it would scarcely yield at once to external temptation. But whether or not we may trust ourselves to such arguments, the early Church supersedes the need of them by explaining, that what

[1] Rev. iii. 18.   [2] Rev. xvi. 15.

Adam lost on sinning, was in fact a supernatural endowment, and agreeably with the view of justification already taken, was nothing less than the inward presence either of the Divine Word, or of the Holy Ghost.

The Catholic fathers, as Bishop Bull has collected their testimony,[1] teach that the principle of sanctity in Adam, to which was attached the gift of immortal life, was something distinct from and above his human nature. That nature, indeed, did look towards such a perfection, but could not in itself reach it. Without this heavenly possession, man was not able to keep the Law according to the Covenant of Life, but with it he could serve God acceptably, and gain the reward set before him.

This interpretation of the Scripture account of man's original nature and fall is confirmed by various passages of St. Paul. For instance, he speaks of man as being by mere creation what he calls a *soul ;* " The first Adam was made a living *soul ;*" now just before, he has used a derived form of the same word, though in our version it does not appear. He says, "there is a *natural* body," that is, "a body with a *soul.*" Elsewhere he says, "the *natural* man," that is, the man with a *soul*, "receiveth not the things of the Spirit of God."[2] Human nature then, viewed in itself, is not spiritual, and that neither in soul nor body. 'Accordingly St. Paul contrasts with this mere natural state that which is spiritual, which alone is pleasing to God, and which alone can see Him. " The natural man receiveth not the things of the Spirit

[1] State of Man before the Fall, p. 115.
[2] 1 Cor. xv. 44, 45 ; ii. 14, 15. 1 Thess. v. 32.

of God ; for they are foolishness unto him, neither can he know them, because they are *spiritually* discerned ; but he that is *spiritual* discerneth all things." In like manner, after saying there is a natural, he adds, "there is a *spiritual* body ;" and after saying that Adam in himself was but a living soul, he adds, that Christ, the beginning of the new creation, is "a quickening *Spirit*." In accordance with this distinction, in another Epistle he prays for his disciples, that their whole *spirit*, and *soul*, and body, may be preserved blameless.

Whatever else, then, Adam had by creation, this seems to have been one main supernatural gift, or rather that in which all others were included, the presence of God the Holy Ghost in him, exalting him into the family and service of His Almighty Creator. This was his clothing ; this he lost by disobedience ; this Christ has regained for us. This then is the robe of righteousness spoken of by Isaiah, to be bestowed in its fulness hereafter, bestowed partially at once : less at present than what Adam had in point of completeness, far greater in its nature ; less in that he had neither decaying body nor infected soul, far more precious in that it is the indwelling and manifestation in our hearts of the Incarnate Word. For what in truth is the gift even in this our state of humiliation, but a grafting invisibly into the Body of Christ ; a mysterious union with Him, and a fellowship in all the grace and blessedness which is hidden in Him ? Thus it separates us from other children of Adam, is our badge and distinction in the presence of the unseen world, and is the earnest of greater good /in store. It is an angelic glory which good spirits honour, which devils tremble at, and which we are bound reverently to cherish, with a careful abstinence from sin, and with the offering of good works. Well then may Prophets and Apostles exult in it as the great gift of Divine Mercy, as the rich garment of salvation, and the enjewelled robe of righteousness ; as linen clean and white, or, as it is elsewhere expressed, as " Christ in us," and " upon us," and around us ; as if it were a light streaming from our hearts, pervading the whole man, enwrapping and hiding the lineaments and members of our fallen nature, circling round us, and returning inward to the centre from which it issues. The Almighty Father, looking on us, sees not us, but this Sacred Presence, even His dearly beloved Son spiritually manifested in us ; with His blood upon our door-posts, in earnest of that final abolition of sin which is at length to be accomplished in us.

Such is the great gift of the Gospel conveyed to us by the ministration of the Spirit, partly now, fully hereafter, and to it a number of passages in the New Testament seem to refer. I shall now proceed to consider it, under two chief designations which are there given to it ; by attending to which we shall conceive more worthily of our privilege, and gain a deeper insight into the sacred text ; I mean *glory* and *power*. Both these titles are applied to the gift in the following passages :—

" It," the human corpse, " is sown in dishonour, it is raised in *glory ;* it is sown in weakness, it is raised in *power;* it is sown a natural body, it is raised a spiritual body."

St. Paul prays to God for his brethren, "that He would grant you, according to the riches of His *glory*, to be strengthened with *power* by His Spirit in the inner man, that *Christ may dwell in your hearts* by faith ; that ye, being rooted and grounded in love, may be able to comprehend with all Saints what is the breadth and length, and depth and height."

"Made *powerful* with all *power*, according to the might of His *glory*, unto all patience and long-suffering with joy, giving thanks unto the Father, who hath made us equal to sharing the inheritance of the saints in *light.*"

" It is impossible for those who were once *enlightened*, and have tasted of the Heavenly Gift, and were made partakers of the Holy Ghost, and have tasted the good word of God, and the *powers* of the world to come, if they shall fall away, to renew them again unto repentance."[1]

3.

Let us then consider this great gift, first as it is *glory*, then as it is *power*.

1. Besides the usual sense which the word *glory* bears in Scripture in relation to our duties to Almighty God, as when we are told to "do all to the glory of God," it has also, I need hardly say, in a number of places a mysterious sense, denoting some attribute, property, virtue, or presence of the Divine Nature manifested

[1] 1 Cor. xv. 43, 44 ; Eph. iii. 16 ; Col. i. 11, 12 ; Heb. vi. 4-6.

visibly. Thus we read of the glory of the Lord appearing over the Tabernacle, and entering into the Temple; and in like manner of the glory of the Lord shining round about the shepherds. Cases of this kind must occur to every attentive reader of the Scriptures. In the places just referred to it seems to mean a presence of God; but sometimes it stands for His moral attributes. Moses gained leave to see the skirts of His glory, and the permission was conveyed in these words, "I will make all My *goodness* pass before thee." Accordingly, Almighty God was proclaimed, as He passed by, as "the Lord, the Lord God, merciful and gracious, long-suffering, and abundant in goodness and truth."

Now as long as Scripture uses the word glory to denote the general awfulness attendant on the presence of Almighty God, there is nothing to surprise us, for every thing that attaches to Him is mysterious; but it becomes remarkable, when we find, as in other passages, the same mysterious attribute, which belongs to Him, ascribed to us.

In considering this point, it is obvious first to mention our Saviour's words to His Almighty Father in His prayer before His passion:—"The glory which Thou gavest Me, *I have given them*." [1]

What is this glory which has passed from Christ to us? It is some high gift which admits of being transferred, as is evident. What it was in Christ, we see in some degree by the following words of St. Paul:—"Like as Christ was raised up from the dead by *the glory of the Father*, even so we also should walk in newness of life."

[1] Exod. xxxiii. 18, 19; xxxiv. 6. John xvii. 22; xi. 40. Rom. vi. 4.

Whatever else it was, it appears hence that it was a presence or power which operated for the resurrection of His body. In this connection it may be well to direct attention to a passage which, otherwise, with our present notions, we should explain (as we should think) more naturally. Before our Lord raises Lazarus, He says to Martha, "Said I not unto thee, that if thou wouldest believe, thou shouldest see the *glory* of God?" What He *had* said before to her was simply, that He was the Resurrection and the Life.

And when granted to us, it is characterized by the same operative power; St. Paul speaks in a text already cited of "the *might* of God's glory in us;" of our being "*strengthened with might* by His Spirit in the inner man, according to the riches of His glory." And elsewhere of "the riches of the glory of His inheritance in the Saints;" and St. Peter of our being called "to glory and virtue;" of the "Spirit of glory and of God *resting* on us;" and St. Paul again of our being "*changed* from glory to glory." The gift then is habitual; both permanent and increasing. Again: "Ye were sometimes darkness, but now are ye light in the Lord; walk as children of light." "Awake, thou that sleepest, and arise from the dead, and Christ shall give thee light." "The God of this world hath blinded the minds of them which believe not, lest the light of the glorious Gospel of Christ, who is the image of God, should shine unto them." To these may be added a text, which we now understand differently, "All have sinned, and come short of," or *are in need of,* "the *glory* of God."[1]

---

[1] Eph. v. 8, 14.   2 Cor. iv. 4.   Rom. iii. 23.   ὑστεροῦνται τῆς δόξης

Lastly, these mentions of glory are distinctly connected with the gift of "righteousness." St. Paul speaks indifferently of the "ministration of the Spirit," and " of the ministration of *righteousness,* exceeding in *glory.*"[1]

Now, without knowing at all what "glory" means, all these passages seem to show that it is a gift directly proceeding from God's nature, and intimately united to the Christian. Here then is additional evidence that an endowment is bestowed upon us distinct from any moral gift, or any mere external title or imputation ; and that this endowment thus distinguished is nothing else than our righteousness.

4.

2. The same general conclusion will follow from considering the gift as *power.*

Properly speaking, the word "power," denotes a divine attribute or prerogative. As glory seems to designate the inherent perfection of Almighty God from eternity (as, for instance, when the Son is called "the brightness of God's glory"), so "power" is a characteristic of that perfection as manifested in time. Creation is the offspring of His *power;* again, He "upholds all things by the word of His *power.*"

Next, it is used to denote the particular attribute manifested in the Economy of Redemption and in the

Egent gloriâ Dei. Vulg.—St. Cyprian makes the sense of the word clearer by reading *claritas* for *gloria,* ad Quir. ii. 27. Also τῆς δόξης ἀποστερῇ · τῶν γὰρ προσκεκρουκότων εἶ · ὁ δὲ προσκεκρουκὼς οὐ τῶν δοξαζομένων, ἀλλὰ τῶν κατῃσχυμμένων, Chrys. *in loc.* "That is, the fruition of God in Glory : " Whitby *in loc.* Vid. also Bucer *in loc.*

[1] 2 Cor. iii. 8, 9.

Person of the Redeemer ; for instance,—" The *power* of the Highest" overshadowed the Blessed Virgin in order to the Incarnation. "Jesus returned in the *power* of the Spirit into Galilee." Christ was "declared to be the Son of God with *power*, according to the Spirit of Holiness, by the resurrection from the dead." St. Paul speaks of "knowing Him and the *power* of His resurrection," "Jesus immediately perceived that virtue" or *power* (for the word is the same in the original), "had gone out of Him." " There went *power* out of Him, and healed them all." " Mighty works do show forth themselves in Him," that is, "these virtues or *powers* do energize, act, live, or work, in Him."[1]

Next, let it be observed that this virtue or power was given by Him to His disciples, and then in our Version the word is commonly translated *miracle*. It is true, it does sometimes mean precisely the miraculous act or work itself ; but it often means, not the work, but as the word *virtue* implies, the faculty or gift of power within the agent which effects the work. For instance : " He gave them *power* and authority over all devils, and to cure diseases." " Ye shall receive the *power* of the Holy Ghost coming upon you." " My speech, and my preaching, was not with enticing words of man's wisdom, but in demonstration of the Spirit and of *power*." In like manner Simon Magus, when he bewitched the Samaritans, was called by them " the great *power* " or virtue " of God."[2]

---

[1] Luke i. 35 ; iv. 14. Rom. i. 4. Phil. iii. 10. Mark v. 30. Luke vi. 19. Mark vi. 14.

[2] Luke ix. 1. Acts i. 8. 1 Cor. ii. 4. Acts viii. 10.

Further, the effects of this indwelling gift in the Apostles are described as similar to those which our Lord allowed to appear in Himself; I mean, it showed itself as a virtue going out of them, so as to take away all pretence of its being considered a mere act of the power of God, external to themselves, accompanying their word or deed, and not an effect through them and from them. Thus of St. Paul it is said, that "God wrought special miracles by the hands of Paul, so that *from his body* were brought unto the sick handkerchiefs and aprons, and the diseases departed from them, and the evil spirits went out of them." Again : "By the hands of the Apostles were many signs and wonders wrought among the people ; insomuch that they brought forth the sick into the streets, and laid them on beds and couches, that at least the *shadow* of Peter passing by might overshadow some of them."[1] The instance of the virtue of Elisha's bones in raising the dead is another remarkable instance of the inward gift of the Spirit, and anticipates Gospel times.

And, lastly, such in kind, though not miraculous (in the common sense of the word), is the gift bestowed upon the Christian Church and its members. The same word being used, we may well believe that it is an inward yet not a moral gift, but a supernatural power or divine virtue. Thus, for instance, our Lord speaks of it as being in the body or Church ; and says, on one occasion, that there were some about Him, "who should not taste of death, till they had seen the kingdom of God come *with power.*" The Gospel is said to be " the *power*

[1] Acts xix. 11, 12 ; v. 12-15.

of God unto salvation ;" Christ, "unto the called, both
Jews and Greeks," is "the *power* of God and wisdom of
God." And so as regards the Apostles and Christians
generally. Thus we read of St. Paul's ministerial power
as a similar inward gift ;—"whereof," he says, that
is, of the Gospel, " I was made a minister, by the gift
of the grace of God, which was given to me by the
inward working of His power." Again, he speaks of
his "striving according to His working, *which worketh in
me* mightily." [1] Again "Most gladly therefore will I
rather glory in my infirmities, that the *power* of Christ
may rest upon me." Now this expression, "rest upon
me," is in the original " rest upon me as in a tabernacle ;"
and is used elsewhere. For instance, in an earlier part
of this same Epistle, the word "tabernacle" has been
used for the mortal body. What, then, St. Paul rejoices
in, is that the power of Christ is upon his tabernacle or
body ; and the weight of this privilege is intimated by
the adoption of the word in the Apocalypse, to describe
the characteristic of future glory, " He that sitteth on
the throne shall tabernacle over them." [2]

To the same purport are the following passages : " I
can do all things through Christ which strengtheneth
me," that is, more literally, " I am every way strong in
the power-imparting Christ," or "in Christ who worketh
power in me." And it is observable, that this power is
said to be the same as wrought the Resurrection, or what
is elsewhere called glory ; St. Paul, as I have said,
prays for the Ephesians, that "the eyes of their under-

<hr/>

[1] 1 Cor. i. 18-24.   Eph. iii. 7.   Col. i. 29.
[2] 2 Cor. xii. 9.   Rev. vii. 15 ; xxi. 3.

standing may be enlightened, that they may know what is the hope of His calling, and what the riches of the glory of His inheritance in the saints, and what is the exceeding greatness of His *power* to us-ward who believe, according to the inward working of the might of His strength, *which He* wrought in Christ when He raised Him from the dead." He returns thanks and praises " unto Him that is able to do exceeding abundantly above all that we ask or think, *according to the power that worketh in us.*" He desires for himself that he " may know Him, and the *power* of His resurrection." He speaks of " the work of faith with *power*." He bids Timothy " be partaker of the afflictions of the Gospel according to the *power* of God."[1] He declares that Christ is made a priest " not after the law of a carnal commandment, but after the *power* of an endless life ;" His eternal and spiritual existence becoming, through His sacerdotal intercession, an inward power to His followers, such as could not be imparted by any mere earthly system. Again, St. Peter speaks of Christians being " kept by the *power* of God through faith unto salvation ;" and of God having given us, "according to His divine *power*," " all things that pertain unto life and godliness."

Here then, as before, I conclude that an endowment is vouchsafed to us, not simply moral, yet internal, so as fitly to answer and corroborate the description I have already given of "the gift of righteousness."

[1] Eph. i. 18-20 ; iii. 20. Phil. iii. 10. 2 Thes. i. 11. 2 Tim. i. 8. Heb. vii. 16. 1 Pet. i. 5. 2 Pet. i. 3.

5.

Since, then, the gift of righteousness is a supernatural presence in our moral nature, distinct from it, yet dwelling in it and changing it, it is not wonderful that the change itself should sometimes be spoken of in Scripture as the gift or as included in the gift. Thus, for instance, the garment of salvation put on us, is such as to cleave to us, and to tend to become part of us; what was at first a covering merely, becomes our very flesh. The glory of the Divine Nature, of which St. Peter says we are partakers, first hides our deformity, then removes it.

Again : our Saviour asked the brother Apostles, whether they were able to drink of His cup, and to be baptized in His baptism? Can a draught be separated from the drinking it, or a bath from being bathed in it? In like manner the gift of righteousness, which is our justification as given, is our renewal as received.

Or again : the seal, mould, or stamp, with which our souls are marked as God's *coin* impresses His *image* upon them. He claims them as His own redeemed property, that is, by the signature of holiness : He justifies us by renewing. How natural this continuance is of the one idea into the other, is shown in the literal sense of the words which I am using figuratively. The word *mark* stands both for the instrument marking, and the figure which it makes. So again, the word *copy* sometimes stands for the pattern, sometimes for the imitation. In like manner, *image* sometimes means the original, sometimes the duplicate or representation. Thus, in one text, man is said to be formed "*after* the image of God;" in another he is said to *be* "the image of Christ."[1] And in like manner, though the inward law commonly stands for the new creature, yet it may be said to justify, as standing also for that Archetype of which the new creature is the copy. And again, we may be said to be "saved" by the "ingrafted Word," that is, the Word which *is* ingrafted, but which for all that does not cease to be what it was when first imparted, the presence of Christ.

The following passage in the Book of Wisdom well illustrates, in the case of the attribute from which it takes its name, what I would enforce,—the indivisible union between the justifying gift of the Divine Presence and the inherent sanctity which is its token.

"All men," says the writer, "have one entrance into life, and the like going out. Wherefore I prayed, and understanding was given me ; I called upon God, and the spirit of wisdom came to me. I loved her above health and beauty, and chose to have her instead of light ; for the light that cometh from her never goeth out. All good things together came to me with her, and innumerable riches in her hands. I learned diligently and do communicate her liberally ; I do not hide her riches ; for she is a treasure unto men that never faileth, which they that use *become the friends of God*, being commended for the gifts that come from learning."[2]

Now, if this were all that were said on the subject, unbecoming complaints would be uttered in some schools of religion, that in this passage an internal gift, called wisdom by the writer, was considered to make us " friends

---

[1] Perhaps there is some difference in the sense of these two phrases. Vid. Petav. Dogm. de Opific. ii. 2.   [2] Wisdom vii. 6-14.

of God," or to justify ; and a tendency to Pelagianism would be freely imputed, and an ignorance that justification was God's act, in spite of the strong expression which occurs of the spirit of wisdom *coming* to the writer, which surely implies a Divine Agent, not an implanted excellence, and in spite of our Lord's plain declaration, that we *are* His friends if we do what He commands us. However, as the description proceeds, it will be found that the Wisdom spoken of is no created gift, no inward renewal, but none other than the Eternal Word Himself, who afterwards took flesh, in order thus supernaturally to be imparted ; and who was announced beforehand by holy men in terms which inspired Apostles in due time adopted.   The sacred writer, then (for so surely he may well be called, considering what he says), proceeds as follows :—" In Her " [Wisdom] " is an understanding spirit holy, *only-begotten*, manifold, subtle, lively, clear, undefiled, plain, incorruptible, a lover of good, keen, free to act, beneficent, kind to man, stedfast, sure, free from care, *all-powerful*, *all-surveying*, and pervading all intellectual, pure, and subtle spirits.   For Wisdom is more moving than any motion ; She passeth and goeth through all things because of her pureness. For she is the *Breath of the power of God*, and a *pure Effluence from the glory of the Almighty;* therefore can no defiled thing fall into her.   For she is the *Brightness of the Everlasting Light*, the *unspotted Mirror of the power of God*, and *the Image of His goodness*.   And being but One, She can do all things ; and *remaining in herself*, She *maketh all things new ;* and in all ages *entering into*

holy souls She maketh them friends of God and prophets."[1]
Here then, while wisdom is said to be our justification, no
clear distinction is made between the created wisdom and
the Increate.

6.

One more illustration shall be adduced ; justification
is the setting up of the Cross within us. That Cross,
planted by Almighty Hands, is our safeguard from all
evil ; dropping grace and diffusing heavenly virtue all
around, and hallowing the spot where before there was
but strife, and death. It is our charm against numberless dangers ghostly and bodily ; it is our refuge against
our accusing and seducing foe, our protection from the
terror by night and the arrow by day, and our passport
into the Church invisible. But how does this Cross
become ours ? I repeat, by being given ; and what is
this giving, in other words, but our being marked with
it ? Let us see what this implies. We know that in
Baptism a cross is literally marked on the forehead.
Now suppose (to explain what I mean) we were ordered
to mark the cross, not with the finger, but with a sharp
instrument. Then it would be a rite of blood. In such
a case justification and *pain* would undeniably go together ; they would be inseparable. You might separate
them in idea, but in fact they would ever be one. One
act would convey both the one and the other. If the
invisible presence of the justifying Cross were conveyed
to you *in* marking it visibly, you could not receive the
justification without the pain. Justification would
involve pain. Now it is in this way that justification

[1] Wisdom vii. 22-27.

actually does involve a spiritual circumcision, a crucifixion of the flesh, or sanctification. The entrance of Christ's sacred presence into the soul, which becomes our righteousness in God's sight, at the same time becomes righteousness in it. It make us travail and be in pangs with righteousness, and work with fear and trembling. Such is the account given of it by the son of Sirach ; who uses the same image of Wisdom already referred to :—" If a man," he says, " commit himself to Her, he shall inherit Her, and his generation shall hold Her in possession. For at the first She will walk with him *by crooked ways* and *bring fear and dread* upon him, and *torment him with her discipline,* till She may trust his soul and try him by her laws." [1]

It is very necessary to insist upon this, for a reason which has come before us in other shapes already. It is the fashion of the day to sever these two from one another, which God has joined, the seal and the impression, justification and renewal. You hear men speak of glorying in the Cross of Christ, who are utter strangers to the notion of the Cross as actually applied to them in water and blood, in holiness and mortification. They think the Cross can be theirs *without* being applied,— without its coming near them,—while they keep at a distance from it, and only gaze at it. They think individuals are justified immediately by the great Atonement, —justified by Christ's death, and not, as St. Paul says, by means of His Resurrection,—justified by what they consider *looking* at His death. Because the Brazen Serpent in the wilderness healed by being looked at,

[1] Ecclus. iv. 16, 17.

they consider that Christ's Sacrifice saves by the mind's contemplating it. This is what they call casting themselves upon Christ,—coming before Him simply and without self-trust, and being saved by faith. Surely we ought so to *come* to Christ ; surely we must believe ; surely we must look ; but the question is, in what form and manner He *gives* Himself to us ; and it will be found that, when He enters into us, glorious as He is Himself, pain and self-denial are His attendants. Gazing on the Brazen Serpent did not heal ; but God's invisible communication of the gift of health to those who gazed. So also justification is wholly the work of God ; it comes from God to us ; it is a power exerted on our souls by Him, as the healing of the Israelites was a power exerted on their bodies. The gift must be brought *near* to us ; it is not like the Brazen Serpent, a mere external, material, local sign ; it is a spiritual gift, and, as being such, admits of being applied to us individually. Christ's Cross does not justify by being looked at, but by being applied ; not by as merely beheld by faith, but by being actually set up within us, and that not by our act, but by God's invisible grace. Men sit, and gaze, and speak of the great Atonement, and think this is appropriating it ; not more truly than kneeling to the material cross itself is appropriating it. Men say that faith is an apprehending and applying ; faith cannot really apply the Atonement ; man,cannot make the Saviour of the world his own ; the Cross must be brought home to us, not in word, but in power, and this is the work of the Spirit. This is justification ; but when imparted to the soul, it draws blood, it heals, it purifies, it glorifies.

7.

With one or two passages from St. Paul in behalf of what I have been saying, I will bring this Lecture to an end. We shall find from the Apostle that the gift of the Justifying Cross as certainly involves an inward crucifixion as a brand or stamp causes sharp pain, or the cure of a bodily ailment consists in a severe operation.

For instance, writing to the Galatians, he says, "God forbid that I should glory save in the Cross of our Lord Jesus Christ;"[1]—what Cross? He goes on to tell us; —"by whom," or, rather, by which "*the world is crucified unto me, and I unto the world*,"—that is, the Cross on Calvary, issuing and completed in its reflection on his own soul. An inward crucifixion was the attendant *process* of justification. This passage is the more remarkable, because St. Paul is alluding to certain bodily wounds and sufferings, *as* being actually the mode, in his case, in which the Cross had been applied. He says to his converts,—"The Jews compel you to be circumcised, but we Christians glory in another kind of circumcision, painful indeed, but more profitable. Our circumcision consists in the marks, the brands, of the Lord Jesus; which effect for us what circumcision can but typify, which interest us in His life while interesting us in His passion." The saving Cross crucifies us in saving.

Again: in a previous passage, "A man is not justified by the works of the Law, but by the faith of Christ."[2] Do we conceive this to be a light and pleasant doctrine, and justification to be given without pain and discomfort on our part? so freely given as to be given

[1] Gal. vi. 14.   [2] Gal. ii. 16, 20.

easily,—so fully as to be lavishly ? fully and freely doubtless, yet conferring fully what man does not take freely.
He proceeds ;—" I am *crucified with Christ,* nevertheless
I live ; yet not I, but Christ liveth in me." O easy and
indulgent doctrine, to have the bloody Cross reared within us, and our heart transfixed, and our arms stretched
out upon it, and the sin of our nature slaughtered and
cast out !

Again ; in the same Epistle, " They that are Christ's
have crucified the flesh with the affections and lusts." [1]
It is remarkable that these three passages are from that
Epistle in which the Apostle peculiarly insists on justification being through faith, not through the Law. It is
plain he never thought of mere faith as the direct and
absolute instrument of it. It should be observed how
coincident this doctrine is with our Saviour's command
to His disciples to " *take up their Cross* and follow Him."
Our crosses are the lengthened shadow of the Cross on
Calvary.

To the same purport are the following texts :—" We
are buried with Him by baptism into death . . . . our old
man is crucified with Him."—" Put ye on the Lord Jesus
Christ, and make not provision for the flesh, to fulfil the
lusts thereof."—" Always bearing about in the body the
dying of the Lord Jesus, that the life also of Jesus might
be made manifest in our body ; for we which live are
alway delivered unto death for Jesus' sake, that the life
also of Jesus might be made manifest in our mortal
flesh." [2]

As then the Cross, in which St. Paul gloried, was not

[1] Gal. v. 24.　　　[2] Rom. vi. 4, 6 ; xiii. 14.　2 Cor. iv. 10, 11.

the *material* cross on which Christ suffered,—so neither is it simply the Sacrifice on the cross, but it is that Sacrifice coming in power to him who has faith in it, and converting body and soul into a sacrifice. It is the Cross, realized, present, living in him, sealing him, separating him from the world, sanctifying him, afflicting him. Thus the great Apostle clasped it to his heart, though it pierced it through like a sword ; held it fast in his hands, though it cut them ; reared it aloft, preached it, exulted in it. And thus we in our turn are allowed to hold it, commemorating and renewing individually, by the ministry of the Holy Ghost, the death and resurrection of our Lord.

But enough has been said on the matter in hand. On the whole, then, I conclude as follows . that though the Gift which justifies us is, as we have seen, a something distinct from us and lodged in us, yet it involves in its idea its own work in us, and (as it were) takes up into itself that renovation of the soul, those holy deeds and sufferings, which are as if a radiance streaming from it.

LECTURE VIII.

RIGHTEOUSNESS VIEWED AS A GIFT AND AS
A QUALITY.

I NOW propose to contrast the view of justification
which has been drawn out in the last Lectures with
that to which certain writers of the Roman School
consider themselves committed by the wording of the
Tridentine Decree, into which also some of our writers
have virtually fallen, and which, moreover, is unfairly
imputed to many of our standard divines. As to the Protestant doctrine, on the other hand, which was a third in
the discussion, I cannot go more deeply into what seems
to me a system of words without ideas, and of distinctions without arguments. If I am told, in reply, that such
a view of it arises from want of spiritual perception,—
those who are blind to heavenly objects not understanding
heavenly words,—I answer, that, though undoubtedly
divine words express divine things, and divine things
are hidden from all but divinely enlightened minds, yet
this does not tell against a man for stumbling at words
which are not divine. Luther's words are his own,
reasoned out from Scripture, which every one of us has
equal right to do. If I receive the doctrine of the
Church Catholic as divine, it is as guaranteed by many
concordant witnesses, which converge to one place and

one time, the day of Pentecost, when the Apostles were
with one accord assembled in one place.[1]   And if I bow
to some individual teacher, as Irenæus or Augustine, it is
not from a notion of his infallibility, but on the ground
of his representing the whole Church, or from a sense
of the authority of men of holy and mortified lives in
questions of religion.   But what binds me to yield a
submission to the sixteenth century, which I withhold
even from the second ? why must I measure spiritual
discernment in myself and others, by our apprehension,
not of Scripture, but of comparatively modern treatises,
and accept terms and distinctions which, over and above
their human origin, have no internal consistence,—no
external proof,—no part or lot in Antiquity ; which, in
short, have but a praiseworthy object for their excuse,
the overthrow, as they think, of Roman error ?   Surely
the reverse of wrong is not right ; yet this doctrine
mainly rests its pretensions upon the errors of a rival
doctrine, assumes itself true because it is serviceable,
proves itself Scriptural by proving Romanism unscriptural, flatters itself that it has a meaning viewed out of

[1] " Nay, moreover, I shall persuade myself, that from this one instance (among many) you will learn from henceforth the modesty of
submitting your judgment to that of the Catholic doctors, when they
are found generally to concur in the interpretation of a text of Scripture, *how absurd soever that interpretation may at first appearance seem
to be ;* for upon a diligent search you will find, that 'aliquid latet, quod
non patet,' there is a mystery in the bottom ; and that what at the
first view seemed even ridiculous, will afterwards appear to be a most
important truth.   Let them, therefore, who reading the Fathers are
prone to laugh at that in them which they do not presently understand,
seriously consider, 'quanto suo periculo id faciant.'"—Bull, *State of
Man before the Fall*, p. 99.

Romanism, and thinks to live and flourish though
Romanism came to an end.

On these grounds, as regards the three doctrines above
drawn out,—of the righteousness of Christ imputed
only, imparted only, and both imputed and imparted by
His real indwelling,—I omit the first in the comparison
between them, which now naturally follows, as being
partly negative, partly extravagant. It is a negative
statement to say that justification is not by works ; it
is extravagant to say that it is by faith as the primary
and sole instrument. Whether a disputant says nothing
positive or nothing literal,[1] in neither case is there room
for discussion, which claims to touch and handle, to sift,
to weigh, to adjust, to distribute. There is nothing precise, nothing to grapple with, when we are told, for
instance, that faith justifies independent of its being a
right and good principle—that it justifies as an instrument not as a condition,—that love is its inseparable
accident, yet not its external criterion,—that good works
are necessary, but not to be called so in controversy or
popular preaching ;[2] and that nothing in us constitutes

---

[1] Melanchthon, the most judicious defender of the chief doctrine of
Protestantism, justification by the apprehensive power of faith, whom
our Church follows, makes that doctrine intelligible and true by admitting that it is not to be taken literally, but as a mode of symbolizing a
protest against the doctrine of human merit. The Confession of Augsburgh (Ed. 1538), which is his composition, says, "Jam bonas mentes
nihil offendat novitas Paulinæ *figuræ*, 'Fide justificamur,' si intelli-
gant *proprie* de misericordia dici ;" on which Bull observes, Ex ipsorum
doctrina liquido liquet . . . *figurata* quidem sed non incommoda
locutione dici posse, nos sola fide justificari.—Harm. Apost. ii. 18, § 6.

[2] Dav. de Just. Habit. 31, who observes also, Multi qui recipiunt
hanc propositionem, "Bona opera sunt fidelibus necessaria," rejiciunt

our being justified. Such a doctrine is, what it makes justification to be, a shadow.

2.

I proceed, then, to suggest some points of contrast between the two other views of justification mentioned, the doctrine of the justifying Presence, which I have been maintaining, and that of justifying obedience, as found among ourselves ; for there certainly has been a school of divines in our Church, who by a very different road have practically approached the doctrine of Rome on this subject. What Roman writers have brought about by insisting exclusively on the effects of grace, many among ourselves have done by disparaging its sacramental means. The former raise man to the capacity, the latter have reduced him to the necessity, of being justified by his obedience and nothing else. By the latter divines I mean the Arminians who rose in Charles the First's time, and have exercised an extensive influence in our Church since 1688. Those who conceive duly of the gift of justification, exalt the sacramental instruments of possessing it, as feeling that nothing short of means ordained of God can convey what is so much above them. Thus their glowing language about the Sacraments is but the measure of their estimation of their spiritual privileges. And if they go on to say that obedience justifies, it never occurs to them to suppose that they can be taken to be

et damnant eandem, si hoc additamentum apponatur "Sunt necessaria *ad justificationem*," vel "sunt necessaria *ad salutem*," . . . E contra reperirentur e Protestantibus *nonnulli*, qui haud verentur concedere, bona opera esse *ad salutem* necessaria.

speaking of anything but *the state of soul* in which the heavenly gift resides, and by which it is retained, not that which really causes, or procures, or purchases it.[1] Thus the high doctrine of the Sacraments held by Rome is a safeguard against any such defective or incomplete view of justification as is sanctioned by certain of her writers. But they who see nothing supernatural and mysterious in the Gift, though in words they refer it to the Sacraments, will practically associate it with that which they do see, and which seems to them naturally connected with it, viz., their own obedience. Not believing in any true sense that they are temples of the Holy Ghost, inhabited by Christ, and members of His Body, they consider their justification properly to consist in works, because they do not discern, they do not believe in, anything else, in which it can consist. Justification by obedience, then, is their distinguishing tenet ; doubtless it is also the doctrine of the English Church, as it is of St. James ; yet not only it, but much more besides. To put a parallel case, one man might say that our bodily *life* consisted in *organization*, or in a certain state of the nerves, or in the circulation of the blood ; and another might ascribe it to *the presence of the soul.* The latter doctrine is the former and something besides ; but the former by itself is defective. He

[1] Davenant grants as much as this :—" Bona opera justificatorum sunt ad salutem necessaria, *necessitate ordinis* non causalitatis, vel planius, *ut via ordinata ad vitam æternam,* non ut causæ meritoriæ vitæ æternæ." He also freely grants that they are " media seu *conditiones* sine quibus Deus non vult justificationis gratiam in hominibus conservare."—c. 31. That is, we are saved neither by faith, nor by works, but as walking *in the way* both of faith and of works.'

who holds the former is not wrong, but he who holds only the former. Religious men may ascribe life to the heart, and thought to the brain; but those who say these are the only constituting causes of life and thought are materialists. In like manner St. Austin and others who, though they place justification in renewal, refer renewal to the indwelling presence of the Holy Ghost, are not to be compared with those who enlarge on what is seen, and explain away the mystery. This analogy holds in many other points; but I confine it to what is before us. I say, then, justification by obedience is anyhow true; it is sound doctrine, if we hold another doctrine too; it is incomplete, if we omit that other doctrine; it becomes erroneous, if we deny it.

When it is held exclusively among ourselves, it often takes the following shape: that God accepts our sincere obedience, as if it were perfect; or that God will save us if we do our part; or that God has done His part in Baptism, and now we must do ours. Such statements are most true and Scriptural, if they are not meant to deny (what may be called) our Sacramental life, the fount of grace which Holy Baptism has stored within us, and the awful realities of Holy Communion, those invisible facts (as I may call them) in which we stand, in which we breathe, on which we feed. For if our Life be verily and indeed hid with Christ in God, it follows, that, though we are bound to do our part and work with Him, such co-operation is the condition, not of our acceptance, or pardon, but of the continuance of that sacred Presence which is our true righteousness, as an immediate origin of it. I believe this distinction is no matter of words, but real and practical, as a few remarks will show.

3.

Now, when you teach as follows. that Christ's Atoning Death, eighteen hundred years since, and our own personal Baptism in our infancy, so changed our state in God's sight once for all, that henceforth salvation depends on ourselves, on our doing our part in the Covenant,—that those gracious events put us indeed on a new footing, wiped out what was passed, set us off fair, and are still operative as gaining for us heaven, if obedient, and present aids if believing, but that faith and obedience are the conditions of grace and glory,—true as all this is to the letter, yet if nothing more is added, we shall seem, in spite of whatever we say concerning the Atonement and the influences of the Holy Ghost if duly sought, to be resting a man's salvation on himself, and to be making him the centre of the whole religious system.[1] All has been done for him ages ago, or when

[1] "God is pleased to grant remission of all past sins, for the sake of His Blessed Son, on account of faith only ; but He requires from those whom He thus graciously receives into His favour, an implicit obedience to His commands in future ; if they *disobey, their pardon is cancelled, the state of acceptance forfeited,* and liability to punishment ensues."—p. 124. . . . "If he really performed these conditions, he continued in a state of justification, and if he persevered to the end of his life, his salvation was secured. But if he did not perform these conditions," etc.—p. 134. The continuance of justification "depends upon their abstinence from those sins which are forbidden, and upon the practice of those virtues which are enjoined in the Gospel. By the indulgence of any criminal passion, or by the neglect of any practicable duty, the state of justification is forfeited."—p. 142.—*Tomline on Calvinism.* It is not insinuated that the author is at all wanting in

he was an infant; and all that *has* been done, seems as though a condition of his existing at all, as benefits on which he cannot be said to repose his mind, because they are presupposed in his being himself, which do not come to him from without, nor admit of being viewed by him objectively. I would not say that this doctrine will so affect men of high religious attainments; but that, viewed as the multitude will view it, it does not come up to the idea of the Gospel Creed as contained in Scripture, does not fix our thoughts on Christ in that full and direct way of which Scripture sets the pattern, as being not only the Author of salvation to the whole race, but the Saviour of each of us individually through every stage of our Christian course, and in every act of our lives. This seems to be the real meaning of the popular saying, that "Christ ought to be preached," and of the anxiety felt by a portion of the community to maintain the supremacy and all-sufficiency of His righteousness.

Hence the charge against Romanism, not unfounded as regards its popular teaching,[1] that it views the influences of grace, not as the operations of a living God, but as a something to bargain about, and buy, and traffic with,

explicit statements concerning the influence of divine grace, nor that what he says is not true, (*e.g.* Jerome thus speaks in Jovinian. ii. 32. fin.), but the prominence he gives to this view of justification makes the doctrine what would popularly be called *cold;* approximates it, theologically speaking, to the *unica formalis causa* of the Council of Trent; and, when analyzed, will be found to arise from a neglect of the doctrine of the Real Presence.

[1] [It requires a considerable acquaintance with the working of the Catholic system to have a right thus to speak of it.]

as if religion were, not an approach to Things above us, but a commerce with our equals concerning things we can master.[1]   And this is the cause of the suspicions entertained in many quarters against those who in any sense teach that obedience justifies, as if it implied we had something in ourselves to rely upon ; whereas, if the Presence of Christ is our true righteousness, first conveyed into us in Baptism, then more sacredly and mysteriously in the Eucharist, we have really no inherent righteousness at all.   What seems to be inherent, may be more properly called *adherent*, depending, as it does, wholly and absolutely upon the Divine Indwelling, not ours to keep, but as heat in a sickly person, sustained by a cause distinct from himself.   If the Presence of Christ were to leave us, our renovation would go with

[1]   " Disdaining to be anticipated by God Himself, [the soul of man] prevents Him in His supernatural gifts by a previous display of her own meritorious deeds, challenging, *as a congruous right*, that which only could have been otherwise conferred as a favour undeserved. Approaching the throne of mercy, not with a conscious sense of frailty, but with a confident persuasion of her inherent dignity, she wrests from a somnivolent Deity, hitherto but a slumbering spectator of her efforts, an ornamental grace, enabling her *to merit that reward by condignity*, which, without any defect of virtue, but *merely by the appointed order of things*, she is incapable of meriting by congruity."—Laurence, Bampt Lect. 4, quoting in the notes the following striking passage of Luther " Quisque Monachus hanc habet imaginationem : ' Ego per observantiam Sanctæ Regulæ possum mereri gratiam de congruo ; operibus autem, quæ post acceptam gratiam facio, tantum meritum accumulare possum, ut non tantum mihi sufficiat pro consequenda vita æterna, sed etiam hoc aliis communicare et vendere possim.' " [Luther's language is vigorous, though slanderous ; but did any one ever come across so elaborate a specimen of pretentious writing, as is this passage of the Bampton Lecturer's ?]

it ; and to say we are justified by renovation, only means that we are interested in Him from whom it flows, that we dwell beneath the overshadowing Power of Him who is our Justifier.

And further, it is not nearly so consoling yet awful a doctrine to say, that we *have* had mercy and *shall* have reward, and are at present in some measure in a middle state, expected to move and promised grace upon moving, as to know, which I conceive is the full truth of the Gospel, that that perfection, which is as yet but begun in our own nature, is anticipated, pledged, and in one sense realized within us by a present gift, and that the centre on which our thoughts must be fixed, and the foundation from which our exertions must proceed, is not ourselves, but His Presence, in whom " we live, and move, and have our being." And though it is most necessary to exhibit to men the severer side of the Gospel, and to dwell on their duties, and responsibilities, and the conditions on which grace is given, yet this is but one side; and when it is exclusively presented to Christians, as it is in the school of divinity in question, a complaint will not unfairly arise against it as cold and narrow, and unlike what it is popular to call "the freeness and fulness " of the Gospel.

4.

And here I am reminded of another objection which may be urged against this same school of theology, viz. that it disparages certain doctrines which are very prominent in Scripture, those of predestination and election. The Gospel is a free gift; it comes to the unworthy, to those who have done nothing to earn it, who can do nothing right towards God before He shows mercy towards them. That spontaneous mercy is abundantly taught in the doctrine of the Atonement itself and the ordinance of Baptism ; but, these being, as I said just now, past events in our own case, and as if conditions of our existence rather than objects presented to us, the Covenant of God's unsearchable grace becomes one of man's free election ; and man has rather to choose Heaven than Heaven man. The great mercies of God are done and over ; and we have now to act, if we would receive additional benefits. Thus, in this view of the Gospel, there is a tendency, which in our Church has been realized, to put out of sight the doctrines of election and sovereign grace ; a circumstance which by itself would separate it, in spite of partial resemblance, from the teaching of St. Austin, who is known to have laid an unprecedented stress on those doctrines, and to have given them a new direction.

Moreover, it is no slight evil in the mode of teaching here censured, that by withdrawing a portion of truth, countenance is given to those false Protestant views now so popular among us. Truth always avenges itself ; and if kept in bondage, it breaks forth irregularly, burying itself with the strong man in the overthrow of its oppressors. And so if our Church has at any time forgotten the Living Presence conveyed in the Sacraments, an opening has been at once. made for the meagre and artificial doctrine of a nominal righteousness. So many passages are there which speak of the Atonement as still living in Christians, that if we will not enforce them literally, we must be content to hear them explained away into a mere imputation of it in God's dealings with us, or into a contemplation of it by our faith.

I say, the view of justification taken by a school of divines in the Roman Church[1] and among ourselves, tends to fix the mind on self, not on Christ, whereas that which I have advocated as Scriptural and Catholic, buries self in the absorbing vision of a present, an indwelling God. And as so doing, it is a more awakening and fearful doctrine even, than that mode of teaching which insists mainly and directly on our responsibilities and duties. For to what does it point as the great and immediate condition of justification? to faith and holiness of our own? or, on the other hand, to the mere title of righteousness, which cannot be literally approached or profaned by us? no,—but to the glorious Shekinah of the Word Incarnate, as to the true wedding garment in which the soul must be dressed. Does not such a view far increase, instead of diminishing, our responsibilities? does it not make us more watchful and more obedient, while it comforts and elevates us? Surely it takes our minds off ourselves, in order to fill us with triumph, awe, and godly fear at what our state is, and what we hold

---

[1] [This school is elsewhere called in these Lectures ultra-Roman or extreme Romanist. Such Catholic divines as Caietan, Vasquez, and Bellarmine were intended by this title, who, by making justification consist in the habit of charity, or again in good works, not in sanctifying grace as an initial and distinct gift from above, seemed to the writer to fix the mind, equally with Anglican Arminians, not on a Divine inward Presence vouchsafed to it, but on something of its own, as a ground to rest upon and take satisfaction in. Of course, such a judgment seems to him now unreal and arbitrary.]

within us. When are we the more likely to dread sinning, when we know merely we ought to dread it, or when we see the exceeding peril of it? When are we the more likely to keep awake and be sober, when we have a present treasure now to lose, or a distant reward to gain? Is it not more dreadful, when evil thoughts assail us, more encouraging and ennobling in affliction, more kindling in danger and hardship, to reflect (if the words may be said) that we bear God within us, as the Martyr Ignatius expresses it, that He is grieved by us or suffers with us, according as we carry or renounce His Cross,—I say, has not this thought more of persuasiveness in it to do and suffer for Him than the views of doctrine which have spread among us? is it not more constraining than that which considers that the Gospel comes to us in name not in power; deeper, and more sacred than a second, which makes its heavenly grace a matter of purchase and trade; more glowing than a third, which depresses it almost to the chill temperature of natural religion?

5.

Such are some of the doctrinal respects in which what I consider the Scriptural view of justification recommends itself to the Christian mind. It is open however at first sight to one objection, which some persons may think not inconsiderable; but which I believe, when examined, will be found rather to be an additional argument in its favour. To this I shall now direct attention.

It may be said then that the doctrine of righteousness

as consisting in the Indwelling of Christ in the soul labours under this difficulty, that, supposing it true, the word "justification" has different senses in the Old and New Testament. If under the Gospel it consists in the inward Presence of the Incarnate Word, therefore, this gift being peculiar to the Gospel, Abraham (for instance) who was justified, was justified in some other way; whereas St. Paul certainly does liken the one justification to the other, as if, whatever the word meant in the Old Testament, such it meant in the New. For instance, it is said that faith "was imputed to Abraham for righteousness ; now it was not written for his sake alone that it was imputed to him, but for us also, to whom it shall be imputed." Here, it may be objected, that faith is said to justify us *as* it justified Abraham ; which it is supposed to do both in the Roman system and in the Protestant, but not in that which has been here explained. Whether faith be taken as a mere instrument, as the Lutherans say, or for a sanctifying element with divine love for its life as the Romanists, in either case righteousness means a state of divine acceptance ; whereas (it may be objected), if it consists under the Gospel in being a temple of Christ, this could not be Abraham's state, who lived before the Son became the Christ; and then the question arises, What did Abraham's justification consist in, and why is it compared to ours ?

As far as this objection relates to an interpretation of Scripture, I do not consider it requires much notice ; since all that St. Paul says is that righteousness or acceptableness is imputed to Abraham and us on faith, which I take as literally as Romanist or Lutheran ; the distinction between Abraham and us relating to a further point, viz. *what* this righteousness is under the Gospel ; or *in what way* this acceptableness is conveyed, whether by a mere act of God's will or by a positive gift on His part? There is nothing contrary to St. Paul's argument in supposing that that same blessing which was conveyed before Christ came in one way, should under the Gospel come to us in another and more precious way. For instance, animal life belongs to men and to brutes ; but, whatever be the mode of its existence in the case of the latter, in the former it lies in the special gift of a rational soul. However, let us consider the state of the case more attentively.

Now this circumstance, which at first sight seems a difficulty, that the attribute of righteousness, however conveyed to the Old Saints, should since Christ's coming be the attendant on a divine gift, even His own sacred Presence, will in truth be found, as I have said, an argument in favour of the doctrine. For such a transformation of shadows into substances, and human acts into divine endowments, far from being anomalous, is the very rule of the New Covenant. Christ came for this very purpose, to gather together in one all the elements of good dispersed throughout the world, to make them His own, to illuminate them with Himself, to reform and refashion them into Himself. He came to make a new and better beginning of all things than Adam had been, and to be a fountain-head from which all good henceforth might flow. Hence it is said that " in the dispensation of the fulness of times" Almighty God "gathered together in one all things in Christ, both which are in heaven, and which are on earth."[1] How He became a new commencement to things in heaven, we know not ; nor know we adequately in what way He recapitulated or ordered anew things on earth. But this we know, that, the world being under the dominion of Satan, and truth and goodness in it being but as gems in the mine, or rather as metal in the ore, He came to elicit, to disengage, to combine, to purify, to perfect. And, further than this, He came to new-create,—to begin a new line, and construct a new kingdom on the earth : that what had as yet lain in sin, might become what it was at the first, and more than that. In His incomprehensible mercy He designed that man, instead of being a child of wrath, should be quickened and impregnated with Divine Life ; and sooner than this should not be, (as the Creed says) He was made man. He took on Him our nature, that in God that nature might revive and be restored ; that it might be new born, and, after being perfected on the Cross, might impart that which itself was, as an incorruptible seed, for the life of all who receive it in faith, till the end of time. Hence He is called in Scripture the Beginning of the Creation of God, the First-begotten of the dead, the First-fruits of the Resurrection.

6.

If this be so, we see how wide and essential a difference there is, there must be, in this life, between good men before His coming and good men after. Whatever they were, however high in God's favour, however influenced by God's secret aids, they could not,

[1] Ephes. i. 10.

while here below, be partakers of that which as yet did
not exist; the Body and Blood of the Incarnate Son.
God had His favoured servants then as afterwards, and
had His own inscrutable ways both of blessing them at
the time, and of incorporating them afterwards into His
Christ. But taking a general view of human nature, and
not dwelling on exceptions, we may say that its highest
piety and devotion, out of Him, though the fruit (as it
surely is) of divine assistance, is but the poor effort
after that righteousness which it never can really reach,
and which He is. Its services at best are but an
imitation, not a likeness, of Him. They do not tend to
that perfection which they testify; like the moonlight
which never rivals, though it comes from the radiance
of the sun. They may be shadows and auguries of God's
merciful purposes; but they cannot rise out of their
feeble selves, or claim to be His work and not man's.
Such is human nature in its fallen state; but at length
its Redeemer came. He left His Father's courts, He was
manifested, He spake; and His voice went out into all
lands. He has taken to Himself His great power and
reigned; and, whereas an enemy is the god and tyrant
of this world, as Adam made it, so, as far as He
occupies it, does He restore it to His Father. Henceforth He is the one principle of life in all His servants,
who are but His organs. The Jewish Church looked
towards Him; the Christian speaks and acts from Him.
What is prior to Him is dark, but all that comes after
Him is illuminated. The Church, before His manifestation, offered to Him material elements "which perish
with the using;" but now He has sent His Spirit to fill

such elements with Himself, and to make them living and availing sacrifices to the Father. Figures have become means of grace, shadows are substances, types are Sacraments in Him. What before were decent ordinances and pious observances, have now not only a meaning but a virtue. Water could but wash the Body in the way of nature ; but now it acts towards the cleansing of the soul. " Wine which maketh glad the heart of man," and " bread which strengthens man's heart," nay, the " oil which maketh him a cheerful countenance," henceforth are more than means of animal life, and savour of Him. Hands raised in blessing, the accents of the voice of man, which before could but symbolize the yearnings of human nature, or avail for lower benefits, have now become the " unutterable intercessions " of the Spirit, and the touch and the breath of the Incarnate Son. The Church has become His Body, her priests His delegates, her people His members.

This is what Christ has done by His coming ; but observe, *while* He did all this for His Church, He claimed all He did *as* His own. Henceforth whatever is done is His doing, and it is called what it is. As He is the unseen Source, so must He be acknowledged as the Agent, the present Object of worship and thanksgiving in all that is done ; and His instruments are not even so much as instruments, but only the outward lineaments of Him. All is superseded by Him, and transmuted into Him. Before He came there were many masters, but henceforth only One ; before He came many Fathers, but He is the One Father of the coming age, as the Prophet styles Him; before He came, all to whom the word of God came were called gods, but He is the One God manifested in the flesh; before He came, there were many angelic appearances with the name of God on them, but now the great Angel of the Covenant is alone to be worshipped; before He came, there were many priests who had infirmity, offering sacrifices year by year continually, but now there is but One High Priest, "who is set on the right hand of the throne of the majesty in the heavens, a minister of the sanctuary, and of the true tabernacle, which the Lord pitched, and not man;"[1] before, there were innumerable sacrifices of bulls and calves which could never perfect the worshippers, now One Immaculate Lamb who taketh away the sin of the world; before, there were judges, kings, and rulers of various ranks, but now there is but One King of kings, and Lord of lords, in His kingdom. Those former kings, prophets, priests, and sacrifices, those masters, teachers, and fathers, not being from Him, were not claimed by Him as His; they were ordained according to the old constitution of nature; they were but little glorious, yet, what they were, they were in themselves, and had a sort of substantive existence, and gained some benefit by their functions. Their priests were real priests, sacrificing real propitiations, and gaining thereby real blessings, namely temporal. Their cities of refuge were really sanctuaries, and saved from death of the body. Their kings were real representatives of God, and suffered and wrought for the real good of their people.

[1] Heb. viii. 1, 2.

There were mediators many, and prophets many, and atonements many. But now all is superseded by One, in whom all offices merge, who has absorbed into Himself all principality, power, might, and dominion, and every name that is named ; who has put His holy and fearful Name upon all, who is in and through all things, and without whom nothing is good. He is the sole self-existing principle in the Christian Church, and everything else is but a portion or declaration of Him. Not that now, as then, we may not speak of prophets, and rulers, and priests, and sacrifices, and altars, and saints, and that in a far higher and more spiritual sense than before, but that they are not any of them such of themselves ; it is not they, but the grace of God that is in them. There is under the Gospel but One proper Priest, Prophet, and King, Altar, Sacrifice, and House of God.[1] Unity is its characteristic sacrament; all grace flows from One Head, and all life circulates in the members of One Body. And what is true of priests and sacrifices, is true of righteous and holy men. It is their very privilege thus to be taken into Christ, to exist in Christ, as already in their mortal life they "have their being" in God. They had indeed before what was more their own than they have now ; but to what did it tend, and how far did it aspire ? It aspired to earthly blessings, and it tended to an earthly end.

---

[1] [It is true that there is but one Priest and one Sacrifice under the Gospel, but this is because the Priests of the Gospel are *one* with Christ, not because they are only *improperly* called Priests. "Christus et Sacerdotes sunt *unus Sacerdos.*"—*Catech. Roman.* ii. 84. "Profiteor in Missa offerri Deo verum, *proprium,* et propitiatorium sacrificium pro vivis et defunctis."—*Profess. Fid. Trident.*]

Better surely to be the mere stones of the Everlasting Pavement, than the head of the corner in the Jewish Temple. Better to be the least in the Kingdom of Heaven, even than the greatest of all that were born of women before it. Far better surely than Solomon in all his glory, is that chosen generation, that royal priesthood, that holy nation, that peculiar people, whose life is hid with Christ in God, who live because He lives in them, who are blessed because He is blessed, who are the fragrance of His breath, the myrrh, aloes, and cassia from His garments; nay, are one spirit with Him, as His dove, " His undefiled one," His sister and spouse," " coming up from the wilderness leaning upon her Beloved."

7.

Now to apply these remarks to our immediate subject, unless this has been sufficiently done in the course of them.—If in other things Christ changed the application of words, it is surely but fitting and natural that He should have in a similar way changed the application of the words " righteousness " and " justification." Priests, I have said, offered sacrifices under the Law : Christian Ministers also offer sacrifices, but it is their privilege to know that those sacrifices are not independent of Christ, or complete in themselves, but continuations, as it were, of His Sacrifice, and shadows cast from His Cross ; and that though, distinct as visible and literal acts, yet, as being instinct with that which they commemorate, they are absorbed and vivified in it. And so in like manner the inherent righteousness of a true Christian, viewed as distinct from Christ's inward presence, is something real, and doubtless far higher than that of a Jew; but why should we so degrade ourselves, so disparage our own high privilege, as to view it separately, to disjoin it from Him through whom we have it, to linger in the thought of it instead of tracing it back to that which is its immediate source; as if a man were to praise the daylight, yet forget the sun? No; whatever might be the righteousness of the Jews, we certainly know what is ours; and it is what they could not have had; it is "Christ," our propitiation, "within us;" on it we rely, not on ourselves. It is our boast thus to look back from the ultimate manifestations of life, in which is our sanctification, upon that Glory within us, which is its fount, and our true justification. It is our blessedness to have our own glory swallowed up in Christ's glory, and to consider our works and our holiness, to avail merely as securities for the continuance of that glory; not as things to be dwelt upon and made much of for their own sake, but as a sort of sacramental rite addressed to Him, for the sake of which He may be pleased still to illuminate us, and as tokens that His grace is not in vain. And after all, what we are, whatever it is, could not avail, were it tried in the balance, for more than this, to prove our earnestness and diligence. Even what is acceptable in us, is still so imperfect that the blood of Christ is necessary to complete what His Spirit has begun; and, as His regenerating grace has infused sweetness into what was bitter, so must His mercifulness overlook the remaining bitterness in what He has made sweet.

In this way then, let me reply to what seems at first sight a specious argument against what I consider to be the Catholic doctrine. It is a more simple theory, doubtless, to say that righteousness should be to the Christian what it was to the Jew ; as it is a more simple theory that we should have real priests, sacrifices, and altars now.[1]   But those who believe that Christ has set up a new creation in unity, and that He Himself is the One principle in His Church of all grace and truth, will not be surprised to find that He has superseded the righteousness, as He has abolished the victims, of the ancient time ; and that as the grace of the Holy Eucharist is the Presence of Christ Crucified, so the justification of those who approach it is the Indwelling of Christ risen and glorified.

[1] [*Vid.* p. 198, note.   The Christian Priesthood is real and proper. "Cum in N. T. Sanctum Eucharistiæ sacrificium visibile ex Domini institutione Catholica Ecclesia acceperit, fateri etiam oportet, in eâ novum esse visibile et externum Sacerdotium, in quod vetus translatum est."—*Conc. Trid. Sess.* 23, cap. 1.]

LECTURE IX.

THAT our justification, or our being accounted righteous by Almighty God, consists in our being grafted
into the Body of Christ or made His members, in God
dwelling in us and our dwelling in God, and that the
Holy Ghost is the gracious Agent in this wonderful
work, — all this has been argued from Scripture in
various ways ; first from righteousness being there spoken
of as a gift internal to the soul ; or, again, from the great
gift of the Gospel (which righteousness confessedly is)
being spoken of as inward ; secondly, on the ground that,
if so high a privilege as God's indwelling be vouchsafed,
it must necessarily involve justification as one of its
benefits ; thirdly, from righteousness being represented
as an ornament of the soul beyond nature, and such an
endowment having actually been lost in Adam,—from
which it seemed to follow, that what is gained in Christ
is a like ornament, which Scripture confirms by speaking
of it as a glory and a power ; and fourthly, from the
analogy of such a view of justification to the special
character of Christian privileges.   In the present Lecture,
following up a consideration already touched upon, I
shall treat the matter thus :—whatever is now given to

us by the Spirit is done within us ; whatever is given us
through the Church since Christ's ascension, is given by
the Spirit ; from which it follows that our justification,
being a present work, is an inward work, and a work of
the Spirit.   This, I conceive, is supported, together with
other passages of Scripture, by the emphatic words of St.
Paul, that He " who was delivered for our offences was
raised again for our justification," for, in saying that
Christ *rose again* for our justification, it is implied that
justification is through that second Comforter who after
that Resurrection came down from heaven.   In considering this view of the subject, I shall, as in the foregoing
Lecture, appeal rather to the harmony of sacred doctrine
and the light which the view in question throws upon
particular texts, than to the passages of Scripture which
prove it, that having been already incidentally done in
the 2d, 6th, and 7th Lectures.

Christ's work of mercy has two chief parts ; what He
did for all men, what He does for each ; what He did once
for all, what He does for one by one continually ; what
He did externally to us, what He does within us ; what
He did on earth, what He does in heaven ; what He did
in His own Person, what He does by His Spirit ; His
death and the water and the blood after it ; His
meritorious sufferings, and the various gifts thereby purchased, of pardon, grace, reconciliation, renewal, holiness,
spiritual communion ; that is, His Atonement, and the
application of His Atonement, or His Atonement and
our justification ; He atones by the offering of Himself on
the Cross ; and as certainly (which is the point before us)
He justifies by the mission of His Spirit.

His Atonement is His putting away the wrath of God for our sins. In order to this, He took flesh ; He accomplished it in His own Person, by His crucifixion and death. Justification is the application of this precious Atonement to this person or that person, and this He accomplishes by His Spirit. For He ceased, I say, to act towards us by His own hand from the day of His ascension ; He sent His Spirit to take His place,—" I will not leave you orphans," He says, "I will come unto you." —" I will pray the Father, and He shall give you another Comforter, that He may abide with you for ever." [1] Whatever then is done in the Christian Church is done by the Spirit ; Christ's mission ended when He left the world ; He was to come again, but by His Spirit. The Holy Spirit realizes and completes the redemption which Christ has wrought in essence and virtue. If the justification, then, of a sinner be a continual work, a work under the New Covenant, it *must* be the Spirit's work and not simply Christ's. The Atonement for sin took place during His own mission, and He was the chief Agent ; the application of that Atonement takes place during the mission of His Spirit, who accordingly is the chief Agent in it.

2.

We know nothing of the reasons of God's wonderful providences ; why an Atonement was necessary, why the Son of God was the sacrifice, why that sacrifice must be applied in order to " wash away the sins" of individuals ; let us accept what is given, adore God's wisdom, and be

[1] John xiv. 16-18.

thankful and silent ;—but, whatever be the deep reasons, this seems to be the rule of His counsels as to our justification ; that, as the Atonement was a work of flesh and blood, a tangible, sensible work, wrought out in this material world,—not, as the heretics said of old, an imaginary act, the suffering (God forgive the blasphemy !) of a phantom, a mere appearance (for such was the heresy which St. John and St. Paul especially opposed)—as Christ really "came in the flesh," which none but deceivers and antichrists can deny, and suffered in the real body and blood of man ;—so on the contrary the communication of this great and adorable Sacrifice to the individual Christian, is not the communication of that Body and Blood such as it was when offered upon the Cross, but, in a higher, glorified, and spiritual state. The Son of God suffered as the man Christ Jesus, "with strong crying and tears,"—"in weakness" and a body of "flesh ;" the crucified Man, the Divine Son, comes again to us in His Spirit. He came once, then He ascended, He has come again. He came first in the flesh ; He has come the second time in the Spirit. He did not come the second time carnally, nor the first time invisibly, but He came first in the flesh, and secondly in the Spirit. As in God's counsels it was necessary for the Atonement that there should be a material, local, Sacrifice of the Son once for all : so for our individual justification, there must be a spiritual, ubiquitous communication of that Sacrifice continually. There was but One Atonement ; there are ten thousand justifications. What was offered "under Pontius Pilate" in flesh and blood, is partaken again and again in every time and place, in the power and virtue of the Spirit. God the Son atoned ; God the Holy Ghost justifies.

Further ; it would appear as if His going to the Father was, in fact, the same thing as His coming to us spiritually. I mean there is some mysterious unknown connection between His departing in His own Person, and His returning in the Person of His Spirit. He said that unless He went, His Spirit would not come to us ; as though His ascending and the Spirit's descending, if not the same act, yet were very closely connected, and admitted of being spoken of as the same. And thus His rising again was the necessary antecedent of His applying to His elect the virtue of that Atonement which His dying wrought for all men. While He was on the Cross, while in the tomb, while in hell, the treasure existed, the precious gift was perfected, but it lay hid ; it was not yet available for its gracious ends; it was not diffused, communicated, shared in, enjoyed. Thus He died to purchase what He rose again to apply. " He died for our sins ; He rose again for our justification ;" He died in the flesh ; He rose again " according to the Spirit of holiness," which, when risen, He also sent forth from Him, dispensing to others that life whereby He rose Himself. He atoned, I repeat, in His own Person; He justifies through His Spirit.

3.

And here I have touched upon another part of the harmony of the Divine Dispensation, which may be profitably dwelt upon. For He Himself was raised again and "justified" by the Spirit ; and what was wrought in Him is repeated in us who are His brethren, and the complement and ratification of His work. What took place in Him as an Origin, is continued on in the succession of those who inherit His fulness, and is the cause of its continuance. He is said to be "justified by the Spirit," because it was by the Spirit that He was raised again, proved innocent, made to triumph over His enemies, declared the Son of God, and exalted on the holy Hill of Sion. It had been declared, "Thou art My Son, this day have I begotten Thee," and in these words He was justified or recognized, and owned before the world as the Dearly-beloved of the Father. This, I say, was His justification; and ours consists in our new birth also, and His was the beginning of ours. The Divine Life which raised Him, flowed over, and availed unto our rising again from sin and condemnation. It wrought a change in His Sacred Manhood, which became spiritual, without His ceasing to be man, and was in a wonderful way imparted to us as a new-creating, transforming Power in our hearts. This was the gift bestowed on the Church upon His ascension; for while He remained on earth, though risen, it was still withheld. During that interval, too, if we may speak without presumption, He seems to have been in an intermediate state, passing by an orderly course from what He had been during His humiliation to what He is in His glory. Then He was neither in His body of flesh simply, nor in His glorified body. He ate in the presence of His disciples; He suffered them to examine His hands and feet, and wounded side. Yet, on the other hand, He now appeared, and now vanished, came into the room, the doors being shut, and on one occasion said, "Touch Me not." When, however, on His ascension, He became a lifegiving Spirit, in the power of His Spirit He came to us, to justify us as He had been justified. Hence the force of St. Paul's expressions, which I elsewhere cited, concerning "the exceeding greatness of God's power to us-ward that believe according to the working of His mighty power, which He wrought in Christ, when He raised Him from the dead ;" and the blessedness of "knowing Him and the power of His resurrection ;" and again, our being "made alive together with Christ, and raised up together, and made to sit together in heavenly places in Christ Jesus."

Here I would observe of this part of the wonderful Economy of Redemption, that God the Son and God the Holy Ghost have so acted together in their separate Persons, as to make it difficult for us creatures always to discriminate what belongs to each respectively. Christ rises by His own power, yet the Holy Ghost is said to raise Him ; hence, the expression in St. Paul, "according to the Spirit of Holiness," as applied to His resurrection, may be taken to stand either for His Divine nature or for the Third Person in the Blessed Trinity. The case is the same as regards the mystery of the Incarnation itself. It was the Word of God who descended into the Virgin's womb, and framed for Himself a human tabernacle, yet the man so born was "conceived of the Holy Ghost." And hence some early writers seem to have doubted whether by "the power of the Highest," and "the Holy Spirit," the Angel Gabriel meant the Second or Third Divine Person ; whether He

who took flesh may not be also spoken of as the Maker
of that flesh which He took ; whether That which
anointed the Manhood of the Saviour with the fulness of
grace, was not rather the Divine Fulness of the Saviour
Himself than the Holy Ghost.[1] I notice this merely by
way of explaining myself, if in speaking upon this most
sacred subject I have said, or may say, anything which
would seem to " confound the Persons " of the Son and
Spirit, which are eternally distinct and complete in
Themselves, though in nature and operation One.   Let
me then proceed to comment on several important texts
of Scripture, which are adapted to throw light on the
main doctrine which is now under review, that our
ascended Lord, in ascending, has returned to us invisibly
in the attributes of a Spirit.

4.

1. In His discourse in the synagogue at Capernaum,
recorded in the sixth chapter of St. John, after saying,
" If any man eat of this Bread, he shall live for ever,
and the Bread that I will give is my flesh, which I will
give for the life of the world," thereby intimating both
the sacrifice of His Sacred Body upon the cross, and the
real and individual communication of it to all who shall
be saved, He was misunderstood to mean that He
intended thereby that what they saw before them, an
extended and material form, was to be eaten carnally
with the teeth.   On this He said, " Doth this offend·

---

[1] *e.g.* Tertullian passim, Cyprian de Van. Idol. fin. (p. 538, ed.
Ven.) Iren. Hær. v. 1.   Just. Apol. 2.   Vid. Grotius on Mark ii. 8,
and Præf. Bened. in Hilar. § 57-67.

you ? *what, and if ye shall see the Son of man ascend up,* where He was before ? It is the Spirit that is the life-giver ; the flesh profiteth nothing ;"—that is, if without presumption we may attempt an explanation of such words, " You, being flesh, understand Me to speak of mere flesh, mortal flesh ; whereas when I speak of My flesh, though I do speak of My body and blood, yet it is not of anything carnal and earthly, it is not of what you see with your eyes, but of this My body and blood, My Humanity, when, having passed through its state of humiliation, and having been perfected upon the cross, It shall ascend to heaven in a new way, the same and not the same, by the power of the Spirit. Then It shall no longer be a substance that can be seen and handled ; It shall be a spiritual body ; It shall be spiritual, and this is that which giveth life. It is the Spirit that quickeneth. This is what I spoke of, when I said that whoso eateth My flesh, and drinketh My blood, shall have eternal life ; I spoke of my spiritual and glorified body. It is the Spirit that is the Life-giver ; when I come to you again in the power of the Spirit, when He imparts My spiritual body, then It shall be eternal life to all who eat of It."

Observe especially, our Lord connects this spiritual coming with His resurrection and ascension. " What and if ye see the Son of man ascend up, where He was before ? " He had been, He was ever, in Heaven ; but His flesh, which He had assumed for our sakes, had not yet been there. When It had overcome death, when It touched the throne of God, It was no longer what It had been. Death had no more dominion over Him. " He liveth unto God."

5.

2. Again: consider St. Paul's words, "There is a natural body, and there is a spiritual body. . . . The first man Adam was made a living soul, the last Adam was made a quickening Spirit. . . . The first man is of the earth, earthy ; the second man is the Lord from heaven. As is the earthy, such are they also that are earthy ; and as is the heavenly, such are they also that are heavenly."[1] And recollect, this is said in answer to the question, "With what body do the dead come?" An objection might be made, then as now, that since the component particles of our body are ever changing during life, since on death they are dissipated to the four winds, the *same* body cannot be raised ; what is *meant* then by its being called the *same* body? St. Paul answers that it will be the same body in the sense that a blade of wheat is the same with the seed ; being contained within it, and at length developed out of it. So also there is a natural body, and a spiritual body ; and the natural body comes first, as the seed does. The spiritual body, how or what we know not, is formed within it, the same as it, yet different in its accidents. Corruption, dissolution, mortality, are but the accidents of the Christian's body, and are separated from it for ever on its rising again. What we see is not the real body, it is but the outward shell ; the real body of the regenerate soul is not only material, but spiritual, of which the seed is now deposited within us.

The Apostle then goes on to say how this takes place, viz. by a new birth from Christ. The first man Adam

[1] 1 Cor. xv. 44-48.

had at first life given him, but he lost it and became earthy ; all who are born from him are earthy like him. Such is the generation of those who are born after the flesh. But the second Man is not merely living, but life-giving ; He is a "quickening or life-giving Spirit ;" the very words (be it observed) which our Saviour had used in His discourse at Capernaum. He is life-giving ; and what He is, such are His followers ; "as is the Heavenly, such are they that are heavenly." As Adam diffused death, so the life-giving Spirit is the seed and principle of spiritual bodies to all who are His. "Flesh and blood," says the Apostle, "cannot inherit the kingdom of God ;" here, too, is a parallel to our Lord's words, "The flesh profiteth nothing." And further, as our Lord referred to His ascension and exaltation, so here again the life-giving Spirit is said to be " the Lord *from heaven*." Thus this passage, equally with the foregoing, speaks of our ascended Lord as a Spirit present in His people, and that, apparently, *because* He has ascended.

6.

3. Another passage of the same description, though the Ascension is not mentioned in it, is St. Paul's declaration to the Corinthians, that " he that is joined to the Lord is one spirit."[1] Taking these words in their context, they have a remarkable force in showing the extent of our Lord's condescension towards us under the Gospel. But I quote them here in order to point out that the gift of the Spirit is none other than the entrance into us of the ascended and invisible Saviour. To be joined as

[1] 1 Cor. vi. 17, 19.

one spirit to Christ and to be a Temple of the Holy
Ghost are spoken of as the same gift. It is to be observed, moreover, that St. Paul, who here speaks of
Christ as a Spirit, elsewhere speaks of Him as still
possessed of a bodily substance, and as communicating
Himself to us as such. "We are members of His Body,
from His flesh and from His bones."[1]

Another remarkable text of the same kind occurs
where St. Paul, after describing the "glorious ministration
of the Spirit," which is "righteousness" or justification,
proceeds : "Now the Lord is that Spirit; and where
the Spirit of the Lord is, there is liberty ; but we all
with open face beholding as in a glass the glory of the
Lord, are changed into the same image from glory to
glory, even as by the Spirit of the Lord."[2] I am not
here concerned to explain the course of the Apostle's
teaching in this chapter ; but it would appear on the
face of it, that the righteousness of the Gospel, which is
also "liberty" and "glory," is "ministered" to us by One
who is first called "the Spirit," and then "the Lord"
Christ. The manner too in which are interchanged the
words, "the Spirit," "the Lord," and "the Spirit of the
Lord," is very observable.

7.

4. That our justification is connected in some unknown way with Christ's ascension and going out of
sight, is also implied in His own words concerning the
Holy Ghost in His last discourse with His disciples.
"When He is come, He will reprove," or convince, "the

---

[1] Eph. v. 30. [2] 2 Cor. iii. 17, 18.

world of sin, and *of righteousness*, and of judgment: of
sin, because they believe not on Me ; *of righteousness,
because I go to My Father, and ye see Me no more."* [1]
Surely it is impossible to doubt that the "righteousness"
so solemnly and emphatically announced in this discourse concerning His coming kingdom, is that "righteousness of God," concerning which St. Paul speaks, and
in which he glories.   Now I do not say the passage
quoted shows *in what* it consists ; but thus much it
seems to show, that our Lord's ascension out of sight is
connected with the gift.   Men had refused to believe,
therefore there was a charge of sin against them ; Christ
had disappeared from the world and gone to God, therefore there was the news of righteousness.   The words
"because I go to My Father, and ye see Me no more,"
seem, I say, in accordance with the other texts quoted,
to connect our justification with some hidden necessity on
the part of the Justifier, of removing from us His corporal
presence and coming to us invisibly.

And here perhaps we may see somewhat of the meaning and depth of the doctrine of justification by *faith*
when rightly understood.   If justification, or the imparting of righteousness, be a work of the Holy Ghost, a
spiritual gift or presence in the heart, it is plain that faith,
and faith alone, can discern it and prepare the mind for it,
as the Spirit alone can give it.   Faith is the correlative,
the natural instrument of the things of the Spirit. [2]
While Christ was present in the flesh, He might be seen
by the eye ; but His more perfect and powerful presence,
which we now enjoy, being invisible, can be discerned and

---

[1] John xvi. 8-10.   [2] Vid. August. Serm. 143.

used by faith only. Thus faith is a mysterious means of gaining gifts from God, which cannot otherwise be gained; according to the text, "If thou canst believe, all things are possible to him that believeth."[1] If it was necessary for our justification that Christ should become a quickening Spirit and so be invisible ; therefore it was as necessary for the same, in God's providence, that we should believe;[2] as necessary a condition, in St. Paul's language, for "the heart to *believe* unto *righteousness*," as any one thing is a necessary condition of another, as (in this world) eating and drinking are necessary for animal life, or the sun for ripening the fruits of the earth, or the air for transmitting sounds. We have no reason for supposing that the supernatural providences of God are not ordered upon a system of antecedents or second causes as precise and minute as is the natural system. Faith may be as a key unlocking for us the treasures of divine mercy, and the only key. I say there is no *à priori* improbability in the idea; and we see, from the nature of the case, that Christ could not enter into the hearts of the ten thousand of the true Israel, till He came

[1] Mark ix. 23.

[2] Luther speaks well on this point : " Fit ut anima, quæ firma fide illis adhæret, sic eis uniatur, imo penitus absorbeatur, ut non modo participet, sed ·saturetur et inebrietur omni virtute eorum. Si enim tactus Christi sanabat, quanto magis hic tenerrimus in Spiritu, imo absorptio Verbi, omnia quæ Verbi sunt, animæ communicat?" And then he diverges to his private conclusion, which is either a truism or a paradox, " Hoc igitur modo anima per fidem *solam, sine operibus*, e Verbo Dei justificatur, sanctificatur, verificatur, pacificatur, liberatur, et omni bono repletur, vereque filia Dei efficitur, sicut Joannes dicit, Dedit eis potestatem filios Dei fieri, iis qui credunt in nomine ejus."— Luther de Lib. Christ. f. 5.

differently from His coming in the flesh,—till He came in the Spirit. And as the Spirit is the only justifier, so faith is the only recipient of justification. The eye sees what is material ; the mind alone can embrace what is spiritual.

8.

5. And these considerations will serve to throw some light on a difficult passage in the end of St. John's Gospel, where our Lord says to St. Mary Magdalen— " Touch Me not, for I am not yet ascended to My Father."[1] The question arises here, *Why* might not our Lord be touched *before* His ascension, and how *could* He be touched *after* it ? But Christ speaks, it would seem, thus (if, as before, we might venture to paraphrase His sacred words)—" Hitherto you have only known Me after the flesh. I have lived among you as a man. You have been permitted to approach Me sensibly, to kiss and embrace My feet, to pour ointment upon My head. But all this is at an end, now that I have died and risen again in the power of the Spirit. A glorified state of existence is begun in Me, and will soon be perfected. At present, though I bid you at one moment handle Me as possessed of flesh and bones, I vanish like a spirit at another ; though I let one follower embrace My feet, and say, ' Fear not,' I repel another with the words, ' Touch Me not.' Touch Me not, for I am fast passing for your great benefit from earth to heaven, from flesh and blood into glory, from a natural body to a spiritual body. When I am ascended, then the change will be completed. To pass hence to the Father

[1] John xx. 17.

in My bodily presence, is to descend from the Father to you in spirit. When I am thus changed, when I am thus present to you, more really present than now though invisibly, then you may touch Me,[1]— may touch Me, more really though invisibly, by faith, in reverence, through such outward approaches as I shall assign. Now you but see Me from time to time; when you see most of Me I am at best but 'going in and out among you.' Thou hast seen Me, Mary, but couldst not hold Me ; thou hast approached Me, but only to embrace My feet, or to be touched by My hand ; and thou sayest, 'O that I knew where I might find Him, that I might come even to His seat! O that I might hold Him and not let Him go!' Henceforth this shall be ; when I am ascended, thou shalt see nothing, thou shalt have everything. Thou shalt 'sit down under My shadow with great delight, and My fruit shall be sweet to thy taste.' Thou shalt have Me whole and entire. I will be near thee, I will be in thee ; I will come into thy heart a whole Saviour, a whole Christ,—in all My fulness as God and man,—in the awful virtue of that Body and Blood, which has been taken into the Divine Person of the Word, and is indivisible from it, and has atoned for the sins of the world,—not by external contact, not by partial possession, not by momentary approaches, not by a barren manifestation, but inward in presence, and intimate in fruition, a principle of life and a seed of immortality, that thou mayest 'bring forth fruit unto God.'"

[1] Vid. Leon. Serm. 74, c. 4, ed. Ballerin. Vigil. Taps. contr. Eutych. iv. *sub fin.*

9.

6. This leads me to offer a suggestion as to the sense of another text, which has no great obscurity on the face of it, yet seems to mean more than cursory readers are apt to consider. I mean St. Paul's words to the Colossians,—" your life is hid with Christ in God." [1]

Now, when we come to consider these words, are they not harsh and strange, if they mean nothing more than what is contained in the popular view of them taken in our day? If life means, what men at present are content that it should mean, the life of religion and devotion, spiritual-mindedness (as it is sometimes called), is it not a very violent phrase to say, " it is hid in God?" Is it not irreverent, taken literally? Can it be made reverent without explaining away its wording? If, however, the foregoing remarks be admitted as true, we are able to take this and similar statements of Scripture literally. For it would seem that, in truth, the principle of our spiritual existence is divine, is an ineffable presence of God. Christ, who promised to make all His disciples one in God with Him, who promised that we should be in God and God in us, has made us so, —has in some mysterious way accomplished for us this great work, this stupendous privilege. It would seem, moreover, as I have said, that He has done so by ascending to the Father; that His ascent bodily is His descent spiritually; that His taking our nature up to God, is the descent of God into us; that He has truly, though in an unknown sense, taken us to God, or

[1] Col. iii. 3.

brought down God to us, according as we view it.[1]
Thus, when St. Paul says that our life is hid with
Him in God, we may suppose him to intimate that our
principle of existence is no longer a mortal, earthly
principle, such as Adam's after his fall, but that we are
baptized and hidden anew in God's glory, in that
Shekinah of light and purity which we lost when Adam
fell,—that we are new-created, transformed, spiritualized,
glorified in the Divine Nature,—that through the
participation of Christ, we receive, as through a channel, the true Presence of God within and without us,
imbuing us with sanctity and immortality. *This*, I
repeat, is our justification, our ascent through Christ to
God, or God's descent through Christ to us ; we may
call it either of the two ; we ascend into Him, He
descends into us ; we are in Him, He in us ; Christ
being the One Mediator, the way, the truth, and the
life, joining earth with heaven. And this is our true
Righteousness,—not the mere name of righteousness,
not only forgiveness or favour as an act of the Divine
Mind, not only sanctification within (great indeed as
these blessings would be, yet it is somewhat more),
—it implies the one, it involves the other, it is the
indwelling of our glorified Lord. This is the one great
gift of God purchased by the Atonement, which is light
instead of darkness and the shadow of death, power
instead of weakness, bondage and suffering, spirit instead
of the flesh, which is the token of our acceptance with

[1] On this subject, *vid.* the Author's Via Media, vol. ii., edit. 1884,
pp. 235, &c.

God, the propitiation of our sins in His sight, and the seed and element of renovation.

10.

7. I will conclude with directing attention to the vision of our Lord to St. John in the book of Revelation, which also seems to me to be an intimation of the doctrine which I have been explaining. We know how our Lord appeared "in the days of His flesh;" in hunger and thirst, in weariness, in sorrow, in pain, in mortality. Such He is described in the Gospels, while His disciples saw Him ; what His Presence is now, when they see Him not, we learn from St. John's vision. First He is said to be "in the *midst of the* Seven Candlesticks," or Churches ; an expression which marks both that He is here and that His presence is spiritual. Then He is described, as follows :—"His head and His hair were white as wool, as white as snow, and His eyes were as a flame of fire, and His feet were like unto fine brass, as if they burned in a furnace, and His voice as the sound of many waters. And He had in His right hand seven stars, and out of His mouth went a sharp two-edged sword, and His countenance was as the sun shineth in his strength." What words could be devised to express more forcibly the power and spirituality of His presence ! It is the same description which is given of Him at His transfiguration, only this is far more fearful. Then He anticipated that spiritual state which was to be after "His decease, which He should accomplish at Jerusalem." And on that occasion the Apostles "fell on their face and were sore afraid ;" but now, St. John him-

self, the beloved disciple, who had undergone the former
vision, and since seen Him risen from the grave, nevertheless at the sight "fell at His feet as dead." Then
Moses and Elias talked of the death "which He should
accomplish ;" but now He said, "I am He which liveth
and was dead, and behold I am alive for evermore, and
have the keys of hell and of death."

Here then is certainly a representation of our Lord,
the risen and glorified Saviour, living and ruling in His
Church. Now it is very remarkable that, though He
thus appears as Christ in the vision, yet in what follows
He is spoken of as the Spirit, not as Christ, though He
still speaks of Himself as Christ ; as if to intimate that
all the gifts His blood has purchased are ministered by
the Spirit, and that what Christ was to His Apostles
when on earth, such, and far more than such, is the
Holy Ghost to us now. Here we seem to see something
of the meaning of the words,—"The Holy Ghost was
not yet given, because that Jesus was not yet glorified ;"
for the gift brought by the Spirit was really this and
nothing else, Jesus Himself glorified, ascended and invisibly returned.

11.

To conclude :—What has been said will serve to
throw light upon a peculiarity of the Apostles' preaching,
which has sometimes caused remark. They insist on
our Lord's Resurrection, as if it were the main doctrine
of the Gospel ; but why so, and not on His Divinity or
the Atonement ? Many good reasons may be given for
this ; as, for instance, that the Resurrection was the
great miracle and evidence of the divinity of the religion ;

or that it is the pledge of our resurrection ; on the other hand, that His Divinity and Atonement were doctrines too sacred to preach to the world. But if, as we have seen, the Resurrection be the means by which the Atonement is applied to each of us, if it be our justification, if in it are conveyed all the gifts of grace and glory which Christ has purchased for us, if it be the commencement of His giving Himself to us for our spiritual sustenance, of His feeding us with that Bread which has already been perfected on the Cross, and is now a medicine of immortality, it is that very doctrine which is most immediate to us, in which Christ most closely approaches us, from which we gain life, and out of which issue our hopes and our duties. Christ is God from everlasting ; He became man under Cæsar Augustus ; He was an Atonement for the world on the Cross ; but He became a Saviour on His resurrection. He was then "exalted to be a Prince and a Saviour ;" to come to us in the power of the Spirit, as God, as Man, and as Atoning Sacrifice.

LECTURE X.

JUSTIFICATION consisting in the Presence of Christ within us, and that Presence manifesting itself in newness of heart and conduct, the question arises, where, under such a view of the doctrine, Faith is found, what is its position, what are its bearings upon the points already settled, and how are its claims satisfied as acknowledged in our Formularies? This is the subject which shall now engage our attention.

Our eleventh Article says that "we are justified *by Faith only;*" agreeably with which we are told in the Homily on the Passion, that Faith is the *one mean and instrument* of justification. "As it profiteth a man nothing," says its very perspicuous author, "to have salve, unless it be well applied to the part affected, so the death of Christ shall stand us in no force, unless we apply it to ourselves in such sort as God hath appointed. Almighty God commonly worketh by means, and in this thing He has also ordained a certain mean whereby we may take fruit and profit to our souls' health. What mean is that? forsooth it is faith. Not an unconstant or wavering faith, but a sure, stedfast, grounded, and unfeigned faith. 'God sent His Son into the world,' says St. John. To what end? 'That whosoever believeth in Him should not perish, but have life everlasting.' Mark these words, 'that whosoever believeth in Him.' Here is the mean, whereby we must apply the fruits of Christ's death unto our deadly wound. Here is the mean, whereby we must obtain eternal life, namely faith." Then, after quoting other texts of Scripture, he continues, " By this, then, we may well perceive that the only mean and instrument of salvation required on our parts is faith, that is to say, a sure trust and confidence in the mercies of God." He adds, towards the end of the Homily, " Let us, then, use that mean which God hath appointed in His word, to wit, the mean of faith, which is the only instrument of salvation now left unto us. Let us stedfastly behold Christ crucified with the eyes of our heart ;" and so he concludes in a very serious and impressive strain.

In the judgment, then, of this Homily, faith is certainly in some distinct and important sense the sole mean and instrument of justification. The question is, in what sense.

2.

Now, on the one hand, I observe, what all will allow, that the faith spoken of is not any faith, but a lively faith. This indeed is implied in the passage just quoted, which speaks as concerning " not an unconstant or wavering faith, but a sure, stedfast, grounded, and unfeigned faith." Faith which does not trust, as the devil's faith,—or faith which does not love, though it could " remove mountains,"—or faith which cannot work, such as his to whom " to will is present," but " not to perform that which is good,"—all such faith does not justify.

It is, then, not mere faith, but faith under certain circumstances or conditions, faith when it trusts, loves, and lives, a fruitful faith, which is the sole mean and instrument of justification.

On the other hand, I do not understand faith to be a general term, meaning nothing more or less than trust, love, life, and all other excellences of the new mind or creature together. When the Homily calls it "the *sole* mean," it speaks by way of contrast with *other* graces. The writer would not call it tne sole *mean,* if it were the sole *grace.* By faith is not meant religiousness generally, nor obedience, nor spiritual life, nor love, nor hope, nor trust ; whatever is meant, something is meant distinct from all these. I do not deny that faith often stands for these in Scripture, in the Homilies themselves, and elsewhere ; nay, I will not deny that the Homily before us, as being a popular discourse, does speak of faith, as if it were something more than faith, viz. trust, confidence, hope, and perseverance, because it is really inseparable from them, and one with them ; still, when it is called the sole instrument of justification, it must stand in contrast with them, and be contemplated in itself, as being one certain property, habit, or act, of the mind. This is explicitly stated by another Homily, when it says that faith " doth not shut out repentance, hope, love, dread, and the fear of God, to be joined with faith in every man that is justified ; but it *shutteth them out from the office* of justifying."[1]

Here I draw an important conclusion ; that the instrumental power of Faith cannot interfere with the

[1] Sermon of Salvation, Part 1.

instrumental power of Baptism ; because Faith is the *sole* justifier, not in contrast to all means and agencies whatever, (for it is not surely in contrast to our Lord's merits, or God's mercy), but to all other *graces.* When, then, Faith is called the sole instrument, this means the sole *internal* instrument, not the sole instrument of any kind.

There would be nothing inconsistent, then, in Faith being the sole instrument of justification, and yet Baptism also the sole instrument, and that at the same time, because in distinct senses ; an inward instrument in no way interfering with an outward instrument. Baptism might be the hand of the giver, and Faith the hand of the receiver. However, this is not the exact relation of faith to baptism, as is plain, for this reason,—that Baptism occurs but once, whereas justification is a state, and faith " abides." Justification, then, needs a perpetual instrument, such as faith can be, and Baptism cannot. Each, then, has its own office in the work of justification ; Baptism at the time when it is administered, and faith ever after. Faith secures to the soul continually those gifts, which Baptism in the first instance conveys. The two Sacraments are the primary instruments of justification ; faith is the secondary, subordinate, or representative instrument. Or we may say, varying our mode of expression, that the Sacraments are its instrumental, and Faith its sustaining cause.[1]

---

[1] [Catholics hold that, not faith only, but faith, hope, and charity, are the " sustaining cause " of justification. " Fides, nisi ad eam spes accedat et charitas, neque unit perfecte cum Christo, neque corporis ejus vivum membrum efficit."—Concil. Trid. Sess. vi. 7.]

Faith, then, being the appointed representative of
Baptism, derives its authority and virtue from that
which it represents. It is justifying because of Baptism ;
it is the faith of the baptized, of the regenerate, that is,
of the justified. Justifying faith does not precede
justification ; but justification precedes faith, and makes
it justifying. And here lies the cardinal mistake of the
views on the subject which are now in esteem. In
those views faith is considered as the sole instrument,
not after Baptism but before ; whereas Baptism is the
primary instrument, and causes faith to be what it is
and otherwise is not, giving it power and rank, and, as
it were, constituting it its own successor.

3.

That this is the doctrine of our Church appears
from the Homilies. These are addressed, not to heathens
but to Christians, they are practical and popular exhortations to Christians. They inform a baptized congregation, or, as they speak, " dear Christians," " good
Christian people," how they may be saved, not how God
will deal with the heathen. They are not missionary
discourses, directing pagans how to proceed in order to
be justified, but are composed for the edification of those
who through God's mercy are already "dearly beloved in
Christ." And, as regards the point before us, they lay
down " what the lively and true faith *of a Christian man*
is." Clear, however, as this is, at first sight, I will make
some extracts from them, to impress it upon the mind.

Take, for instance, the very passage I quoted in the
opening, in which faith is called the sole instrument of

justification; it will be found that the writer is teaching a Christian congregation what they must do. He does not, cannot, say with St. Peter, " Be baptized every one of you for the remission of sins ;" that sacred remedy has been long ago applied, and may not be repeated. What is left, then, after sinning, but, as it were, to renew our Baptism, at least its virtue, by faith, as " the only instrument of salvation *now left unto us* " ? And this is why stress is laid upon " a stedfast, not a wavering faith ;" he does not simply say lively, but stedfast, because faith is to be the abiding, sustaining means of justification, or, in the words of St. Paul, " By faith we stand ;" as Moses' uplifted hands continued on the victory of his people over Amalek. The writer says so in express words, " Here we must take heed that we do not halt with God through an unconstant and ·wavering faith, but that it be strong and stedfast *to our lives' end.* . . . . . Peter coming to Christ upon the water, because he fainted in faith, was in danger of drowning. So we, if we begin to waver or doubt, it is to be feared lest we should sink, as Peter did, not into the water, but into the bottomless pit of hell-fire." All this, I say, shows that, when the Homily speaks of faith as an instrument, it means a sustaining instrument ; what the primary instrument is, being quite a separate question. Those who now speak of faith as the sole means of justification, too commonly consider the mass of Christians unregenerate, and call them out of their supposed heathen state *through* faith, as the sole *initiation* into Christ's kingdom. How different is the tone of this Homily ! Attend to the very words which precede the strongest of the passages cited above. "Therefore, dearly beloved, if we chance *at any time*, through frailty of the flesh, *to fall* into sin . . . . and if we feel the heavy burden thereof to press our souls . . . . let us *then* use that mean which God hath appointed in His word, to wit, the mean of faith, which is the *only* instrument of salvation now left unto us."

But, it may be said, there is nothing about Baptism here ; let us then turn to the Homily on Salvation or Justification, to which the 11th Article refers, where we shall find that doctrine clearly stated, though it does not enter' into the scope of the Homily already cited. "Infants, being baptized and dying in their infancy, are by this Sacrifice washed from their sins, brought to God's favour, and made His children, and inheritors of His kingdom of heaven. And they which in act or deed do sin *after their Baptism*, when they turn again to God unfeignedly," that is, come to God *in faith*, as the Homily forthwith goes on to say, "they are *likewise* washed by this Sacrifice from their sins." Here is distinct mention of faith justifying *after* Baptism, but no mention of its justifying *before* Baptism ; on the contrary, Baptism is expressly said to effect the first justification. The writer proceeds : " *This* is that justification or righteousness which St. Paul speaks of, when he saith, ' No man is justified by the works of the Law, but freely by faith in Jesus Christ.' " So it seems that St. Paul too, when he speaks of justification through faith, speaks of faith as subordinate to Baptism, not as the immediate initiation into a justified state.

And as Holy Baptism, in the judgment of the

Homilies, is the immediate initiation into God's grace, so is Holy Communion, not the initiatory, but still an immediate and proper instrument of receiving it also; though this is not the place for proving it.[1] Here the question before us simply is, in what sense *faith* is the " sole instrument ; " and I have answered it by showing from the Homilies, that it is the sole, not as opposed to external means, but to the other graces, and as preceded and made an instrument by the secret virtue of Baptism. As to the Holy Eucharist, in whatever sense it justifies, certainly faith, as taking the place of Baptism, can as little interfere with its office as Baptism itself interferes. One proof, however, may be mentioned by the way, that our Church assigns to faith the same subordinate function as regards the second Sacrament, as it bears towards the first.[2] I mean the Rubric in the Service for the Communion of the Sick ; which instructs us that faith, so far from superseding, is to represent

---

[1] " Thus much we must be sure to hold, that in the Supper of the Lord there is no vain ceremony, no bare sign, no untrue figure of a thing absent. . . . . Thus much more the faithful see, hear, and know ; the favourable mercies of God sealed, the satisfaction by Christ towards us confirmed, and the remission of sin established. . . . . Take, then, this lesson, O thou that art desirous of this Table, of Emissenus, a godly Father, that when thou goest up to the reverend Communion, to be satisfied with spiritual meat, then look up with faith upon the Holy Body and Blood of thy God, then marvel with reverence, then touch it with thy mind, then receive it with the hand of thy heart, and then take it fully with thy inward man."—Sermon concerning the Sacrament, *Part I.*

[2] " That faith is a necessary instrument *in* all these Holy Ceremonies, we may thus assure ourselves, for that, as St. Paul saith, ' without faith it is impossible to please God.' When a great number of the Israelites were overthrown in the wilderness, Moses, Aaron, and

the Eucharist, only when, from whatever cause, it cannot be obtained.   It continues on and pleads in God's sight the sick person's former reception of it.

Faith, then, considered as an instrument, is always secondary to the Sacraments.   The most extreme case, in which it seems to supersede them, is found, not in our own, but in the Ancient Church ; in which the faith of persons, dying in the state of Catechumens, was held to avail to their reception on death into that kingdom, of which Baptism is the ordinary gate.   How different is the spirit of such a guarded exception, from the doctrine now in esteem, that faith, *ipso facto,* justifies, the Sacraments merely confirming and sealing what is complete without them !

4.

Let us proceed to Scripture, which will be found distinctly to declare the same general doctrine.   And here I cannot desire a more cogent argument than is furnished by the account of St. Paul's conversion, who surely, if any one, would have received justification, not in Baptism, but before it ; I mean at the time of Christ's appearance to him, or during his three days' fasting and prayer.   Faith surely would have been immediately justifying in his case, if in any ; yet, so far from it, Ananias, after pointedly referring to his having seen "*that Just One,*" who is also "the justifier of him that believeth," still bade him be baptized " and wash away

Phineas, did eat manna, and pleased God," etc.—*Ibid.* And so the 28th Article.   "The *mean* whereby the Body of Christ is received and eaten in the Supper, is *Faith.*"

his sins." The Apostle himself teaches the same doctrine to the Galatians, when, after discoursing at large concerning faith as justifying, and that as a very observable and important truth, he ends thus : " Ye are all the children of God *by faith* in Christ Jesus ; *for* as many of you as have been *baptized* into Christ, have put on Christ." That is, ye *are* God's children by faith, *because* ye *have* put on Christ in Baptism. Putting on Christ by Baptism has brought you into the condition of being God's children by faith. Or, in other words, Faith justifies, *because* Baptism has justified. Again, he says to the Hebrews, " Let us draw near with a true heart, in full assurance of *faith*, having been sprinkled in heart from an evil conscience, and *having been washed in body with pure water."* Why is this cleansing of the conscience, and baptismal washing mentioned, except as a *warrant* in order to drawing near in assurance of faith ? To the same purport is St. Peter's teaching, that God " hath *begotten* us again unto a lively hope," and " to an inheritance incorruptible," and that they who are thus chosen " are *kept* by the power of God *through faith.*"[1] Lively faith comes after regeneration, not before it.

In these passages faith is made a permanent or sustaining means, and not the beginning of justification ; with which agree others, which speak of our faith as securing our *state* of favour. For instance, " By faith ye stand." Again : " Because of unbelief they were broken off, and thou *standest by faith.*" Again : " I declare unto you the Gospel which I preached unto you, which also

[1] Acts xxii. 14, 16. Gal. iii. 26, 27. Heb. x. 22. 1 Pet. i. 3-5. Vide also Acts x. 47.

ye have *received,* and *wherein ye stand.*" And again :
" By whom also we have access *by faith* into this grace,
wherein we stand." Once more : " Yet a little while and
He that cometh will arrive, and will not tarry ; now the
just shall *live by faith,* but if he *draw back,* My soul shall
have no pleasure in him."

These passages also prove that only faith has this
sustaining power, from the circumstance that while it is
so repeatedly ascribed to faith, and that absolutely and
without contrast, it is not ascribed to other graces.   If
by "standing" be meant, as I conceive, being in a justified state, faith surely, and not any other grace, is that
which operates in keeping us in it.   Why it does so, is
altogether a distinct question, and one perhaps which we
cannot adequately determine.   But, whatever be God's
inscrutable reasons for thus connecting faith immediately
with His evangelical gifts, so has He done.

Moreover, it will be observed that the greatest and
most sacred gifts are again and again ascribed to faith,
and not to other graces ; as if there certainly were some
special connection between those gifts and faith, though
we may be unable to define what it is.   For instance, the
forgiveness of sins :—" Whom God has set forth to be
a propitiation through *faith* in His blood, to declare His
righteousness for the *remission of sins* that are past."
The presence of the Spirit :—"That we might receive the
promise of the Spirit through *faith.*"   Sanctification :—
" Purifying their hearts by *faith.*"   Perseverance :—"Who
are kept by the power of God through *faith.*"   The resurrection of the body :—"He that *believeth* in Me, though
he were dead, yet shall he live."   Eternal life :—" That

whosoever *believeth* in Him, should not perish, but have everlasting life." The Body and Blood of Christ :—" I am the Bread of Life ; he that cometh to Me shall never hunger, and he that *believeth* on Me shall never thirst." Or, as all God's ineffable gifts may be compendiously stated in one word, justification :—"That He might be just, and the justifier of him that believeth in Jesus."[1]

And here a strong confirmatory argument is afforded by Christ's conduct, when on earth, to those who came to Him to be healed. What faith was in the "days of the Son of Man" for temporal blessings, such surely is it now under the ministration of the Spirit for heavenly. So strict, then, it would seem, was the necessity of faith as a mean of receiving His bounty, that when the sick person did not or could not show it, it was exacted of the parties who brought him. Our Lord said to the woman with an issue of blood, who touched His garment, " Thy *faith* hath made thee whole ;" to the blind men, " *Believe* ye that I am able to do this ?" and " according to your *faith*, be it unto you ;" to the woman of Canaan, " O woman, great is thy *faith ;* be it unto thee even as thou wilt." Seeing the *faith* of those who let down the paralytic through the roof, He said to the sick man, "Son, thy sins be forgiven thee ;" in His own country, " He did not many mighty things, *because of their unbelief ;*" nay, " He *could* do there no mighty works, save that He laid His hands upon a few sick folk, and healed them." In like manner, St. Paul at Lystra, "stedfastly beholding" the cripple, " and perceiving he had *faith* to be healed,

[1] Rom. iii. 25, 26. Gal. iii. 14. Acts xv. 9. 1 Pet. i. 5. John xi. 25 ; iii. 16 : vi. 35.

said with a loud voice, Stand upright on thy feet." And
St. Peter also, fastening his eyes upon " the lame man at
the Beautiful gate," and saying, " Look on us," " took him
by the right hand, and lifted him up ;" and in consequence, he says presently, that Christ's " Name, through
faith in His Name, hath made this man strong." Moreover, our Lord lays down on several occasions this broad
doctrine: " If thou canst believe, all things are possible to
him that believeth ;"[1] " If ye have faith as a grain of
mustard-seed, ye shall say to this mountain, Remove
hence to yonder place, and it shall remove ; and nothing
shall be impossible unto you." " All things whatsoever
ye shall ask in prayer, believing, ye shall receive." Our
Lord's words seem to have become proverbial, for St.
Paul speaks of faith " removing mountains." [2] Surely, it
is not without the purpose of a permanent lesson in the
Church, that the inspired word has thus uniformly recorded this connection between faith and the gifts of the
Gospel ; surely, what is true of its visible miracles, is
true also of its invisible, which still remain to us. It is
not love nor humility which has the special office of
co-operating with God's outward signs, with the divine
" breathing " and " touching," with the divinely tempered
" clay," or the divine word, but faith. And let it be
observed that this assignment of a particular office or a
special blessing to a certain grace, is quite according to
the analogy of Scripture ; so that, even could we see no
reasons at all for it, it need not surprise us, that the re-

[1] Matt. ix. 22, 28, 29 ; xiii. 58 ; xv. 28 ; xvii. 20 ; xxi. 22. Mark
ii. 5 ; vi. 5 ; ix. 23. Acts iii. 4, 7, 16 ; xiv. 9, 10.

[2] 1 Cor. xiii. 2.

ception of God's grace should be a prerogative of Faith Thus, "the pure in heart" "shall *see* God ;" and "the meek" "shall *inherit the earth.*"

On all accounts, then, from the instances, statements, and analogy of Scripture, we may safely conclude that there is a certain extraordinary and singular sympathy between faith and the grant of Gospel privileges, such as to constitute it, in a true sense, an instrument of receiving them, that is, of justification, which includes them all ;—in a true sense, which is to be determined by that same Scripture, and not by antecedent arguments, as if the definition of faith implied it, or the condition of man required it (man being unequal to works, or faith being "apprehensive," or trusting to our own merits being perilous and uncertain, or comfort being thus secured to us),—not clashing with other truths, such as the instrumentality of the Sacraments,—nor superseding conditions, such as repentance and obedience,—nor inconsistent with the priority of love to faith, at least implicitly, both in order of nature and of time.[1]

5.

While then we reserve to Baptism our new birth, and to the Eucharist the hidden springs of the new life, and to Love what may be called its plastic power, and to Obedience its being the atmosphere in which faith breathes, still the divinely appointed or (in other words)

---

[1] [Catholics hold that, whereas faith, as a disposing condition, is prior to justification, love or *charitas* is posterior to it. It is a *pia affectio* and a *bona voluntas*, not *charitas*, which precedes faith. On the "pia affectio," vid. the next Lecture.]

the mysterious virtue of Faith remains. It alone coalesces with the Sacraments, brings them into effect, dissolves (as it were) what is outward and material in them, and through them unites the soul to God.[1] It alone, while it develops, also sanctifies in God's sight all other graces,—like salt or incense on sacrifices, which neither buys the victim, nor supersedes it, but recommends it to God's acceptance. Such is justifying faith, justifying not the ungodly, but the just, whom God has justified when ungodly; justifying him under God, and under God's means ; justifying the just, as being the faith of the justified, who through Baptism first were justified, when as yet they were unjust. And hence the Gospel is called "the law of faith," and discipleship "the obedience of faith ; " for though faith is the principle of all religion, yet under the Gospel it has a special office, and that with an evident fitness *so far* as it is formally assigned it, though we dare not antecedently decide *how far* it is so.

It may indeed be objected to this doctrine that faith, thus restricted in its office, is after all only a higher kind of condition, or what is called *sine qua non*, in justification, instead of a positive instrument ; that, whereas the Sacraments convey the gift, faith has but the negative office of not impeding its bestowal, and this office any other grace has equally, for, if love, or purity, or repent-

---

[1] Δείξας ἀνόνητα τῆς νομικῆς ἱερουργίας τὰ εἴδη, ὑπισχνεῖται τῶν ἁμαρτημάτων τὴν ἄφεσιν· ἣν διὰ τοῦ παναγίου βαπτίσματος ἐδωρήσατο· 'Εγώ εἰμι ὁ ἐξαλείφων τὰς ἁμαρτίας, κ. τ. λ. (Is. xlii. 25), οὐ γὰρ δὴ δι' ἔργων ἀξιεπαίνων, ἀλλὰ διὰ μόνης πίστεως τῶν μυστικῶν τετυχήκαμεν ἀγαθῶν.—Theod. Adv. Gent. viii. p. 892.

ance were absent, the Sacraments would not savingly operate, and that it is unmeaning to make faith more than a condition and less than an immediate and proper instrument. But I would reply that this is but to indulge in the same antecedent sort of reasonimg as before. What do we know of the instruments, means, qualifications, and conditions of salvation? What do we know of the real efficacy of anything we do? What of the mode in which prayer operates? What of the means through which actions change the character? What of the sense in which Adam's sin is our sin? Let us not think God's system narrow, because we are ignorant. Let us believe, if His word so intimates, that faith has an office for which we have not a word, as not having a definite idea; that, without its being that on which solely and immediately God grants His heavenly gifts, still there is some connection between it and them, more than ordinary;—as, to take a parallel instance, gaining blessings for the Church is associated by our Lord and His Apostles with perseverance in prayer.

6.

It may be said, however, that there are passages of Scripture which distinctly speak of faith as justifying, not after, but before Baptism. Such are the following: " Being justified by faith we have peace with God," Baptism not being named; or, where both are mentioned, " He that believeth and is baptized shall be saved ;" or, in the way of precept, " Believe in the Lord Jesus, and thou shalt be saved ;"—and how can these be reconciled with the doctrine which I have been maintaining?

Now if this objection is worth anything, its force must lie in this; that, not in laying down principles, as the first of these (for in such passages truth is stated in an abstract way), but in precepts and directions, as in the last, faith is pointed out as the instrument of justification apart from Baptism. The first of these texts then may be at once dismissed from the discussion ; the last may fairly be urged, but nothing will follow from it. The words " Believe, and thou shalt be saved," as little negative the use of a divine instrument, (such as Baptism), intervening between faith and its reward, as the Centurion's faith, such as was not in Israel, dispensed with our Lord's speaking the word that his servant might be healed. The jailor to whom St. Paul spoke *was* baptized forthwith ; if St. Paul's silence about Baptism be an argument against its instrumental power, it would be an argument also against its administration ; that is, the objection proves too much. Texts, then, in which Baptism is not mentioned, prove nothing, so long as there are texts in which it is mentioned ; else the omission of faith in St. Peter's exhortation on another occasion to "repent and be baptized," is a valid argument against the necessity of faith. And as to the second of the three passages quoted, in which faith comes *first* and Baptism follows, such passages as little prove that faith and not Baptism is the true instrument of grace, as our Saviour's call to "repent and believe the Gospel" shows that repentance justifies, and not faith. Such texts, then, as the three instanced, neither prove the one doctrine nor its opposite : they may be taken either way. The state of the case is this : there *are* texts which speak of Baptism as the *beginning* of a state of grace ; are there any which so speak of faith ? The new birth is an *act*, an initiatory act, forgiveness is an *act ;* but justification is a *state*, being in God's favour is a *state*. It is nothing to the purpose then to show that faith is connected in Scripture with justification, or with God's favour. How is it connected with the new birth, with the washing away of sin ? this is the question. Now Baptism *is* an act, an initiatory act and nothing beyond, and therefore a fit attendant on an inward initiatory act, such as regeneration ; whereas faith, though an act, is something beyond an act, it is an abiding habit, and therefore more fitly constituted to attend upon an abiding state. And next, I repeat, the act of justifying *is* expressly ascribed to Baptism as an immediate means ; is it anywhere ascribed to faith ? Ananias bids St. Paul be baptized and *wash away* his sins ; but we are told in the text I have already quoted, " By faith ye *stand*." Are we anywhere said to *rise up* by faith, as well as to stand ? Is faith ever said to wash away sins, as Baptism is ? to effect our new birth, as Baptism is ? to *begin* that new life, which doubtless it *sustains*, to *gain* what it certainly *holds ?* The silence of Scripture on this point is the more remarkable from the circumstance that so many high gifts—sanctification, eternal life, and resurrection of the body—*are* connected in Scripture with faith; all but the new birth ; all but the first step, and this is in other passages said to be through Baptism.

But it may be replied, that in matter of fact faith does come before Baptism ; men are not baptized till they believe ; whatever then be the office of faith, it has

that office independently of Baptism; and if it be an
instrument of justification, it is not made so by Baptism.
I answer, that though faith comes before Baptism, yet
before Baptism it is not the instrument of justification,
but only one out of a number of qualifications necessary
for being justified. Nothing is said in Scripture of faith
before Baptism, that is not said of repentance, or of the
resolve to lead a new life, which also are necessary conditions, together with faith, in order to Baptism; but
before Baptism, it, as well as they, is without "availing"
power, without life in the sight of God, as regards our
justification. *After* all these preparatives (as they may
be called), not *in* and *through* them, comes Gospel grace,
meeting, not co-operating with them, by a distinct process
and with an interval. "As many as *received* Him," says
the Evangelist, "to them *gave He power* to become the
sons of God, even to them that believe on his name."
Their faith was their *coming;* is coming the *instrument*
of a beggar's receiving alms, or rather a necessary
previous step? is it the same as the hand that takes, or
the hand that gives? Those who believe, says St. John,
are thereupon born of God; yet he does not say, "as
many as had faith in Him, they, *ipso facto*, were born
again," but "as many as received Him, they received
power to be born again." There was an intervening step
in the process; that step was reception into His Church
or Kingdom. Faith then must not be called the new
birth, till Scripture is proved to say so; and this is
why we hear so much in Protestant schools and congre-
gations of "*apprehending*," "*applying*," "*appropriating*,"
"*interesting oneself in*" Christ by faith; words not in

Scripture, and *instead* of Scripture terms which cannot be found.

But it may be urged in answer to this, that to consider faith first as a condition, and then as the instrument of justification, and Baptism as the means of changing it from the one to the other, is an arbitrary and unnatural view of the subject; that, in fact, it is the same fault which in another connection I charged on those who give two senses to the word *righteous*, in order to obviate a difficulty in the way of their particular theory. But the answer is obvious; I objected to giving two *senses* to the word *righteous* as being unreasonable; but I do not assign two *senses* to the word "faith," but two *offices*. What is there unreasonable in holding that, whereas all we have and all we are is exalted by Baptism, the office of faith is exalted also? that, while faith is renewed in knowledge, upon Christ being revealed as an Object, it should also be renewed in power, upon Christ being imparted as a Spirit? that, as it is variously exercised in the Law and the Gospel, so it should be variously endowed also? that, when it has changed its character, it should also change its function? Surely it is not at all strange that faith, when a grace, should do more than faith when but a human virtue; when lively, than when it "willed" without "performing." Rather it is strange that faith, before Baptism, like the jailor's, full of terror and disquiet, or that of his household, vague and dull-minded,—that feeble, sickly, wayward, fitful, inoperative faith, should be taken even as a condition, except that a man "is accepted according to that he hath, not according to that he hath not ;" that the principle of faith is capable of great things, though it be nothing till Christ regenerate it ; and that when it comes for Baptism, it is on the point of being rid of itself and hid in Him. It comes to the Fount of life to be made alive, as the dry bones in the Prophet's vision were brought together in preparation for the Breath of God to quicken them ; and He who "makes all things new," and takes into Him, and assimilates unto Him, all that is "in heaven and earth," as He makes sinners righteous, their persons "pleasant," their works "acceptable," and their alms, instead of a mere "memorial," a "sweet-smelling sacrifice," so also by His presence, converts what is a condition of obtaining favour into the means of holding and enjoying it.

The faith then of the justified continues and preserves his justification ; the faith of the sinner prepares the way for his justification. From the first it is a condition, and afterwards it is an instrument, its office varying in importance with its character. — However, there is a point of view in which both its character and its office are the same always, and its relation towards justification one and the same. With some notice of this I shall conclude.

7.

Unless, indeed, it were substantially the same habit of mind under all circumstances, it would not be called faith ; and so far as it is the same habit, it always has the same office, of which one especial characteristic is this, that it magnifies the grace of God, and is a sort of witness of its freeness and largeness. In consequence it is a *symbol* of the nature and mode of our justification, and of its history; and hence is said by Protestant divines to "justify alone," that our minds may be *affected* with a due sense of our inability to do any good thing of ourselves. This is Melanchthon's view, in which he is followed by parts of our Homilies ;—and now to explain it.[1]

I say, then, that when Melanchthon and his school speak of faith only justifying, they neither say with Luther that it is the *primary instrument* (which it is not), nor with our Homilies, that it is an *instrument after* Baptism (which it is), but with parts of our first book of Homilies, that it is an *emblem* or *image* of the free grace of our redemption. To say we are justified by faith only was in that Reformer's mouth a lively mode of speech (he calls it figurative), for saying that we are justified neither by faith nor by works, but by God only. I do not deny that such a figure has some-

---

[1] " Cum dicitur, Fide justificamur, *non aliud* dicitur, quam quod propter Filium Dei accipiamus remissionem peccatorum et reputemur justi . . . . Intelligatur ergo propositio correlative, Fide sumus justi, id est, *per misericordiam* propter Filium Dei sumus justi seu accepti."—Melanchth. Loc. Theol. de voc. Fidei (f. 199, 2).

" In ecclesiis nostris dicitur, Fide sola justificamur, quod sic intelligimus et declaramus, Gratis propter solum Mediatorem, non propter nostram contritionem, seu alia nostra merita, donamur remissione peccatorum et reconciliatione."—Confess. Eccl. Saxon. (ibid. f. 126).

"Sancti patres sæpe dicunt, nos per misericordiam salvari. Quoties igitur fit mentio misericordiæ, sciendum est quod fides ibi requiratur, quæ promissionem misericordiæ accipit. Et rursus quoties nos de fide loquimur *intelligi volumus objectum*, scilicet misericordiam promissam."—Apol. Confess. August. de Justif. (ibid. f. 64).

thing refined about it, but it served effectually to excul-
pate the doctrine, which he had received from Luther, from
the charge of superseding good works, as showing that
really and practically it had nothing to do either with
faith or works, but with grace. And since when thus
explained it was most true, and was a protest against
errors, which then were said to be widely spread in the
Church, it was adopted by our Reformers, without aban-
doning the modified *instrumental* sense of it as above
commented on.

A few illustrations will bring out its meaning. We
speak of " the Throne," or " the Crown," when we mean
the King. " The rights of the Crown " is a phrase,
absurd, if analyzed literally, but intelligible as a figure.
Such, according to Melanchthon, is justification by faith
only.

Again : faith is the tenure on which we enjoy the
gifts which Christ has merited for us ; as one who had
served his country might receive from it large possessions
for his children on the condition of some yearly acknowledgment on their part, the presentation of a banner
or the like, worthless in itself, but, under the circumstances, a memorial both of his claims and of his dependence on his country for the fulfilment of them. We
might speak of their holding their estates *by* such acknowledgment, without meaning more than that it was
the sole symbol, not in any sense the sole condition of
enjoying them, or the original means of gaining them.

Again : our Lord commits to St. Peter the keys of
the kingdom of heaven, and gives him the name of *rock*,
or foundation. This does not exclude the other Apostles

from holding the keys and being foundations also : indeed they are expressly so called. He is not sole among them, or the channel through whom they are Christ's Apostles. Why, then, is he singled out by our Lord? Protestants answer that he is a specimen of what all the Apostles are, and a type and symbol of them all. His *name* expresses what all of them, including himself, really *are*,—foundations. In like manner, according to the explanation before us, faith is *said* to justify, not that it really *does* justify more than any other grace ; but it has this peculiarity, that it signifies, in its very nature, that *nothing* of ours justifies us, or it typifies the freeness of our justification. Faith heralds forth divine grace, and its name is a sort of representation of it, as opposed to works. Hence it may well be honoured above the other graces, and placed nearer Christ than the rest, as if it were distinct from them, and before them, and above them, though it be not. It is suitably said to justify us, for the very reason that it says itself that it does not justify, if one may so speak ; as a sort of reward made to it. In so determining, the Reformers are not laying down a practical direction how to proceed *in order* to be justified, what is required of us *for* justification, but a large abstract principle or doctrine ever to be held and cherished, viz. that in ourselves we deserve eternal ruin, and are saved by Christ's mercy, and that not through faith only, but through faith and all other graces.

8.

Now about this interpretation of the doctrine I will only say, first, that nothing can be more scriptural than the sense thus elicited from it; next, that it is more suited to the Schools, than to the taste of a people like the English at the present day; but, lastly, that if our Reformers have chosen thus to express what is in itself true, and to transmit it to us, it is right to maintain it, as Bishop Bull has incidentally done in his instructive Harmony of St. Paul with St. James.

Let us then now turn to the first book of Homilies; which will be found clearly to teach, not with Luther that faith is solitary at the time when it first justifies, but with Melanchthon that, whereas it never is solitary, it is but *said* to be the sole justifier, and that with a view to inculcate another doctrine *not* said, viz. that all is of grace.

"This *sentence*, that we be justified by faith only, is not so meant by them," the Fathers, "that the said justifying faith is alone in man, without true repentance, hope, charity, dread and the fear of God, *at any time or season.*" Again, in a passage which has been already cited, we are told, "Faith *doth not shut out* repentance, love, dread and the fear of God, to be joined with faith in every one that is justified, but it shutteth them out from the *office* of justifying."

What is the office here spoken of? not the office of conveying, but of symbolizing justification. For instance: "As great and godly a virtue as the lively faith is, yet it *putteth us from itself,* and remitteth or *appointeth* us unto Christ, for to have *only by Him* remission of our sins or justification. So that our faith in Christ (as it were) *saith unto us* that, 'It is not I that take away your sins, but it is Christ only, and to Him only *I send you* for that purpose, forsaking therein all your good virtues, words, thoughts, and works, and only putting your trust in Christ.'" It is plain that, according to this Homily, "faith only" does not apprehend, apply, or appropriate Christ's merits ; it does but *preach* them ; and thus surely conveys a "most wholesome doctrine, and very full of comfort."

The formula, then, "justification by faith only," on this interpretation, is not a practical rule, but an abstract principle. Accordingly, it will be observed, the Homilies do not attempt to explain it *literally*, but declare it to be a *sentence, saying,* or *form* of *speech,* one too, which, when drawn out, assumes quite a new shape, as far as its letter is concerned.

For instance : " *This saying,* that we be justified by faith only, freely, and without works, is spoken *for to take away* clearly all merit of our works, as being unable to deserve our justification at God's hands ;" let it be observed, the *drift* of "the saying," is given, not an *interpretation.* The writer proceeds, "and *thereby most plainly to express* the weakness of man and the goodness of God ; the great infirmity of ourselves, and the might and power of God ; the imperfectness of our own works, and the most abundant grace of our Saviour Christ ; and *thereby wholly to ascribe* the merit and deserving of our justification unto Christ only, and His most precious blood-shedding."[1] Can words be clearer to prove that faith is

[1] Sermon of Salvation, part ii.

In like manner, "Justification is the office of God only, and is not a thing which we render unto Him, but which we receive of Him ; not which we give to Him, but which we take of Him, by His free mercy,

considered to justify not as an instrument, but as a symbol? it is to *do* nothing, but it is to "*say*," to "*express*," to "*ascribe*," to *warn*, to *bring good tidings*.

In like manner, in the third part of the same Homily : "The very true meaning of this *proposition or saying*, We be justified by faith only (according to the meaning of the old ancient authors) is this, We put our faith in Christ, *that we be justified by Him only*." [1] Justification

and by the only merits of His most dearly beloved Son, our only Redeemer, Saviour, and Justifier, Jesus Christ ; so that *the true understanding* of this doctrine, we be justified freely by faith without works, or that we be justified by faith in Christ only, is *not*, that this our own act to believe in Christ, or this our faith in Christ, which is within us, doth justify us,"—let it be observed, we are told what the words do *not* mean,—in what sense it is *not* true that faith justifies, viz. *not* by having any real merit ; it would have been natural then to have gone on to say in what sense faith *does* justify. Instead, however, of thus closing with the words, and sifting their meaning, well understanding they are the emblem of a principle, not a literal statement, the writer continues :—"but *the true understanding and meaning thereof is*, that *although* we have faith, hope, charity, repentance, dread and fear of God within us, and do never so many good works thereunto, yet we must *renounce the merit* of all our said virtues, of faith, hope, charity, and all our other virtues and good deeds which we either have done, shall do, or can do, as things that be far too weak and insufficient, and imperfect, to deserve remission of our sins, and our justification ; and therefore we must trust only in God's mercy, and that Sacrifice which our High Priest and Saviour, Christ Jesus, the Son of God, once offered for us upon the Cross." It must be recollected that Melanchthon (vide note, *supra*, p. 181) calls justification by faith, "Paulina *figura*."

[1] Again : "Because faith doth *directly* send us to Christ for remission of our sins, and that by faith given us of God we *embrace the promise* of God's mercy and of the remission of sins (which thing none other of our virtues or works properly doth), therefore Scripture *useth to say*, that faith without works doth justify." Here is the reason for saying "*faith* only," and not "love only," or "obedience only,"

by faith only is here said to be a *saying* ; consider how astonished and pained we should be, were the doctrine of the Atonement or of Christ's divinity insisted upon merely as a proposition, saying, or form of speaking.

This last-mentioned title is actually given it in another passage :—" *This form of speaking* use we, in the humbling of ourselves to God, and to give all the glory to our Saviour Christ, who is best worthy to have it."

9.

Enough has now been said upon the symbolical office of faith. If more were needed, it might be further observed that such a view of it is congenial to the tone of thought which the Reformers discover in other matters. As they considered prayers as *lectures*, Absolutions as *declarations*, the Eucharistic Commemoration as a *visible memento*, Mystical Rites as *edifying exhibitions* (which they certainly are also), so they regarded faith as the *symbol* of justification. Of course this is not the highest view of the doctrine ; and our own Homilies, in another portion of the Book, go on to the higher, according to which it is an instrument, as has been shown. Well would it have been if all Protestant writers had done the same ; but others, following out the view which was more peculiarly their patrimony as Protestants, have ended in

because *faith* directly "*sendeth* us to," or *preaches* "Christ." Observe, too, that still, as in the former cases, the Homily does not so much affirm that faith only *does* justify, "but is *said* to justify." Elsewhere faith is compared to the Baptist, who "did put the people from him, and appointed them unto Christ." Was St. John an instrument, or only a preacher ? "*I* indeed baptize you with water unto repentance," etc.

the notion, that justification is the feeling of satisfaction which belief in God's mercy inspires, and nothing more.

To sum up what has been said :—the question has been in what sense faith *only* justifies, for that it is *necessary* to our justification, all parties allow. I answer, it justifies only, in two ways, as the only inward *instrument*, and as the only *symbol.* Viewed as an instrument, it unites the soul to Christ through the Sacraments ; viewed as a symbol it shows forth the doctrine of free grace. Hence it is the instrument of justification after Baptism ; it is a symbol both before and after.[1]

---

[1] The reader will find several statements contained in this and in the 4th and 6th Lectures, more or less confirmed by Waterland (*on Justification,* Works, vol. ix.)

LECTURE XI.

THE NATURE OF JUSTIFYING FAITH.

A FTER considering the office of Faith, it fitly follows
to inquire what it is, both in itself, and as existing
in the regenerate. This I propose now to do, and in
doing it shall have the guidance of a text, which approaches as nearly as any statement in Scripture to a
formal definition :—"Faith is the substance of things
hoped for, the evidence of things not seen." Our Church
has nowhere defined faith. The Articles are entirely
silent ; and though the Homilies contain many popular
descriptions, they present, as is natural, nothing consistent and accurate.

Religious faith is "the substance," or the realizing of
what as yet is not here, but only "hoped for ;" it is the
making present what is future. Again : it is "the evidence" of what is not seen, that is, the ground or medium of
proof, on or through which the unseen is accepted as really
existing. In the way of nature, we ascertain the things
around and before us, by sight ; and things which are to
be, by reason ; but faith is our informant about things
present which we do not see, and things future which we
cannot forecast. And as sight contemplates form and
colour, and reason the processes of argument, so faith rests

on the divine word as the token and criterion of truth. And as the mind trusts to sense and reason, by a natural instinct, which it freely uses prior to experience, so in a parallel way, a moral instinct, independent of experience, is its impelling and assuring principle in assenting to revelation as divine. By faith then is meant the mind's perception or apprehension of heavenly things, arising from an instinctive trust in the divinity or truth of the external word, informing it concerning them.[1] Whether it acts upon that knowledge so obtained, depends upon something beyond with which we are not now concerned, —its particular moral state in a given case.

In other words, faith, as such, is not a practical principle or peculiar to religious men. Thus, in matters of this world, men believe, but are not influenced, unless they feel the matter to be important. On the other hand, if they are interested in it, they believe what they otherwise would not believe. So far, then, from faith directly causing action, action in a particular case may depend on circumstances on which faith also depends. Accordingly, there is nothing in the text to confine its definition to religious faith, except the indirect expression "hoped for;" which no one would say was strictly part of the definition. None, doubtless, but religious men can hope for what God's word announces ; but leaving out this incidental word, the text might even be taken to describe the faith of evil spirits, which St. James both recognises as faith, and discriminates from religious faith. Reli-

---

[1] ὥσπερ ὀφθαλμὸς δεῖται φωτὸς ἐπιδεικνύντος τὰ ὁρατὰ, οὕτω δὴ αὖ καὶ ὁ νοῦς δεῖται πίστεως ἐπιδεικνυούσης τὰ θεῖα, καὶ τὴν περὶ τούτων δόξαν φυλαττούσης βεβαίαν.—Theodor. adv. Gent. i. p. 714.

gious men believe and "*hope ;*" "the devils believe and *tremble.*" They believe in a judgment to come, for on one occasion they exclaimed against being "tormented before their time ;" and on what, but on God's infallible word announcing it? Thus dread and despair are inseparable attendants upon the devils' faith ; hope and trust upon religious faith ; but both are in their nature one and the same faith, as being simply the acceptance of God's word about the future and unseen. Religious faith is nothing else but the faith of the religious, and despairing faith is the faith of the despairing. Dead faith is the faith of the dead ; lively faith is the faith of the living. Justifying faith, strictly speaking, is not trust, or adherence, or devotedness, though in familiar language it allowably be so called, but faith,—the faith of trusting, adhering, devoted minds.

Faith, then, is not a virtue or grace in its abstract nature ; else evil spirits could not possess it. It is so only under circumstances or in the particular case ; Abraham's faith involved self-denial, the Blessed Virgin's faith implied love and hope. Faith is but an instrument, acceptable when its possessor is acceptable. And in this respect it differs from most other virtues, that it is not an excellence, except it be grafted into a heart that has grace. The devils cannot have love, humility, meekness, purity, or compassion,—they have faith. When, however, it is so grafted, then it makes progress, and the last becomes the first. "He raiseth up the poor out of the dust, and lifteth up the beggar from the dunghill, to set them among princes, and to make them inherit the throne of glory." And then it becomes the instrument of securing that favour which more properly attaches to the soul exercising it ; as the eye is said to see, whereas it is the organ of the mind.

2.

But though faith, considered by itself, is not a grace, it must be borne in mind that it never does exist by itself ; it always exists *in* this person or that, and, as exercised by the one or the other, it must be either a grace or not. Faith in the abstract does not exist except as a mere conception of our minds. The devils believe, and Christians believe ; we may compare the two together, and observe that the outline of the faith in each is the same ; they both realize the unseen and future on God's word. But an outline never exists by itself ; it ever exists in a certain body or substance. One man is said to be the same as another man, when the mind contemplates them *as* man ; yet after all the mind can but contemplate, it cannot create or alter what is external to it. In spite of our arbitrary abstractions, each existing man exists to himself, as an individual, complete in himself, independent of all others, differing from all others, in that he is he, and not they nor one with them, except in name. No one thing can be another thing ; faith in this man is not faith in that ; nay, the one is not necessarily like the other, except in outline, or as one kind of animal, for instance, is like another, or as a good spirit is like an evil one. An animal in the abstract, is neither man nor brute, but then there is no such thing as an abstract animal ; every animal must be man *or* brute ; and so faith, as actually existing, either is an excellence or it is not, though considered in its abstract nature it has no positive character.[1]

Or, to take another illustration :—the animal nature, when found in man, is the organ of doing what neither the soul can do without it, nor it can do without the soul. It sees, and enables us to read ; yet no one would so confuse the case, as to say that the animal nature, *as such*, reads, because we read *through* it. In some such way does faith stand towards a right state of mind. Together they make up religiousness ; the one reports, the other feels and acts on the report. Moral rectitude without faith is a soul without eyes ; faith without moral rectitude is perception without appreciation. It may see, but it cannot read the message of mercy, though it gaze ever so hard ; it is said to do so, as the eye is said to read, but it does not of itself really appreciate or obey that message from above.

It would seem, then, that Luther's doctrine, now so popular, that justifying faith is trust, comes first, justifies by itself, and then gives birth to all graces, is not tenable ;—such a faith cannot exist, and if it could would not justify. For, as faith cannot exist except in this or that mind, so it cannot be as much as trust, without being also hope,[2] nor hope without having some

---

[1] Vid. the author's Essay on Assent, ch. viii. § 2, pp. 272-275.

[2] Luther and Calvin both virtually grant that faith and hope are inseparable, or parts of one thing, though Luther, and perhaps Calvin, deny this of faith and love. " Reipsa igitur fides et spes vix discerni possunt, et tamen est aliquod discrimen inter ipsas. .... Sicut .....
in politia prudentia sine fortitudine vana est, ita fides in Theologia sine Spe nihil est, quin spes fert et perdurat in malis et vincit ea. Et vicissim, sicut fortitudo sine prudentia temeritas est, ita spes sine fide

portion of love. Mere trust as little gives birth to other graces as mere faith. It is common indeed to say that trust in the mercy of God in Christ ensures all other graces, from the fertilizing effect of the news of that mercy on the heart. But surely that blessed news has no such effect unless the heart is *softened* to receive it ; that softening then is necessary to justification, and by whatever name it is called, religiousness, or love, or renewal, it is something more than trust.[1] That is, something more than trust is involved in justifying faith ; in other words, it is the trust of a renewed or loving heart. But after all, it is an abuse of terms to go so far as to define faith to be trust, unless one might also

præsumptio in spiritu.—Luth. in Gal. v. 5. Fieri non poterit quin spem æternæ salutis comitem secum habeat *individuam*, vel potius ex se gignat et exerat, etc.—Calv. Instit. iii. 2, § 42. As to faith *producing* hope, this, supposing they are parts of one, is a distinction merely in the way of viewing it.

[1] Calvin attempts to overcome this obvious inference thus : Quoniam res maxime dubia est, uno verbo statuimus, eos inepte loqui quum fidem formari dicunt, accessione piæ affectionis ad assensum facta ; quum assensio quoque pia affectione constet.—Instit. ii. 2, 8. That is, assent is not made justifying by the presence of spiritual feeling, *because* justifying assent consists in spiritual feeling. Bucer is not more successful. Vera utique fides, certaque de Dei erga nos *bonitate* persuasio, illico ex se ejus *quoque* summum *amorem* ac reverentiam gignit, studiumque omnium quæ Deo probantur, et odium eorum quæ ille detestatur.—Enar. in Matt. viii. f. 83. Jackson puts the case clearly in his definition of faith, as "a firm and constant assent or adherence unto the mercies and loving-kindness of the Lord, or generally to the spiritual food exhibited in His sacred word, ... *grounded upon a taste or relish of their sweetness*, wrought in the soul or heart of man by the Spirit of Christ."—B. iv. c. 9, p. 667. Jackson, however, does not allow this "taste of their sweetness" to involve love ; but this seems a question of words. (Vide *supra*, p. 236, note.)

call the devil's faith despair. Faith is neither trust nor despair, but faith ; though it takes the colour of trust or of despair, according to the mind into which it is received. But this is a subject which admits of fuller statement.

3.

Justifying faith, then, may be considered in two main points of view; either as it is in itself, or as it exists in fact in those who are under grace. In the former point of view it is not necessarily even a moral virtue ; but when illuminated by love, and ennobled by the Spirit, it is used as a name for all graces together, as having them all as its attendants and companions. In the alternative, then, of thus narrowing and of thus extending its meaning, our Homilies have chosen the latter course and the Romanists the former. The Roman schools define it almost in its bare distinctive outline, as it is in itself viewed apart from all circumstances or states of mind, as found in good and bad, as living and dead. They consider it *an assent* of the mind to God's word. On the other hand, our Homilies seem to consider that grace so changes its nature, that a description which answers to it, both before and after justification, is but a verbal generalization and a practical fallacy, as if a living body and a corpse were called by one name ; and therefore they teach that faith must not be called *real* unless it is *living*. Accordingly, instead of attempting a strict definition, they enlarge upon its properties or adjuncts in the regenerate, and set it before us in all the health, energy, and fulness of stature which grace bestows. Each party appeals to St. Paul, but Roman controversialists stop short at the words "substance" and "evidence," as including the whole essence of faith, which in consequence is nothing more than evil spirits may have. Our Homilies, on the contrary, writing popularly, describe it to be trust and obedience as well as bare faith; as if arguing, that St. Paul speaks of it as the substance of things *hoped for*, and appealing for its practical character to the various instances of obedience which follow in the course of the Chapter.

This will be plain to any one who consults the Homilies ; which, as far as the words go, speak of faith, not in its characteristic features, but as instinct with the whole "mind of the Spirit," as illustrated by the entire assembly of graces which belong to the regenerate. For instance, first they develop it into *trust* and *hope*, laying it down that a quick and living faith "is *not only* the common *belief* of the Articles of our faith, but it is *also* a true *trust and confidence* of the mercy of God through our Lord Jesus Christ, and a stedfast *hope* of all good things to be received at God's hand." [1] Of course this does not mean that faith is hope, or that, strictly speaking, faith is trust, which would be a misuse of words, but that that faith which justifies, is not mere faith, but faith in trust and hope, and trust and hope in it. Next, they say "Dead faith is not the sure and substantial faith which saveth sinners. Another faith there is in Scripture, which is not, as the foresaid faith, idle, unfruitful, and dead, but '*worketh by charity*,' as St. Paul declareth Gal. v." Here then is another element of lively faith, *love ;* mere faith does not justify,

[1] Sermon of Faith, Part I.

but faith which is one with love, animated and impregnated with love, and pouring itself out into trust or hope without ceasing to be faith. They continue : " This is the true, lively, and unfeigned Christian faith, and is not in the mouth and outward profession only, but it liveth and stirreth inwardly in the heart. And this faith is not without hope and trust in God, nor without the love of God and of *our neighbours;* nor without *the fear of God,* nor without the *desire to hear* God's word, and to *follow* the same, *eschewing* evil, and *doing* gladly all *good works.*" Thus faith, according to these Homilies, is one with a spirit of godly fear and holy obedience also ; and what makes this passage clearer is the circumstance that, whereas faith is here said to be " *not without* hope and trust," it was in the former passage said to *be* hope and trust, which shows that hope and trust are not to be taken as mere additions or consequences, but as characteristic appendages of justifying faith itself ; therefore that godly fear and that holy obedience, which in this last passage it is said not to be " without," are to be taken as characteristics also.   Elsewhere they are still more express : " There is one work *in the which be all good works,* that is, faith which worketh by charity.   If thou have it, thou hast the *ground* of all good works ; for the *virtues* of strength, wisdom, temperance, and justice, be all referred unto this same faith."[1]   Thus all "virtues," which are the " ground " of good works, exist in and with the faith that justifies.

[1] Of Good Works, Part I.   [This is "fides formata," which *is* justifying.]

Such is the view taken of justifying faith in the Homilies, as extended out into that circle of graces of which it becomes the outline and peculiarity; whereas the Roman Church views it in that outline taken separately. The Homilies, being popular discourses, speak of it practically; Rome, speaking theologically, traces it to its elements. The one views it in the abstract, the other as it is in fact; the one considers it as the faith of the regenerate, the other as regenerate faith. Either notion is intelligible, whichever is the more advisable; but what is not at all intelligible is the notion of the Protestant schools, which makes it neither the one nor the other, but more than one, and less than the other, something between abstract and concrete, not mere assent to God's word, yet not so much as obedience, not bare faith, yet not living. Its upholders indeed boldly call their justifying faith, living, and reject the notion of its being bare faith; so far is well; but then they go on to define it to be mere *trust*, or a fiduciary apprehension of Gospel mercy, which, though certainly more than bare faith, is not necessarily living. It will be said that our Homilies sometimes so speak of it; certainly they do, but they are popular addresses. It is quite another thing when statements, which contain a true and impressive teaching, are taken as adequate and accurate *definitions* of the matter in hand. No such statements occur in our Articles; they do occur in the German Confessions[1] from which the

[1] Et fidei vocabulum, non solum cognitionem historiæ de Christo significat, sed etiam credere et assentiri huic promissioni, quæ est Evangelii propria, in qua propter Christum nobis promittuntur remissio peccatorum, justificatio, et vita æterna. — Conf. August. 2,

Articles are taken. The silence then of the Articles is significant. What I am here speaking of is a *formal declaration* that faith is trust; and I ask on what intelligible principle is it that the Divines who make it, leave *assent* without going on to *obedience?* Why, if they begin to tint their outline, do they not finish the colouring? why, if they will consider it as confident assurance, do they not allow it, as the Homilies allow it, to represent hope, love, joy, peace, thanksgiving, devotedness, and all kinds of virtue, whatever indeed is necessary for "the measure of the stature of the fulness of Christ"? Why do they say it only works *by* love and results *in* obedience, if they maintain that it *is* trust? why must trust be part of its essence, yet love and obedience external to it? why must trust be any more than its necessary exhibition, if obedience is to be considered as nothing more? why should it cease to be justifying faith if called love or obedience, yet not if it be called trust? Yet such is the way of viewing it, to which multitudes have accustomed themselves. They escape from the strict definition, then pitch

1540. Illa fides, quæ justificat, non est tantum notitia historiæ sed est assentiri promissioni Dei.—Apol. Conf. August. Hæc fides simul est fiducia acquiescens in Mediatore. —Confess. Saxon. Jackson says that "confidence, fiducia, or trust," is "so nearly allied to faith, that some include it in the essence or formal signification of the word in the learned tongues ; which opinion may seem to have some countenance from the Book of Homilies. But what there is said of faith to this purpose is a popular description, not an accurate or artificial definition, like as also we may not think the author of those Homilies meant formally and essentially to define faith, when he said that 'faith is a firm hope,' for so in the same place doth he describe it."—B. iv. ch. 10, s. 6, p. 673. Jackson differs in some points from the view contained in these Lectures.

their tent in the very middle of their route, dread to go forward, and fire up at the very notion of going back, and have recourse to cries of alarm, protestations, and threats, if any the most gentle persuasion or most intelligible reasonings be used to turn them one way or the other.

4.

This then is the false position, if I may so speak, which the schools in question have taken up. Their idea of faith is a mere theory, neither true in philosophy nor in fact; and hence it follows that their whole theology is shadowy and unreal. I do not say that there is no such thing as a trusting in Christ's mercy for salvation, and a comfort resulting from it. This would be resisting what we may witness daily, and what, under circumstances, it is our duty to exercise. Bad and good feel it. What *is* so unreal, is to say that it is necessarily a holy feeling, that it can be felt by none but the earnest, that a mere trust, without anything else, without obedience, love, self-denial, consistent conduct, conscientiousness, that this mere trust in Christ's mercy, existing in a mind which has as yet no other religious feeling, will necessarily renew the soul and lead to good works. This is the mere baseless and extravagant theory I speak of. Men may be conscious they trust; they may be conscious they gain comfort from trusting; they cannot be conscious that such a trust is of a practical character; they cannot be conscious that it changes the heart. The event alone determines this. That it raises present emotions they may be conscious; that it is such as permanently to impress their inner man they cannot know, except they be prophets ; for that is a thing future. It may, or it may not ; and it is pernicious to say it must. However, to enter into its practical results is beside my present subject.

Viewed in its theological aspect, in which it is now before us, the Protestant account will be found to give a character of vagueness and equivocation to the whole system built upon it. What indeed can be expected but arbitrary distinctions and unreal subtleties in the conformation of a theology, which has a flaw in its leading principle, which starts with maintaining that faith is, what nothing ever was or can be, an abstraction in actual existence,—an object or thing which contains in it in fact only what the name contains,—an aspect, side, quality, and property standing by itself,—and, as if this were not enough, which lays down, when we go on to inquire *what* faith is, that it is mere *trust*, and yet necessarily *spiritual ?* Hence, not unnaturally, it is a source of never-ending disputes between persons who seem to agree together, yet go away and act differently, and still wonder why they differ. I describe faith, and another describes it, and perhaps we even use the same terms, yet agree in nothing else. Why is this ? because I aim at contemplating things as they are, and must be, in their embodied form ; and he, on the contrary, has a notion that he may seize a certain portion of the idea conveyed by the word faith, more than assent, less than obedience, and may give it a substantive existence, and carry it on to results such as he pleases to assign to it.

The one view then differs from the other as the likeness of a man differs from the original. The picture re-

sembles him ; but it is not he. It is not a reality, it is
all surface. It has no depth, no substance; touch it, and
you will find it is not what it pretends to be. When I
assign an office to faith, I am not speaking of an abstraction or creation of the mind, but of something
existing. I wish to deal with things, not with words.
I do not look to be put off with a name or a shadow.
I would treat of faith as it is actually found in the
soul ; and I say it is as little an isolated grace, as a
man is a picture. It has a depth, a breadth, and a thick-
ness ; it has an inward life which is something over and
above itself ; it has a heart, and blood, and pulses, and
nerves, though not upon the surface. All these indeed
are not *spoken* of, when we make mention of faith ; nor
are they painted on the canvas ; but they are implied
in the word, because they exist in the thing. What has
been observed above, of the distinction between the
meaning of the word and of the thing, *righteousness*,
applies here. Love and fear, and heavenly-mindedness,
and obedience, and firmness, and zeal, and humility, are
as certainly one with justifying faith, considered as a
thing existing, as bones, muscles, and vital organs, are
necessary to that outward frame of man which meets
the eye, though they do not meet it. Love and fear and
obedience are not really posterior to justifying faith for
even a moment of time, unless bones or muscles are formed
after the countenance and complexion. It is as unmeaning to speak of living faith, as being independent of
newness of mind, as of solidity as divisible from body,
or tallness from stature, or colour from the landscape.
As well might it be said that an arm or a foot can exist

out of the body, and that man is born with only certain portions, head or heart, and that the rest accrues afterwards, as that faith comes first and gives birth to other graces. This illustration holds with only one limitation ; that faith, though connatural with other graces, has a power of reacting upon them, by placing more constraining objects before them, as motives to their more vigorous exercise.

This then is what is meant by the doctrine that faith is not justifying unless informed or animated by love ; isolated or bare faith being impossible in a Christian, or in any one else, and existing only in our conceptions, and not being a grace or virtue when so conceived. That such is the doctrine of Scripture has been variously shown in the discussion of the subjects which have come before us. Here I will but cite two celebrated passages from St. James and St. Paul. St. Paul says, " Though I have *all faith,* so that I could remove mountains, and have *not love,* I am nothing." And St. James, after warning his brethren against " holding the *faith* " of Christ " in respect of persons," that is, in an *unloving* spirit, as the context shows, proceeds to say, that it is " *perfected* by works," and that " without works " it is " dead," as a body without the soul. That is, as the presence of the soul changes the nature of the dust of the earth, and makes it flesh and blood, giving it a life which otherwise it could not have, so love is the modelling and harmonizing principle on which justifying faith depends, and in which it exists and acts.

5.

I conclude, then, by stating what *is,* as I conceive, the

special fruit or work of faith under the Gospel, and its influence upon the Christian; in doing which I shall assume, what this is not the place to prove, that it is an original means of knowledge, not resolvable into sense, or the faculty of reasoning, confirmed indeed by experience, as they are, but founded on a supernaturally implanted instinct; an instinct developed by religious obedience, and leading the mind to the word of Christ and of His Apostles as its refuge.

The Gospel, then, as contrasted with all religious systems which have gone before and come after, even those in which God has spoken, is specially the system of faith and "the law of faith," and its obedience is the "obedience of faith," and its justification is "by faith," and it is a "power of God unto salvation to every one that believeth." For at the time of its first preaching the Jews went by sight and the Gentiles by reason; both might believe, but on a belief resolvable into sight or reason,—neither went simply by faith. The Greeks sought after "wisdom," some original and recondite philosophy, which might serve as an "evidence" or ground of proof for "things not seen." The Jews, on the other hand, "required a sign," some sensible display of God's power, a thing of sight and touch, which might be "the substance," the earnest and security "of things hoped for." They wanted some carnal and immediate good, as "the praise of men;" for this they did their alms, fasted and prayed, not looking on to witnesses unseen, but for an earthly reward; or, if they wrought for God, it was in a grudging, calculating way, as if to make their services go as far as possible, resting in them as ends, and suspicious of God as of a hard or unjust Master. Such was the state of the world, when it pleased Almighty God, in furtherance of His plan of mercy, to throw men's minds upon the next world, without any other direct medium of evidence than the word of man claiming to be His ; to change the face of the world by what the world called "the foolishness of preaching" and the unreasoning zeal and obstinacy of faith, using a principle in truth's behalf which in the world's evil history has ever been the spring of great events and strange achievements. Faith, which in the natural man has manifested itself in the fearful energy of superstition and fanaticism, is in the Gospel grafted on the love of God, and made to mould the heart of man into His image.

6.

The Apostles then proceeded thus :—they did not rest their cause on argument ; they did not rely on eloquence,' wisdom, or reputation ; nay, nor did they make miracles necessary to the enforcement of their claims.[1] They did not resolve faith into sight or reason ; they contrasted it with both, and bade their hearers

---

[1] Vid. Acts xvii. 23 ; xxiv. 25. Paley, whose work on the Evidences is founded on the notion that the miracles wrought by Christ and His Apostles are to be *the ground* of our faith, feels the difficulty that *in fact* they were not so accounted in early times. After quoting passages of the Fathers in his favour, he adds, "I am ready, however, to admit that the ancient Christian advocates did not insist upon the miracles in argument *so frequently as I should have done*. It was their lot to contend with notions of magical agency, against which the mere production of the facts was not sufficient for the convincing of their adversaries. *I do not know whether they themselves thought it quite de-*

believe, sometimes in spite, sometimes in default, sometimes in aid, of sight and reason. They exhorted them
to make trial of the Gospel, since they would find their
account in so doing.[1] And of their hearers "some
believed the things which were spoken, some believed
not." Those believed whose hearts were "opened,"
who were "ordained to eternal life;" those did not
whose hearts were hardened. This was the awful
exhibition of which the Apostles and their fellow
workers were witnesses; for faith, as a principle of
knowledge, cannot be exactly analyzed or made intelligible to man, but is the secret, inexplicable, spontaneous
movement of the mind (however arising) towards the
external word,—a movement not to the exclusion of
sight and reason, for the miracles appeal to both, nor of
experience, for all who venture for Christ receive daily
returns of good in confirmation of their choice, but
independent of sight or reason before, or of experience
after. The Apostles appealed to men's hearts, and,
according to their hearts, so they answered them. They
appealed to their secret belief in a superintending providence, to their hopes and fears thence resulting; and
they professed to reveal to them the nature, personality,

cisive of the controversy."—Part iii. c. 5, fin. Then on what *did* they
believe? Again: are not philosophical objections as cogent now
against miracles as the belief in magic then?

[1] πότερον βέλτιόν ἐστιν αὐτοῖς ἀλόγως πιστεύουσι κατεστάλθαι πως τὰ
ἤθη καὶ ὠφελῆσθαι, διὰ τὴν περὶ τῶν κολαζομένων ἐπὶ ἁμαρτίαις καὶ τιμω-
μένων ἐπὶ ἔργοις χρηστοῖς πίστιν, ἢ μὴ προσίεσθαι αὐτῶν τὴν ἐπιστροφὴν
μετὰ ψιλῆς πίστεως, ἕως ἂν ἐπιδῶσιν ἑαυτοὺς ἐξετάσει λόγων; . . . .
ἡ περὶ τοῦ τὰ κρείττονα καὶ τὰ κατ' εὐχὴν ἀπαντήσεσθαι πίστις τολμᾷν
πάντας ποιεῖ, καὶ ἐπὶ τὰ ἄδηλα καὶ δυνατὰ ἄλλως συμβῆναι.—Orig. in
Cels. i. 9-11.

attributes, will, and works of Him "whom their hearers ignorantly worshipped." They came as commissioned from Him, and declared that mankind was a guilty and outcast race,—that sin was a misery,—that the world was a snare,—that life was a shadow,—that God was everlasting,—that His Law was holy and true, and its sanctions certain and terrible ;—that He also was all-merciful,—that He had appointed a Mediator between Him and them, who had removed all obstacles, and was desirous to restore them, and that He had sent themselves to explain how. They said that that Mediator had come and gone ; but had left behind Him what was to be His representative till the end of all things, His mystical Body, the Church, in joining which lay the salvation of the world. So they preached, and so they prevailed ; using indeed persuasives of every kind as they were given them, but resting at bottom on a principle higher than the senses or the reason. They used many arguments, but as outward forms of something beyond argument. Thus they appealed to the miracles they wrought, as sufficient signs of their power, and assuredly divine, in spite of those which other systems could show or pretended. They expostulated with the better sort on the ground of their instinctive longings and dim visions of something greater than the world. They awed and overcame the passionate by means of what remained of heaven in them, and of the involuntary homage which such men pay to the more realized tokens of heaven in others. They asked the more generous-minded whether it was not worth while to risk something on the chance of augmenting and perfecting those precious elements of good which their hearts still held ; and they could not hide what they cared not to "glory in," their own disinterested sufferings, their high deeds, and their sanctity of life. They won over the affectionate and gentle by the beauty of holiness, and the embodied mercies of Christ as seen in the ministrations and ordinances of His Church. Thus they spread their nets for disciples, and caught thousands at a cast ; thus they roused and inflamed their hearers into enthusiasm, till "the Kingdom of Heaven suffered violence, and the violent took it by force." And when these had entered it, many of them, doubtless, would wax cold in love, and fall away ; for many had entered only on impulse ; many, with Simon Magus, on wonder or curiosity ; many from a mere argumentative belief, which leads as readily into heresy as into the Truth. But still, those who had the seed of God within them, would become neither offences in the Church, nor apostates, nor heretics; but would find day by day, as love increased, increasing experience that what they had ventured boldly amid conflicting evidence, of sight against sight, and reason against reason, with many things against it, and more things for it, they had ventured well. The examples of meekness, cheerfulness, contentment, silent endurance, private self-denial, fortitude, brotherly love, perseverance in well-doing, which would from time to time meet them in their new kingdom,—the sublimity and harmony of the Church's doctrine,—the touching and subduing beauty of her services and appointments,—their consciousness of her virtue, divinely imparted, upon themselves, in subduing,

purifying, changing them,— the bountifulness of her
alms-giving,—her power, weak as she was and despised,
over the statesmen and philosophers of the world,—her
consistent and steady aggression upon it, moving forward
in spite of it on all sides at once, like the wheels in the
Prophet's vision, and this in contrast with the ephemeral
and variable outbreaks of sectarianism,[1]—the unanimity
and intimacy existing between her widely-separated
branches,—the mutual sympathy and correspondence of
men of hostile nations and foreign languages,—the simplicity of her ascetics, the gravity of her Bishops, the awful
glory shed around her Martyrs, and the mysterious and
recurring traces of miraculous agency here and there, once
and again, according as the Spirit willed,—these and the
like persuasives acted on them day by day, turning the
whisper of their hearts into an habitual conviction, and
establishing in the reason what had been begun in the
will. And thus has the Church been upheld ever
since by an appeal to the People,—to the necessities of
human nature, the anxieties of conscience, and the
instincts of purity ; forcing upon Kings a sufferance or
protection which they fain would dispense with, and
upon Philosophy a grudging submission and a reserved
and limited recognition.

---

[1] ἔσβεστο μὲν γὰρ αὐτίκα, πρὸς αὐτῆς ἐνεργείας ἀπελεγχόμενα τὰ τῶν
ἐχθρῶν ἐπιτεχνήματα, ἄλλων ἐπ' ἄλλαις αἱρέσεων καινοτομουμένων· ὑπορ-
ρεουσῶν ἀεὶ τῶν προτέρων, καὶ εἰς πολυτρόπους καὶ πολυμόρφους ἰδέας
ἄλλοτε ἄλλως φθειρομένων· προῄει δ' εἰς αὔξησιν καὶ μέγεθος, ἀεὶ κατὰ τὰ
αὐτὰ καὶ ὡσαύτως ἔχουσα, ἡ τῆς καθόλου καὶ μόνης ἀληθοῦς ἐκκλησίας
λαμπρότης, τὸ σεμνὸν καὶ εἰλικρινὲς καὶ ἐλευθέριον, τό τε σῶφρον καὶ
καθαρὸν τῆς ἐνθέου πολιτείας τε καὶ φιλοσοφίας εἰς ἅπαν γένος Ἑλλήνων τε
καὶ βαρβάρων ἀποστίλβουσα.— Euseb. Hist. iv. 7, fin.

7.

Such was the triumph of Faith, spreading like a leaven through the thoughts, words, and works of men, till the whole was leavened. It did not affect the substance of religion ; it left unaltered both its external developments and its inward character ; but it gave strength and direction to its lineaments. The sacrifice of prayer and praise, and the service of an obedient heart and life, remained as essential as before ; but it has infused a principle of growth. It has converted grovelling essays into high aspirings,—partial glimpses into calm contemplation,—niggard payments into generous self-devotion. It enjoined the law of love for retaliation ; it put pain above enjoyment ; it supplanted polygamy by the celibate ; it honoured poverty before affluence, the communion of Saints before the civil power, the next world before this. It made the Christian independent of all men and all things, except of Christ ; and provided for a deeper humility, while it supplied an overflow of peace and joy.

LECTURE XII.

I NOW proceed to show that though we are justified, as St. Paul says, by faith, and, as our Articles and Homilies say, by faith only, nevertheless we are justified, as St. James says, by works ; and to show in what sense this latter doctrine is true, and that, not only in the case of works of righteousness, but also of ritual services, such as Baptism, as St. Paul and St. Peter teach. Of course I do not forget St. Paul's declaration that "a man is justified by faith without the deeds of the Law," but he does not thereby assert that justification is independent of the deeds of the Gospel, as a few remarks will suffice to show.

Now, I say at first sight it is no contradiction of St. Paul to assert that we are justified by faith *with* evangelical works, unless St. James contradicts him also. Those who object to the doctrine of justification through good works, must first object to St. James's Epistle, which they sometimes have done ; on the other hand, the temper of Christian reverence which will lead the disciple of St. Paul to submit to St. James, is also a spirit of charity towards those who speak with St. James, from a fear lest in condemning them it should resist an Apostle. With those then who judge severely of the maintainers

of justification by works, I would expostulate thus :
—Why be so bent upon forcing two inspired teachers
into a real and formal discordance of doctrine? If you
could prove ever so cogently that when St. Paul said,
"deeds of the Law," he meant to include Christian
works, you would not have advanced one step towards
interpreting St. James, or impairing his authority ; you
would have only plunged into a more serious perplexity.
Difficult if it be to account for St. Paul insisting on faith,
and St. James at a later date insisting on works, surely
it is a greater difficulty when it is insisted on that St.
Paul excludes the very works which St. James includes.
Is our Gospel like the pretended revelation of the
Arabian impostor, a variable rule, the latter portion con-
tradicting the former ? Let men speak out then : what is
their latent theory, which is sufficient to reconcile their
minds to this *primâ facie* difficulty, and inspirits them,
under cover of a presumed contrariety in Scripture, to
move forward against Catholic and Apostolic truth?

I believe the latent view to be this : that the Scripture question was settled once for all three centuries
since, when the words of both the Holy Apostles were
harmonized and merged in the formula of "justification
by faith only ; " which henceforth, in spite of the supposed liberty of private judgment, is practically a dogma
to Protestants, as the canons of the Tridentine Council
are binding on the faith of Roman Catholics ; and further, that because our Articles and Homilies contain the
phrase " by faith only," therefore they must mean by that
phrase all that the Protestant schools have meant by it.
But surely, while we accept fully this form of speech, as

has been done in the foregoing Lectures, we may reasonably maintain that an assent to the doctrine that faith alone justifies, does not at all preclude the doctrine of works justifying also. If indeed I said that works justify in *the same sense* as faith only justifies, this would be a contradiction in terms ; but faith only may justify in one sense, good works in another,—and this is all that I here maintain. After all, does not Christ only justify? How is it that the doctrine of faith justifying does not interfere with our Lord's being the sole justifier? It will of course be replied that our Lord is the meritorious· cause, and faith the means ; that faith justifies in a different and subordinate sense. As then Christ alone justifies, *in the sense* in which He justifies, yet faith also justifies us in its own sense, so works, whether moral or ritual, may justify us in their own respective senses, though in the sense in which faith justifies, it only justifies. The only question is *what* is that sense in which works justify, so as not to interfere with faith only justifying? It may indeed turn out on inquiry, that the sense alleged will not hold, either as being unscriptural or for any other reason ; but, whether so or not, at any rate the apparent inconsistency of language should not startle men; nor should they so promptly condemn those who, though they do not use *their* language, use St. James's. Indeed, is not this argument, as has been suggested already, the very weapon of the Arians in their warfare against the Son of God? They said, Christ is not God, because the Father is called the " *Only* God."

2.

I might seem just now to grant that St. Paul's words, at first sight, countenanced the extreme Protestant view of them ; but this was not at all my meaning. The truth is, we put a particular sense upon those words, from having heard it again and again assigned to them, and thus every other interpretation comes to seem unnatural. The state of the case is as follows :—The Jews sought to be justified by works done in their own unaided strength, by the Law of Nature, as it was set before them in the Mosaic Covenant ; and the Apostle shows them a more excellent way. He proposes to them the Law of Faith, and says that a man is justified by faith without the deeds of the Law ; moreover, that in thus teaching, so far from making the Law void through faith, He establishes it. He means then to speak to the Jews as follows :—"Throw yourselves on God's mercy, surrender yourselves to Him ; the Law in which you pride yourselves, holy as it is in itself, has been to you but an occasion of sin. You are in bondage ; you have no real sanctity, no high aims, no inward growth, no power of pleasing God. Instead of having done anything good, you have everything to be forgiven. You must begin over again ; you must begin in a new way, by faith ; faith only, nothing short of faith, can help you on to a justifying obedience. But faith is fully equal to enabling you to fulfil the Law. Far then from invalidating the Law by the doctrine of faith, I establish it." Now I do not ask whether there is no other possible interpretation of his words besides this (though I do think this the only natural one), but whether, at least, it is not natural, whatever becomes of others ; and then, whether it is not perfectly consistent with St. James's doctrine. It concerns those who are dissatisfied with it to assign one equally unexceptionable in itself, equally consistent with the rest of Scripture.

Justification comes *through* the Sacraments ; is received *by* faith ; *consists* in God's inward presence; and *lives* in obedience. Let us take some parallel cases.

Supposing one saw a Pagan or Mahometan at his devotions, or doing works of charity, and were to say, " Alas ! your prayers and works will profit you nothing ; you must believe on Christ ; which will stand you in stead of all that you now do ;" would any one suppose it to be meant that Christians said no prayers, or gave no alms ? or only that prayers and alms, when separate from Christ, were but dead and vain ?

Again : Scripture says that " the prayer of the *wicked* is an abomination to the Lord ;" does this prove that the prayer of the righteous is an abomination also ?

Again : when Almighty God says by the prophet, " I will have mercy, and not sacrifice," does this mean that the Jews were thenceforth to leave off their sacrifices, or that sacrifices were useless unless they *also* showed mercy ?

Again : when our Lord censures the " long robes" of the Pharisees, does He censure such garments as are worn at present by His ministers in Church ?

Again : when St. Paul declares that the Jewish Sabbath is abolished, does this prove there is no Christian Sabbath, or Lord's day ?

This then is a mode of arguing, which would carry us

much further than we dare to go. It does not follow that works done in faith do not justify, because works done without faith do not justify ; that works done in the Holy Ghost, and ordinances which are His instruments, do not justify, because carnal works and dead rites do not justify. There is nothing in the text I have quoted to exclude the Works and Sacraments of faith ; all that can be said is that they are not mentioned. St. Paul is urging upon his brethren the one *way* to salvation, which, as it is Christ Himself in God's sight, so it is faith on our part. He tells them they must be justified on a new principle ; new, that is, as being used under the Gospel for higher purposes than heretofore, and because publicly recognized as the one saving principle. He guides them to heaven along a path by which alone they can ascend the mountain of the Lord, and which is called the way of faith, not that it does not lie through hope and charity too, but faith is the name designating the track. The principle of faith directed and sanctified their services : did it follow from this that it was (what is called) substantive, and could stand by itself, instead of being a quality or mode of obedience ? or that obedience itself, or what St. James calls works, could not be that substance ? If we refuse, not to modify, but even to complete one text of Scripture by another,—if we will not admit the second, merely because we prefer an interpretation of the first which contradicts it,—if we will not hold two doctrines at once, merely because the text that declares the one does not also declare the other,—if we will not say with St. James that works of faith justify, merely because St. Paul says that faith justifies and

works without faith do not justify,—if we will demand
that the whole of the Gospel should be brought out into
form in a single text,—then surely we ought to hold
that Baptism is sufficient for salvation, because St. Peter
says it "saves us,"—or hope sufficient, because St. Paul
says "we are saved by hope,"—or that only love is the
means of forgiveness because our Lord says, "Her sins
are forgiven, for she loved much,"—or that faith does not
save, because St. James asks, "Can faith save him?"—or
that keeping the commandments is the whole Gospel,
because St. Paul says it has superseded circumcision.
Nothing surely is more suitable than to explain justifying
faith to be a principle of action, a characteristic of obedience, a sanctifying power, if by doing so we reconcile St.
Paul with St. James, and moreover observe the while the
very same rule of interpretation which we apply to
Scripture generally.

3.

Thus much at first view of the subject; now let us
take separately the two parts into which it divides,
gospel ordinances and gospel works; and show in each
case more distinctly their relation to faith.

1. It is objected, then, that under the Gospel, Ordinances are of little account, and that to insist on them
is to bring the Church into bondage; that if Baptism
convey regeneration, or the Apostolical Succession be the
warrant for the Ministry, or Imposition of hands be a
spiritual benefit, or Consecration be required for giving
and receiving the Eucharist, or its Celebration involve a
sacrifice, in a word, if outward signs are necessary means

of gospel grace, then St. Paul's statement does not hold that we are "justified by faith without the deeds of the Law."

Now, I observe, that this argument, on the face of it, proves too much ; it proves that Christian rites should altogether be superseded as well as Jewish. Faith superseded circumcision ; it did not sup rsede Baptism ; there is then, on the face of the matter, some difference between Jewish and Christian Ordinances ; and if the latter be *necessary* under the Gospel and the former not, perhaps they are necessary *for some certa 1 pi rpose*, and perhaps that purpose is *justification.* Whether they are or not is another matter ; but certainly the text in question is not inconsistent with such a doctrine, or else is inconsistent with much more. If faith is compatible with their *use*, it may be compatible with their *virtue.*

But here it may be urged that, specious as this mode of arguing may be, it does not touch the real reluctance of religious persons to believe in the power of Sacraments under the Gospel, or the grounds of their considering such belief unscriptural ; that, as every one knows, there are explanations of the sacred text, which, however specious, are felt to be evasions ; and that the interpretation proposed is utterly subversive of St. Paul's doctrine, and uncongenial with his spirit. No one can doubt, it may be said, that by the doctrine of Faith he meant to magnify God's grace, to preach Christ's Cross, to inculcate its all-sufficiency for pardon and renewal, and our dependence on the aid of the Holy Spirit for the will and the power to accept these blessings ; that, on the other hand, to say that Sacraments are the means of

justification, obscures the free grace of the Gospel, and is
"putting a yoke on the necks of the disciples." Now
certainly, this argument, in its place, demands attention ;
I say in its place, lest I should seem to allow of its being
used, after the fashion of these later centuries, as a
"leading idea" of the Christian Dispensation, and a
short and easy way into a comprehensive view of it. No ;
we must abandon all such methods, if we would enter
in at the strait and lowly gate of the Holy Jerusalem ;
bowing our heads and bending our eyes to the earth, not
thinking to command the city, or letting the eye range
over its parts, or flattering ourselves we can "mount up
with eagles' wings," before we have first "waited on the
Lord." Philosophizing upon the inspired text is a very
poor method of interpreting it, though it be allowable
under due limitations, after gaining its meaning in a
legitimate way. With this caution, I proceed to consider the objection which has been stated.

4.

I say then, that fully allowing, or rather maintaining
that the scope of St. Paul's words is to show the nothingness of man and the all-sufficiency of Christ, and that this
is the proper meaning of the doctrine of justification by
faith, yet so far is the Catholic doctrine concerning
Sacraments from interfering with this undeniable truth,
that I might apply the Apostle's words, and say, "Do we
make void faith through the Sacraments ? yea, we establish faith." The proof of this is simple.

I allow then that faith exalts the grace of God ; this
is its office and charge ; accordingly, whatever furthers

this object, co-operates with the Gospel doctrine of faith ; whatever interferes with this object, contradicts the doctrine. Salvation by faith only is but another way of saying salvation by grace only. Again, it is intended to humble man, and to remind him that nothing he can do of himself can please God ; so that " by faith " means, " *not* by works of ours." If then the Sacraments obscure the doctrine of free grace, and tempt men to rest upon their own doings, then they make void the doctrine of faith ; if not, then they do not ; if they magnify God and humble man, then they even subserve it. This was the evil tendency of the Jewish rites when Christ came, that they interfered between Christ and the soul. They were dark bodies, eclipsing the glorious Vision which faith was charged to receive. Now I would say, that the Sacraments have a directly reverse tendency, and subserve the object aimed at by the doctrine of faith, as fully as the Jewish ordinances counteracted it. If this be so, the doctrine of justification by Sacraments is altogether consistent, or rather coincident with St. Paul's doctrine, when he says, that we are justified by faith without the deeds of the Law.

Upon Adam's fall, the light of God's countenance was withdrawn from the earth, and His presence from the souls of men ; nor was the forfeited blessing restored but by the death of Christ. The veil which hung before the Holy of Holies, was a type of the awful " covering " which was " cast over all people ;" and, when the Atoning Sacrifice was made, it rent in twain. Henceforth, heaven was opened again upon man, not on rare occasions, or in the instance of high Saints only, but upon all who believe. Such being the state of things before Christ came and such the state after, the Law which was before could not be the means of life, because life as yet was not; it was not wrought out, it was not created; it began to be in Christ, the Word Incarnate. The Law could not justify, because, whatever special favour might be shown here and there by anticipation, Gospel justification was not yet purchased in behalf of all who sought it. God justified Abraham, and He glorified Elijah; but He had not yet promised heaven to the obedient, nor acceptance to the believing. He wrought first in the few what He offered afterwards to all; and even in those extraordinary instances, He acted immediately from Himself, not through the Jewish Law as His instrument. Abraham was not justified through circumcision, nor Elijah raised by virtue of the Temple. Judaism had no life, no spirit in its ordinances, to connect earth and heaven.

Accordingly, the ceremonies of the Law, though given by God, were wrought out by man; I mean, as has been explained before, they were men's acts, not God's acts. They were done towards God, in order (if so be) to approach that which was not yet accorded; and thus were tokens, not of the presence of grace, but of its absence. Sacrifices and purifications, circumcision and the sabbath, could not take away sins, could not justify. Visible things are but means of grace at best; and they were not so much, before grace was purchased. They were attempts in a bad case towards what was needed; they were the humble and anxious representation of nature, making dumb signs for the things it needed, as we provide pictures and statues when we have not the originals.

Such was human nature in its best estate before Christ came ; its worst was when it mistook the tatters of its poverty for the garments of righteousness, and, as in our Lord's age, prided itself on what it was and what it did, because its own,—its sacrifices, ceremonies, birth-place, and ancestry,—as if these could stand instead of that justification which it needed. This was that reliance on the works of the Law, which St. Paul denounces, a reliance utterly incompatible of course with the doctrine of free grace, and, in consequence, of faith.

5.

This then was the condition of the Jews ; they had been told to approach God with works, which could not justify, *as if* they could ; and the carnal-minded among them mistook the semblance for the reality. But when Christ came, suffered, and ascended on high, then at length the promised grace was poured out abundantly, nay, for all higher purposes, far more so than on Adam upon his creation. What, therefore, to the Jews was impossible even to the last, is to us imparted from the first. They might not even end where we begin. They wrought towards justification, and we from it. They wrought without the presence of Christ, and we with it. They came to God with rites, He comes to us in Sacraments.

Now supposing, when any one desired and prayed for the gospel gifts, they were conveyed to him through the visible intervention of an Angel, would that Angel's presence be a memento of free grace, or a temptation to self-righteousness ? Or did Naaman's bathing in Jordan naturally lead to self-trust and a practical forgetfulness

of God's power? Did the necessity of coming to the
Apostles for a cure inculcate the law of works or of faith?
But it may be answered that such appointments *are*
capable of being used in a superstitious dependence.
Angels may be worshipped; Apostles venerated, as if
they were not "also men." Let me then put the
question in another shape,—does the *possibility* of the
abuse destroy the *natural and direct meaning* of the appointment? Was not the Brazen Serpent worshipped
in a corrupt age? yet our Lord still appeals to its
legitimate meaning as a token of God's free grace. If
the ordinance of the Brazen Serpent, which had been
abused, still conveyed the doctrine coupled with it by
Christ Himself, of "everlasting life" to those that
"believe," surely Baptism, which had not been abused,
might in St. Paul's mind be deemed consistent with the
doctrine of justification "by faith without deeds of the
Law;" surely he might discard those deeds without meaning to include Baptism among them. St. Peter teaches us
the same lesson after curing the lame man; he and St.
John had been the visible means of the cure; "all the
people ran together unto them greatly wondering." If
there be a tendency anywhere superstitiously to rest in
the outward part of Baptism or of the Lord's Supper, or
in their circumstances, or in other Christian rites, with
that "amazement" which the Jews felt towards the
Apostles, why must we deny their instrumentality in
order to our giving glory to God? why is it not enough
with St. Peter, to lead the mind, not from, but through
the earthly organ to the true Author of the miracle, not
denying a subordinate truth in order to enforce a higher?

" Ye men of Israel," he says, " why marvel ye at this? or why look ye so earnestly on us, as though by *our own* power or holiness we had made this man to walk ?" And surely, what St. Peter proclaimed by word of mouth, that the Sacraments proclaim from the first by their symbolical meaning and their simplicity. Nay, and independent of this, surely what is professedly a channel of mercy, is an emblem of that mercy ; what conveys a gift, speaks of a gift. Under the Law, God was in " clouds and darkness ;" in heaven, "the Lord God will lighten" the Temple face to face ; but under the Gospel, He is as upon the Mount of Transfiguration, in "a bright cloud over-shadowing" us ; and as well may such a cloud be said to obscure the sun which gilds it, as Sacraments to obscure that grace which makes them what they are. Hence Baptism was even called of old the Sacrament of faith, as being, on the part of the recipient, only an expression by act of what in words would be " I believe and I come." And what is meeting together for prayer but an act of faith and nothing more ? What the Jews by journeying up to Jerusalem were wont, not to receive, but to ask, is brought home to us, almost to our very doors, not in promise merely, but in substance ; according to our Saviour's condescending words, " If any man hear My voice and open the door, I will come in to him, and will sup with him, and he with Me." And all this is " without money and without price ;" expensive sacrifices were required of the Jews, and intricate rules prescribed ; but the Gospel rites are so simple, that the world despises them for their very simplicity.

In a Jewish ordinance, then, man worked and God

accepted ; in a Christian, God speaks the word, and man
kneels down and is saved.   Such is the relation between
Faith and Sacraments ; — in considering which I have
taken "faith" in the sense in which the objection uses
it, not in its proper sense of submission to what is unseen, but as trust founded upon that submission ; and
it appears, that while the Sacraments are an exercise of
submission, they are also a lesson of trust.   Faith is in-
culcated in their outward sign, and required for their
inward grace ; and is as little disparaged by the Catholic
doctrine concerning them, as Christ Himself by the
doctrine of faith.

6.

2. Now let us proceed to the second part of the subject, the relation between Faith and Works, which,
though quite distinct from the former, may be con-
veniently considered in connection with it.

St. Paul says that we are "justified by faith without
the deeds of the Law ;" and St. James, "not by faith only
but by works ;" are these statements inconsistent?
Now, as I said before, to condemn works without faith
is surely quite consistent with condemning faith without
works.   St. James says, we are justified by works, not
by faith only ; St. Paul implies, by faith, not by works
only.   St. Paul says, that works are not available before
faith ;   St. James, that they are available after faith.
And now I will make this clearer.

(1.) St. Paul says, we are justified without works ;
what works? "works of," or done under, "the Law," the
Law of Moses, through which the Law of Nature spoke

in the ears of the Jews. But St. James speaks of works done under what he calls "the royal Law," "the Law of liberty," which we learn from St. Paul is "the Law of the Spirit of Life," for "where the Spirit of the Lord is, there is liberty;" in other words, the Law of God, as written on the heart by the Holy Ghost. St. Paul speaks of works done under the letter, St. James of works done under the Spirit. This is surely an important difference in the works respectively mentioned.

Or, to state the same thing differently : St. James speaks, not of mere works, but of works of faith, of good and acceptable works. I do not suppose that any one will dispute this, and therefore shall take it for granted. St. James then says, we are justified, not by faith only, but by *good* works. Now St. Paul is not speaking at all of good works, but of works done *in the flesh,* and of themselves "deserving God's wrath and damnation." He says, "without *works;*" he does not say without *good* works; whereas St. James is speaking of good works solely. St. Paul speaks of "works done before the grace of Christ and the inspiration of His Spirit;" St. James of "good works which are the fruits of faith and follow after justification." Faith surely may justify without such works as, according to our Article, "have the nature of sin," and yet not justify without such as "are pleasing and acceptable to God in Christ."

Now in proof of this distinction it is enough to observe, that St. Paul never calls those works which he says do not justify "good works," but simply "works,"— "works of the Law,"—"deeds of the Law,"—"works not in righteousness,"—"dead works;" what have these to do with works or fruits of the Spirit? Of these latter also St. Paul elsewhere speaks, and by a remarkable contrast he calls them again and again "good works." For instance, "By grace are ye saved through faith, . . . not of *works*, lest any man should boast ; for we are His workmanship, created in Christ Jesus unto *good* works." This surely is a most pointed intimation that the works which do not justify are not good, or, in other words, are works *before* justification. As to works after, which *are* good, whether they justify or not, he does not decide so expressly as St. James, the error which he had to resist leading him another way. He only says, against the Judaizing teachers, that our works must begin, continue, and end in faith. But to proceed ; he speaks elsewhere of " abounding in every *good* work," of being " fruitful in every *good* work," of being " adorned with *good* works," of being " well reported of for *good* works," " diligently following every *good* work," of " the *good* works of some being open beforehand," of being " rich in *good* works," of being " prepared unto every *good* work," of being " throughly furnished unto all *good* works," of being " unto every *good* work reprobate," of being "a pattern of *good* works," of being "zealous of *good* works," of being " ready to every *good* work," of being " careful to maintain *good* works," of " provoking unto love and to *good* works," and of being " made perfect in every *good* work." [1]   Now surely this is very remarkable. St. James, though he means good works, drops the epithet, and only says

[1] 2 Cor. ix. 8.   Eph. ii. 10.   Col. i. 10.   2 Thess. ii. 17.   1 Tim ii. 10 ; v. 10, 25 ; vi. 18.   2 Tim. ii. 21 ; iii. 17.   Tit. i. 16 ; ii. 7 14 ; iii. 8, 14.   Heb. x. 24 ; xiii. 21.

works. Why does not St. Paul the same? why is he always careful to add the word *good*, except that he had also to do with a sort of works with which St. James had not to do,—that the word *works* was already appropriated by him to those of the Law, and therefore that the epithet *good* was necessary, lest deeds done in the Spirit should be confused with them?[1]

St. Paul, then, by speaking of faith as justifying without works, means without corrupt and counterfeit works, not without good works. And he does not deny what St. James affirms, that we are justified in good works.

7.

Such has ever been the Catholic mode of reconciling the two Apostles together, and certainly without doing violence to the text of St. Paul. But now, before proceeding, let us for a moment inquire, on the other hand, what attempts have been made on the side of Protestant writers to reduce the language used by St. James to a Lutheran sense.

"By works," says St. James, "a man is justified, and not by faith only." Now, let me ask, what texts do their opponents shrink from as they from this? do they even attempt to explain it? or if so, is it not by some harsh and unnatural interpretation? Next, do they not proceed, as if distrusting their own interpretation, to pronounce the text difficult, and so to dispose of it? yet who can honestly say that it is in itself difficult? rather, can words be plainer, were it not that they are forced into connection with a theory of the sixteenth century; and

[1] Bull, Harm. ii. 12, § 3.

then certainly they become as thick darkness, "as a book that is sealed, which men deliver to one that is learned, saying, Read this, I pray thee ; and he saith, I cannot, for it is sealed."[1] If St. James is difficult, is St. Paul plain ? will any one say that St. Paul is plainer than St. James ? Is it St. James in whose Epistles are "some things hard to be understood ?" What then is this resolute shutting of the eyes to an inspired Apostle, but the very spirit which leads the Socinian to blot out from certain texts, as far as his faith is concerned, the divinity of Christ ? If we may pass over "By works a man is justified, and not by faith only," why may we not also, "I and My Father are One"? Can we fairly call it self-will to refuse the witness of the latter text, while we arbitrarily take on ourselves to assign or deny a sense to the former ? What is meant by maintaining the duty of a man's drawing his Creed from Scripture for himself, and yet telling him it is a deadly heresy to say, just what St. James says, and what St. Paul (to say the least) does not deny ? But in truth, after all, men do not make up their mind from Scripture, though they profess to do so ; they go by what they consider their inward experience. They fancy they have reasons in their own spiritual history for concluding that God has taught them the doctrine of justification without good works ; and by these they go. They cannot get themselves to throw their minds upon Scripture ; they argue from Scripture only to convince others, but you may defeat them again and again, without moving or distressing them ; they are above you, for they do not depend on

[1] Isaiah xxix. 11.

Scripture for their faith at all, but on what has taken place within them.[1] But to return :—

8.

(2.) A clearer view of faith and works will be gained by considering that faith is a *habit* of the soul: now a habit is a something permanent, which affects the character ; it is a something in the mind which develops itself through acts of the mind, and disposes the mind to move in this way, not in that. We do not know what it is in itself, we only know it in its results ; relatively to us, it exists only in its results. We witness certain deeds, a certain conduct, we hear certain principles professed, all consistent with each other, and we refer them to something in the mind as the one cause of what is outwardly so uniform. When we speak of a bountiful man, we mean a man who thinks and does bountifully ; and if we were to say that God will reward bountifulness, we should mean bountiful acts. In like manner then, when we speak of a believer, we mean a man who thinks and does,—that is, of a mind that acts, —believingly ; and when we say that God justifies by faith on our part, we mean by acts of whatever kind, deeds, works, done in faith.

It will be replied that this is true indeed, but that the acts in which faith shows itself are not actions, deeds,

[1] A candid writer has confessed this :—" It is difficult," says Milton, " to conjecture the purpose oi Providence in committing the writings of the New Testament to such uncertain and variable guardianship, unless it were to teach us, by this very circumstance, that the Spirit which is given to us is *a more certain guide than Scripture*, whom therefore it is our duty to follow."—*Christian Doctrine*, i. 30.

works, but good feelings, thoughts, aspirations, and the like. Let it be so ; let us so take it for argument's sake. The acts then in which faith shows itself are to be considered, not as deeds or services, but what are popularly called spiritual desires, and a willingness to renounce self and adhere to Christ. Let us suppose this ; even then, it seems, *some* manifestations are required. So much is this felt by the persons against whom I am arguing, that they consider baptized infants cannot be regenerate, because they show no *signs* of regeneration ; a poor reason truly, for habits may exist without showing themselves to us, and, for what we know, God may bestow on infants in Baptism the element of justifying faith, though by reason of their tender age it be latent and undeveloped, as the Lutherans themselves have before now maintained (though now, such is the course of error, they rather deny them regeneration than attribute to them faith) ; however, this insisting upon signs and tokens at least proves how strongly the persons in question hold that faith cannot exist without its manifestations. They do certainly think both that faith only justifies, and yet that faith does not justify, does not exist, except in certain manifestations. Now supposing St. James had spoken thus : " What doth it profit, my brethren, though a man say he hath faith, and has no experience of the love of Christ, no spiritual-mindedness, no renewed taste, and holy affections? can faith save him ? If he has no knowledge of his sin and deadness, if he has not brought himself to renounce his own merit and fly for safety to the appointed refuge for sinners, what doth it profit ! Even so faith, if it be not truly warm and experimental,

is dead. . . . Ye see then, my brethren, that a man is
justified by having a renewed and converted heart, and
not by faith only." I say, supposing St. James had thus
spoken, would they have found any repugnance between
his doctrine and St. Paul's ? would they have denied the
Epistle to be genuine, or maintained it was difficult, or
gone into this or that rival extravagance of interpretation
in order to cripple an Apostle into Lutheranism ? No,
surely, they would have taken its words as they stand,
and thought them a powerful argument in behalf of what
they miscall "spiritual religion." As then they would
not have declined the inspired message, had it said that
faith without a change of heart was dead, not justifying,
why should there be any insuperable difficulty, any contradiction to St. Paul, in its saying that good works are
necessary concomitants of the faith that justifies, as
they themselves make spiritual emotions to be ?—that
its life is like the life of other graces, of benevolence,
or zeal, or courage, not good feelings only, but services or
works ? What contradiction indeed is there between St.
Paul and St. James but one of their own making, arising
from their assumption that faith, unlike benevolence or
courage, manifests itself or lives, not in deeds, but in
passive impressions ?

9.

(3.) And that this assumption, contrary as it is to
philosophy, is contrary also to revealed truth, is plain,
from this one circumstance, which should be carefully
noticed :—that whereas St. Paul says we are justified by
faith, and St. James by works, yet St. Paul's *illustrations*

of justification by faith are taken from occasions, not on which men *felt* anything unusual, but when they did something unusual. St. Paul, instancing justifying faith, does not say, Abraham said he was "dust and ashes," (which he did say), and so was justified ; Moses desired to see God's glory, and so was justified ; David, as his Psalms show, was full of holy aspirations, and so was justified ;—no, but Abraham and the Patriarchs, Moses and the Prophets, David and the Confessors, did strong deeds of righteousness : they not only "*confessed* they were strangers and pilgrims upon earth," but they "*obeyed ;*" they "went out," they "chose affliction with the people of God :" they "stopped the mouths of lions, quenched the violence of fire, waxed valiant in fight ; they wandered about in sheepskins and goatskins, in deserts and in mountains, and in dens and caves of the earth ; they had trial of cruel mockings and scourgings, of bonds and imprisonment ; they were tortured, they were stoned, they were sawn asunder, they were slain with the sword ;" —these are the acts of justifying faith, these are its life, and no one can deny that they are deliberate and completed works ; so that, if faith be justifying, it justifies in and by acts, and not when divested of them.

(4.) But this is not all ; St. Paul uses the *same* instances as St. James. He says, "By *faith* Abraham, when he was tried, offered up Isaac ;" and St. James, "Was not Abraham our father justified by *works*, when he had offered Isaac his son upon the altar ? St. Paul, "By *faith*, the harlot Rahab perished not with them that were disobedient, when she had received the spies with peace ;" St. James, "Likewise also was not Rahab the harlot justified by *works*, when she had received the messengers, and had sent them out another way?" Do not these parallels show that faith is practically identical with the works of faith, and that *when* it justifies, it is as existing in works? And farther, the Apostles are so coincident in expression, as to lead forcibly to the notion, which obtained in the early Church, that St. James was alluding to St. Paul's words, and fixing their sense by an inspired comment. Nor yet is this all ; as if with a wish to show us how to harmonize his teaching with St. Paul's, he uses words, which exactly express and sanction the very mode of reconciliation which I have been enforcing. "Seest thou," he says, "how faith *wrought with* his (Abraham's) works, and by works was faith *made perfect ?*" Thus works are the limit and completion of faith, which gives them a direction and gains from them a substance. He adds to the same purport : " As the body without the spirit is dead, so faith without works is dead also ;" action is the very life of a habit

10.

(5.) The same doctrine is contained all through Scripture ; in which God's mercies are again and again promised to works, sometimes of one kind, sometimes of another, though in all cases as acts and representatives of faith. For instance, Solomon speaks of alms-giving as justifying : "By *mercy* and truth iniquity is purged." So does Daniel, saying to Nebuchadnezzar, "Break off thy sins by righteousness, and thy iniquities by showing mercy to the poor." Our Lord also, "Rather give alms of such things as ye have, and behold all things are clean unto you." And St. James, "mercy rejoiceth against judgment."[1]

In the Prophet Isaiah justification is ascribed to good works generally. He proclaims the gracious message that, "though our sins be as scarlet, they shall be as white as snow," and "though they be red like crimson, they shall be as wool." Here is an evangelical promise ; why then is there nothing about justifying faith ? why, but that faith is signified and is secured by other requisites, by good works ? Accordingly the Prophet thus introduces the message of pardon :—"Wash you, make you clean, put away the evil of your doings from before Mine eyes, cease to do evil, learn to do well, seek judgment, relieve the oppressed, judge the fatherless, plead for the widow." In like manner, Ezekiel : "If the wicked restore the pledge, give again that he had robbed, walk in the statutes of life, without committing iniquity, he shall surely live, he shall not die ; none of his sins that he hath committed *shall be mentioned* unto him."[2] Here again the promise must be evangelical ; for under the Jewish Law there were no "statutes of life."

Phinehas, the son of Eleazar, was justified by an act of zeal : "Then stood up Phinehas and executed judgment, and so the plague was stayed. And that was counted unto him for righteousness unto all generations for evermore."[3]

Zacharias and Elizabeth were "both righteous before God, walking in all the commandments and ordinances

---

[1] Prov. xvi. 6.   Dan. iv. 27.   Luke xi. 41.   James ii. 13.

[2] Isa. i. 16-18.   Ezek. xxxiii. 15, 16.

[3] Ps. cvi. 30, 31.

of the Lord blameless." [1]   Words cannot be stronger to express the justification of these holy persons, than that they were " blameless and righteous *before God ;* " yet this gift is not coupled with faith, but with acts of obedience paid to the special and particular commandments of God.

In like manner St. John teaches, that " walking in the light" justifies us : " If we walk in the light, as He is in the light, we have fellowship one with another, *and the blood* of Jesus Christ His Son cleanseth us from all sin." [2]

To these may be added particular texts in the Gospels, such as Christ's warning to the two brethren of the consequences of becoming His disciples ; His bidding us count the cost of following Him, and to take up our cross, deny ourselves, and come after Him ; moreover in His going into the wilderness, whither the multitudes had to seek Him at the price of privation and suffering.

(6.) And as works are acts of faith, so the mental act of faith is a difficult work.   Thus our Saviour says to the father of the demoniac, " If thou canst believe, all things are possible to him that believeth ;" and he answers, " Lord, I believe ; help Thou mine unbelief." In like manner St. Paul speaks of Abraham " staggering not at the promise of God through unbelief, but being strong in faith, giving glory to God, and being fully persuaded what He had promised He was able also to perform."   " And *therefore,*" he adds, " it was imputed to him for righteousness."

[1] Luke i. 6.   [2] 1 John i. 7 ; iii. 7.

11.

(7.) Lastly, leaving Scripture, I will quote a passage from Luther, in which he will be found to corroborate by his testimony what has been said; not willingly as the extract itself shows, but in consequence of the stress of texts urged against him. I take him, then, for what he says, not for what he does not say:—

"[1] It is usual with us," he says, "to view faith, sometimes apart from its work, sometimes with it. For as an artist speaks variously of his materials, and a gardener of a tree, as in bearing or not, so also the Holy Ghost speaks variously in Scripture concerning faith; at one time of what may be called abstract faith, faith as such: at another of concrete faith, faith in composition, or embodied. Faith, as such, or abstract, is meant, when Scripture speaks of justification, as such, or of the justified. (Vid. Rom. and Gal.) But when it speaks of rewards and works, then it speaks of faith in composition, concrete or embodied. For instance: 'Faith which worketh by love;' 'This do and thou shalt live;' 'If thou wilt enter into life, keep the commandments;' 'Whoso doeth these things, shall live in them;' 'Cease to do evil, learn to do well.' In these and similar texts, which occur without number, in which mention is made

---

[1] Deinde hoc modo etiam distinguere solemus fidem, quod fides aliquando accipiatur extra opus, aliquando cum opere. Ut enim artifex varie de sua materia, et hortulanus de arbore vel nuda vel gestante fructum loquitur, ita et Spiritus Sanctus in Scriptura varie de fide loquitur, jam de fide (ut sic dicam) abstracta vel absoluta, jam de fide concreta, composita, seu incarnata, etc. etc.—In Gal. iii. 10. Vid also f. 347 (1 and 2) Gerh. de Justif. p. 570.

of doing, believing doings are always meant ; as, when it
says, 'This do and thou shalt live,' it means, 'First see
that thou art believing, that thy reason is right and thy
will good, that thou hast faith in Christ ; that being
secured, work.'" Then he proceeds :—" How is it wonderful, that to that embodied faith, that is, faith working,
as was Abel's, in other words, to believing works, are
annexed merits and rewards ? Why should not Scripture speak thus variously of faith, considering it so
speaks even of Christ, God and man ; sometimes of His
entire Person, sometimes of one or other of His two
natures, the Divine or human ? When it speaks of one
or other of these, it speaks of Christ in the abstract ; when
of the Divine made one with the human in one Person, of
Christ as if in composition and incarnate. There is a
well-known rule in the Schools concerning the 'com-
municatio idiomatum,' when the attributes of His divinity
are ascribed to his humanity, as is frequent in Scripture;
for instance, in Luke ii. the Angel calls the infant born of
the Virgin Mary, 'the Saviour' of men, and 'the Lord'
both of Angels and men, and in the preceding chapter,
'the Son of God.' Hence I may say with literal truth,
That Infant who is lying in a manger and in the Virgin's
bosom, created heaven and earth, and is the Lord of
Angels. . . . . As it is truly said, Jesus the Son of Mary
created all things, so is justification ascribed to faith incarnate or to believing deeds."

12.

Such, then, is justifying faith ; why the gift of
justifying has been bestowed upon it, and what its con-

nection is with hope, love, and universal holiness, has
been discussed in former Lectures ; here I am speaking
of its relation to works, and I say that, viewed as justifying, it lives in them. It is not (as it were) a shadow
or phantom, which flits about without voice or power,
but it is faith developed into height and depth and
breadth, as if in a bodily form, not as a picture but as
an image, with a right side and a left, a without and a
within ; not a mere impression or sudden gleam of light
upon the soul, not knowledge, or emotion, or conviction,
which ends with itself, but the beginning of that which
is eternal, the operation of the Indwelling Power which
acts from within us outwards and round about us, works
in us mightily, so intimately with our will as to be in a
true sense one with it ; pours itself out into our whole
mind, runs over into our thoughts, desires, feelings,
purposes, attempts, and works, combines them all together
into one, makes the whole man its one instrument, and
justifies him into one holy and gracious ministry, one
embodied lifelong act of faith, one " sacrifice, holy, acceptable to God, which is his reasonable service." Such is
faith, springing up out of the immortal seed of love, and
ever budding forth in new blossoms and maturing new
fruit, existing indeed in feelings but passing on into acts,
into victories of whatever kind over self, being the
power of the will over the whole soul for Christ's sake,
constraining the reason to accept mysteries, the heart
to acquiesce in suffering, the hand to work, the feet to
run, the voice to bear witness, as the case may be.
These acts we sometimes call labours, sometimes endur-
ances, sometimes confessions, sometimes devotions, some-

times services ; but they are all instances of self-command, arising from Faith seeing the invisible world, and Love choosing it.

It seems, then, that whereas Faith on our part fitly corresponds, or is the correlative, as it is called, to grace on God's part, Sacraments are but the manifestation of grace, and good works are but the manifestation of faith ; so that, whether we say we are justified by faith, or by works or by Sacraments, all these but mean this one doctrine, that we are justified by grace, which is given through Sacraments, impetrated by faith, manifested in works.

NOTE ON LECTURE XII.

FROM what has been said, it would seem that, while works before justification are but conditions and preparations for that gift, works after justification are much more, and that, not only as being intrinsically good and holy, but as being fruits of *faith.* And viewed as one with faith, which is the appointed instrument of justification after Baptism, they are,—(as being connatural with faith and indivisible from it, organs through which it acts and which it hallows),—instruments with faith of the continuance of justification, or, in other words, *of the remission of sin after Baptism.* Since this doctrine sounds strange to the ears of many in this day, and the more so because they have been taught that the Homilies, which our Church has authoritatively sanctioned, are decidedly opposed to it, I make the following extracts from that important work, for the accommodation of the general reader who may not have it at hand. Deeply is it to be regretted that a book, which contains " doctrine " so " godly and wholesome and necessary for *these* Times," as well as for the sixteenth century, should popularly be known only by one or two extracts, to the omission of such valuable matter as shall now be quoted :—

" Our Saviour Christ in the Gospel teacheth us, that it profiteth a man nothing to have in possession all the riches of the whole world, and the wealth and glory thereof, if in the mean season he lose his soul, or do that thing whereby it should become captive unto death, sin, and hell-fire. By the which saying, he not only instructeth us how much the soul's health is to be preferred before worldly commodities, but it also serveth to stir up our minds and to prick us forwards to seek diligently and learn by *what means* we may preserve and keep our souls ever in safety, that is, *how we may recover our health* if it be lost or impaired, and how it may be defended and maintained if once we have it. Yea, He teacheth us also thereby to esteem that *as a precious medicine* and an inestimable jewel, that *hath such strength and virtue in it,* that can either procure or preserve so incomparable a treasure. For if we greatly regard that medicine or salve that is able to heal sundry and grievous diseases of the body, much more will we esteem that which hath *like power over the soul.* And because we might be better assured both to know and to have in readiness *that so profitable a remedy,* He, as a most faithful and loving teacher, showeth Himself both what it is, and where we may find it, and *how we may use and apply it.* For, when both He and His disciples were grievously accused of the Pharisees, to have defiled their souls in breaking the constitutions of the Elders, because they went to meat and washed not their hands before, according to the custom of the Jews, Christ, answering their superstitious complaints, teacheth them *an especial remedy how to keep clean their souls,* notwithstanding the breach of such superstitious orders ; ' *Give alms,*' saith He, ' and behold all things are clean unto you.'

" He teacheth, then, that to be merciful and charitable in helping the poor, *is the means* to keep the soul pure and clean *in the sight of God.* We are taught therefore by this, that *merciful almsgiving is profitable to purge the soul from the infection and filthy spots of sin.* The same lesson doth the Holy Ghost also teach in sundry other places of the Scripture, saying, ' Mercifulness and almsgiving purgeth from all sins, and delivereth from death, and suffereth not the soul to come into darkness.' [1] *A great confidence* may they have *before the high God,* that show mercy and compassion to them that are afflicted. The wise Preacher, the Son of Sirach, confirmeth the same, when he saith, that ' as water quencheth burning fire, even so mercy and alms resisteth and reconcileth sins.' And sure it is, *that mercifulness quaileth the heat of sin so much,* that they shall not take hold upon man to hurt him ; or *if ye have by any infirmity or weak-*

[1] Tobit iv.

ness been touched and annoyed with them, straightways shall mer-cifulness wipe and wash them away, as salves and remedies to heal their sores and grievous diseases. And therefore that holy father Cyprian taketh good occasion to exhort earnestly to the merciful work, to giving alms and helping the poor, and then he admonisheth to consider how wholesome and profitable is it to relieve the needy and help the afflicted, *by the which we may purge our sins* and heal our wounded souls."

Such is the virtue of works, not before justification, but after, as the means of keeping and restoring, not of procuring it, as fruits of faith done in the grace of Christ and by the inspiration of His Spirit, not as dead works done in the flesh, and displeasing to God. Attention should be especially called to a parallelism between one sentence in this extract and what was quoted in Lecture X. (pp. 223, 224) from the Sermon on the Passion, as showing how our Reformers *identified* faith and works, not in idea, but in fact. The one Homily says "It remaineth that I show unto you how to apply Christ's death and passion to our comfort as a *medicine to our wounds.* . . . Here is the mean, whereby we must apply the fruits of Christ's death unto our deadly wound, . . . namely, faith." The other speaks of alms as "a precious *medicine*, a profitable *remedy*," which we are to "use and apply," "*salves* and *remedies* to heal" our "sores and grievous diseases."

It must be observed, moreover, that though faith is the appointed means of pleading Christ's merits, and so of cleansing (as it were) works done in faith from their adhering imperfection, yet that after all those works, though mixed with evil, are good in themselves, as being the fruit of the Spirit. Hence, in the passage which follows what has been quoted, very slight mention is made of faith, and the grace of God is made all in all, as "working in us both to will and to do," and "giving us power to get wealth;"[1] the contrast lying not between faith and works, but between God's doings and man's doings. Nay, even when the image of the tree and fruit is introduced, it is interpreted of the *grace* of God the Holy Ghost in us, and of the *effects* in us of His gracious Indwelling.

[1] Deut. viii. 18.

"But here some one will say unto me, If alms-giving and our charitable works towards the poor be able to *wash away sins*, to *reconcile us to God*, to *deliver us from the peril of damnation*, and *make us sons and heirs of God's kingdom*, then are Christ's merits defaced, and His blood shed in vain, then are we justified by works, and by our deeds may we merit heaven ; then do we in vain believe that Christ died for to put away our sins and that He rose for our justification, as St. Paul teacheth." Now, here let us observe, this is the very objection urged against our Divines, such as Bishop Wilson, for words far short of those admitted by the Homily as true. Let us see how the writer answers it. "But ye shall understand, dearly beloved, that neither those places of Scripture before alleged, neither the doctrine of the Blessed Martyr Cyprian, neither *any other* godly and learned man,"—for instance, those excellent writers now so unworthily censured,—"when they, in extolling the dignity, profit, fruit, and effect of virtuous and liberal alms, do say that it washeth away sins and bringeth us to the favour of God, do mean, that our work and charitable deed is the *original cause* of our acceptation before God, or that *for the dignity or worthiness thereof* our sins be washed away, and we purged and cleansed from all the spots of our iniquity ; for that were indeed to deface Christ, and to defraud Him of His glory. But they mean this, and this is the understanding of these and such like sayings, that God, of His mercy and especial favour towards them whom He hath appointed to everlasting salvation, hath so offered His grace especially, and they have so received it fruitfully, that although, by reason of their sinful living outwardly, they seemed before to have been the children of wrath and perdition, yet now *the Spirit of God mightily working in them*, unto obedience to God's will and commandments, they declare by their outward deeds and life, in the showing of mercy and charity (which cannot come but of the Spirit of God and His special grace), that they are the undoubted children of God appointed to everlasting life. . . . For as the good fruit is not the cause that the tree is good, but the tree must first be good before it can bring forth good fruit, so the good deeds of man are not the cause that maketh man good, but he is first made good by the Spirit and grace of God that effectually worketh in him, and afterward he bringeth forth good fruits. . . . . As the true Christian man, in the thankfulness of his heart for the redemption of his soul, purchased by Christ's death, showeth kindly by the fruit of his faith his obedience to God, so the other, as a merchant with God, doth all for his own gain, thinketh to win heaven by the merit of his works, and so defaceth and obscureth the price of Christ's blood, who only wrought our purgation. The meaning then of these sayings in Scripture, ' alms-deeds do wash away our sins,' and ' mercy to the poor doth blot out our offences,' is, that *we doing these things* according to God's will and our duty, *have* our sins indeed washed away and our offences blotted out, not for the *worthiness* of them, but by the grace of God which worketh all in all, and that *for the promise* that *God hath made to them that are obedient unto His commandments,* that He which is the Truth might be justified in performing the truth due to His true promise." (This seems an allusion to a statement of St. Austin's) :—" Alms-deeds do wash away our sins, because God doth vouchsafe then to *repute us* as clean and pure " (that is, justify), " *when* we do them for His sake, and not because they deserve or merit our purging, or for that they have any such strength and virtue in themselves. . . . The godly do learn that when the Scriptures say that by good and merciful works we are *reconciled to God's favour,* we are taught then to know what Christ by His intercession and mediation obtaineth for us of His Father *when we be obedient* to His will ; yea, they learn, in such manner of speaking, a comfortable argument of God's singular favour and love, that attributeth that unto us, and to our doings, that He by His Spirit worketh in us, and through His grace procureth for us. . . . Thus they humble themselves and are exalted of God ; they count themselves vile, and of God are counted pure and clean ; they condemn themselves, and are justified of God ; they think themselves unworthy of the earth, and of God are thought worthy of heaven."—Sermon of Alms-deeds, Part II.

　　To add passages to this most striking testimony would be

unnecessary, were it not important to show that our Formularies consistently put forth the doctrine contained in it. For instance, in the first Sermon on the Passion, justification is said to be gained through forgiveness of injuries and mutual forbearance : " Let us then be favourable one to another, and pray we one for another that we may be healed from all frailties of our life, the less to offend one the other ; and that we may be of one mind and one spirit, agreeing together in brotherly love and concord, even like the dear children of God. *By these means* shall we *move* God to *be merciful to our sins ;* yea, and we shall be hereby the more ready to receive our Saviour and Maker in His blessed Sacrament, to our everlasting comfort and health of soul." Again, soon afterwards : " Unless we forgive other, we shall never be forgiven of God. No, not all the prayers and good works of other can pacify God unto us, unless we be at peace and at one with our neighbour. Not all our *deeds* and *good works* can *move* God to forgive us our debts to Him except *we forgive to other.'* Now it is presumed the word " move," used in these passages, implies that forgiveness of injuries is an immediate means or instrument of our forgiveness at God's hand ; not indeed mere forgiveness accorded from any motive, but forgiveness which is of faith.

Again, at the end of the Sermon of Charity :—" If we thus direct our life by Christian love and charity, *then* Christ doth promise and assure us, that He loveth us, that we be the children of our heavenly Father, *reconciled to His favour,* very members of Christ."

To the same purpose surely are such exhortations as the following from the Sermon on the Resurrection :—" Apply yourselves, good friends, to *live in Christ, that* Christ may *still* live in you, whose favour and assistance if ye have, then have ye everlasting life already within you, then can nothing hurt you." Godly and holy living was the *immediate tenure* of Christ's inward presence, or of justification in God's sight.

On turning to the Prayer Book, what first calls for remark is the collection of introductory Sentences prefixed to the Exhortation. It is quite evident that these Sentences are intended to proclaim God's *forgiveness of sin*, as a fit introduction to the Confession. They are a sort of gospel herald, inviting all who hear to come to Christ. Now is faith mentioned as *the* mean by which pardon and acceptance after sinning may be obtained ? by a singular chance (so to speak) it is not mentioned in any one of them ; most singular and observable indeed, considering the Sentences are the selection of the Reformers, who, if any men, were alive to the necessity of faith in order to justification. Nothing can show more clearly that, while they considered it the only instrument of justification, they considered also that good works (of whatever kind) were in fact the coming to God, and the concrete presence of faith. Certainly, the view of religion popular in this day would have confined itself to such texts as are most impressively cited in the Communion Service,[1] instead of putting forth the profitableness of " turning away from the wickedness we have committed," of " acknowledging our transgressions," and of " a broken spirit." Contrition, confession, humiliation, deprecation, repentance, and amendment, are separately urged upon us ; faith is omitted,—not as unnecessary, but as being implied *in* all of these.

In like manner in the Exhortation we are enjoined to confess our sins " with a *humble, lowly, penitent,* and *obedient* heart, to the end that we may obtain forgiveness of the same." Why are we not told to " come in faith, and to apprehend and appropriate the free gift ?"

Again, in the Collect for Ash Wednesday, we pray God to " *create and make in us new and contrite hearts, that* we worthily *lamenting* our sins and acknowledging our wretchedness, may obtain *perfect remission and forgiveness.*" Are not renewal, contrition, and confession, here represented as the *immediate* causes or instruments, on our part, of justification ?

So again, in the Visitation of the Sick, the directions given to the sick person in order to the forgiveness of his sins, are " accusing and condemning himself of his own faults," " believing the Articles of our Faith," " repenting of his sins," " being in charity

---

[1] John iii. 16 etc.

LECTURE XIII.

IT may be asked, What was the fault of the Jews in their use of their Law, which led them to reject Christ when He came? That Law was from God; they honoured it as such; they were told to adhere to it, and they did adhere; they thanked God for it; they thanked God for the power of obeying it; they thanked God for the electing grace which had given them in it a pledge of His favour above the rest of mankind. All this surely, it may be said, was right and praiseworthy; it was proceeding in the way of God's commandments, and seemed to promise, that when His perfect truth was revealed, it would be obeyed as dutifully as that portion of it which had already been given. This might have been expected; yet when Christ came, He was rejected.

We all know how to answer this question, viz. by explaining that the Jews considered their Law, not imperfect, as it was, but perfect; not as a means, but as the end. They rested in it, and though they nominally expected a Messiah, they did not in their thoughts place Him above the Law, or consider Him the Lord of the Law, but made their Law everything, and "the Desire of all nations" nothing. He was the true mode of approaching God, the sole Justifier of the soul; they considered their Law to be such. And so, in the words

LECTURE XIII.

IT may be asked, What was the fault of the Jews in their use of their Law, which led them to reject Christ when He came? That Law was from God; they honoured it as such; they were told to adhere to it, and they did adhere; they thanked God for it; they thanked God for the power of obeying it; they thanked God for the electing grace which had given them in it a pledge of His favour above the rest of mankind. All this surely, it may be said, was right and praiseworthy; it was proceeding in the way of God's commandments, and seemed to promise, that when His perfect truth was revealed, it would be obeyed as dutifully as that portion of it which had already been given. This might have been expected; yet when Christ came, He was rejected.

We all know how to answer this question, viz. by explaining that the Jews considered their Law, not imperfect, as it was, but perfect; not as a means, but as the end. They rested in it, and though they nominally expected a Messiah, they did not in their thoughts place Him above the Law, or consider Him the Lord of the Law, but made their Law everything, and "the Desire of all nations" nothing. He was the true mode of approaching God, the sole Justifier of the soul; they considered their Law to be such. And so, in the words

of the Apostle, "they, being ignorant of God's righteousness, and going about to establish their own righteousness, did not submit themselves unto the righteousness of God." They imagined that they could be both
justified and sanctified by the Law, whereas Christ was
the end of the Law both for holiness and acceptance.
Now it is a very common charge against the Ancient and
Catholic view of the Gospel, that it throws us back into
a Jewish state, and subjects us to the dominion of the
Law. On the other hand, from various remarks made
in the course of these Lectures, it may be seen that that
modern system, whose very life and breath (as I may
say) consist in the maintenance of this charge, is itself
not altogether free from the error which it denounces.
Rather, as I would maintain, it is deeply imbued with it,
having fallen, after the usual manner of self-appointed
champions and reformers, into the evil which it professed
to remedy. This, then, shall be our subject in this
concluding Lecture, in which I shall suggest some
remarks on the imputation of *legalism*, as it is called,
wrongly urged against Catholic Truth, rightly urged
against Protestant error ;—not that I propose to enter
upon a formal discussion of it, which would carry us far
away from our main subject.

2.

1. It may be objected, then, that, as Judaism interposed the Mosaic Law between the soul and Christ,
turning a means into an end, a resting-place into an
abode, so the Christian Church, Ancient and Catholic,
also obscures the sight and true worship of Him, and

that, by insisting on Creeds, on Rites, and on Works ;—
that by its Creeds it leads to Bigotry, by its Rites to
Formality, and by its doctrine concerning Works to Self-
righteousness.   Such is the charge.

Now here I most fully grant that those who in their
thoughts substitute a Creed, or a Ritual, or external
obedience, for Christ, do resemble the Jews.   Nay, I do
not care to deny (what, however, I leave it for others to
prove), that there are, and have been, Catholic Christians
open to the charge of forgetting the " One Thing needful,"
in their over-anxiety about correct faith, ceremonial
observances, or acts of charity and piety.   But I will
say this :—that, on the face of the case, such an error is
a great *inconsistency;* and no system can be made
answerable for consequences which flow from a neglect
of its own provisions.   When, for instance, the Church
bids us be accurate in what we hold concerning the
Person of Christ, she is thereby declaring that Christ is
the Object of our worship ; when she bids us frequent
His House, she implies that He is in it ; when she says,
good works are acceptable, she means acceptable to Him.
The Church has never laid it down that we are justified
by Orthodoxy only, or by Baptism only, or by Works
only ; much less by some certain spiritual feelings or
experiences ; and less still has she decided that to
believe this was the one fundamental truth of religion.
And if this be turned into a charge against her, that
whereas there is One only Saviour Invisible, she has
made the visible instruments and means of approaching
Him many, and so by their very multiplicity has hidden
Him, I reply, that if this were a fair argument, it ought

to tell against the Mosaic Law also, as if its divinely
appointed ceremonies themselves were to blame for the
blindness of the Jews ; but if the Jews themselves were
in fault, and not their Law, so there is no antecedent
objection against Catholic Christianity, (and such objections only have I here to consider), for its insisting on
Baptism and Orthodoxy and Works, and many things
more, even though in individual cases it has occasioned
forgetfulness of Him, by whom these conditions and
channels of grace have been appointed.

So much at first sight : now let us descend into
particulars.

3.

(1.) As to the doctrine of works leading to self-righteousness, I pass it over here, though much might be said
about it, both because I have incidentally answered the
charge in the foregoing Lectures, and in various Sermons,
and because it is a mere theory set up to frighten the
mind from strict obedience, which a man will best refute
for himself, by obeying, and trying whether he becomes
self-righteous, except so far as all we are and all we do
will be used as weapons against our souls by our spiritual
enemy, unless we are on our guard. So I pass on.

(2.) Next, as to the Creeds of the Church ; I grant
that the Athanasian Creed certainly may be taken by
careless readers to imply that orthodoxy is the ultimate
end of religion ; but surely it will seem otherwise on due
consideration. For no one can deny, looking at it as a
whole, that it is occupied in *glorifying* Father, Son, and
Holy Ghost, in declaring Their infinite perfections ; so
much so, that it has sometimes been considered what it

really is in form, a Psalm or Hymn of Praise to the Blessed Trinity, as the Te Deum is, rather than a Creed. Nay, this is its characteristic, not only in its general structure, but in its direct enunciation of the Sacred Mystery ; which is put forth not as an end in itself, but evidently in order to glorify God in His incomprehensible majesty, and to warn us of the danger of thinking of Him in a chance way, and of speculating concerning Him without reverence.   For instance, it begins by stating that the purpose of the Catholic Faith is, not intellectual accuracy, but "that we *worship* One God in Trinity, and Trinity in Unity ;" and ends its confession with a similar intimation, that "in all things, as is aforesaid, the Unity in Trinity, and the Trinity in Unity, is to be *worshipped.*" And this agrees with what we know historically, that doctrinal statements on these high subjects are negative rather than positive ; intended to forbid speculations, which are sure to spring up in the human mind, and to anticipate its attempts at systematic views by showing the ultimate abyss at which all rightly conducted inquiries arrive, not to tell us anything definite and real, which we did not know before, or which is beyond the faith of the most unlearned.   Or, again, they are safeguards, summing up in brief what the *whole* Scripture doctrine on the subject implies, and thus directing us as landmarks in speaking and teaching on the subject. Thus, for instance, the statement "Not by conversion of the Godhead into flesh, but by taking of the Manhood into God," has somewhat the same drift as the formula of "justification by faith only," as explained by Melanch-thon and adopted by our Church ; except that the latter expresses a principle, and the former a fact. However, they both are framed by the mind's reflecting, in the latter case on Christ's work, in the former on His Person. By resting on our mere knowledge of the one or the other, and making the statement itself our end, we become bigots ; and not less in the latter case than in the former. As, then, the doctrine of justification, as held by our Church, is not answerable for such abuse of itself, neither, on the other hand, is the statement in the Athanasian Creed. Each may be used as a touchstone or measure of doctrine ; neither has a direct and immediate reference to practice. I shall say no more on this part of the subject either ; but pass on to the consideration of the Ordinances.

(3.) The Ordinances of the Church then are specially accused of detaining the worshipper from Him towards whom they profess to lead, and of causing *formality* and *superstition.* Now it must be borne in mind, that whether our doctrine concerning them is *superstitious* or not, depends simply on the circumstance whether it is true or not. If it be not true, I grant it becomes *ipso facto* superstitious. To ascribe regeneration to the Word and Water in Baptism, is either a Scripture duty, or a virtual breach of the second commandment.

Superstition is the substitution of human for divine means of approaching God. Before He has spoken, it is religious to approach Him in what seems the most acceptable way ; but the same principle which leads a pious mind to devise ordinances, when none are given, will lead it, under a Revelation, to adhere to those which are given. He who made the creature, gives it its uses ;

He can make bread of stones, or bid the fig-tree wither.
Things are what He makes them, and we must not
"make to ourselves," lest we make idols. Thus it was
a superstition in the Jews to use other than the appointed
rites under the Law, and a superstition to observe
those rites under the Gospel; a superstition to sacrifice
to Baal then, and to keep the Sabbath now. It was a
superstition to worship graven images, no superstition to
"rise up and worship" towards "the cloudy pillar" when
it "descended."[1]   It is a superstition in the Christian
Church to assign such a virtue to penance or to an indulgence as Christ has not given; it is a superstition to pay
an honour to images, which Christ has forbidden. Superstition, then, keeps the mind from Christ, because it origi-
nates in a plain act of self-will : a rite is not properly
superstitious, unless it is such will-worship. And hence
it is but one form of presumptuousness or profaneness,
as the history of the Jews shows us. It is superstitious
to ascribe power to the creature where God has not given
it ; and profane to deny it where He has. If, then, to
look for regeneration through Baptism be superstitious,
as it would be, supposing God has not made Baptism
the channel of it, so, if He has, it is profane not to look
for it through that rite. The question lies in this alternative of profaneness or superstition. If the Catholic
doctrine be true, it is not superstitious ; if the Anti-
catholic be not true, it is profane. This is the real state
of the case, and can be settled only by an appeal to the
matter of fact, whether the doctrine is or is not revealed.
Hence it is plainly nugatory to urge against us that our

[1] Exod. xxxiii. 10.

ordinances *are* superstitious, for this is (what is called)
"to beg the question." The only real definition of a
superstitious ordinance is, that it is one which God
has actually or virtually forbidden ; so the objection
when drawn out will really stand thus :—"The Catholic
ordinances are mere inventions of man *because* they are
superstitious ; and they are superstitious, *because* they
are not divine appointments." When they are proved to
be not divine, we will grant, without the intermediate
step, that they are human.

However, it may be objected that we are open to
the charge of *formality* at least, whatever difficulties may
beset the question of superstition ; that any system of
religion which so multiplies and diversifies its visible
means of grace, as thereby to deny the direct communion of God with the soul, effectually shuts out the
thought of Him ; that it makes the worshipper practically dependent on things sensible, and introduces a
Pantheistic spirit into the Gospel. Whatever be the
force of this antecedent objection in a question of *fact*, such
as that concerning the contents of a Revelation, let those
answer to whom it applies. If there be a Church system
anywhere, which makes itself co-extensive with the Gospel Dispensation, which professes to be the mirror of all
that passes before the Divine Mind, and the organ of His
diversified dealings with the conscience of man, which
keeps pace with what is infinite and eternal, and ex-
hausts the Abyss of grace, such a system is certainly
open to the objection. And as far as any theology, such
as that of the Roman Schools, has approximated to such
an assumption in practice, so far it is concerned to

answer it.   But how does it apply to our own, which on
the face of it has never so represented the Church's
office, or claimed for her so vast a delegation of power?
It is often said of us, by way of reproach, that we leave
Dissenters to the " uncovenanted mercies of God ;" nay,
in a sense, we leave ourselves ; there is not one of us
but has exceeded by transgressions the revealed Ritual,
and finds himself in consequence thrown upon those
infinite resources of Divine Love which are stored in
Christ, but have not been drawn out into form in the
appointments of the Gospel.   How can we be said to
place the Church instead of Christ, who say that there
is no other ordained method on earth for the absolute
pardon of sin but Baptism ; and that Baptism cannot be
repeated ?   Surely, while English divines deny the existence of any Sacrament like Baptism after Baptism,
whatever objections are brought against them, they cannot be accused of substituting the Church for Christ.

4.

But it may be said that the real objection to Forms
lies, not in their number, be they many or few, nor in
their being unauthorized, though this of course is an
aggravation, but in this, that they *are* forms ; that by a
form is meant a standing rule, a permanent ordinance ;
and that it is this which keeps the soul from God, whatever degree of spiritual benefit, greater or less, be ascribed
to the observance of it.   Whatever Baptism be supposed
to effect, if it effects anything, if it is necessary for any
blessing, if it be of continual obligation in the Church,
so far it throws a shadow, not light, upon her.

All we mean by one thing being the cause of another, it may be said, is its being its invariable antecedent. As we all call the Sun the cause of summer, because its presence is the one necessary condition of summer, with as good a reason may Baptism be called the cause of regeneration, if it must always precede regeneration. And if even educated persons are found to consider the Sun the cause of light, and forget God, much more will the imagination of the multitude practically substitute Baptism for regeneration. Accordingly this, it may be argued, is the great advantage of considering preaching as the ordinary means of regeneration and conversion, that it obviates the possibility of an invariable condition, and the formality consequent thereupon. Preaching cannot be called a form, because it is not of a permanent and uniform character. Preachers rise and fall, come and go ; no two are alike ; no two speak in the same way ; they allow us the liberty of judging for ourselves concerning them, and of depending on our own convictions. They do but stimulate and feed our mind, —they do not oppress it with a yoke of bondage. They are amenable to their flocks ; and are honoured, not for their office-sake, but for their usefulness ; whereas the ministers and rites of the Church are idols, worse than pagan, because the worshipper cannot break them at his will.

Now it is plain that such a line of reasoning would prove, did not our senses convince us otherwise, that the Sun could not be constituted as the fountain of light and heat. Were the arguments for considering Baptism an ordained means of grace ever so insufficient, the danger

of its superstitious use would be no proof against its being so ordained, while the miserable idolatries are on
record which have been directed towards the Sun. Moreover, this argument from the abuse of a thing against
the use, comes with a bad grace from an age, in which,
more than in any other, the powers of nature are extolled
to the neglect of Divine Providence and Governance.
If the doctrines of the Church are chargeable with having led to reliance on the creature, are not the useful arts
much more? Does not Baptism, even when most mistaken and abused, remind us more of heaven, than do
those physical sciences, and mechanical and other inventions, which are now regarded as almost the long sought
summum bonum of the species? If Catholic teaching
has led to superstition, has not the new philosophy led
to profaneness?

This objection is still more unreasonable when applied
to the visible instruments of religion, because neither
under the Law nor under the Gospel have they been,
strictly speaking, of an abiding nature, not permanent in
actual and material form, but only in the abstract ordinance. The means, through which the gifts are conveyed,
are transitory; as our Lord's appearances after His resurrection. His glory in the cloud, at which the people
"rose up and worshipped," was but now and then and
according to his will; the manna might not be kept till
the morning; again, of the Paschal Lamb nothing was
to remain till the morning; and the Brazen Serpent,
which for a moment they were bid "look upon," that
they might live, became an idol on being kept, and was
broken by Hezekiah because honoured "*unto those days,*"

and therefore, as was thereby necessarily implied, not as a mere symbol, but for its own sake, and with idolatrous worship. In like manner our ordinances are transitory ; and it is remarkable, that the imputation of idolatry cast by Protestants upon the Church of Rome mainly arises from her giving a permanence to objects or instruments of devotion, as an examination of her religious observances obviously suggests.

Moreover, it may fairly be questioned whether religion does not necessarily imply the belief in such sensible tokens of God's favour, as the Sacraments are accounted by the Church. Religion is of a personal nature, and implies the acknowledgment of a particular Providence, of a God speaking, not merely to the world at large, but to this person or that, to me and not to another. The Sacred Volume is a common possession, and speaks to one man as much and as little as to his neighbour. Our nature requires something special ; and if we refuse what has been actually given, we shall be sure to adopt what has not been given. We shall set up calves at Dan and Bethel, if we give up the true Temple and the Apostolic Ministry. This we see fulfilled before our eyes in many ways ; those who will not receive Baptism as the token of God's election, have recourse to certain supposed experiences of it in their hearts. This is the idolatry of a refined age, in which the superstitions of barbarous times displease, in consequence of their grossness. Men congratulate themselves on their emancipation from forms and their enlightened worship, when they are but in the straight course to a worse captivity, and are exchanging dependence on the creature for dependence on self.

5.

2. And thus we are led to the consideration of the opposite side of the question before us, that is, whether at this day it is not rather the accusing party itself than the Church that is accused, to which the charge of Judaism properly attaches. At first sight a suggestion of this kind will look like a refinement, or as only a sharp retort urged in controversy, and not to be seriously dwelt on. But I wish it dwelt on most seriously, and if rejected, rejected after being dwelt on. I observe, then, that what the Jews felt concerning their Law, is exactly what many upholders of the tenet of "faith only," feel concerning what they consider faith ; that they substitute faith for Christ ; that they so regard it, that instead of being the way to Him, it is in the way ; that they make it a something to rest in ; nay, that they alter the meaning of the word, as the Jews altered the meaning of the word Law ; in short, that, under the pretence of light and liberty, they have brought into the Gospel the narrow, minute, technical, nay, I will say carnal and hollow system of the Pharisees. Let me explain what I mean.

I would say this then :—that a system of doctrine has risen up during the last three centuries, in which faith or spiritual-mindedness is contemplated and rested on as the end of religion instead of Christ. I do not mean to say that Christ is not mentioned as the Author of all good, but that stress is laid rather on the believing than on the Object of belief, on the comfort and persuasiveness of the doctrine rather than on the doctrine itself. And in this way religion is made to consist in contemplating ourselves instead of Christ ; not simply in looking to Christ, but in ascertaining that we look to Christ, not in His Divinity and Atonement, but in our conversion and our faith in those truths.

Of course nothing is more natural or suitable than for a Christian to describe and dwell on the difference between one who believes and one who does not believe. The fault here spoken of is the giving to our "experiences" a more prominent place in our thoughts than to the nature, attributes, and work of Him from whom they profess to come,—the insisting on them as a special point for the consideration of all who desire to be recognized as converted and elect. When men are to be exhorted to newness of life, the true Object to be put before them, as I conceive, is "Jesus Christ, the same yesterday, to-day, and for ever ;" the true Gospel preaching is to enlarge, as they can bear it, on the Person, natures, attributes, offices, and work of Him who once regenerated them, and is now ready to pardon ; to dwell upon His recorded words and deeds on earth ; to declare reverently and adoringly His mysterious greatness as the Only-begotten Son, One with the Father, yet distinct from Him ; of Him, yet not apart from Him ; eternal, yet begotten ; a Son, yet as if a servant ; and to combine and to contrast His attributes and relations to us as God and man, as our Mediator, Saviour, Sanctifier, and Judge. The true preaching of the Gospel is to preach Christ. But the fashion of the day has been, instead of this, to preach conversion ; to attempt to convert by insisting on conversion ; to exhort men to undergo a change ; to tell them to be sure they look at Christ, instead of simply holding up Christ to them ; to tell them to have faith, rather than to supply its Object; to lead them to stir up and work up their minds, instead of impressing on them the thought of Him who can savingly work in them ; to bid them take care that their faith is justifying, not dead, formal, self-righteous, and merely moral, whereas the image of Christ fully delineated of itself destroys deadness, formality, and self-righteousness ; to rely on words, vehemence, eloquence, and the like, rather than to aim at conveying the one great evangelical idea whether in words or not. And thus faith and (what is called) spiritual-mindedness are dwelt on as *ends,* and obstruct the view of Christ, just as the Law was perverted by the Jews.

6.

I will take two passages from writers of the last century, out of a hundred which might be selected, in illustration of this over-earnest dwelling upon the state of our minds, with a view to effect in us real and spiritual conversion.

The following is an extract from a letter addressed to a person ignorant of the truth, and whom the writer was endeavouring to enlighten. After having mentioned the doctrine of the Trinity, he says, " I believe, that, whatever *notions* a person may take up from education or system, no one ever did, or ever will, *feel* himself and own himself to be such a lost, miserable, hateful sinner, unless he be powerfully and supernaturally convinced by the Spirit of God." Doubtless ; but the question is whether we should simply preach the doctrine of the Trinity, trusting to God to rescue it from being a mere notion, and to bring it home with power to the mind, or whether we are more likely to prevent its being a notion by cautioning men against its being a notion. To proceed : "There is, when God pleases, a *certain light* thrown into the soul, which differs not merely in degree, but in kind, *toto genere,* from anything that can be effected or produced by moral suasion or argument. But, (to take in another of your queries), the Holy Spirit teaches or reveals no new truths, either of doctrine or precept, but only enables us to *understand* what is already revealed in Scripture." Most true ; but to tell a person so is not the way to convert him. We do not affect people by *telling* them to weep or laugh ; let us preach Christ, and leave the effect to God, to prosper it or not. He continues : "Here a *change* takes place ; the person that was spiritually blind begins to *see.* The sinner's character, as described in the word of God, *he finds* to be a description of himself ; that he is afar off, a stranger, a rebel ; that he has hitherto lived in vain. Now he begins to see the necessity of an Atonement, an Advocate, a Shepherd, a Comforter ; he can no more trust to his own wisdom, strength, and goodness ; but accounting all his former gain but loss, for the excellency of the knowledge of Christ, he renounces every other refuge, and ventures his all upon the person, work, and promises of the Redeemer. . . . . *Without this awakened state of mind* a divine, reputed orthodox, will blunder

wretchedly even in defending his own opinions."[1]   Now
that no effect follows upon such representations I am
very far from saying; experience shows the contrary.
But for the most part it will be produced by sympathy,
and will consist in imitation.   Men will feel this and
that, because they are told to feel it, because they think
they ought to feel it, because others say they feel it
themselves; not spontaneously, as the consequence of
the objects presented to them.   And hence the absence
of nature, composure, unobtrusiveness, healthy and un-
studied feeling, variety and ease of language, among
those who are thus converted, even when that conversion
is sincere.   Convulsions are in their view the only real
manifestation of spiritual life and strength.

The other passage which I proposed to quote runs as
follows :—" *Beware of mistaking mere external works for
true holiness.*   Holiness is seated in the heart ; every act
receives its goodness from the principles from which it
flows, and the end to which it is directed.   The external
works of the generally esteemed, devout, decent, and
charitable, are usually as far from being acts of real holiness, as any of the enormities of those who proclaim their
shame as avowed children of disobedience : they proceed
from as unrenewed hearts, from as unchristian tempers,
and are directed to as unsanctified ends."   Still, supposing it, the question is whether one tends ever so little

---

[1] Newton's Cardiphonia, Letter II. to Mr. S.   Again : "As you
tell me you *never remember a time* when you were not conscious before
God of great unworthiness, and intervals of earnest endeavours to serve
Him, though not with the same success, yet something in the same
way as at present ; this is but saying in other words, *you never remember a time when old things passed away, and all things became new.*"

to escape the danger of having counterfeit holiness instead of true in consequence of this sort of warning. Just the reverse ; the more you fasten men's thoughts on themselves, the more you lead them to unconscious show, pretence, and duplicity. To proceed : "You may attend your Church twice on Sunday ; you may go on week-days too. You may frequent the Sacrament. You may say prayer in your house and alone. You may read the Psalms and Lessons for the day. You may be 'no extortioner or unjust.' You may be in many things unlike other men ; neither given to swear, nor drink, nor lewdness, nor extravagance. You may be a tender parent, a careful master, and what the world calls an honest man ; yea, you may withal be very liberal to the poor ; be regarded in the world as a pattern of piety and charity, and respected as one of the best sort of people in it ; and yet, with all this, be the very character, which, ' though highly esteemed amongst men, is an abomination in the sight of God.'

"For if you have never seen" (not your Saviour, but) " *your* ' *desperately wicked heart,*'—been united to Christ" (by His love and grace ? no, but) " *by faith,—renounced* your own righteousness to be found in Him, and *receive* from Him newness," (receive, as if the great thing was not His giving but our taking), "if you *know not experimentally what is meant* by 'fellowship with the Father and His Son Jesus Christ ;' " (observe, not " if you *have* not fellowship," but "if you *know* not you have ;" and this self-seeking, as it may be truly called, is named *experimental* religion ;) "if your *devotion* hath not been inspired 'by faith which worketh by love ;' if your *worship* hath not been in 'spirit and truth,' from a real *sense* of your wants, and an earnest *desire* and *expectation* of receiving from Him 'in whom all fulness dwells ;' if this hath not been your case, your devotions have been unmeaning ceremony, your book, not your heart, hath spoken : and instead of the fervent effectual prayer of the righteous man, your babblings have been no better than the sounding brass and tinkling cymbal."[1]   Poor miserable captives, to whom such doctrine is preached as the Gospel!   What! is *this* the liberty wherewith Christ has made us free, and wherein we stand, the home of our own thoughts, the prison of our own sensations, the province of self, a monotonous confession of what we are by nature, not what Christ is in us, and a resting at best not on His love towards us, but in our faith towards Him !   This is nothing but a specious idolatry ; a man thus minded does not simply think of God when he prays to Him, but is observing whether he feels properly or not ; does not believe and obey, but considers it enough to be conscious that he is what he calls warm and spiritual ; does not contemplate the grace of the Blessed Eucharist, the Body and Blood of His Saviour Christ, except—O shameful and fearful error!—except as a quality of his own mind.[2]

---

[1] Haweis' Sermons, p. 221-3.

[2] A remarkable contrast between our Church's and this false view of religion is afforded in the respective modes of treating a death-bed in the Visitation of the Sick, and a popular modern work, the Dairyman's Daughter.   The latter runs thus :—" My dear Friend, do you not FEEL *that you are supported?*   The Lord deals very gently with me, she replied.—Are not His promises *very precious to you?*   They are all yea and amen in Christ Jesus.—Are you in much bodily pain ?   So little,

Even Luther, in his zeal against the undue estimation
of works in his own day, teaches his followers a lesson

that I almost forget it.—How good the Lord is! And how unworthy
am I. . . . Do you *experience any doubts or temptations* on the subject
of your eternal safety? No, sir; the Lord deals very gently with me,
and gives me peace.—What are your *views* of the dark valley of death,
now that you are passing through it? *It is not dark,"* etc. etc. Now,
if it be said that such questions and answers are not only in their place
innocent, but natural and beautiful, I answer, that this is not the point
here, but this: viz. they are evidently intended, whatever their merits,
as a pattern of *what death-bed examinations should be.* Such is the
Visitation of the Sick in the 19th century. Now let us listen to the
nervous and stern tone of the 16th. In the Prayer Book the Minister
is instructed to say to the person visited,—" Forasmuch as after this
life there is *an account* to be given unto the *Righteous Judge,* etc. . . .
I require you to examine yourself and your estate, both towards God
and man; so that, etc. Therefore I shall rehearse to you *the Articles
of our Faith, that you may know whether you do believe* as a Christian
man should, or no. Dost thou believe in God the Father Almighty?"
etc. . . After mentioning the Objects of faith, the service proceeds to
speak of the Works: "Then shall the Minister examine whether he
repent him truly of his sins, and be in *charity* with all the world; ex-
horting him to *forgive* from the bottom of his heart all persons who
have offended him; and if he hath offended any other to *ask them forgiveness;* and where he hath done injury or wrong to any man, that he
make amends to the utmost of his power. . . . . The minister should
not omit earnestly to move such sick persons as are of ability, to be
liberal to the poor." Then the sick man is to be "moved to make a
special *confession* of his sins, if he feel his conscience troubled with any
weighty matter.'" Creeds and Works! let but Rites be added, and
then we shall have all three offences, as men now speak, Bigotry,
Superstition, and Self-righteousness; and in truth the third stumbling-
block does follow. "After which Confession, the Priest shall *absolve*
him, if he humbly and heartily desire it, after this sort; 'Our Lord
Jesus Christ, who hath left power to His Church to absolve all sinners
who truly repent and believe in Him,' etc. Such is the contrast
between the "dreamy talk" of modern Protestantism, and "holy fear's
stern glow" in the Church Catholic.

here. Commenting on the text, " Yet *not I*, but Christ liveth in me," he uses the following energetic words :—
"[1] Here," says he, "the Apostle clearly shows how he lives ; and he teaches what Christian righteousness is, viz. that with which Christ lives in us, not that which is in our own person. And so when we treat of Christian righteousness, we must altogether put away our person. . . . . . . If I look at myself only, Christ being excluded, *it is over with me.* For then immediately the thought comes across me, ' Christ is in heaven, thou upon earth, how wilt thou now come to Him ?' I will live spiritually, and do as the Law demands, and so as to enter into life. Here *reflecting on myself*, and considering what is the quality of my mind, or what it *ought to be*, also what I ought to do, *I let go Christ from my eyes*, who is my sole righteousness and life. . . . . We should accustom ourselves, *turning from ourselves*, in such distress of conscience, from the Law and works, *which only force us to reflect on ourselves*, simply to turn our eyes to the Brazen Serpent, Christ fixed to the Cross, on whom fixing our earnest gaze we may be sure that He is our righteousness and life." What Luther wrote against the conscience-stricken Catholic of his day, applies still more forcibly

---

[1] Ibi ostendit clare, quomodo vivat. Et docet, quæ sit justitia Christiana, ea scilicet, qua Christus in nobis vivit, non quæ est in persona nostra. Itaque cum disputandum est de justitia Christiana, prorsus abjicienda est persona. Nam si in persona hæreo, vel de ea dico, fit ex persona, velim, nolim, operarius Legi subjectus. Sed hic oportet Christum et conscientiam meam fieri unum corpus, ita ut in conspectu meo nihil maneat nisi Christus crucifixus et resuscitatus. Si vero in me tantum intueor, excluso Christo, actum est de me, etc. etc. —In Gal. ii. 20.

to the unduly triumphant Protestant ; for surely it is better not to have Christ and to mourn, than to let Him go and to think it gain.

To the same purpose is a passage from the Homily on Salvation :—" Our faith in Christ, as it were, saith unto us thus : It is not I that take away your sins, but it is Christ only, *and to Him only I send you for that purpose, forsaking therein* all your good virtues, *words, thoughts,* and works, and only putting your trust in Christ."

7.

And now if we proceed to inquire where the real difference lies between this view, which our Church does hold, and that which pretends to be hers, it will be found to be this, which it is worth while insisting on ;— that the Church considers the doctrine of justification by faith only to be a *principle,* and the religion of the day takes it as *a rule of conduct.* Principles are great truths or laws which embody in them the character of a system, enable us to estimate it, and indirectly guide us in practice. For instance, " all is of grace," is a great principle of the Gospel. So are the following :—" we conquer by suffering,"—" the saints of God are hidden,"—"obedience is of the spirit not of the letter,"—"the blood of the Martyrs is the seed of the Church,"—" to gain happiness we must not seek it." It is a characteristic of such statements of principles to be short, pointed, strong, and often somewhat paradoxical in appearance. Such, for example, is the political maxim, which has a clear and true meaning, but in form is startling, " The King can do no wrong ;" or in physics, that "nature abhors a vacuum." They are laws or exhibitions of general truths ; and not directly practical. I mean, a man will be sure to get into difficulty or error if he attempts to use them as guides in matters of conduct and duty. They mean nothing, or something wide of the truth, taken as literal directions. They are like the Sun in the heavens, too high, too distant, to light your lamp by, though indirectly and secondarily useful even for that.

Proverbs, again, are of the same nature ; we recognize their truth in the course of life, but we do not walk by them. They come after us, not go before. They confirm, they do not explore for us. They are reflections upon human conduct, not guides for it. Thus " Honesty is the best policy," suggests the natural reward of honesty, not the way to be honest.

Such are principles :—rules, on the other hand, are adapted for immediate practice ; they aim at utility, and are directed and moulded according to the end proposed, not by correctness of reasoning or analysis. We follow blindly ; content, so that we arrive where we propose, whether we know how or not. We take them literally and without reasoning, and act upon them. Thus, if I ask my way, I shall be told, perhaps, to go first right forward, then to take a bend, then to watch for a hill or a river. There is no room for philosophy here ; it were out of place ; all is practical.

Now justification by faith only is a principle, not a rule of conduct ; and the popular mistake is to view it as a rule. This is where men go wrong. They think that the long and the short of religion is to have faith ; that is the whole, faith independent of every other duty;

a something which can exist in the mind by itself, and from which all other holy exercises follow ;—faith, and then forthwith they will be justified ; which will as surely mislead them as the great principle that "the Saints are hidden" would mislead such as took it for a rule, and thought by hiding themselves from the eyes of the world to become Saints. They who *are* justified, certainly are justified by *faith ;* but having faith is not more truly the *way* to be justified, than being hidden is the way to be a Saint.

The doctrine of justifying faith is a summary of the whole process of salvation from first to last ; a sort of philosophical analysis of the Gospel, a contemplation of it as a whole, rather than a practical direction. If it must be taken as a practical direction, and in a certain sense it may, then we must word it, not, "justification through faith," but, "justification by Christ." Thus, interpreted, the rule it gives is, "*go* to Christ ;" but taken in the letter, it seems to say merely, " Get *faith ;* become spiritual ; see that you are not mere moralists, mere formalists, see that you feel. If you do not feel, Christ will profit you nothing : you must have a spiritual taste ; you must see yourself to be a sinner ; you must accept, apprehend, appropriate the gift ; you must understand and acknowledge that Christ is the 'pearl of great price ;' you must be conscious of a change wrought in you, for the most part going through the successive stages of darkness, trouble, error, light, and comfort." Thus the poor and sorrowful soul, instead of being led at once to the source of all good, is taught to make much of the conflict of truth and falsehood within itself as the pledge of God's love, and to picture to itself faith, as a sort of passive quality which sits amid the ruins of human nature, and keeps up what may be called a silent protest, or indulges a pensive meditation over its misery. And, indeed, faith thus regarded cannot do more ; for while it acts, not to lead the soul to Christ, but to detain it from Him, how can the soul but remain a prisoner, in that legal or natural state described by the Apostle in the seventh of Romans ?—a passage of Scripture which the upholders of this doctrine confess, nay boast that they feel to be peculiarly their own.   Such is their first error, and a second obviously follows.   True faith is what may be called colourless, like air or water ; it is but the medium through which the soul sees Christ ; and the soul as little really rests upon it and contemplates it, as the eye can see the air.   When, then, men are bent on holding it (as it were) in their hands, curiously inspecting, analyzing, and so aiming at it, they are obliged to colour and thicken it, that it may be seen and touched. That is, they substitute for it something or other, a feeling, notion, sentiment, conviction, or act of reason, which they may hang over, and doat upon.   They rather aim at experiences (as they are called) within them, than at Him that is without them.   They are led to enlarge upon the signs of conversion, the variations of their feelings, their aspirations and longings, and to tell all this to others ;—to tell others how they fear, and hope, and sin, and rejoice, and renounce themselves, and rest in Christ only ; how conscious they are that their best deeds are but "filthy rags," and all is of grace, till in fact they have little time left them to guard against what

they are condemning, and to exercise what they think
they are so full of. Now men in a battle are brief-spoken;
they realize their situation and are intent upon it. And
men who are acted upon by news good or bad, or sights
beautiful or fearful, admire, rejoice, weep, or are pained,
but are moved spontaneously, not with a direct consciousness of their emotion. Men of elevated minds are
not their own historians and panegyrists. So it is with
faith and other Christian graces. Bystanders see our
minds; but our minds, if healthy, see but the objects
which possess them. As God's grace elicits our faith, so
His holiness stirs our fear, and His glory kindles our
love. Others may say of us "here is faith," and "there
is conscientiousness," and "there is love;" but we can
only say, "this is God's grace," and "that is His holiness,"
and "that is His glory."

8.

And this being the difference between true faith and
self-contemplation, no wonder that where the thought of
self obscures the thought of God, prayer and praise
languish, and only preaching flourishes. Divine worship
is simply contemplating our Maker, Redeemer, Sanctifier,
and Judge; but discoursing, conversing, making speeches,
arguing, reading, and writing about religion, tend to
make us forget Him in ourselves. The Ancients
worshipped; they went out of their own minds into the
Infinite Temple which was around them. They saw
Christ in the Gospels, in the Creed, in the Sacraments
and other Rites; in the visible structure and ornaments
of His House, in the Altar, and in the Cross; and, not
content with giving the service of their eyes, they gave

Him their voices, their bodies, and their time, gave up their rest by night and their leisure by day, all that could evidence the offering of their hearts to Him. Theirs was not a service once a week, or some one day, now and then, painfully, as if ambitiously and lavishly given to thanksgiving or humiliation ; not some extraordinary address to the throne of grace, offered by one for many, when friends met, with much point and impressiveness, and as much like an exhortation, and as little like a prayer, as might be ; but every day and every portion of the day was begun and sanctified with devotion. Consider those Seven Services of the Holy Church Catholic in her best ages, which, without encroaching upon her children's duties towards this world, secured them in their duties to the world unseen. Unwavering, unflagging, not urged by fits and starts, not heralding forth their feelings, but resolutely, simply, perseveringly, day after day, Sunday and week-day, fast-day and festival, week by week, season by season, year by year, in youth and in age, through a life, thirty years, forty years, fifty years, in prelude of the everlasting chant before the Throne, — so they went on, " continuing *instant* in prayer," after the pattern of Psalmists and Apostles, in the day with David, in the night with Paul and Silas, winter and summer, in heat and in cold, in peace and in danger, in a prison or in a cathedral, in the dark, in the day-break, at sun-rising, in the forenoon, at noon, in the afternoon, at eventide, and on going to rest, still they had Christ before them ; His thought in their mind, His emblems in their eye, His name in their mouth, His service in their posture, magnifying Him, and

calling on all that lives to magnify Him, joining with
Angels in heaven and Saints in Paradise to bless and
praise Him for ever and ever. O great and noble system,
not of the Jews who rested in their rights and privileges,
not of those Christians who are taken up with their own
feelings, and who describe what they should exhibit, but
of the true Saints of God, the undefiled and virgin souls
who follow the Lamb whithersoever He goeth! Such is
the difference between those whom Christ praises and
those whom He condemns or warns. The Pharisee
recounted the signs of God's mercy upon and in Him;
the Publican simply looked to God. The young Ruler
boasted of his correct life, but the penitent woman
anointed Jesus' feet and kissed them. Nay, holy Martha
herself spoke of her "much service;" while Mary
waited on Him for the "one thing needful." The one
thought of themselves; the others thought of Christ.
To look to Christ is to be justified by faith; to think of
being justified by faith is to look from Christ and to fall
from grace. He who worships Christ and works for
Him, is acting out that doctrine which another does but
enunciate; his worship and his works are acts of faith,
and avail to his salvation, because he does not do them
as availing.

9.

But I must end a train of thought, which, left to
itself would run on into a whole work. And in doing
so I make one remark, which is perhaps the great moral
of the history of Protestantism. Luther found in the

Church great moral corruptions countenanced by its highest authorities ; he felt them ; but instead of meeting them with divine weapons, he used one of his own. He adopted a doctrine original, specious, fascinating, persuasive, powerful against Rome, and wonderfully adapted, as if prophetically, to the genius of the times which were to follow. He found Christians in bondage to their works and observances ; he released them by his doctrine of faith ; and he left them in bondage to their feelings. He weaned them from seeking assurance of salvation in standing ordinances, at the cost of teaching them that a personal consciousness of it was promised to every one who believed. For outward signs of grace he substituted inward ; for reverence towards the Church contemplation of self. And thus, whereas he himself held the proper efficacy of the Sacraments, he has led others to disbelieve it ; whereas he preached against reliance on self, he introduced it in a more subtle shape ; whereas he professed to make the written word all in all, he sacrificed it in its length and breadth to the doctrine which he had wrested from a few texts.

This is what comes of fighting God's battles in our own way, of extending truths beyond their measure, of anxiety after a teaching more compact, clear, and spiritual, than the Creed of the Apostles. Thus the Pharisees were more careful of their Law than God who gave it ; thus Saul saved the cattle he was bid destroy, " to sacrifice to the Lord ;" thus Judas was concerned at the waste of the ointment, which might have been given to the poor. In these cases bad men professed to be more zealous for

God's honour, more devotional, or more charitable, than the servants of God ; and in a parallel way Protestants would be more spiritual. Let us be sure things are going wrong with us, when we see doctrines more clearly, and carry them out more boldly, than they are taught us in Revelation.

APPENDIX.[1]

ON THE FORMAL CAUSE OF JUSTIFICATION.

THE formal cause of a thing is generally explained to be that which constitutes it what it is; thus the soul may be said to be that which changes the dust of the earth into an organized and living body; or, again, heat may be considered the cause of a hot substance being hot, or that in which its state as hot, consists. Comparing the formal cause to other so-called causes or antecedents, it is the last in the series by which a thing is brought to be, or the ultimate state of the process which intervenes between the will of the originator and its performance; at least this will convey a notion of what is meant, sufficient for the matter in hand. Thus, according to the Council of Trent, justification, the work of God, is brought into effect through a succession of the following causes: the mercy of God the *efficient* cause, Christ offered on the Cross the *meritorious*, Baptism the *instrumental*, and the principle of renewal in righteousness thereby communicated the *formal; upon* which immediately follows justification. Or again, Faith is, by various parties, considered successively as a disposing

[1] [The purpose of this Appendix is to show that the cardinal question to be considered by Catholics and Protestants in their controversy about Justification is, What is its *formal cause?* When this is properly examined, it will be found that there is little or no difference of view between the disputants, except when the Protestant party adheres to the paradox of Luther :—" Sola fides, non fides formata charitate, justificat : fides justificat sine et ante charitatem," and refuses to assign a formal cause.]

cause, the instrumental, or the formal cause of justification, thus being brought nearer and nearer to that of which it is the cause, till it (as it were) falls into and coincides with it. Hence the form is that, between which and the thing in question nothing can be interposed in our ideas ; and accordingly it is sometimes really distinct from that effect, sometimes not, though it is always supposed to be distinct. Thus, to take one of the instances given, if the renovation in righteousness which follows Baptism, or the " justitia Dei qua nos justos facit," as the Council speaks, be considered as the *principle* of renewal, as I have expressed it, it is the formal cause of our renewed state itself as well as of justification ; and is or is not really distinct from that renewed state, according as we believe the principle of renewal to be a mere abstraction of the mind contemplating it, or a definite divine gift residing in the soul. Again : heat, the formal cause of a hot iron, is or is not really distinct from and antecedent to its being hot, according as we view caloric as an idea or as a substance. When what is considered the formal cause is a mere abstraction of the mind, then it nearly coincides with the logical *differentia*, or *proprium*, or *inseparable accident*. Thus whiteness is at once the form and the *accident* of a white wall ; and animality is the *form* and the *generic difference* of man as distinguished from a vegetable.

The ordinary meaning of the word *form* serves to illustrate this scientific use of it. What discriminates a body from everything else is its shape ; which is the development of that of which it is composed, into and unto a certain determinate lineament and structure. The Form then is some such disposition or result, constituting a thing to be what it is. For instance, the matter of a science is its objective truth, its form is that truth when it has become subjective, or *knowledge*, which is a sort of determinate embodying of what was till then unappropriated.

Other instances of the formal cause are as follows :—
The muscles, claws, teeth, intestines, etc. of a beast of prey
so intimately harmonize with each other, as forcibly to
suggest the notion that they are necessary results of some
one element or principle, or that there is a certain latent
type on which its whole structure is formed and from which
it is developed. This, if it exists, will be the formal cause
of what we mean by a beast of prey.

Again :—It is often a difficult question in pathology to
determine the *seat* of diseases. Fever, for instance, manifests
itself in certain symptoms, as quickness of pulse, restlessness,
etc. ; and, speaking in a vague way, we might say that it
consisted *in* those symptoms, but it is natural to investigate
whether there be not some simple disarrangement of one or
other organ or function or department of the animal frame,
to which these symptoms may be referred. Thus insanity
has been supposed to consist in,—*i.e.* to have for its formal
cause,—a certain determination of blood to the head ; gout
to be an inflammation of the membrane which covers the
bones, etc. etc. In like manner, it has lately been a subject
of controversy in the medical world, whether the seat of
disease generally, and therefore its formal cause, was to be
sought in the solids or in the fluids.

Again :—If man be defined to be a rational animal, we
do not gain any real and tangible account of him, nor
advance in our knowledge of him ; it is an ideal, not a real
view of him ; but if we are told that virtue is a power
of ruling the passions, or that happiness, as Aristotle says,
lies in action, we have brought before us, more or less clearly,
how virtue or happiness, come to be, or of what they are
the issue ; that is, we approximate to their formal cause.
When Cicero suggests that " omne bonum in honestate
consistit " (Tuscul. Disp. v. 42), or that " honestas " is that
quality of a thing on account of which it is called good, he
is assigning the formal cause of goodness.

Again :—It is often debated in what the union of Church

and State consists; whether in the Church rates, or in the legal protection of endowments, or in its Bishops having seats in parliament, or in the Sovereign being an *ex officio* member of it, and bound to support it; that is, what is the formal cause.

Once more :—Every one knows what is *meant* when we speak of "endowments;" but a question may arise as to a particular institution, object, or country, *what* in fact its endowments consist in. For instance, the endowment of a certain hospital may consist in land; of a certain bishopric in tithes; of a certain preachership in railroad shares. These may be considered as the respective formal causes of "endowment" in the particular cases, as being the real things in which the endowments in question lie.

2. This being the meaning of the term employed, it is plain that to determine what is the formal cause of our justification, or what it is which under the Christian covenant constitutes us just in God's sight, or what it is in us in which our justification consists, or what it is immediately upon which we receive God's justification, is as important an undertaking as any one in the controversy, whatever difficulties may attend it, whatever chance there be of verbal disputes (as there is almost the certainty), and whatever danger, in consequence, of men finding themselves on contrary sides, who are in reality like-minded. The question may be thrown into the following more practical shape : What is it which God will look on at the last day and accept us in? what will be the immediate antecedent in our souls to the words, "Come, ye blessed." Supposing a religious man, unversed in controversy, to be asked this question, the answer would at once rise on his tongue, which is suggested by the passage of Scripture referred to, viz. the recognition of our *good works* on the part of God; "Come, ye blessed, *for* I was an hungered," etc. Next, on consideration he might correct his answer so far as to say, that since works are not good except done in a certain way, and

persevered in to the end, it is not the mere having done certain works, but the presence of a renewed state of mind developing itself in works, which is that upon which acceptance or justification falls. Further; after a little more thought, recollecting the parable of the Pharisee and Publican, he might add, that of course he did not mean to say that our works or our inward state was such as to be able in itself to stand the scrutiny of a Just and Holy God, but that whatever was accepted in us must be accepted for the sake of Christ's merits and under the covenant of mercy. Lastly, recollecting the language of Hezekiah and Nehemiah, and St. Paul's about "the rich storing up for themselves a good *foundation*," and about his own "good fight," and St. Luke's remark that Zacharias and his wife were "righteous *before God*," and Zacharias's prophecy about Gospel "holiness and righteousness *before Him*," and St. Paul's appeal to his *conscience*, he would add further, by way of caution, that Christ's merits did not supersede the necessity of our doing our part.

3. Here suppose two disputants to interpose, they would perhaps each claim the speaker as on his own side. The one would urge that he had decided that the formal cause of justification was either our good works, or our inward holiness, as the case was viewed. The other, that on the contrary he had spoken of the necessity of Christ's merits coming between us and God's sentence; these merits then, after all, were the immediate antecedent of justification, that upon and in which justification came, or its formal cause. The former would rejoin that those merits were not the *immediate antecedent* of justification, but the presupposed ground-work of justification all along, without which there would be no covenant, no works, no reward at all; not the last step before justification, but the first step towards it:[1] not the formal cause, but the meritorious

[1] Vide Vasquez, Disp. 222.

And here they would join issue; viz. whether Christ's merits, which are the original cause of our holiness and works, are to be considered as the medium (as it may be called) of the covenant *in which* we act, or the *proximate* cause of our entering into life.[1] Such is the question on which some remarks are now to be attempted, and which has been viewed by different schools in a variety of ways; such as the following:—(1) It has been said that we are justified directly and solely *upon* our holiness and works wrought in us *through* Christ's merits *by* the Spirit; or (2) upon our holiness and works *under* the covenant of Christ's merits, or, in other words, sanctified and completed by Christ's merits; or (3) that our faith is mercifully appointed as the substitute for perfect holiness, and thus is the interposing and acceptable principle between us and God; or (4) that Christ's merits and righteousness are imputed as ours, and become the immediate cause of our justification, superseding everything else in the eye of our Judge. Of these the first is the high-Roman view; the last the high-Protestant; and the two intermediate are different forms of what is commonly considered the high-Church view among ourselves, and very nearly resemble Bucer's, among the Protestants, and that of Pighius, Mussus, and many others of the Roman school.

4. Indeed, it is no point of faith with the Roman Catholics to take the view which I have called Roman,[2]

---

[1] Quando formalem causam quærimus justificationis nostræ, id quærimus *propter quod* peccator in gratiam Dei recipitur, *per quod immediate* Deo gratus et ad æternam vitam acceptus stat.—Daven. *Just. Hab.* 22. Statuendum est hanc justitiam sive hoc meritum Christi non intervenire solummodo in prima nostra justificatione, sed *semper objici* divino judicio, ita ut *ejus intuitu* non modo recipiamur in gratiam ab initio, sed stemus in gratia ac perducamur ad finem gratiæ, nempe ad gloriam.—*Ibid.* p. 28.

[2] [It was laid down in the Council of Trent that the "unica formalis causa" of justification is "justitia Dei, qua nos justos facit,"

but still I shall so call it, as holding the place among them which our so-called high-Church doctrine does among us, that is, as being the generally received, orthodox, and legitimate exposition of their formularies. Romanists then consider that that on which justification at once takes place, in which it consists, or its formal cause, is inherent right-eousness (whether habitual or of works, which is an open question) ; and they argue that it is so, on the plain ground that no interposition of mercy between it and justification is required, and therefore none is made. If justification is the issue of inherent righteousness at all, there is no reason, they say, why it should not be the immediate issue of it. If it be replied to them, that nothing we can do, though proceeding from the grace of Christ, is such as to stand the scrutiny of God's judgment ; so that the most perfect human righteousness cannot possibly proceed to justification as its legitimate result, but even though real, and though not infected with sin, yet as being but inchoate and incomplete, needs to be pardoned, they deny it, and argue as follows : —Nothing exposes us to God's wrath but sin, and a state of sin is incompatible with the existence at all of grace in the soul.[1] To deny this, they say, is almost a contra-diction in terms ; hence a habit of grace *occupies* the soul, to the exclusion, not of infirmities, imperfections, and venial sins,[2] but of everything which interferes with a state of reconciliation with God ; it may grow towards perfection, and it tends to destroy all that remains of an earthly nature

or renovation of spirit and the good works thence proceeding ; for there can be only one form of any thing, and this inward righteousness being that on which justification immediately follows, is therefore that one form. At the same time there may be many improper forms ; as (according to the illustration used *infra*) the soul is the true form of the body, and yet its organization in some sense its form also.]

[1] Vid. Jerom. Adv. Jovinian. ii. 2.

[2] About venial sins, vid. Vasquez, Disp. 222, ii. 17.

in the soul, but by the fact of entering into the soul it expels
at once all that is hateful to God.   The renewed soul is *in* a
state of favour, else it would not be renewed ; Christ's merits
have been applied when it was renewed, and their virtue
lasts while the renewal lasts.   If a man commits a mortal
sin, he is at once thrown out of this state both of favour
and renewal ; and if he so died would die out of justification ;
but, while he is in it, he is by the very force of the words
only in the commission of such sins as are not mortal, and
do not incur God's wrath and damnation.   And in this the
Roman schools differ from Luther, who taught that no sin
throws the soul out of a state of grace but unbelief, that is,
distrust.   It appears then that they hold two things—that
the presence of grace implies the absence of mortal sin ;
next, that it is a divine gift bringing with it the property
of a continual acceptableness, and thus recommending the
soul to God's favour, so as to anticipate the necessity of
any superadded pardon.

Nay, some writers speak of the presence of the Holy
Ghost Himself, who is in the righteous, as being the formal
cause of their inherent righteousness, who of course may
easily be understood as continually applying to them Christ's
merits, while He continually sustains their spiritual life.
But whether we consider the presence of the Holy Spirit as
the form of righteousness, or grace as the form, or grace as
the "justitia" which is mentioned as the form in the Council,
or even if grace be taken to be the same habit as love
viewed differently, yet in all these cases an inward gift is
supposed immediately from God, doing that for the soul,
which, whatever be its actual proficiency in holiness, it must
need, washing it in Christ's blood, and so presenting it to
God blameless and glorious without spot or wrinkle or
blemish.   This doctrine seems expressed in the Canon of
the Council of Milevis (A.D. 416), in the time of St. Austin :
" Placuit, ut quicunque dixerit gratiam Dei, *in quâ justifica-*

mur per Jesum Christum Dominum nostrum, ad solam remissionem peccatorum valere quæ jam commissa sunt, non etiam ad adjutorium ut non committantur, anathema sit." To the same effect, when Bucer in the Ratisbon Conference objects to his opponent, as saying, " Homines non eo justos quia non eis imputentur, sed quia legem Dei impleant," the Roman writer of the Acts observes, "Sed hoc non ita posuerat Malvenda ; sed quia *gratiam* habent *delentem peccata*, et vires suggerentem ad implendam legem."

5. This doctrine of a real distinction, to be drawn between the divinely imparted principle of righteousness, even after it has been imparted, and the actual righteousness or renewed state of our minds, is allowed in the Church of Rome and held by Roman divines, both before the Council of Trent and after.   Lombard even held that for justification the indwelling of the Spirit takes the place of the *habit* of love, etc. (Vasquez, Disp. 203, c. 1 ; Bellarm. de Gratia, i. 8.) Again, St. Thomas contends that the " gratia justificans " is not the same as the habit of love ; the latter belonging to the will, and the former to the substance of the soul.   In which opinion he is followed by Caietan, Conradus, Soto, and others.   Bonaventura assents, so far as to consider that there is a formal distinction between them.   (Vasquez, Disp. 198, c. 2.)   This alleged distinction was a subject of dispute at the Council of Trent between the Franciscans and Dominicans (Sarpi, Hist. lib. ii. p. 187); on all which accounts it was left unsettled by the Fathers there assembled. " Observandum præterea est," says Pallavicino, Hist. viii. 14, § 2, " cum e Scholasticis aliqui putarent, hominem reddi justum per gratiam a charitate distinctam, alii per ipsam charitatem, præter quam non insit alia gratia quæ justum faciat, *adhibitam data opera fuisse a Patribus vocem nunc gratiæ nunc charitatis et interdum etiam utramque*, velut in Canone undecimo, ut se abstinerent ab ea declaratione, duæ res an una eademque res illæ forent."   Indeed it may be

obviously argued, that unless the habits of grace and of love
are distinct, infants cannot be justified. Vasquez and
Bellarmine indeed, though they treat it as an open question,
consider that *grace* and *love* are one and the same, which
would resolve the inward justifying principle into a quality
of our minds ; but even then arises the question in reserve,
whether that love does not after all arise from the presence
of the Holy Spirit, who, therefore, and nothing of ours,
whatever strong terms be used about love, will be the true
justifier ; and among moderns, Petavius, no mean authority,
does not scruple to call the Holy Ghost the formal cause of
the righteousness imparted to us.

This is so remarkable as to justify the insertion of
several passages out of the many which might be quoted
from his De Trinitate, lib. viii. " Sic igitur cum fidelibus
ac justis impertiri communicarique Spiritus Sanctus legitur,
non ipsamet illius persona tribui, sed ejus efficientia videri
potest, idque communis fere sensus habet eorum, qui in
Patrum veterum lectione minus exercitati sunt. Quos qui
attente pervestigare voluerit, intelliget occultum quendam
et inusitatum missionis communicationisque modum apud
illos celebrari, quo Spiritus Ille Divinus in justorum sese
animos insinuans cum illis copulatur ; eumque non acciden-
tarium, (ut ita dicam) esse,—hoc est, qualitate duntaxat illa
cœlesti ac divina perfici, quam in pectora nostra diffundit
idem cœlestium donorum largitor ac procreator Spiritus,—sed
οὐσιώδη, hoc est substantialem ; ita ut substantia ipsa Spiritus
Sancti nobiscum jungatur, nosque sanctos et *justos*, ac Dei
denique *filios efficiat.*"—4, § 5. " Omnino itaque per occultam
quandam *infusionem substantiæ suæ* justificare homines Spiritum Sanctum Didymus arbitratus est. Eadem et apud
Paschasium et Bernardum leges de participatione illa substantiæ Spiritus Sancti, *qua* boni vel sapientes *efficimur*, hoc
est *justi* et sancti."—Ibid. § 15. " Evidens est ex eorum
[Patrum] decretis, *justitiæ* ac sanctitatis *statum* non creata re

ulla vel qualitate, sed ipsa Spiritus Sancti substantia, *tanquam principali forma, in nobis perfici.*"—5, § 1. " Ac valde
sunt illa consentanea Cyrilli, aliorumque Patrum sententiis
. . . . quæ Spiritum Sanctum *ποιότητα* velut quandam
divinitatis esse demonstrant, aut *formam* quæ *ποιούς τινας*
reddit eos in quibus inest."—Ibid. § 15. " Relegantur
omnia veterum Patrum testimonia, quæ superius exposita
sunt, et quod iis præstantius est Scripturæ loca illa recen-
seantur, quæ cum *justis* conjungi vel in iis *habitare,* aut
Deum simpliciter, aut privatim Filium, docent, inveniemus
eorum pleraque testari per Spiritum Sanctum hoc fieri, velut
proximam causam et ut ita dixerim *formalem.*"—6, § 8. It
would seem then as if there were *two* formal causes of justification admitted by Romanists, love or inherent righteousness, and grace or the presence of the Holy Spirit indwelling.
Nor does Vasquez take an objection to the notion of thus
viewing the subject ; on the contrary, he says, " Neque enim
incommodum aliquod est, constituere *duas formas,* per quas
homo justificari possit apud Deum, nempe duos habitus." [1]
Disp. 198, c. 3. Indeed, such a determination of the matter
is just as intelligible and reasonable, as if the form of bodily
life were said to be either a certain organization, or the
presence of an animating spirit.

This admission of a double form in justification is worth
noting, as it points towards that doctrine which I shall
presently notice as more exact and satisfactory than the

---

[1] [Sporer goes further. In defending the thesis, that "justificatio
est effectus formalis gratiæ sanctificantis ex ordinatione divinâ," he says,
not indeed that there are two formal causes of justification, since there
is "unica formalis causa," but that the causa is of a composite nature,
including an external and internal Divine act. " Qualitas inhærens
seu habitus charitatis *et* ordinatio seu favor Dei constituunt integraliter
unam causam formalem nostræ justificationis." And he appeals to
the words of the Council of Trent for this view.—*Theol. Moral. Suppl.*
p. 286.]

extreme Roman; nor does the argument urged by Vasquez against it, that where one is enough, it is superfluous to suppose two, tell for much, on the hypothesis that the gift of grace is really the form, and inherent righteousness but improperly so.

6. But to return: such then is, on the part of the extreme Romanists, the resolution of the question *how* inherent righteousness stands the scrutiny of divine holiness and constitutes our acceptance; they answer, that it consists in an inward divine quality, which has the power of apply-ing, or springs from the application of Christ's merits, and so effects or pre-supposes the cleansing of all sin in us. Protestants, on the other hand, are accustomed to consider that the immediate antecedent to justification is an act of pardon from without upon the soul to be justified, which act, in consequence, is considered its formal cause. Now there are many difficulties attending this theory, but its strength in argument with Romanists lies in the authorities which can be brought against them from among their own friends. Some of these shall be mentioned, before we consider the theory itself. A remarkable testimony, for instance, of this kind is St. Austin's, who thus speaks in his De Civitate Dei: " Ipsa nostra justitia, *quamvis vera sit* prop-ter veri boni fidem ad quem refertur, tamen tanta est in hac vita, *ut potius peccatorum remissione constet quam perfectione virtutum*. Testis est oratio totius Civitatis Dei, quæ pere-grinatur in terris, per omnia quippe membra sua clamat ad Deum, Dimitte nobis debita nostra."—xix. 27. And St. Jerome: "Tunc ergo justi sumus, quando nos peccatores fatemur; justitia nostra non ex proprio merito, sed *ex Dei consistit misericordia.*" — contra Pelag. (vol. ii. p. 179). Against such statements it seems hardly in point to urge passages from the Fathers on the other side which speak of inherent righteousness as justifying; the sole question being whether, *granting this*, it justifies after being sprinkled with

the blood of Christ, which passages such as the above seem
clearly to imply. So again St. Ambrose : "Non gloriabor,
quia justus sum, sed quia redemptus sum ; gloriabor, non
quia vacuus peccatis sum, sed quia mihi remissa sunt peccata ; non quia profui, neque quia profuit mihi quisquam,
sed quia pro me Advocatus apud Patrem Christus est, sed
quia pro me Christi sanguis effusus est."—de Jacob et vit.
beat. i. 6. And Pope Gregory : "Justus Advocatus noster
justos nos defendet in judicio, quia nosmet ipsos et cognos-
cimus et accusamus injustos. Non ergo in fletibus, non in
actibus nostris, sed in Advocati nostri allegatione confidamus."—In Ezek. lib. i. hom. 7, *fin.* And so St. Bernard
on his sick-bed, as Hooker after him : "Fateor, non sum
dignus ego, nec propriis possum meritis regnum obtinere
cœlorum ; cæterum duplici jure illud obtinens Dominus
meus, hæreditate scilicet Patris et *merito passionis*, altero
ipse contentus, alterum mihi donat ; *ex cujus dono jure illud
mihi vendicans non confundor.*"—Vit. S. Bern. i. 12, col. 1084.
And so again the words of the present Roman Mass, "intra
quorum [sanctorum] nos consortium, *non æstimator meriti
sed veniæ* quæsumus, *largitor* admitte." These passages are
not inconsistent indeed with the Roman view of the doctrine,
still they differ in tone from it. Lists of similar passages will
be found in Gerhard de Just. §§ 8, 213, etc. ; de Leg. § 189 ;
Field, Of the Church, iii. Append. ch. 2 ; J. White's Way to
the Church, Digress. 35 ; Davenant de Just. Habit. c. 29.
Of these I shall only cite in addition the testimony of
Bellarmine himself, often quoted in the controversy, and
remarkable because he advocates the high Roman view.
After saying that the Catholic Church goes along a middle
way, teaching that our *chief* hope and confidence must be
placed in God, yet *some* in our services, he proves from
Scripture and the Fathers three propositions ;—that the
confidence of the Saints in God arises not from faith alone,
but from good works : that when our services are *proved*

really to deserve the name, we may put some confidence in them, *so that we beware of pride ;* and thirdly, which is the statement in question, " Propter *incertitudinem* propriæ justitiæ et periculum *inanis gloriæ, tutissimum* est *fiduciam totam in sola Dei misericordia et benignitate reponere.*" And then he explains this by saying that he means, not that we should not pursue good works with all our might, not that they are not a true ground of confidence, are not real righteousness, or are unable to sustain God's judgment, but that it is *safer* in a manner to *forget* what we have done, and to look solely at God's mercy, because no one can know, except by revelation, whether or not he has done any good works, or whether he shall persevere, and because the contemplation of his good works, even if he could know of them, is dangerous, as being elating.—Vide de Just. v. 7.

7. On this subject may be consulted to advantage Le Blanc's Theological Theses, *de Rel. bon. op.* part. 2, Thes. 1, who carefully discusses the views of the Roman doctors concerning the value of good works, and shows that, in spite of their doctrine *ex condigno,* many of them hold one or other of the following opinions distinct from that of Vasquez, which has been chiefly spoken of above :—that the merit of the works of the regenerate depends on God's covenant, even regarded as works of the Spirit ; that these works are not accepted for the reward of eternal life, except as *sprinkled with the blood of Christ ;*[1] that the word merit is not meant to apply in the standard of justice but of *mercy ;* and that when the justice of God is spoken of in this relation His *faithfulness* is meant, or *conformity to the dictates of His wisdom.* Moreover he says, that they all confess that the meritorious works in question are not such in themselves,

---

[1] Vid. also Davenport. " Nos dicimus nostram justitiam, si præscindas acceptationem divinam et justitiam Christi, à quâ suam dignitatem meritorie derivat, parum valere."—Franc. à Sanct. Clar. Tractat. 26.

but as done by the *persons of the regenerate,* who are God's sons, not servants, and that good works are not meritorious of life, in the sense in which bad works are meritorious of death. In a word, they do not consider our holiness or good works a cause in the *way of nature,* but in the mind and dealings of a gracious God ; though, at the same time, as is hardly necessary to add, the Roman doctors often use language most grating and revolting to our ears, and (as we cannot but think) very perilous to those who acquiesce in it.

To these authorities must be added the testimony of many of the schoolmen, who distinctly state as general doctrine what Bellarmine considered only to be safer to the individual, that the regenerate cannot trust in the view of God's judgment on anything good in them, or any good works of theirs. Vasquez makes mention of these writers and of others of later date, in the following very observable words, which have often been quoted :—" Non possum non mirari antiquos scholasticos, quos hactenus memoravi, quod de justitia nobis inhærente ita abjecte senserint, ut veram ei adscribere *formidaverint* rationem justitiæ et sanctitatis inhærentis quæ suapte natura Deo necessario placeat ; recentiores vero theologos multo magis miratus sum, quod post præclaram Concilii Tridentini definitionem, quam inferius explicabo, tam *exilem* justitiam inhærentem justis concesserint, ut ex se non habeat virtutem tergendi maculas peccatorum, nec eas purgare valeat, nisi favore et condonatione Dei relaxentur."—Disput. 204, c. 2, p. 469.

8. Such are the confessions, or, it may be said, concessions, of Roman Divines, towards the doctrine of Protestants on the subject of justification. But far from being content with them, Luther, Calvin, and their followers, have maintained that nothing is really granted, while good works or holiness are in *any* respect made the formal or constituting cause of justification ; and then their difficulty begins, for they have forthwith to *construct* a doctrine of their own.

whereas Protestants seem by the force of their name to disclaim the office of framing any positive theology.[1] The question is, what is the formal cause of our justification?— now let us grant that any divinely imparted sanctity, any good works are not the immediate antecedent to our being justified; that justification does not depend on, or consist in, anything we are or can do; that Christ's merits must ever interpose or intercede between us and God, and so preclude the righteousness inherent in us from being the formal cause; the question recurs, what *is* the formal cause of our justification? and on this question we shall find in the writings of Protestants great diversity of opinion and little satisfaction. Some say that faith is the formal cause, some forgiveness of sins, some the imputation of Christ's righteousness, and some that there is no formal cause at all.

9. Perhaps the best choice that can be made out of these answers, is to say that it is faith. Such was the answer originally given by the Lutherans, but they retracted it. And such is the answer virtually given by Bishop Bull and many others of our divines who have chosen to express themselves in what may be called the *calculus* of Protestantism. By faith, according to Bishop Bull, is meant *fides formata charitate et operibus,* or the obedience which is of faith; a doctrine which one is glad to find was admitted in the deliberations of the Council of Trent,[2] and differs from the view I have called properly Roman, in this, that by calling inherent righteousness by the name of *faith,* it implies that it is only in Christ that that righteousness is accepted, being unable to stand God's judgment unless sprinkled with His Atoning blood. But, returning to Luther, I observe that he too sometimes speaks of faith as our "formalis justitia." "Ubi ergo vera fiducia cordis est, ibi adest Christus ipsa

---

[1] There is a dissertation on the formal cause of justification in Pareus's Miscell. Catechet. vii. p. 171, but it does not help us in our present inquiry.   [2] Pallavic. Hist. viii. 4, § 3.

nebula et fide. Eaque est *formalis justitia, propter* quam homo justificatur, non propter charitatem, ut sophistæ loquuntur."—In Gal. ii. 16. " Hoc [tribuere Deo gloriam] ratio non facit, sed fides ea consummat divinitatem, et, ut ita dicam, creatrix est divinitatis, non in substantia Dei, sed in nobis. . . . Ideoque illam gloriam posse tribuere Deo, est sapientia sapientiarum, *justitia justitiarum,* religio religionum, et sacrificium sacrificiorum. Ex hoc intelligi potest, quanta *justitia* sit fides, et per antithesin quantum peccatum incredulitas."—In Gal. iii. 6.[1] And Illyricus, writing against Osiander, ascribes to Luther the doctrine, "*fiduciam* in Christum esse nostram *formalem justitiam* seu imputari nobis in justitiam."—E. 3, p. 6. Calvin says the same ; by way of showing that works are not a cause of salvation, he observes that of the four received kinds of causes, " Efficientem . . . vitæ æternæ nobis comparandæ causam ubique Scriptura prædicat Patris cœlestis misericordiam et gratuitam erga nos dilectionem ; materialem vero Christum cum sua obedientia, per quam nobis justitiam acquisivit ; *formalem* vel *instrumentalem* quam esse dicemus nisi fidem ?"—Instit. iii. 14, § 17. This solution of the question, however, seems to have been soon given up, and the *apprehensive* notion of faith substituted. Gerhard, de Justif. § 163, argues that faith cannot be the formal cause of justification ; " cum justificatio sit actio Dei ;" which is to miss the question (vide above, Lecture IV. pp. 96, 97), and says, §§ 197, 201, that it is so called by Lutherans, nothing more is meant than that faith is the means of apprehending Christ, who is our righteousness in God's sight.

10. This latter doctrine, which is Luther's, is reduced by Gerhard from *Christus* fide apprehensus est justitia nostra, § 163, to *Christi justitia,* next to Christi obedientiæ *imputatio,* then to justitiæ per Christum *partæ imputatio,* and lastly to *remissio peccatorum,* §§ 16, 197, 198 ; maintaining, as he does,

[1] Vide also Melanchth. Apol. vol. i. f. 77.

that imputatio justitiæ per Christum partæ is identical with remissio peccatorum, § 199, and the one formal cause of justification. Calvin, on the other hand, assenting to the doctrine that the imputatio justitiæ, or non-imputatio or remissio peccatorum, is the formal cause (Instit. iii. 11, §§ 2, 4 ; Antidot. p. 323 ; Eccles. Reform. Rat. p. 368 ; Chamier, de Justif. xxii. 13, § 5), and that sanctification is not the formal cause, but a "necessary accident," present in justification *comitanter* not *formaliter*,—a distinction difficult to master, since a form need not be intrinsic,—(vide Calvin, Antid. p. 324 ; Davenant de Just. Hab. fin.) determines with more candour that Christus, or the obedientia Christi, is the *matter* of justification.[1]   (Vide passage above quoted, and Instit. iii. 11, § 7 ; Chamier de Justif. xxi. 1, § 19.)   But what he gains thereby in truth, he loses in the argument ; for whereas the formal cause must be from its nature intimately connected (whether accidentally or essentially) with that of which it is the cause, this solution of the question gives up the notion of such a connection altogether, as substituting with Gerhard for the passive sense of justification that active sense which belongs to God.   (Vide Chamier, loc. cit.)   To tell us that *justifying* consists in God's pardoning sin, does not help us one step towards determining what it really is to be *justified ;* whereas the phrases " Christus justitia nostra," " Christus in cordibus inhabitans," etc., of the Lutherans are better adapted to create at least a semblance of some real and intimate characteristic, and thus, granting nothing more than Calvin, to break the force of an opponent's argument.

The Lutherans then argue that a form need not be anything essential or internal ; that the form, for instance, of a *sunny bank* is the sun's shining, the form of *news* lies in

---

[1] It is remarkable that Davenant animadverts on Bonaventura's making the merits of Christ the matter of justification, which he says at once throws us upon inherent righteousness as the form.—*De Just Hab.* ch. 28, fin.

him to whom it is news; moreover that love, the form, as their opponents say, of justifying faith, is extrinsic only. Vasquez grants this (Disput. 202, c. 3), but argues that still there is always some real connection between a thing and such extrinsic form; for instance, it is part of the Catholic doctrine of the Incarnation that our Lord's human nature is holy from its union with the Divine Nature as an extrinsic form; here, however, the union between the two natures is *personal;* what then, in like manner, is that real connection between Christ and the justified, whatever be its precise nature, which will allow us to call Him the form of our righteousness? The Lutherans make answer that *faith* is such a connection; to which Vasquez replies by asking, whether a man is called rich who by faith apprehends riches? or noble who so apprehends nobility? What do they mean, in short, when they say that an act of our minds changes our *real* state in God's sight? Gerhard answers (in controversy with Bellarmine), § 238, that it is a mystery; a sufficient account, if his school kept to it, instead of going on, as they do, to explain how it was, and turning the justifying power of faith into a weapon against all mysteries, such as the Sacraments.

Further, Bellarmine goes on to urge (de Just. ii. 7), that, even though the formal cause be extrinsic, still where there is an intrinsic also, that is more *properly* the form (for instance, it is more exact to say that fluidity is the form of melting wax than its exposure to the fire); that a negro dressed in white would still be called a black man; and that a sinner to whom the righteousness of Christ is but imputed, has for his truer form the sin which is in him, not the perfection which is counted to him; (and, in like manner, if he is really made righteous by inherence, whether infection be left or not, that inherent righteousness is more properly the form of his justification than a mere imputed righteousness which is without him); whereas, in the case of *fides formata* which is alleged by Lutherans as an *argumentum ad hominem*, no other form can be assigned but an external one, namely love, whatever be the form of faith as such, and love, far from being separated from faith, is united with it by the closest and most real of all connections, as existing with it in one and the same soul. To this Gerhard answers, that the reason why the justified sinner is said to be in a state of righteousness, because of what is external to him, rather than of sin from what is internal, is that he is not really a sinner in the same sense in which he was before; for sin in the regenerate has lost its formal part, which is guilt, and has only its matter remaining, and even that is under process of mortification. Further: he protests against the notion that the Protestant doctrine of imputation is nominal, shadowy, and putative. Davenant makes a similar complaint; yet, desirous as one may be to be fair to the theory, it is difficult to speak of it in any other terms. Davenant's words are these :—" Imputatio non fictionem cogitationis humanæ denotat, sed *efficacissimam Dei ordinationem* et *validissimam rei donationem.* Si Bellarminus nolit advertere quid intersit inter fictionem et donationem justitiæ Christi, dignus est qui coram tremendo illo tribunali sistatur, non alia justitia indutus quam sua inhærente."—c. 34. This surely is unfair, as well as severe; a gift or a possession is of two kinds, personal, and for use and enjoyment; gold or jewels put into one's hands is the former, and landed property is the latter. Davenant means that the justitia Christi is ours in the latter sense. He says (c. 28, fin.), "Christi justitia imputata nihil aliud est quam Christi justitia applicata et donata nobis *ad spiritualem aliquem effectum producendum.*" He does not regard it at all as a personal possession; and Calvin grants as much, when he considers the formal cause of justification, *not* the justitia Christi, but remission of sins, that is, the spiritual *consequence* of His righteousness. Bellarmine then assumes no more than

Calvin grants; that we are *said* to be or *named* as having
Christ's righteousness in order to have the fruits of that
righteousness. Only he goes on to argue that such a mere
nominal and not real gift, or to make use of the foregoing
distinction, a gift not personal, cannot be called a formal
cause. Yet Davenant dispenses very different justice to his
acute opponent and his clear-headed and candid Master.
While he uses language which one would wish to forget,
because Bellarmine says that the imputation which is by
faith, by the very force of the terms used, cannot be a
personal characteristic of the soul, yet when Calvin says that
Christ's righteousness is but the matter, not the form of
justification, and only is applied to us in its effects, in the
remission of sins, he says, " ut itaque *seponamus* philosophicas
speculationes de natura causæ formalis," etc. Yet he is just
beginning a dissertation of eight chapters upon it! The
subject may be treated in a philosophical, or a common-sense
way; but must not be taken up and put down in one or
the other at pleasure. All this *ambiguity*, as I must call it,
is to be imputed not to Bishop Davenant, whose work is full
of noble passages, but to his system.

11. Another answer still more explicit than Calvin's, is
that there is no formal cause of justification at all. Such is
the final evolution of the Protestant theory, which beginning
in the bold, nay correct language of Luther, that Christ
Himself is the form of our justification, is gradually attenu-
ated till the very notion of a form vanishes. This is the
ground taken by those of our writers who are not Calvinists,
yet retain partially the language of Protestantism. Jackson
plainly puts forward this view in the following words :—
" To demand of us what is the formal cause of Justification,
by which our sins are formally remitted, is as if we should
ask one of our young pupils, what were Latin for *manus.*
Justification *taken* (as we do) *for remission of sins,* not by inherent righteousness, or aught within us immediately incom-

patible with them, but *by the external merits of Christ,* is a form or entity as simple as any formal cause can be, and simple or uncompounded entities can neither have formal causes, or aught in proportion answering to them. Wherefore, as I said, it is either the folly or knavery of our adversaries to demand a formal cause of their justification, that deny themselves to be formally just in the sight of God."— Book iv. ch. 7, init. Yet surely, with deference to so great a writer, if a justified state, or, as he expresses it, a state of remission of sins by the external merits of Christ, consist in anything, if he who is in that state differs from him who is not, that in which it consists, that in which he differs from the other, is a kind of formal cause : and he would be the last to deny that there are such characteristics attaching to a person justified. Yet from a fear of the Roman doctrine of merit, and from a principle of maintaining, as far as might be, their inherited doctrine, some of our most revered divines have virtually denied with Jackson that there is any formal cause of justification ; that is, they have avoided the question.[1] Thus Hooker, in a note on the Christian Letter, which asks, " Tell us whether you think, that not faith alone, but faith, hope, and love, be the *formal cause* of our righteousness ? " answers, " Is faith then the formal cause of justification ? and faith alone a cause in this kind ? who hath taught you this doctrine ? " but he does not tell us what the formal cause is.—Eccles. Pol. lib. i. n. 58, Ed. 1836. Again, Bull, Taylor, and others who hold the doctrine of " fides formata charitate," and Barrow, Tillotson, Wake, and a number of supporters of the same doctrine, nevertheless do not, as far as I can discover, venture to speak of "justificatio formata fide," though by calling faith, or faith and obedience, the

[1] Romanists are equally perplexed to determine the matter in Penance ; the Council of Trent calls contrition, etc., the "*quasi materia ;*" just as Davenant calls Christ's righteousness *instar causæ formalis.*—c. 28, p. 369.

condition of justification, they call it the form virtually. Indeed Bull, Apol. iv. 8, expressly recognizes the "remission of sins and acceptation to eternal salvation" as the formal cause of justification. In spite of this, Grabe, in *Harm.* i. 1, §§ 6 and 8, and Wells also, *Covenants,* p. 2, ch. 2, *fin.,* do not scruple to call faith the formal cause.

12. The reluctance, which writers like those just mentioned show, from the prudence necessary for their times, becomes in all who are imbued with the proper Protestant theory a feeling of zeal against a view, which, though existing in the Roman system, is not false, unless exclusively held. Such divines go a step further yet than has been noticed, and maintain not simply that there is no formal cause of justification, but that any one who says there is, is thereby assigning not a formal but a meritorious cause. Christ is acknowledged on all hands to be the sole meritorious cause of our justification: but the question is not, who is the Author or Agent, or other cause of it more or less subordinate, but simply what justification consists in, what immediately constitutes us righteous in God's sight ? This question, we will suppose, had been abused to the neglect of God's grace and Christ's merits, and to an idolatrous reliance on the creature, just as the doctrine that life consists in certain physical conditions, or the brain is the organ of thought, or the system of gravitation, may be perverted to a denial of God's creative and overruling power, or of the immateriality of the soul. Going into the opposite extreme, Protestants, when asked what it is which constitutes us righteous before God, not only refuse to answer explicitly, but assume the offensive ; and when any one does venture to answer, accuse him of substituting the merit of works for the true Source of all acceptance and grace. Whenever one speaks of conditions, they explain it of merits ; whenever one says, that the pure in heart shall see God, they answer that, contrariwise, none are justified but those who are drawn by God's

grace ; and when one says that only the obedient shall be saved, they cry out that the doctrine of justification by faith only is the " articulus stantis vel cadentis Ecclesiæ."

Such are some of the difficulties of the Protestant doctrine on this point ; in suggesting which, if I have ventured to differ from some of our standard writers, it has been on a point not of faith, and on which they differ from each other ; and if I have here or elsewhere spoken freely of Luther and Calvin, I will observe, that those who spoke as they did of all who went before them, have no claim on the reverence of those who come after.[1]

13. To sum up what has been said :—the form into which we cast the original question was this, are our holiness and works done in Christ accepted or not without a fresh imputation upon them of Christ's merits? does the personal state of Christians, or do Christ's merits, come next before the act of God justifying them ? The Romanist answers, that Christians are justified in their holiness and works without any fresh pardon; and explains himself to mean, not that Christ's merits are not imputed, but that either they have been imputed once for all on the original justification, or that their continual imputation accompanies that inward gift of grace by which Christians are holy and do good works. The Protestant maintains that we are saved merely by that imputation, because even granting our holiness and works were in themselves good, which the strict followers of both Luther and Calvin deny altogether even of the fruit of the Spirit,[2]

---

[1] Luther, on the text, "Behold I Paul say unto you," etc., Gal. v. 2, says, "Is locus terribile fulmen est contra totum regnum Papæ. Nam omnes sacerdotes, monachi, eremitæ, etc. (*de optimis loquor*), non Christo, quem summa injuria et blasphemia fecerunt iratum judicem accusatorem, et damnatorem, sed suis operibus, justitiis, votis, et meritis confisi sunt." As to Calvin's arrogance, even against the Nicene Fathers, it needs no proof.—Vid. in Valent. Gentil. p. 780, col. 2.

[2] Quanta quæso blasphemia est, opera facta ex fide et gratiâ

yet that after all they would be but inchoate and incomplete.

Now in the case of those who say that the fruit of the Spirit in us is in no degree good, and that we have no inherent righteousness at all, this difference is not verbal ; the one party says that we are justified entirely by what is without us, because there is nothing within us which can justify, and the other says by what God plants within us, completed by His merciful imputation. But those who even, though admitting the infection of sin to remain in the regenerate, deny that it is a mortal matter, or "deserves God's wrath and damnation ;" or even if they hold that it is mortal, yet that it may be through God's grace subdued, seem to have no irreconcilable difference on this point with the Romanists. And this view of sin has ever been virtually and practically the prevalent doctrine in the English Church; nay, Le Blanc, in his *Theses Theologicæ*, maintains that Protestants generally have no difference with Romanists on this subject. "Quum mentem suam distinctius explicant [Scholæ Romanæ Doctores] in eundem plane sensum cum Theologis Reformatis incidunt."—De Justit. inhær. 27. But however this may be, at least English divines teach that our holiness and works done in the Spirit are something towards salvation, but not enough ; or that we are justified by obedience under the Covenant of mercy, or by obedience sprinkled with or presented in the Atoning Sacrifice. According to them then we are saved in Christ's righteousness, yet not without our own ; or considering Christ's righteousness as a formal cause, we are saved by two contemporaneous formal causes, by a righteousness, meritorious on Christ's part, inchoate on ours.

Now it happens that this doctrine appears to have been held by Bucer as distinct from the other Reformers ; it is

Christi, stercora nominare (Phil. iii. 8) quæ ad Gal. v. fructus Spiritûs ipse idem vocat Apostolus !—Bellarm. de Justif. i. 19. Even Chemnitz seems to have been open to this charge.

also the doctrine of the Canons of Cologne in their Antidi-dagma of 1544 ; it was held by Pighius, Seripando, and others, at the Council of Trent ; and we have already heard the confession of Vasquez, that it was virtually held by many schoolmen and divines of his Church, both in ancient and later times. In this then I conceive to lie the unity of Catholic doctrine on the subject of justification, that we are saved by Christ's imputed righteousness, and by our own inchoate righteousness at once.

14. First let us hear the Antididagma of Cologne, which was a considerable document at the time it appeared. It was drawn up by the Clergy of that See against Herman their Archbishop, who with Bucer and Melanchthon was meditating a reform of his Church. (Vid. Sleidan. Hist. Reform. xv.) It cannot then be accused of a Protestant leaning. It speaks as follows :—

" Justificamur a Deo *justitia duplici tanquam per causas formales et essentiales.* Quarum una et prior est *consummata Christi justitia ;* non quidem quomodo extra nos in ipso est, sed sicut et quando eadem nobis (dum tamen fide apprehen-ditur) ad justitiam imputatur. Hæc ipsa ita nobis imputata justitia Christi, præcipua est et summa justificationis nostræ causa, cui principaliter inniti et fidere debeamus. Aliter vero *justificamur formaliter per justitiam inhærentem ;* quæ remissione peccatorum simul cum renovatione Spiritus sancti et diffusione charitatis in corda nostra, secundum mensuram fidei uniuscujusque nobis donatur, infunditur, et fit propria ; atque ita per fructus spiritus exercetur, efficiturque in nobis propria quædam justitia qua afficiamur. Cui tamen inhæ-renti justitæ (quod sit imperfecta) non innitimur princi-paliter ; sed ea tanquam interiori quodam experimento certificamur, nobis (qui talem renovationem spiritus nostri in nobis sentimus et experimur) remissionem peccatorum factam Christi consummatam justitiam nobis imputari atque ita Christum per fidem in nobis habitare."—f. **13.**

The statement of the Bishop of Bitonto, in the deliberations at Trent, is to the same general effect : " Bituntinus
ita disputavit : Duo intervenire cum impius justitiam accipit,
liberationem ab injustitiæ statu et justitiæ adeptionem : *illam
huic antecedere*, intelligens, ut arbitror, eam quam *antecessionem naturæ* Scholæ nominant, perinde ac Solis adventus
suæ lucis effusionem antecedit. Is itaque fortasse censuit
per hujusmodi quam dicunt naturæ antecessionem *prius*
condonari peccatum per divinam *extrinsecus* remissionem,
tum vero, sed *eorum* [*eodem*] *temporis momento*, cessante in
nobis peccati obice, gratiam infundi qua Dei filii constitui-
mur. Hinc ipse aiebat *antecedentem hujusmodi justificationem*
ex eo haberi, quod *nobis imputetur Christi justitia*, qui veniam
nobis impetrat ; at subsequentem obtinet per justitiam
interius nobis infusam, non autem per Christi justitiam
nobis extrinsecus imputatam, quod Lutherani contendebant."
—Pallavicin. Hist. Conc. Trid. viii. 4, § 14. To this may be
added that of Seripando, the Augustinian General, which
agrees with the Antididagma more closely still. " *Duplicem*
postea justitiam statuebat. Partem quidem *nobis intimam*
. . . . Secundam justitiam *extra nos* sitam volebat, nempe
justitiam ac merita Redemptoris, quæ ex divinâ commisera-
tione nobis imputentur quasi nostra ; non quidem integra, sed
secundum eum gradum et ad ea efficienda quæ Deo placuis-
sent."—Pallav. Hist. viii. 11, § 4. Such too was the doctrine
of Pighius (vid. Bellarm. de Just. ii. 1), from whose work on
the Ratisbon Conference I make the following extract :—
" Justificat ergo nos Deus Pater bonitate sua gratuita qua
nos in Christo complectitur, dum eidem insertos, innocentia
et justitia Christi nos induit ; quæ una, ut vera et perfecta
est, quæ Dei sustinere conspectum potest, ita unam pro
nobis sisti oportet tribunali divini judicii, et velut causæ
nostræ intercessorem eidem repræsentari," etc.—Controv.
Ratispon. ii. G. iii. " Nos dicimus, nec fide, nec charitate
nostra nos justificari coram Deo, si *formaliter* et *proprie*

loquamur, sed *una Dei in Christo justitia,* una Christi nobis communicata justitia, una ignoscente nobis peccata nostra Dei misericordia . . . Ut vero intelligamus nos justificari seu fide seu charitate, velut dispositionibus aut mediis quibusdam in nobis ad justificationis gratiam a Deo obtinendam necessariis, nos utramque et fidem et charitatem necessario requirimus, sed hanc non illam esse *dispositionem proximam et inseparabilem* a justificationis gratia etiam a nobis demonstratum est."—*ibid.* I. Vide also the language of Contarini, Hosius, Stapleton, etc. etc., as found in Field and Gerhard as above, p. 355. The same is the doctrine of Valentinus, Bishop of Hildesheim, in a work written in 1535, with a view of composing the controversies of the day, and presented to the Emperor about the time of the Diet of Worms, 1545. I give an extract of it as it is preserved by Seckendorf. Comm. iii. 31, § 121. "Addit," says that writer, " quæ Lutheranæ doctrinæ propius accedere videntur, donatam nobis *justitiam Christi,* ejusque merita nostra esse, et nobis imputari ; sed mox subjungit, præter hanc imputativam meritorum Christi justitiam, *justitiam aliam,* voluntati nostræ nempe inhærentem, justitiam, id est, propriam a nobis per charitatem recipi ; *his duabus justitiis* simul hominem justificari *easque separari non* posse, et priorem amitti nisi altera sequatur." Valentinus assented, moreover, to the doctrine that fides formata justifies. Cassander's doctrine is the same in his Consultatio : " De ipsa autem justitia qua justificamur, magna hactenus certamina exstiterunt, aliis in sola Christi justitia nobis imputata, aliis in justitia novæ vitæ nobis communicata justificationis formam ponentibus, cum postea a doctissimis viris observatum sit, ex Apostolica doctrina et Patrum traditione *utramque justitiam* in justificationis ratione conjungi debere. . . . . . . Justificari hominem non sola imputatione sed etiam veræ justitiæ participatione manifeste declarat analogia illa peccati et justitiæ ex inobedientia et obedientia unius hominis, quæ explicatur a Paulo, Rom. v."—*ap.* Grotium,

Oper. vol. v. He then proceeds to say that this was Bucer's opinion, who, however, shall now speak for himself.

15. Bucer's opinion is of some importance to those who judge of the doctrine of the English Church by the views of the men who conducted its Reformation in the 16th century. I shall therefore give some considerable extracts from his writings :—He will be found to speak like a Lutheran concerning the office of faith under the gospel ; but that does not interfere with his doctrine on the point in question, of there being two forms in justification :—

The following is the statement presented by the Emperor's directions to the Conference at Ratisbon, A.D. 1541, and assented to by Bucer among others :—" Firma itaque est et sana doctrina, per fidem *vivam et efficacem* justificari peccatorem. Nam per illam Deo grati et accepti sumus propter Christum. Vocamus autem fidem vivam, motum Spiritus sancti, quo vere pœnitentes veteris vitæ eriguntur ad Deum, et vere apprehendunt misericordiam in Christo promissam, ut jam vere sentiant, quod remissionem peccatorum et reconciliationem propter meritum Christi gratuita Dei bonitate acceperunt ; et clamant ad Deum, Abba Pater. Id quod tamen nulli obtingit, *nisi etiam simul infundatur caritas,* sanans voluntatem, ut voluntas sanata, quemadmodum Divus Augustinus ait, *incipiat implere legem.* Fides ergo viva est, quæ et apprehendit misericordiam in Christo ac credit justitiam quæ est in Christo, sibi gratis imputari, et quæ simul pollicitationem Spiritus et caritatem accipit. Ita quod fides quidem justificans est illa fides, quæ est efficax per caritatem, sed interim hoc verum est, quod hac fide eatenus justificamur, id est, acceptamur et reconciliamur Deo, quatenus apprehendit misericordiam et justitiam, quæ nobis imputatur propter Christum et ejus meritum, non propter dignitatem seu perfectionem justitiæ nobis in Christo communicatæ. Etsi autem qui justificatur justitiam accipit, et habet per Christum etiam inhærentem, sicut dicit Apostolus, Abluti

estis, sanctificati estis, justificati estis, etc. (quare Sancti
Patres justificari etiam pro eo quod est inhærentem justitiam
accipere, usurparunt) tamen anima fidelis huic non innititur,
sed soli justitiæ Christi, nobis donatæ, sine qua omnino
nulla esse potest justitia. Et sic fide in Christum justificamur seu reputamur justi, id est, accepti per ipsius merita,
non propter nostram dignitatem aut opera; et propter
inhærentem justitiam eo justi dicimur, quia quæ justa sunt
operamur, juxta illud Joannis, Qui facit justitiam justus
est."—Liber. Propos. ad Comp. Rel. It is observable that
this statement was as a whole considered so little Protestant,
that a complaint was made to Luther by the Elector of
Saxony against Melanchthon for having signed it. It was
thought to be an undoing of the Confession of Augsburgh,
and especial offence was taken at the word *efficax* applied
to " fides," as if it implied " fides formata." The account is
contained in Seckendorf Comm. iii. 23, § 87. It should be
noticed that, while Luther casts off Bucer, expressly declaring his suspicions of him, Cassander, in the work already
referred to, claims him as agreeing with himself.

But Bucer's opinion is more clearly stated in his own
words four or five years afterwards in the second Conference
at Ratisbon, in which he drew up a paper stating the points
of agreement, dissent, and ambiguity, between him and the
Romanists. He says, " Hanc . . . . *inchoatam justitiam*, justitiam non esse eam qua justi sumus apud Deum, ita ut *propter*
illam vita æterna nobis debeatur. Cum *ex parte* tantum et
imperfecta sit, nec legi Dei satisfaciat dum hic vivimus; ideo
aliam in nobis nempe Dei justitiam esse qua Christo Domino
confidamus," etc.—Acta Coll. Rat. Ult. (Lovan. 1547). Again:
" Tum ille orsus (Bucerus) multis verbis de fide apprehen-
dente dicere, qua apprehendamus Christi justitiam, quæ vera
perfectaque hominis justificatio sit. Hanc *vitæ justitiam* nominari a Paulo, quam porro sequatur *nostra illa inhærens atque
inchoata justitia*," etc.—*Ibid.*

In the following passage he speaks of justification through spiritual obedience, as strongly as St. Austin in the passages quoted in Lecture II.:—"Non est igitur ex Lege *justitia;* imo qui ex operibus Legis sunt, execrationi existunt obnoxii, Gal. iii. 10, id est, qui *nihil præter Legem et suas vires* habuerint, ut opera eorum tantum a Lege sint extorta, non ultro nec Spiritu edita, hi execrationi sunt obnoxii ; quia nequeunt omnia quæ Lex exigit, præstare. Tales autem ipsa Lex testatur execratos esse. Lex vetat ea ad quæ natura propensissima est, scilicet, amorem nostri et quæ hic quærit. . . . . Ita a Lege bona et sancta, institutaque ad vitam, nihil nobis *nondum Spiritu vivificante donatis,* quam ut peccati cognitio, ita et incrementum ac consequenter ira Dei nostrique condemnatio provenit. . . . . Legem igitur abolemus per fidem ? Absit, sed Legem stabilimus. . . . . Necessarium . . . . ut ante pestifer hic animi morbus tollatur. Id quum Lex præstare nequeat, et ex sola gratia Dei donantis bonum Legis amantem *Spiritum* nobis contingit, *consequens est nos ex gratia et haudquaquam ex Lege justificari.* Hanc itaque *gratiam* quum Christus nobis meruerit, ipse unus Author est nostræ justificationis."—Enar. in Matt. v. 19. Vid. also Enar. in xv. 10-20.

As might be expected, he holds the doctrine of fides formata, nay, he condemns the use of the word sola as dangerous ; he says, " Quia vero danda est opera, ne quem vel verbulo offendamus, nemo gravari debet (cum videt offendi homines quod sancti scribunt, nos sola fide justificari), adjicere viva, *formata,* per dilectionem efficaci, aut quid hujusmodi. . . . Ut igitur nemo ne veris quidem offendendus est, ita satis habebo vocibus uti Scripturæ et dicere, Justum fide vivere ; fide nos justificari et salvari, omisso quod tantopere offendit, Sola."—In Psalm. 2. Vid. also a passage quoted by Bull, Harm. ii. § 8.

16. So much space has been given to Bucer's doctrine, because he is in no small degree connected with our own

Reformation; and such as his has been the current doctrine of the English Church. Our divines, though of very different Schools, have, with a few exceptions, agreed in this, that justification is gained by obedience in the shape of faith, that is, an obedience which confesses it is not sufficient, and trusts solely in Christ's merits for acceptance; which is in other words the doctrine of two righteousnesses, a perfect and imperfect; not of the Roman schools, that obedience justifies without a continual imputation of Christ's merits; nor of the Protestant, that imputation justifies distinct from obedience; but a middle way, that obedience justifies *in* or *under* Christ's Covenant, or sprinkled with Christ's meritorious sacrifice. It would be easy to show this in the case of Bull, Taylor, Barrow, Tillotson, and Wake, who goes so far as to imply his agreement with Bossuet on this point, Expos. Art. 5. Nay, it is almost the opinion of the Calvinists, which is worth remarking. Davenant, for instance, grants the doctrine of " justitia inchoata." He grants that it is true righteousness in the same sense in which a white wall, though not perfectly white, has whiteness (vid. *supra*, note, p. 84), and he grants that inherent righteousness is justification in a *passive* sense, or what he calls *justifaction*, c. 22; that is, in fact, we have two righteousnesses, a perfect and an imperfect, Christ's and our own; the point in which he differs being merely this, whether this inchoate righteousness can be said to tend towards justification, or to serve us in any stead in God's sight. And this would seem to be very much a question of words; for if he means to deny it is such as we can *trust* to, Bucer confesses this distinctly; but that there is something good in it, he surely cannot deny unless he will contend there is no whiteness in a wall that is partially white. Nay, in one place he confesses as to a kindred point, " Non igitur cum Patribus *neque cum hisce sanioribus Pontificiis* lis ulla nobis erit de nudo meriti vocabulo (quanquam multo melius et tutius est ab hoc vocabulo abstinere), sed contra nuperos Papistas dimicabimus."—De Just. Act. c. 53.

To the same effect Hooker, whose view of justification is supposed to be adverse to Bucer's and Bull's : " I will not in this place dispute . . . whether truly it may not be said, that penitent both weeping and fasting are means to blot out sin, means whereby, through God's unspeakable and undeserved mercy, we obtain or procure to ourselves pardon ; *which attainment unto any gracious benefit by Him bestowed, the phrase of Antiquity useth to express by the name of merit.*"—Eccl. Pol. v. 72, § 9. Hooker then holds, or at the very least suffers, the doctrine, that God has not only made his son righteousness to us by imputation, but that He does for us *still more;* He *begins* actually to *make* us in this life what Christ is, righteous. That doctrine surely is neither derogatory to God's grace nor an incentive to man's pride, which, while it *adds* a gift, does not tend to dispense with the utter necessity of Christ's merits for our justification. Or again, let the following extract from our Homily, which has been quoted at length elsewhere, be considered : " Mercifulness quaileth the heat of sin so much, that they shall not take hold upon man to hurt him ; or if ye have by any infirmity or weakness, been touched and annoyed with them, straightway shall mercifulness wipe and wash them away, as salves and remedies to heal their sores and grievous diseases."—Of Almsdeeds, 2. In like manner Chamier makes this curious confession :—" Nos . . . non negamus justitiam nostram aliquo modo *constare justitia inhærente ;* quod sæpe testati sumus ; nimirum quia necesse sit nos mori peccatis et vivere Deo. Sed iidem justitiæ *proram et puppim* constituimus *in remissione peccatorum ;* nimirum, quia hæc nos apud Deum constituit justos quod perfectio virtutum non potest. Quid ergo discriminis est ? nimirum, quia ut *duas formales* causas ita duas distinguimus justitias ; *quia* absurdum sit, unius ejusdemque rei geminam formam esse, itaque justitiam nostram, quatenus constat remissione peccatorum, cum Paulo justificationem, eam autem quæ perfectione virtutum, sanctificationem appellavimus."—xxi. 19, 9. (Vid. Davenant de Just. Hab. xxv. p. 360.) Just before he has found fault with the Council of Trent for assigning " unica," one only, formal cause, in opposition to St. Austin, who made two, and made not the inherent but the imputed righteousness the chief. In another place he hails Bellarmine's explanation of the phrase, " Christ our righteousness," (by which that author seems to assign a double formal cause to justification), as all but the same as his own. " Certe si pauca vel demas vel commode interpreteris, nihil est in hac Bellarmini solutione quod non libenter admittamus."—xxi. 17, § 25. " Nostram in Bellarmini verbis mentem læti agnoscimus, et optamus, ut vere sic sentiant Jesuitæ, sic sentiant omnes Papistæ."—*ibid.* § 38. This is not the first passage which has already been referred to from Bellarmine, about trusting to works, in which he comes near to an agreement with the Protestants. In like manner, while Bellarmine and the Romanists call love the extrinsic, and therefore *accidental form* of justifying faith, Calvin calls it its *inseparable accident*, and says that justification and sanctification are as inseparable as light and heat in the sun. His words are as follows : " Neque tamen interea negandum est quin perpetuo conjunctæ sint ac cohæreant duæ istæ res, sanctificatio et justificatio : sed perperam inde infertur unam ac eandem esse ; exempli gratia, solis lumen, etsi nunquam separatur a calore, non tamen calore existimandus est, nemoque tam rudis invenitur qui non unum ab altero distinguat."—Calvin. Antid. p. 324. The *extent* then of the doctrinal error he opposes, is the confessing indeed that the Sun of righteousness is both light and heat, but speaking of the Sun*shine warming* us. As to the *practical* corruptions of Roman Catholics, that is another matter ; here the question is about a certain *doctrine* held by them and others. The statement of the Bishop of Bitonto at Trent, quoted above, p. 369, seems identical with Calvin's, except that the former attributes *more* to justification, comparing it to the Sun's *presence*, not merely his heat. All this being considered, it does not seem rash to say with Grotius, that, provided we acknowledge that man does not procure remission of sins by anything he can do, and nevertheless, is retained in God's favour by obedience "cætera quæ disputantur, sunt Scholastica, et Metaphysicalia."—Animadv. in Rivet. 4.

17. To sum up again, that we may not lose ourselves : —All parties seem to agree that there are two main essential conditions, or constituting causes, of a soul being in the state of justification, God's bounty and our sanctification ; and there are two extreme opinions, both dangerous, and at first sight paradoxical ; the one that God's bountiful acceptance of the regenerate is independent of that Atonement through which of course they become regenerate, the other that their holiness is not really and intrinsically good, even considered as the work of the Holy Ghost. Putting these two extravagances, as they may be called, aside, all parties will be found to agree together, that is, *theologically* speaking, and *so far as this doctrine is concerned* (for I am not going to the question of moral differences, or differences in creeds, in existing parties and individual writers),—with this one point of controversy, viz. whether God's mercy, considered as the form of justification, is an external form or not. To say that the proper form of justification is external to us, seems, on the face of it, unnatural ; yet, on the other hand, hów shall we say that it is within us, without confusing it with our own inherent righteousness ? The multitude of controversialists then have taken this side or that, according as they were on the one hand clear-minded, or on the other hand sensitively alive to their own moral deficiency and unprofitableness. Great divines, however, have approximated to an agreement ; thus Lombard and St. Thomas, and, in modern times, Petavius, declare that

grace, or the Holy Spirit Himself indwelling, is the formal cause of justification, and thus appear to have avoided an intellectual difficulty without falling into what is a worse moral one. On the other hand, it is remarkable that Hooker, in his Treatise on Justification, in spite of his just abhorrence of the *practical* corruptions of Romanism on this point, virtually confesses the same doctrine with the divines last mentioned. After speaking of three kinds of righteousness, Imputed, Habitual, and Actual, he proceeds : " If here it be demanded which of these we do *first* receive, I answer that the Spirit, the virtue of the Spirit, the habitual justice which is ingrafted, the external justice of Jesus Christ which is imputed, these we receive all at one and the same time : whensoever we have any of these we have all ; they go together ; yet sith no man is justified except he believe, and no man believeth except he has faith, and no man except he hath received the Spirit of adoption hath faith, forasmuch as they do necessarily infer justification, and justification doth of necessity pre-suppose them, we must needs hold that *imputed righteousness,* in dignity being the chiefest, is, notwithstanding, *in order the last of all these.*"— § 21. Here it is said that whereas *in time* these separate gifts go together, yet *in order* imputation *comes upon* the gift of the Spirit ; what is this, divested of verbal differences, but to say expressly that the Holy Spirit is the formal cause of justification ? Now, turning from Hooker to the following statements of Mr. Knox, let the reader decide whether there is any great difference between them on the particular point which is before us. " Our being reckoned righteous coram Deo always and essentially implies a *substance of* . . . *righteousness previously implanted in us ;* and . . . our reputative justification is the strict and inseparable *result* of this previous moral justification. I mean that the reckoning us righteous indispensably *pre-supposes* an inward reality of righteousness, *on which* this reckoning is founded."—

Remains, vol. i. p. 278. Now if Mr. Knox means that we are in matter of *fact* and *time* sanctified before we are justified, then he differs from Hooker, as also from St. Austin's famous maxim, Sequuntur opera justificatum, etc. ; but if he means in order of nature (as when we say that wisdom is "first pure, then peaceable"), then I conceive he agrees with Hooker. And in p. 265 he expressly declares that he means *in order of nature.* Or again, let the coincidence of doctrine between Calvin and the Council of Trent be observed in the following passages :—Calvin : "Admonet [Petrus], ne irrita sit sacri illius *sanguinis* effusio, *arcana Spiritus irrigatione* animas nostras *eo purgari."*—Instit. iii. 1, § 1. The Council : "Quanquam enim nemo possit esse justus, nisi cui *merita passionis* Domini nostri Jesu Christi *communicantur*, id tamen in hoc impii justificatione fit, *dum* ejusdem sanctissimæ passionis merito *per Spiritum sanctum charitas Dei diffunditur* in cordibus eorum qui justificantur." —Sess. 6, c. 7. With these passages let the words of the Homily on Almsdeeds be compared : "We, *doing* [as if *dum* facimus] these things, according to God's will and our duty, have our sins indeed washed away, and our offences blotted out, not for the worthiness of them, but by *the grace of God, which worketh all in all,* and that for the promise, etc. Almsdeeds do wash away sins, because God doth vouchsafe then to repute us clean and pure, *when* we do them for His sake, and not because they deserve or merit our purging, etc." The same dependence of justification upon the gift of the Spirit is maintained by Baxter. "Though most Protestants say that justification is a sentence of God, they are not agreed what that sentence is. . . . Some think, etc. . . . Others say that by a sentence is meant God's secret mental estimation. Mr. Lawson noteth that (as all confess that God hath no voice but a created voice, and therefore useth not words as we, unless what Christ as man may do in that we know not ; so), His *sentence* is nothing but His declaration that He esteemeth us pardoned and just in title, *which is principally, if not only, by his execution*, and taking off all penalties of sense and loss, and using us as pardoned in title ; and so that *the giving of His Spirit is His very sentence of justification* in this life, as it is His declaration as aforesaid. . . . . There is much truth in most of the foresaid opinions inclusively, and much falsehood in their several exclusions of all the rest, unless their quarrel be only *de nomine*, which of all these is fitliest called justification. . . There is no doubt that God doth esteem them just, *that are first made just*, and no other, because he erreth not . . . . and that God doth begin such execution [of His sentence] in this life, and that *His giving the Spirit* is thus *His principal pardoning and justifying act*, and yet that this is but part, and not the whole, of our present executive pardon, and that glorification in this sense is the highest and noblest justification or pardon."—*Life of Faith*, p. 3, ch. 8. The whole passage is worth consulting. Waterland speaks of the operation of the Spirit as the *efficient* cause, but the general sense is evidently the same :—" The *Holy Ghost* is here to be considered *as the immediate efficient cause* [of justification] ; for proof of which, we need not go farther than our Lord's own words, that ' except a man be born of water and of the Spirit, he cannot enter into the kingdom of God,' which is as much as to say, he cannot have a title to salvation, cannot be justified."—*On Justification*, p. 434. " The merits of Christ *applied* in Baptism *by the Spirit*, and received by a lively faith, *complete our justification* for the time being," p. 440. Barrow is still more to the point : " To each person sincerely embracing the gospel, and continuing in stedfast adherence thereto, God doth afford His Holy Spirit as a principle productive of all inward sanctity, and virtuous dispositions in his heart, enabling and quickening him to discharge the conditions of faith and obedience required from him, and undertaken by him, that *which is by some termed,* making a person just, infusion into his soul of right-eousness, of grace, of virtuous habits. In the Scripture style it is called, 'acting by the Spirit,' 'bestowing the gift of the Holy Ghost,' 'renovation of the Holy Ghost,' 'creation to good works,' sanctification by the Spirit,' etc., which phrases denote partly the collation of a principle enabling to perform good works, partly the design of religion tending to that performance. Now all these acts (as by the general consent of Christians, and according to the sense of the ancient Catholic Church, so) by all considerable parties seeming to dissent, and so earnestly disputing about the point of justification, are acknowledged and ascribed unto God; but with which of them the act of justification is solely or chiefly coincident, whether it signifieth barely some one of them, or extendeth to more of them, or compre-hendeth them all (according to the constant meaning of the word in Scripture), are questions coming under debate, and so eagerly prosecuted: of which questions, whatever the true resolution be, *it cannot methinks be of so great consequence* as to cause any great anger or animosity in disputes one toward another, seeing they all conspire in avowing the acts, whatever they be, meant by the word justification, although in other terms, seeing all the dispute is about the precise and adequate notion of the word justification; whence *those* questions might well be waived as unnecessary grounds of contention, and it might suffice to understand the points of doctrine which it relateth to in other terms laying that aside as ambiguous and litigious."—Barrow, *Of Just. by Faith.*

Such then are the decisions of divines of very various schools of opinion; and it will be observed, moreover, that, as far as they decide that justification consists in the pre-sence of the Holy Spirit, they explain how it is that *two* formal causes can be assigned to it; which could not be if each were complete in itself and independent: whereas, incipient righteousness, which is the improper form, is but the necessary attendant on the Divine Presence, which is the proper.

18. In the foregoing Lectures a view has been taken substantially the same as this, but approaching more nearly *in language* to the Calvinists; viz. that Christ indwelling is our righteousness; only what is with them a matter of words I would wish to use in a real sense as expressing a sacred mystery; and therefore I have spoken of it, in the language of Scripture, as the indwelling of Christ *through the Spirit.* Stronger words indeed cannot be desired than those which the Calvinists use on the subject; so much so, that it may well be believed that many who use it, as the great Hooker himself at the time he wrote his Treatise, mean what they say. For instance, the words of a celebrated passage which occurs in it, taken literally, do most entirely express the doctrine on the subject which seems to me the Scriptural and Catholic view.—" Christ hath merited righteousness for as many as are found in Him. In Him God findeth us, if we be faithful; for by faith we are incorporated into Christ. Then, although in ourselves we be altogether sinful and unrighteous, yet even the man which is impious in himself, full of iniquity, full of sin, him being found in Christ through faith, and having his sin remitted through repentance, him God beholdeth with a gracious eye, putteth away his sin by not imputing it, taketh quite away the punishment due thereunto by pardoning it, and accepting him in Jesus Christ, as perfectly righteous, as if he had fulfilled all that was commanded him in the Law; shall I say more perfectly righteous than if himself had fulfilled the whole Law? I must take heed what I say; but the Apostle saith, God made Him to be sin, etc. Such we are in the sight of God the Father, as is the very Son of God Himself," etc. Or again, Davenant speaks thus:—" Christi Mediatoris in nobis *habitantis* atque per *Spiritum sese nobis unientis* perfectissima obedientia, est formalis causa justificationis

nostræ."—De Just. Habit. 22. And Calvin still more strongly:—" Conjunctio igitur illa capitis et membrorum, *habitatio Christi in cordibus nostris,* mystica denique unio a nobis in summo gradu statuitur; ut Christus, noster factus, donorum quibus præditus est nos faciat consortes. *Non ergo eum extra nos procul speculamur,* ut nobis imputetur ejus justitia, *sed quia ipsum iuduimus,* et insiti sumus in ejus corpus, unum denique nos secum efficere dignatus est, ideo justitiæ societatem nobis cum eo esse gloriamur."—Instit. iii. 11, § 10. Many striking passages might be extracted from Luther to the same effect: as, for instance, one about Baptism, quoted by Dr. Pusey in his Work, ed. 1, p. 28; or again, vid. Bucer on the text, "All have sinned and come short of the glory of God."

But above all, attention must here be drawn to a most important passage in the Homily on the Resurrection, or rather to the greater part of that Homily, which precisely and formally lays down the doctrine which I have advocated. The writer of the Homily in question incidentally alludes to the Sacrament of the Lord's Supper; but with this further view of the doctrine we are not here concerned. He is enlarging on St. Paul's words, that " Christ died for our sins and *rose again for our justification,*" and he says,—" It had not been enough to be delivered by His death from sin, except by His resurrection we had been endowed with right-eousness. And it should not avail us to be delivered from death, except He had risen again to open for us the gates of heaven, to enter into life everlasting. . . . Thus hath His resurrection wrought for us life and righteousness. He passed through death and hell, to the intent to put us in good hope that by His strength we shall do the same. He paid the ransom of sin, that it should not be laid to our charge. He destroyed the devil and all his tyranny, and openly triumphed over him, and took away from him all his captives, and hath raised and set them with Himself among the heavenly citizens above. He died to destroy the rule of the devil in us, and He rose again *to send down His Holy Spirit to rule in our hearts, to endow us with perfect righteousness.*"

Thus a *justifying righteousness,* viz. that of which St. Paul speaks as gained by Christ's resurrection, is ascribed to the work of the Holy Spirit in our hearts. The Homily continues :—

" Thus it is true that David sung ['Truth hath sprung out of the earth, and righteousness hath looked down from heaven ']. The truth of God's promise is in earth to man declared ; or, from the earth is the Everlasting Verity, God's Son, risen to life ; and the *true Righteousness of the Holy Ghost,* looking out of heaven, and in most liberal largess dealt upon all the world. Thus is glory and praise rebounded upwards to God above for His mercy and truth. And thus is peace come down from heaven to men of good and faithful hearts. ' Thus is mercy and truth,' as David writeth, ' together met ; thus is peace and righteousness embracing and kissing each other.' If thou doubtest of so great wealth and felicity that is wrought for thee, O man, call to thy mind that therefore hast thou received into thine own possession the Everlasting Verity, our Saviour Jesus Christ, to confirm to thy conscience the truth of all this matter. Thou hast received Him, if in true faith and repentance of heart thou hast received Him ; if in purpose of amendment thou hast received Him for an everlasting gage, or pledge of thy salvation. Thou hast received His body which was once broken, and His blood *which was shed for the remission of thy sin.* Thou hast received His Body, *to have within thee the Father, the Son, and the Holy Ghost, for to dwell with thee,* to endow thee with grace, to strengthen thee against thine enemies, and to comfort thee with their presence. *Thou hast received His Body to endow thee with everlasting righteousness,* to assure thee of everlasting bliss, and life of thy soul."

Thus justification consists in " righteousness," and righteousness consists in the inward presence of God, in " receiving" within us Christ's " body which was broken " and " blood which was shed for the remission of sins ;" which moreover communicates, " to dwell in us," the Father, the Son, and the Holy Ghost. To proceed :—

" Doubt not of the truth of this matter, how great and high soever these things be. It becometh God to do no small deeds, how impossible soever they seem to thee. Pray to God that thou mayest have faith to perceive this great *mystery* of Christ's resurrection ; that by faith thou mayest certainly believe nothing to be impossible with God. Only bring thou faith to Christ's Holy Word and Sacrament. . . Thus, good Christian people, forasmuch as ye have heard these so great and excellent benefits of Christ's mighty and glorious resurrection, as how that He hath ransomed sin, overcome the devil, death and hell, and hath victoriously gotten the better hand of them all, to make us free and safe from them, and knowing that we be by this benefit of His resurrection risen with Him by our faith unto life everlasting, being in full surety of our hope, we shall have our bodies likewise raised again from death, to have them glorified in immortality, and joined to His glorious body, having in the mean while His Holy Spirit within our hearts, as a seal and pledge of our everlasting inheritance, by whose assistance we be *replenished with all righteousness,* by whose power we shall be able to subdue all our evil affections rising against the pleasure of God ; these things, I say, well considered, let us now in the rest of our life declare our faith that we have in this most fruitful article, by framing ourselves thereunto, in rising daily from sin to *righteousness and holiness of life.*"

This last extended sentence, be it observed, is describing the " benefits of Christ's resurrection," that is, according to St. Paul's words on which the Homily is commenting, " our *justification,*" or our " endowment with perfect righteousness," as the Homily itself calls it, ascribing it to the operation of the Holy Ghost. This then is *the* great gift of the Gospel, manifold, but one, of which justification and sanctification are the two principal effects, divisible however only in our idea of them, not in fact; and that this one gift, considered in itself, is the sacred presence of the Word Incarnate within us, as both righteousness and renewal, as cleansing from guilt and from sin, is stated still more forcibly than hitherto in the words which follow :—

" What a shame were it for us, being *thus* so clearly and freely *washed from our sin,* to return to the filthiness thereof again ! What a folly were it, *thus endowed with righteousness,* to lose it again ! What madness were it to lose the inheritance that we be now set in, for the vile and transitory pleasure of sin ! And what unkindness should it be, where our Saviour Christ of His mercy is come to us, to *dwell within us* as our guest, to drive Him from us and to banish Him violently out of our souls, and, instead of Him, *in whom is all grace and virtue,* to receive the ungracious spirit of the devil, the founder of all naughtiness and mischief! How can we find in our hearts to show such extreme unkindness to Christ, which hath now so gently called us to mercy, and offered Himself unto us, and *He now entered within* us ? Yea, how dare we be so bold to renounce *the presence of the Father, the Son, and the Holy Ghost* (for where one is, there is God all whole in majesty, together with all His power, wisdom, and goodness), and fear not, I say, the danger and peril of so traitorous a defiance and departure ? "

Now surely there is something very striking and arresting in this *repeated* mention of the Divine Indwelling, over and above its being mentioned at all. Nor is this the last reference to it; after a while the Homily continues:— " Apply yourselves, good friends, to live in Christ, *that Christ may still live in you,* whose *favour and assistance if ye have,*"—

favour and assistance, be it observed, denote, in other words, a state of justification and of renewal :—" whose favour and assistance if ye have, then have ye everlasting life already *within* you, then can nothing hurt you. Whatsoever is hitherto done and committed, Christ, ye see, *hath offered you* pardon, and clearly received you *into His favour again;* in full surety whereof ye have Him now *inhabiting and dwelling within you.*"—Sermon, of the Resurrection.

19. It may be proper to observe that the doctrine which has been adopted after the Homily in this Volume, and which Petavius ascribes to the Fathers generally, was advocated, or something not unlike it, at the time of the Reformation, by A. Osiander ; and a few words shall here be added on the subject of his opinions. His *Confessio de Justificatione* was published in Latin and German, but neither it nor any of his other works have fallen in my way. The following statement is made from his son L. Osiander's sketch of his history and opinions, in A. Osiander's (the grandson's) *Disputationes* xiii. on the Liber Concordiæ, A.D. 1611, pp. 147-150 ; from M. Flaccius Illyricus's Answer to the *Confessio,* 1552 ; Bayle's Dictionary, *art.* Stancar ; Petavius *de Incarn.* xii. 3, § 2 ; Calvin, *Institut.* iii. 11, § 5 ; and Bellarmine *de Justif.* ii. 5. If one accepts the testimony of Calvin and Illyricus, Osiander held almost a Manichæan doctrine, but it is unnecessary to advance so grave a charge against him. Illyricus accuses him also of favouring the Roman view ; but he does not seem to have done more than oppose, without owning it, the doctrine of Luther. The same author also accuses him, fairly or unfairly, of teaching that the Son, or Word, is the inward counsel of God concerning the redemption of man, *i.e.* of Sabellianism. He gave rise to three distinct controversies among the Lutherans ; the first of which was in consequence of his maintaining what had been admitted as a question into the schools, that the Incarnation would have been necessary

though man had not sinned; but which happily came to nothing. He next gave offence by teaching that repentance was confession and detestation of sin with purpose of amendment and hope of pardon, whereas Melanchthon considered it to consist in contrition and faith; and by insisting on the doctrine of the Divine Indwelling as a motive against sin: but Melanchthon took his part here, and this disturbance also came to an end. Then followed his controversy about Justification, in which his two main positions were, first, that man is justified by the essential justice of God dwelling in him; and secondly, that Christ is our righteousness, according to His divine, and not His human nature. Of these two the latter is untenable, and actually led to Arianism; but the former, with which we are here concerned, is, with some explanation, not very different from the doctrine of Petavius. Osiander seems to have argued after the manner of the Calvinists, that Christ's death did but save us from punishment, and that His righteousness is still necessary to entitle us to heaven. To His manhood he ascribed the atonement, and to His God-head justification. He proceeded to maintain that the formal cause of our justification was something in us, and therefore that it was the essential righteousness of Christ as God dwelling in us; or again (if Illyricus may be credited), that it was the "love which God is, infused into us." And lastly, he maintained that it was a "horrible error" to assert that the word *justify* stands for "declare just." In order to show the approximation of some of these statements to Catholic doctrine, amid much that is of a very suspicious character, one additional passage shall be quoted from Petavius, in spite of the ample extracts above given. "Illud imprimis memoriâ tenendum, . . hanc bene multorum ex antiquis esse sententiam, *justos* homines et sanctos ac Dei filios adoptivos fieri *applicatione ipsâ Spiritûs Sancti*, hoc est οὐσιωδῶς et substantivè *non* ἐνεργείᾳ solâ Spiritûs ipsius, ut ait Gregorius Nazianzenus, neque per creatam rem ullam, ut scribit Cyrillus Alexandrinus, nempe sic *tanquam primariam formam*, atque hanc præferogativam Novi esse Testamenti propriam."—*De Incarn.* xi. 7, § 11.

20. And so much on the *proper* formal cause of justification, which, with the Roman Divines, I would consider as an inward gift, yet with the Protestant, as not a mere quality of the mind. Numerous passages might be cited from the Fathers in point, but it would be scarcely to the purpose to do so, for Scripture itself is as clear, as far as words go, on the doctrine of a Divine Indwelling, as the Fathers can be; and the question is, as to its *interpretation*, whether it should be literal or not. And if its forcible statements can be explained away, so may those of the Fathers, who, the subject not being one of controversy in their day, do not speak with more scientific exactness than Scripture itself. And we have already seen Petavius's strong testimony to the fact, that the Fathers generally held that the Holy Spirit Himself, as substantially indwelling, is the formal cause of our being just. However, I will refer the reader to some passages from their writings; and that with this purpose, to show that they considered Christians to have a gift under the Gospel, not moral, yet inward.—Iren. Hær. v. 6, et seq. Cyprian. ad Donat. init. Cyril. Hieros. Cat. xvii. 8 (15). Greg. Naz. Orat. xl. *passim.* Basil. Hom. de Bapt. 3; in Eunom. v. fin. Ambros. de Isaac. et An. c. v,· Chrysost. Hom. 40, in 1 Cor. xv. 29; in 2 Cor. iii. 18; in Gal. iii. fin.; in Col. ii. Hom. 6. Greg. Nyss. de Beatitud. iii. p. 798-9, in Cant. v. 2, 5, 13, vi. 4, pp. 633, 644, 676, 697. August. in Psalm xviii. En. i. 8, in 1 Joann. iii. Tract. 5, § 10; iv. Tract. 8. Cyril. Alex. in Isa. lib. iv. orat. 2, p. 591; v. t. 2, pp. 759, 760; v. t. 5, pp. 867-9, de Trin. vi. p. 595.

But as to the other part of the subject, the question of the *improper* formal cause of justification, something may be advantageously said as to the mode in which the Fathers view it, because it has been recently made a question. I consider they held our inherent righteousness as really righteousness, and really availing as far as it goes; that it has a value as being wrought by the Spirit; or, in other words, that it is like a reflection of the sun's light, a real illumination, yet as little superseding the sun as the moon does. Or to take a sacred illustration, which must be used as an analogy, not as an exact similitude; as the Word Incarnate is infinitely holy, and yet His manhood has its own essential holiness too, though finite, so we are made absolutely acceptable to God through the propitiatory indwelling of His Son, yet are not without the beginnings of inherent acceptableness wrought in us by that indwelling. I feel myself obliged to refer to the Fathers' doctrine on this point, because a question, as I have observed, has been lately raised about it by a writer whom every member of the English Church must mention with respect and gratitude, Mr. Faber. He considers, if I understand him rightly, in his "Primitive Doctrine of Justification," that our holiness and works can in no sense be said to justify us in God's sight. It would be disrespectful, in writing on this subject, to pass over a protest such as Mr. Faber's without notice; but whatever I shall say, which will be very little, must be considered as merely defensive, not spoken controversially.

I observe then, that the point is not, whether we can have any real righteousness *before* God justifies us, nor whether we are not justified by Christ's righteousness *imputed*, nor whether our own righteousness is pure enough to be acceptable without a continual imputation of His (on all which the Fathers are clear), but whether they do not also teach that our righteousness *after* justification, as far as it goes, is *real*, tending to fulfil the perfect Law, and such as to be a beginning, outset, or ground on which, when purified and completed by Christ's righteousness, God may

justify us. That they do teach this, the passages which, in
the notes appended to my second Lecture, I brought from
St. Augustine, the special Doctor of Grace, are sufficient to
show ; but I will here add the testimonies of three other
Fathers, separated from each other in place and time, as
specimens of the unanimous teaching of the early Church.

21. First, St. Cyprian, to whose doctrine assent is given
in the Homily on Almsdeeds, says—" Cum Dominus adveniens sanasset illa quæ Adam portaverat vulnera, et venena
serpentis antiqua curasset, legem dedit sano et præcepit ne
ultra jam peccaret, ne quid peccanti gravius eveniret.
Coarctati eramus et in angustum innocentiæ præscriptione
conclusi. Nec haberet quid fragilitatis humanæ infirmitas
atque imbecillitas faceret, nisi iterum pietas divina subveni-
ens, *justitiæ* et *misericordiæ operibus* ostensis, *viam* quandam
tuendæ salutis aperiret, *ut sordes postmodum quascunque con-
trahimus eleemosynis abluamus.* Loquitur in Scripturis
divinis Spiritus Sanctus et dicit, 'Eleemosynis et fide delicta
purgantur.' Non utique illa delicta quæ fuerant ante
contracta ; nam illa Christi sanguine et sanctificatione purgantur. Item denuo dicit :—'Sicut aqua extinguit ignem,
sic eleemosyna extinguit peccatum.' Hic quoque ostenditur
et probatur quia sicut lavacro aquæ salutaris gehennæ ignis
extinguitur, ita et eleemosynis atque operationibus justis
delictorum flamma sopitur. Et quia semel in Baptismo
remissa peccatorum datur, *assidua et jugis operatio* Baptismi
instar imitata Dei rursus indulgentiam largitur."—De Op.
et Eleemos. init.

St. Hilary, in like manner, declares in the following
passage, both the *value* of good works yet their *insufficiency.*
"Spes in *misericordia* Dei, in sæculum et in sæculum sæculi
est." Non enim *ipsa* illa justitiæ opera *sufficient* ad *perfectæ*
beatitudinis *meritum, nisi* misericordia Dei etiam in hac
justitiæ voluntate humanarum demutationum et motuum
vitia non reputet. Hinc illud Prophetæ dictum est, Melior

est misericordia tua super vitam; quia quamvis *probabilis* per justitiæ operationem vita justorum sit, tamen per misericordiam Dei *plus* meriti consequetur. Ex hac enim vita in vitam proficit æternam; et operationem justitiæ in tantum misericordia Dei muneratur, ut miserans justitiæ voluntatem, æternitatis quoque suæ justum quemque tribuat esse participem.—Tract. in Ps. 51, § 23.

The third, St. Chrysostom, is admonishing his hearers neither outwardly nor inwardly to pride themselves on their good deeds; but, in doing so, he takes for granted, and every now and then affirms the worth, or what the Roman divines call the merit, of such deeds, according to the covenant of grace. I have abridged the passage :—

"If thou wouldst show thy good deed to be great, be not great about it, and then thou hast made it greater. Deem thyself to have done nothing, and thou hast achieved everything. For if, when we are sinners, on deeming ourselves what we are, we become righteous, how much more will this happen, if, when we are righteous, we still deem ourselves sinners !

"Do not then spoil thy labours, nor stultify thy toils, nor, after a thousand courses on the race-ground, run in vain, and make thy efforts nought; for, better than thou doth thy Master know those good deeds of thine. Though thou givest but a cup of cold water, not even this doth He overlook; if thy alms be but an obolus, if thou dost but heave a sigh, in His great lovingkindness doth He accept everything, and remember everything, and assign it a great wage. He has no wish that thy labours shall be made less. Made less ? nay, He does everything, He is ever busy, that thou mayest have the crown even of little services, and He goes about seeking excuses why thou shouldest be rescued from hell. And though thou workest but the eleventh hour, the wage which He giveth is a whole wage.

"So let us not be lifted up; let us call ourselves

worthless that we may come to have worth. It is a necessity for us to forget our good deeds. You will say, ' How is this possible to be ignorant of what we know?' What! thou art ever offending thy Master, and art in comfort and merriment, and hast no sense of thy having sinned, for then thou hast utterly forgotten it all; and canst thou not rid thyself of the memory of thy good deeds? This is extreme madness, and the greatest of losses to any one who is heaping such deeds up. The only safe store-house of good deeds is to forget them. Ask then no wage from God, that thou mayest gain a wage; confess thou art saved by grace, that He Himself may confess that He is thy debtor, a debtor not only for thy good deeds, but also for that good disposition."—Hom. iii. in Matt. t. vii. p. 39.

This passage well illustrates the compatibility of the two positions quoted from Bellarmine (*supra*, p. 356), that the good works of the regenerate really deserve the name, and have a claim on God's justice, but that we personally, nevertheless, must rely on our Lord's merits only for salvation.

22. But on this subject the confessions of Protestants, perhaps, are worth more than the collection of certain passages from the Fathers: so let us turn to their testimony: and first of Luther :—" Philip Melanchthon said to me, the opinion of St. Austin of Justification (as it seemeth) was more consistent when he disputed not, than it was when he used to dispute; for thus he saith, We ought to hold that we are justified by faith, that is, by our Regeneration, or by being made new creatures. Now, if it be so, then we are not justified only by faith, but by all the gifts and virtues of God given unto us. That is St. Austin's opinion. From hence cometh also that gift of grace of the school-divines, grace which maketh accepted. They allege also that love is the same grace that maketh us acceptable before God. Now what is your opinion, sir? do you hold that a man is

justified by this Regeneration, as is St. Austin's opinion? I answered and said, I hold this, and am certain, that the true meaning of the Gospel and of the Apostles is, that we are justified before God *gratis,* for nothing, only by God's mere mercy, wherewith, and by reason whereof, He imputeth righteousness unto us in Christ."—Table Talk, c. xiii. Next Calvin :—" Scholæ in deterius semper aberrarunt, donec tandem præcipiti ruina devolutæ sunt ad quendam Pelagia-nismum. Ac ne *Augustini quidem* sententia, vel saltem loquendi ratio *per omnia* recipienda est. Tametsi enim egregie hominem omni justitiæ laude spoliat, ac totam Dei gratiæ transcribit, *gratiam tamen ad sanctificationem refert,* qua in vitæ novitatem per Spiritum regeneramur."—Instit. iii. 11, § 15. Bucer says, " Patres *plerique* justificare pro justum facere accipiunt."—In Eph. ii. p. 63. Chemnitz : "Patribus . . . licet *plerumque* verbum justificare accipiant pro renovatione qua efficiuntur in nobis per Spiritum opera justitiæ, non movemus litem, ubi juxta Scripturam recte et commode tradunt doctrinam," etc. p. 129. It must be observed that Chemnitz holds with Bucer the doctrine of inchoate right-eousness, so that in saying that the Fathers differ from him in the use of the words, he does not mean to say they deny that Christians are really righteous. Gerhard : " Scriptura verbum justificandi accipit in significatione forensi pro absolutione a reatu peccatorum, sed Patres *quandoque* secuti grammaticam vocis compositionem pro donatione inhærentis justitiæ usurpant." — De Justif. § 245. Chamier, after speaking of St. Bernard's doctrine, says, " Concedam justi-ficationem intelligi pro infusione ; quod, etsi *crebrum* est apud Patres, non est ex stilo Pauli."—xxi. 19, § 16. Davenant more cautiously, but to the same effect: " *Si aliquis Patrum,* propter arctam illam cognatam et *individuam* concatenationem gratiæ infusæ sive inhærentis cum gratia remissionis ac imputatione justitiæ Christi, hæc inter se commiscere videatur, non debemus nos idcirco illa confundere, quæ Spiritus Dei in Sacris Scripturis accurate solet distinguere. . . . . Neque huic sententiæ nostræ reclamare patres illico judicandi sunt, si justificandi vocabulum ad justitiæ infusionem aliquando referant; nam idem vocabulum diverso sensu, non modo a Patribus, sed etiam ab ipsis Scripturis quandoque usurpatur. Non itaque jam quærimus de diversis hujus vocabuli justificationis apud Patres significationibus; sed (quod theologicæ disquisitionis proprium est) de ipso dogmate justificationis quid illi senserint indagamus."—De Just. Hab. c. 25. Barrow speaks as follows: "It may be objected that St. Austin and some others of the Fathers do use the word commonly according to the sense of the Tridentine Council. I answer that, the point having never been discussed, and they never having thoroughly considered the sense of St. Paul, might unawares take the *word* as it sounded in Latin, especially the *sense* they affixed to it, signifying a matter very true and certain in Christianity. The like hath happened to other Fathers in other cases; and might happen to them in this, not to speak accurately in points that never had been sifted by disputation. More, I think, we need not say in answer to their authority."—Barrow, *of Justif. by Faith.*

Barrow, it will be observed, accounts for the difference between the Primitive and the Protestant modes of speech, by saying that the subject of justification was never accurately discussed. Now it is remarkable that Roman Catholics on their part also both express dissatisfaction with the statements of the Fathers, and account for them in the same way. Vasquez speaks of "ea quæ pertinent ad formalem causam nostræ justificationis," as being "difficillima eorum quæ de justificatione nostra tractari solent, *neque præteritis sæculis tam exacte a patribus discussa*, quam ea quæ de necessitate auxilii gratiæ ad operandum et recte vivendum hactenus a nobis sunt disputata."—Quæst. 112, Disp. 202, c. 1, init. Father Paul goes further, observing that "the opinion of

Luther concerning justifying faith, that it is a confidence and certain persuasion of the promises of God, with the consequences that follow, of the distinction between the Law and the Gospel, and of the quality of works depending on the one and the other, was *never thought of by any school writer, and never confuted or discussed.*"—Hist. ii. 75, transl. Now supposing, as Bucer and his Roman opponents of Cologne, and again as Valentinus and Seripando, strenuous opponents of the Lutherans, maintain, as the Calvinists Chamier and Davenant, and the Lutherans Melanchthon and Chemnitz, almost grant, and as the body of English divines imply, the Fathers held two formal causes of justification, a proper and an improper, this dissatisfaction of both Roman and Protestant controversialists with their writings is accounted for.

23. Mr. Faber has drawn up a list of passages from them in favour of the view he maintains against Mr. Knox. How far they avail against that original and instructive writer, it falls to others to decide ; they do not seem to militate against what has been maintained in these Lectures, as an instance will best show. This shall be the Epistle of St. Clement of Rome, which I select, because it is the earliest of the Fathers' writings, and the shortest, and insisted on by Mr. Faber, and as favourable a witness for the Lutheran side as any that can be taken.

Clement speaks as follows :— οὐ δι' ἑαυτῶν δικαιούμεθα, οὐδὲ διὰ τῆς ἡμετέρας σοφίας ἢ συνέσεως, ἢ εὐσεβείας, ἢ ἔργων ὧν κατειργασάμεθα ἐν ὁσιότητι καρδίας, ἀλλὰ διὰ τῆς πίστεως.—c. 32. Now here the point in controversy is whether, when St. Clement says, ἔργων ὧν κατειργασάμεθα ἐν ὁσιότητι καρδίας, he means works done *since* faith and regeneration, or *before.* Mr. Faber considers that works *after* faith and regeneration are spoken of ; and he thence concludes, what in that case irresistibly follows, that, according to St. Clement, works after justification do *not* justify, but merely faith. And his reason for considering that St. Clement means works after justification, is, that no holy works at all are possible before justification. " What are the works done in holiness of heart," he asks, " which Clement thus carefully shuts out from the office of justifying, quite as much as wisdom, and understanding, and piety ? Indisputably, *by the very force and tenor of their definition,* they are works performed *after* the infusion of holiness into the heart by the gracious Spirit of God."—p. 83. Mr. Faber, then, does not deduce his proof *from the text* of St. Clement, but from *the force of a definition of his own,* that is, from these two doctrines together,—first, that no works are holy but those which are done through the Holy Spirit; and next, that no works are done through the Holy Spirit before justification.

Granting, however, for argument, both of these without entering into explanations, still the words in question need not refer to the holiness of the justified, and, as I think the text itself shows, do not.

First, let it be observed, St. Clement changes his tense, " We *are* not justified by works which we *did* (not, ' *have done,*' as Mr. Faber translates) in holiness of heart."

Next, he omits the article; he says δι' ἔργων, and thus naturally, I do not say necessarily, implies he is speaking of an hypothetical, not a real case. He says in fact, " We are not justified by holy works which we did, for we did *none ;*" or, in St. Jerome's words, afterwards quoted by Mr. Faber, p. 122, " Convertentem impium per solam fidem justificat Deus, non per opera bona *quæ non habuit.*" Again, ἐν ὁσιότητι καρδίας is scarcely more than an adverb meaning " piously," " holily." Thus St. Paul speaks, Tit. iii. 5, οὐκ ἐξ ἔργων τῶν ἐν δικαιοσύνη ὧν ἐποιήσαμεν ἡμεῖς ἔσωσεν ἡμᾶς ; not, διὰ τῶν ἔργων. What makes this stronger is that St. Clement has just before been speaking of the legal righteousness of the Jews, which was *not* hypothetical, and has s.id it did not justify ; and then he speaks thus :— πάντες οὖν ἐδοξάσθησαν καὶ ἐμεγαλύνθησαν, οὐ δι' αὐτῶν, ἢ τῶν ἔργων αὐτῶν τῆς δικαιοπραγίας ἧς κατειργάσαντο.

But next, if, leaving the particular passage, we examine St. Clement's epistle throughout, we shall find that he nowhere speaks of Christ's righteousness, or of faith as the instrument of apprehending it; but he speaks again and again of faith as a *moral* virtue, and joined to other moral virtues, and in one place he speaks of *love* remitting sin, and in another of justification by *works.* If so, this early Father holds that "fides formata charitate" justifies; in other words, that "fides formata," or holy obedience, is a formal or constituting cause of justification, or that the righteousness of the regenerate is real. *E.g.* τίς γὰρ παρε- πιδημήσας πρὸς ὑμᾶς τὴν πανάρετον καὶ βεβαίαν ὑμῶν πίστιν οὐκ ἐδοκίμασεν ; c. i.—πανάρετος is but another word for *formata.* Ἐνδυσώμεθα τὴν ὁμόνοιαν, ταπεινοφρονοῦντες, ἐγκρατευόμενοι, ἀπὸ παντὸς ψιθυρισμοῦ καὶ καταλαλιᾶς πόῤῥω ἑαυτοὺς ποιοῦντες, ἔργοις δικαιούμενοι καὶ μὴ λόγοις.—c. 30. Μακάριοί ἐσμεν, ἀγαπητοί, εἰ προστάγματα τοῦ Θεοῦ ἐποιοῦμεν ἐν ὁμονοίᾳ ἀγάπης, εἰς τὸ ἀφεθῆναι ἡμῖν δι' ἀγάπης τὰς ἁμαρτίας ἡμῶν. Γέγραπ- ται γάρ· μακάριοι ὦν ἀφέθησαν αἱ ἀνομίαι, καὶ ὦν ἐπεκαλύφθησαν αἱ ἁμαρτίαι.—c. 59. St. Paul applies the passage in the Psalm here referred to, to justification by *faith ;* St. Clement then, his "fellow-labourer," when interpreting it of remission through *love,* explains faith to be "fides formata charitate."

Other passages in the Epistle, as soon as they mention faith, go on to mention obedience of one kind or other in connection with it, or interpret the "righteousness" which follows upon faith to be inherent holiness; clearly implying that faith justifies as being of a moral nature, not as *appre- hensive,* and is "taken for righteousness," not as its *substi- tute* but as the seed, earnest, and anticipation of it—being taken for what under God's grace it will be in due time : *E.g.* the Apostles are called ἐκκλησίας πιστοὶ καὶ δικαιότατοι στύλοι.—c. 5. St. Paul, τὸ γενναῖον τῆς πίστεως αὐτοῦ κλέος ἔλαβεν, δικαιοσύνην διδάξαι ὅλον · τὸν κόσμον.—*ibid.* λάβωμεν Ἐνὼχ, ὃς ἐν ὑπακοῇ δίκαιος εὑρεθεὶς μετετέθη. . . . Νῶε πιστὸς εὑρεθεὶς διὰ τῆς λειτουργίας αὐτοῦ παλιγγενεσίαν κόσμῳ ἐκήρυξεν.—

c. 9. Ἀβραὰμ ὁ φίλος προσαγορευθείς, πιστὸς εὑρέθη, ἐν τῷ αὐτὸν ὑπήκοον γενέσθαι τοῖς ῥήμασι τοῦ Θεοῦ.—c. 10. διὰ πίστιν καὶ φιλοξενίαν ἐδόθη αὐτῷ υἱὸς ἐν γήρᾳ, καὶ δι᾽ ὑπακοῆς προσήνεγκεν αὐτὸν θυσίαν τῷ Θεῷ.—Ibid. διὰ φιλοξενίαν καὶ εὐσέβειαν Λὼτ ἐσώθη ἐκ Σοδόμων.—c. 11. διὰ πίστιν καὶ φιλοξενίαν ἐσώθη Ῥαὰβ ἡ πόρνη.—c. 12. After speaking of humility, subordination, mutual kindness, dutifulness, etc., he says, ταῦτα δὲ πάντα βεβαιοῖ ἡ ἐν Χριστῷ πίστις.—c. 22. τίνος χάριν εὐλογήθη ὁ πατὴρ ἡμῶν Ἀβραὰμ, οὐχὶ δικαιοσύνην καὶ ἀλήθειαν διὰ πίστεως ποιήσας. —c. 31. After speaking of brotherly love, he says, πύλη γὰρ δικαιοσύνης ἀνεῳγυῖα εἰς ζωὴν αὐτή. Then, after quoting Ps. cxviii. "Open Me the gates of righteousness," etc., he proceeds : πολλῶν οὖν πυλῶν ἀνεῳγυιῶν, ἡ ἐν δικαιοσύνη αὕτη ἐστὶν ἡ ἐν Χριστῷ ἐν ᾗ μακάριοι πάντες οἱ εἰσελθόντες, καὶ κατευθύνοντες τὴν πορείαν αὐτῶν ἐν ὁσιότητι καὶ δικαιοσύνη.—c. 48. All this is not in the *tone* of a Lutheran Protestant.

What has been explained of St. Clement's Epistle, might, it seems to me, be easily applied to the rest of Mr. Faber's extracts. Some of them teach what the foregoing Lectures have aimed at enforcing, that our justification consists primarily in Christ's righteousness, or (to speak more definitely) in Christ Himself the righteous, present in us ; but none go to show that Christ does not gradually impart to us that righteousness which He is. For instance, Augustine says, "per fidem [hominem] posse justificari, etiamsi Legis opera non præcesserint; *sequuntur* enim justificatum, non præcedunt justificandum."—De Fid. et Op. 14. Let it be granted most fully that works before justification do not at all in themselves tend to justify,—nor does faith ; both faith and works are but preliminary conditions for justifying Baptism, but neither till then "avail." After Baptism both are justifying, *i.e.* both partake in the righteousness of Christ imputed, and tend towards a perfect justification ; faith, however, more properly and intimately than works, not as being apprehensive, which is a human subtilty, but as being their root, and as having a special unexplained connection with the invisible world. And so much upon the doctrine of the Fathers.

24. As I have throughout these remarks implied that the modern controversy on the subject of justification is not a vital one,' inasmuch as all parties are agreed that Christ is the sole justifier, and that He makes those holy whom He justifies, it may be right, in conclusion, to give the decisions of some of our divines on this subject, that it may be seen how far such an opinion is safe. With this view, I will appeal in conclusion to the three who have sometimes been considered the special lights of our later Church, Hooker, Taylor, and Barrow; of whom two will be found to sanction me, and the third, though apparently pronouncing the other way, to withdraw his judgment while he gives it.

Barrow, whose judgment on the matter has already incidentally been given, speaks thus:—"In former times among the Fathers and the schoolmen, there doth not appear to have been any difference or debate about it; because, as it seems, men commonly having the same apprehensions about the matters, to which the word is applicable, did not so much examine or regard the strict propriety of expression concerning them; consenting in things, they did not fall to cavil and contend about the exact meaning of words. They did indeed consider distinctly no such points of doctrine as that of Justification, looking upon that word as used incidentally in some places of Scripture, for expression of points more clearly expressed in other terms; wherefore they do not make much of the word, as some divines now do.

"But in the beginning of the Reformation, when the discovery of some great errors, from the corruption and ignorance of former times crept into vogue, rendered all things the subjects of contention and multiplied controversies, then did arise hot disputes about this point; and the right stating thereof seemed a matter of great importance ; nor scarce was any controversy prosecuted with greater zeal and earnestness : whereas, yet, so far as I can discern, about the real points of doctrine, whereto this word, according to the sense pretended, may relate, there hardly doth appear any material difference ; and all the questions depending chiefly seem to consist about the manner of expressing things which all agree in ; or about the extent of the signification of words capable of larger or stricter acceptation : whence the debates about this point, among all sober and intelligent persons, might, as I conceive, easily be resolved or appeased, if men had a mind to agree and did not love to wrangle ; if at least a consent in believing the same things, although under some difference of expression, would content them so as to forbear strife." [1]

In like manner Bishop Taylor, recounting the chief points on which the controversy about Justification has turned :—" No man should fool himself by disputing about the philosophy of justification, and what causality faith hath in it, and whether it be the act of faith that justifies or the habit? whether faith as a good work or faith as an instrument? whether faith as it is obedience, or faith as it is an access to Christ? whether as a hand or as a heart? whether by its own innate virtue, or by the efficacy of the object? whether as a sign or as a thing signified? whether by introduction or by perfection? whether in the first beginnings, or in its last and best productions? whether by inherent worthiness or adventitious imputations? . . . . These things are knotty and too intricate to do any good : they may amuse us, but never instruct us ; and they have already made men careless and confident, disputative and troublesome, proud and uncharitable ; but neither wiser nor better. Let us therefore leave these weak ways of troubling ourselves or others, and directly look to the theology of it, the

[1] Sermon V. of Justification by Faith.

direct duty, the end of faith, and the work of faith, the conditions and instruments of our salvation, the just foundation of our hopes, how our faith can destroy our sin, and how it can unite us unto God, how by it we can be made partakers of Christ's death, and imitators of His life. For since it is evident, by the premises, that this article is not to be determined or relied upon by arguing from words of many significations, we must walk by a clearer light, by such plain sayings and dogmatical propositions of Scripture, which evidently teach us our duty and place our hopes upon that which cannot deceive us, that is, which require obedience, which call upon us to glorify God, and to do good to men, and to keep all God's commandments with diligence and sincerity." [1]

Such is the concordant testimony of Taylor and Barrow; Hooker, however, the third great divine mentioned, decides the contrary way, declaring not only for one special view of justification (for his particular opinion is not the point in question here), but that the opposite opinion is a virtual denial of gospel truth. The Romanists, he says, profess "that they seek salvation by the blood of Christ; and that humbly they do use prayers, fastings, alms, faith, charity, sacrifice, sacraments, priests, only as the means appointed by Christ, to apply the benefit of His holy blood unto them; touching our good works, that in their own natures they are not meritorious, nor answerable to the joys of heaven; it cometh of the grace of Christ, and not of the work itself, that we have by well-doing a right to heaven and deserve it worthily. If any man think that I seek to varnish their opinions, to set the better foot of a lame cause foremost, let him know, that since I began thoroughly to understand their meaning, I have found their halting greater than perhaps it seemeth to them which know not the deepness of Satan, as the Blessed Divine speaketh."—*Justif.* § 33

[1] Sermon on Fides formata, vol. vi. p. 271.

This passage, it must be candidly confessed, is by implication contrary to the sentiments maintained in the foregoing
pages ; but it does not avail the least as authority against
them, for the following plain reason :—because this great
author, in the very Treatise in which he so speaks, himself
confesses that he is not acquiescing in the theology of the
early Church ; and, since we are not allowed to call any man
our master on earth, Hooker, venerable as is his name, has
no weight with any Christian, except as delivering what is
agreeable to Catholic doctrine, which, as being unanimous
and concordant, is Christ's doctrine. Did he indeed state
his belief on any theological point, and declare that it *was*
the voice of Catholic consent, we might defer to his judgment ; or did he but keep silence whether it was or no, we
might take for granted that it was so : but in the instance
before us, far from transmitting ancient doctrine, he even
declares that, according to the views which he then held, or
rather, which, by the clamour of the Puritans, he was made
to believe he held, the Greek Fathers were involved by
implication in the heresy of Pelagianism ; and he excuses
them merely upon the plea of their having anticipated
that error in ignorance. To accuse a number of Greek
Fathers of mistake on this point, will be found virtually to
accuse all of them ; and to accuse the Greek Fathers, virtually to oppose Catholic consent. His words are as follows :
"The heresy of free-will was a mill-stone about the Pelagians'
neck : shall we therefore give sentence of death inevitable
against all those Fathers in the Greek Church, which, being
mispersuaded, died in the error of free-will?" The doctrines
of grace and justification are too closely connected to make
it possible for an author to judge rightly of the importance of
questions concerning the latter, who is in error in his view
of the former. I conceive, then, that Hooker makes for the
foregoing statements as truly as Taylor and Barrow : for he
shows us, as by a special instance, that a divine cannot make

the Protestant doctrine of justification a fundamental of faith, without involving himself in an accusation of those, whose concordant decisions carry with them a weight greater than that of even the greatest individual teacher. But there is enough in Hooker's writings and history to show that this valuable Treatise, written before his views were fully matured, and published after his death, is not to be taken on all points as authority.